THE BOSTON RENAISSANCE

THE BOSTON RENAISSANCE

Race, Space, and Economic Change in an American Metropolis

BARRY BLUESTONE AND
MARY HUFF STEVENSON

WITH CONTRIBUTIONS
FROM MICHAEL MASSAGLI,
PHILIP MOSS, AND CHRIS TILLY

A VOLUME IN THE MULTI-CITY STUDY OF
URBAN INEQUALITY

RUSSELL SAGE FOUNDATION | NEW YORK

The Russell Sage Foundation

Library of Congress Cataloging-in-Publication Data

The Boston renaissance : race, space, and economic change in an American metropolis / Barry Bluestone and Mary Huff Stevenson.
  p. cm — (The multi-city study of urban inequality)
Includes bibliographical references and index.
ISBN 0-87154-808-9
  1. Boston (Mass.)—Conditions. 2. Boston (Mass.)—Economic conditions.
3. Boston (Mass.)—Ethnic relations. 4. Boston (Mass.)—Race relations.
5. Boston (Mass.)—Population. I. Bluestone, Barry. II. Stevenson,
Mary Huff, 1945– III. Series.

HN80.B7 B67 2000
306'.09774'61—dc21   99-462260

RUSSELL SAGE FOUNDATION
112 East 64th Street, New York, New York 10021
10 9 8 7 6 5 4 3 2 1

The Multi-City Study of Urban Inequality

The Multi-City Study of Urban Inequality is a major social science research project designed to deepen the nation's understanding of the social and economic divisions that now beset America's cities. It is based on a uniquely linked set of surveys of employers and households in four major cities: Atlanta, Boston, Detroit, and Los Angeles. The Multi-City Study focuses on the effects of massive economic restructuring on racial and ethnic groups in the inner city, who must compete for increasingly limited opportunities in a shifting labor market while facing persistent discrimination in housing and hiring. Involving more than forty researchers at fifteen U.S. colleges and universities, the Multi-City Study has been jointly funded by the Ford Foundation and the Russell Sage Foundation. This volume is the fourth in a series of books reporting the results of the Multi-City Study to be published by the Russell Sage Foundation.

Contents

About the Authors

BARRY BLUESTONE is the Russell B. and Andrèe B. Stearns Trustee Professor of Political Economy and director of the Center for Urban and Regional Policy at Northeastern University.

MARY HUFF STEVENSON is associate professor of economics at the University of Massachusetts, Boston, and senior fellow at its McCormack Institute of Public Affairs.

MICHAEL MASSAGLI is research and development director at the Picker Institute.

PHILIP MOSS is professor in the Department of Regional Economic and Social Development at the University of Massachusetts, Lowell.

CHRIS TILLY is University Professor in the Department of Regional Economic and Social Development at the University of Massachusetts, Lowell.

Preface

Unlike diamonds, which are supposed to be forever, cities and their surrounding regions seldom stay the same for long. Populations expand and contract; neighborhoods transform; some industries thrive, while others fail; economic boundaries shift, even if political boundaries do not. All these changes have enormous implications for the quality of city life and for the public policies that can affect it.

As a consequence, cities, regions, and their people need to be revisited and reexamined on a regular basis. Alterations in the demographic and industrial landscape need to be considered; the attitudes and opinions of the citizens who live in the region, both new and old, need to be probed; the success and failure of the region's labor markets need to be constantly appraised. These needs are the motivation behind this study of the Greater Boston Metropolitan Area. Undertaken in the late 1990s, it is almost certainly the last effort in the twentieth century to consider how the region has changed in the post–World War II era and what this means for the diverse populations who live there. We were particularly interested in how these changes have affected the way racial and ethnic groups treat each other in their communities and at work; how migration and immigration have affected the pattern of housing segregation; and how changes in the region's industrial structure have affected the absolute and relative labor market success of individual racial and ethnic groups.

The Ford Foundation and Russell Sage Foundation–funded Multi-City Study of Urban Inequality, initiated in 1993, provided the opportunity to carry out this research. Boston was chosen—along with Detroit, Atlanta, and Los Angeles—as a site for a major household survey to investigate racial and ethnic attitudes, patterns of residential segregation, and labor market outcomes. In addition to the Greater Boston Social Survey (GBSS) of households, the foundation provided the resources for a separate survey of regional firms, many of which were chosen because they employed respondents in the household survey. The results from these two surveys comprise the raw data we analyze in the second half of this book, while an investigation of dozens of historical studies and the decennial censuses from 1950 on provide much of the context we provide in the first half.

Whether you have lived in the Boston area your whole life, visited it as a tourist, or never even been there, the analysis contained in these pages will reveal some surprising phenomena. And while Boston is certainly unique in many ways, we believe there are lessons to be learned here that will prove useful elsewhere. Boston's triple revolution—in demography, industrial structure, and space—that underlies contemporary racial attitudes, patterns of residential segregation, and the distribution of success in the labor market, has its counterparts in other cities and regions.

A project of this magnitude can never be successfully undertaken without the help of dozens of researchers and colleagues. We benefited immensely from all those who helped develop and carry out the Greater Boston Social Survey and analyzed this enormously rich source of data. In particular, we would like to thank the Center for Survey Research at the University of Massachusetts, Boston. The center's staff of researchers and interviewers worked tirelessly to gather the information on which much of the analysis in this volume is based. We also received a great deal of help in the design of the survey from those who carried out comparable studies in Atlanta, Detroit, and Los Angeles. In addition, three of the chapters of this book were written by our colleagues Michael Massagli, Philip Moss, and Chris Tilly. Mike was responsible for chapters 6 and 7. Philip and Chris undertook the Boston survey of employers and drafted chapter 10.

We would also like to thank the following colleagues and friends. Miren Uriarte, James Jennings, Edwin Meléndez, Paul Watanabe, and Peter Kiang provided initial assistance in framing the questions for the project. Bess Beatty and Susan Porter provided assistance on the history chapters. Maggie Aguilar, Barbara Hamilton, Carson Tsao, Jane West, and Randall Wilson prepared wonderful analyses of census data which helped inform our understanding of Boston's triple revolution. James Butler, a master of Maptitude, prepared the maps that helped us convey the drama of the region's spatial transformation. Russell Williams helped prepare the industry-occupation data we used in the labor market analysis, and Alan Clayton-Matthews served as a consultant on a range of knotty technical issues that cropped up throughout the study's statistical analysis. We also express appreciation to Reynolds Farley for assistance on the residential segregation section of the book.

In terms of the final editing and preparation of the manuscript, we give our thanks to our Russell Sage editor, to Steve Fraser, and to Charles Euchner for a terrific job of providing suggestions on how to make this book as readable as a volume packed with statistics might be. Thanks also to Mark Breslow, who helped edit the chapters on racial and ethnic attitudes and residential segregation. Also, out there someplace are three anonymous reviewers who read the original manuscript painstakingly and gave us detailed comments on how to improve it. Edward Wolff and Marlene Kim carefully read and commented on chapter 8's labor market analysis when it first appeared as a shorter article in the *Eastern Economic Journal*. Amy Dolphin patiently completed the extensive bibliography.

Finally, we thank Mel Oliver and Ron Mincy of the Ford Foundation, Eric Wanner, David Haproff, Nancy Casey, and Alice O'Connor of the Russell Sage Foundation, and Charlotte Kahn of the Boston Foundation for providing both financial and moral support during the seven-year gestation of this Herculean project.

BARRY BLUESTONE
MARY HUFF STEVENSON

1

GREATER BOSTON IN TRANSITION

WHEN we consider how cities and regions change, we normally think in terms of evolution, not revolution. Yet Boston is undergoing a demographic, industrial, and spatial revolution of enormous proportion—if, by *revolution*, we mean something that changes dramatically in a brief space of time. Today's visitor to Boston will no doubt be surprised to learn that this booming metropolitan region was considered a veritable urban basket case less than two decades ago. Its central city was hemorrhaging people, and the entire region was losing jobs. Violent crime was on the rise, and the city government was running out of money. White parents were heaving epithets and rocks at school buses, which, under court-ordered integration, were carrying black children to what had been predominantly white schools and transporting white (mostly Irish and Italian) children to the city's black ghetto. In the surrounding industrial towns and cities, immense red brick mill buildings were boarded up, still sturdy but emptied of the thousands of textile, machine parts, and other manufacturing workers who had earned their living there for decades. America in the early 1970s was still celebrating the last of its postwar glory days, but the glory seemed to have passed from Boston well before. It was a metropolitan area in distress and in decline.

What is stunning about Boston is how quickly this history has been reversed. Few today would suggest that this city—or most of the 154 cities and towns that comprise the Greater Boston Consolidated Metropolitan Statistical Area (CMSA) (see map 1.1)—is suffering from the same level of urban decay found in many of the older cities of the industrial Midwest or in the New York, New Jersey, and Pennsylvania region. To be sure, a number of central-city neighborhoods in the region still have high levels of poverty. But it is rare to find the wholesale deprivation and hopelessness that describe the population in large parts of Detroit, Gary, Philadelphia, Los Angeles, or Chicago.

It is within this context of a depressed region turned prosperous

MAP 1.1   *Greater Boston Social Survey Study Area, 1993 to 1994*

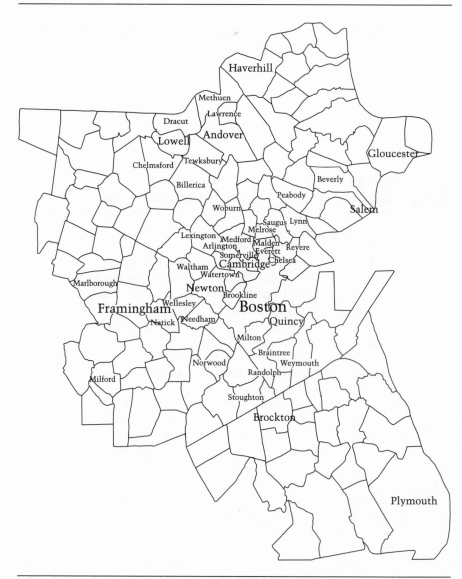

Source: Greater Boston Social Survey 1995.
Note: Named cities and towns of 25,000 population or more in 1990.

that we embark on a grand tour of how Greater Boston's workers and families fared at the end of the twentieth century. Based on a large amount of census data, going back to the 1950s—and on a new survey of 1,820 households in the Greater Boston region carried out in 1993 to 1994—this book asks whether a rising tide has lifted all boats. In particular, how are African Americans and Hispanics doing in the region relative to whites? Do they feel they are being treated fairly in the housing market? Are they able to obtain the same kinds of jobs and the same wages as white workers in the metropolitan area when they have the same objective "human capital" characteristics?

The 1970s: Distress and Decline

The statistics of the 1970s conveyed an even bleaker portrait than what the tourist would have encountered then. In a critically acclaimed study of America's largest urbanized communities published by the Brookings Institution in 1982, Boston was evaluated as one of the 154 largest cities in the United States. The authors of the study, Katherine Bradbury, Anthony Downs, and Kenneth Small (1982), developed indexes of urban distress, decline, and disparity from census data as well as other government sources. The *distress* index was based on such measures as the unemployment rate, the incidence of violent crime, per capita income, and poverty rate in the mid-1970s. *Decline* was based on changes in these measures during the early 1970s, as well as changes in city government indebtedness. *Disparity* measured the gap in these social indicators between the central cities and their surrounding Standard Metropolitan Statistical Areas (SMSA).

On a scale running from −4 to +4, the Brookings study rated the city of Boston −4 in terms of city decline. On the urban distress scale from −5 to +5, Boston ranked −5. The entire Boston SMSA fared just as badly, ranking −4 on the regional decline index and −5 in terms of regionwide disparity. This put Boston at the very bottom of urban America, in the company of Jersey City and Paterson, New Jersey; Hartford, Connecticut; and Dayton, Ohio. Indeed, Boston ranked *below* Detroit, Gary, Newark, Miami, and Oakland. Boston and its SMSA were in the most disadvantaged third of all metropolitan areas on twenty-two of twenty-five individual indicators of urban life.

In the words of the authors of the Brookings study:

Based on data from the early 1970s, Boston suffered from high and rising unemployment and violent crime rates; high percentage poor, old housing, and tax disparity; rising city government debt burden; and falling real per capita income. The entire metropolitan area also suffered from serious

3

functional decline. Nevertheless, many people consider Boston a very attractive city, with excellent cultural, educational, and environmental amenities. This paradox implies both that a highly regarded city may still be
suffering from serious underlying problems and that these problems do not
necessarily make a city unlivable. [Bradbury, Downs, and Small 1982, 50]

Still, the authors note, "Boston's attractiveness was apparently not
strong enough to overcome these underlying problems, since both the
city and its SMSA lost population from 1970 to 1980." The Brookings
study was hardly alone in placing Boston on the docket of most troubled
cities. In a paper prepared for the National Urban Policy Roundtable,
Boston showed up prominently in a compilation of several authors' lists
of problem cities (Stanley 1976).

The Great Turnaround

In 1996, the Center for Urban Policy Research at Rutgers State University, under contract from the U.S. Department of Housing and Urban
Development, issued a thick volume of statistics ranking the seventy-
seven largest metropolitan areas in the country along hundreds of social
and economic dimensions (Glickman, Lahr, and Wyly 1996). The center
relied on census data as well as dozens of special reports from government and private agencies covering a wide range of issues, from education level to urban pollution. Its urban rankings are based mainly on
1990 data and changes between 1980 and 1990. Here is a sampling of
how Boston was doing by 1990—only eight years after the publication of
the Brookings study.

Income and Earnings

While the city of Boston ranked seventeenth in median family income
in 1989, it was number one in the country in terms of fastest-growing
family income during the 1980s. Meanwhile, the towns and suburbs beyond Boston's borders ranked number two in terms of family-income
growth within suburban America. Such improvement in material living
standards was rooted in both rapidly rising wages and an unusually low
dependency rate. Greater Boston's wage earners enjoyed the fourth fastest increase in earnings during the 1980s, and they had to support a
relatively small number of dependents. By 1990, only 30 percent of the
city's population were below age eighteen or above age sixty-four. Only
five major cities in the nation had lower dependency ratios (Glickman,
Lahr, and Wyly 1996).

The gains in family income have not been restricted to white families, according to a related study completed in 1996 (Drennan, Tobier,
and Lewis 1996). Black household income rose by 40.2 percent during

the 1980s, the fastest of any urban black population in the country. Indeed, black families saw their incomes grow a bit faster than the rate for all households in Boston. In Houston, Cincinnati, Detroit, Pittsburgh, Milwaukee, and Cleveland, black family income *declined* by more than 15 percent during the decade. Boston's black family income growth exceeded even that of some of the nation's fastest-growing cities, including San Jose, San Diego, and Charlotte, North Carolina. As a result, in 1989 Boston's black families had a median income 22 percent *higher* than the national median for urban black families. Only a decade earlier, Boston's black families had had a median income 6 percent *lower* than the national African American average.

Booming Industries and Employment Growth

The sharp improvement in the economic position of Boston's households is due in no small measure to a new industrial base that is rapidly filling the void left by an earlier manufacturing structure. By 1990, the city of Boston itself ranked number five among the top seventy-seven cities in its employment share in producer and business services—the set of industries that supplies the rest of the economy with everything from accounting and legal services to software installation and hardware maintenance. Moreover, the share of the city's total employment in these service industries was the seventh fastest growing in the nation.

Similarly, the city stood out in terms of employment in the booming finance, insurance, and real estate industries. It was ninth in the country and had the eighth fastest growth. The city and its suburbs also ranked high (seventh and eighth, respectively) in employment in health and education services. Each of these industries offers a diverse range of employment opportunity, providing jobs not only for professionals but for large numbers of less-skilled support personnel (Glickman, Lahr, and Wyly 1996).

After a sharp downturn in the late 1980s, employment expanded so quickly in Boston that joblessness fell to one of the lowest levels in the country. Between 1992 and 1998, nearly a quarter of a million net new jobs were created in the Boston Primary Metropolitan Statistical Area (PMSA), an area covering Boston and its immediate suburbs. As a result, since 1984, the unemployment rate for the Boston PMSA has averaged only 4.6 percent—and except for the recession period from 1991 to 1993, has never been above 6 percent. It has been as low as 2.7 percent in 1987 and 3.4 percent in 1998. Even the city of Boston itself has experienced exceptionally low unemployment for a central city, averaging only 4.7 percent between 1995 and 1998 (Division of Employment and Training 1999a, 1999b). In such a labor market, employers have had to reach deep into

5

the workforce queue to come up with the labor supply they need, creating job opportunity for even some of the most disadvantaged in the region.

Educational Expenditures and Attainment

Despite rising wages and a tight labor market, Greater Boston continues to attract employers to the region, largely because of the education and training of the region's labor force. On average, municipalities in Greater Boston spent over $7,400 per pupil on K–12 schooling from 1991 to 1992, making it second highest among metropolitan areas in the nation. With its many universities and colleges, the city of Boston ranks fifth in the proportion of its citizens with a college degree. The metro region as a whole ranks eighth (Glickman, Lahr, and Wyly 1996). Even for a large proportion of its immigrant workforce the education level is quite high, owing to the fact that many immigrants have come to Boston to pursue graduate degrees or to take jobs requiring a graduate level of training.

The Darker Side of Boston's Renaissance Region

There is a downside to all this newfound prosperity, however. A number of disturbing trends accompany the region's swift turnaround from basket case to high-tech and services paragon. The home ownership rate in Boston is very low—71st in the nation—not surprising for a region where the cost of housing is very high. Median household rent in 1990 placed the city of Boston as the fourth most expensive place to rent, with the metro region as a whole in ninth place. With its economy taking off, the price of housing rose faster in Boston between 1980 and 1990 than in any other city in the nation, while metrowide home prices placed second. By the second quarter of 1999, the median sale price of an existing single family home was $235,200—76 percent higher than the national median of $133,500. Adding in rental units pushes the cost of housing even higher relative to the rest of the nation. The overall cost of housing is 114 percent higher than the national median (Metropolitan Area Planning Council 1999).

With the cost of housing leading the way, the overall cost of living in the region is extremely high. In 1990, Boston was the second most costly place to live among the major urban areas of the nation (Glickman, Lahr, and Wyly 1996). Adjusted for the cost of living, its rapidly rising median family income barely keeps ahead of rising costs.

Poverty

Income in the Greater Boston region is distributed unevenly. As a result, despite its booming economy and rapidly rising family incomes, Boston falls in the middle ranks of cities when it comes to the proportion of families below the poverty line. The city of Boston ranks 32nd in the country, and more than two out of five of its female-headed families with children are poor.

Nonetheless, relative to other central cities, black poverty is remarkably low. Boston ranks 61st in the nation, with 24 percent in poverty. What keeps Boston's poverty rate high is the level of its Hispanic and Asian households. The city of Boston ranks 11th in terms of Hispanic poverty, with over a third of Latino families officially poor. Outside the central city of Boston, throughout towns like Lawrence and Somerville, Hispanic poverty is no lower, and ranks a very high fourth in the nation. Similarly, Asian poverty is high in Boston (30 percent) and relatively high in the other cities and towns throughout the region, where it ranks sixth in the country at 16 percent (Glickman, Lahr, and Wyly 1996). In contrast, the white poverty rate is 14 percent in Boston and only 6 percent regionwide. The juxtaposition of Boston's high cost of living with high poverty rates for Hispanics and Asians makes living there particularly difficult for many new immigrants. By the standards of the countries they left, they are doing well. By the standards of their newly adopted home, they are impoverished.

Residential Segregation

Greater Boston, like most metropolitan areas, remains a racially segregated region. A commonly used index of segregation (measuring the proportion of residents required to move to achieve perfect integration) reveals that 81 percent of all black residents of the region would have had to move to white neighborhoods to achieve racial balance in 1970. By 1990, the proportion was down to 68 percent (Massey and Denton 1993) a significant improvement, but still a high level of residential segregation.

Moreover, for decades, it has been well recognized in Boston that racial segregation extends beyond the community and neighborhood. The region may have a fascination with sports, music, and fine art, but one is apt to encounter a sea of white faces at a Red Sox or Celtics game, a Boston Symphony event, or an opening at the Museum of Fine Arts. Only when Boston's pitching sensation, Pedro Martinez, is on the mound do you find a large contingent of Latinos at Fenway Park.

Thus, at the turn of the twenty-first century, the Greater Boston region has made enormous strides in terms of an economic renaissance.

But the renaissance is uneven and incomplete. Understanding these features of the region and their impact on families and communities of color is a critical objective of this study.

Greater Boston's Triple Revolution

The economic renaissance that has taken place in the Greater Boston region since the 1970s is reflected in what we call a triple revolution that has swept through the city and its surrounding metropolitan area, changing almost everything in its wake. Demographically, the Greater Boston region has moved from a white ethnocentric to a diverse multicultural community. Industrially, it has been transformed from a mill-based to a mind-based economy. And spatially, the central city has shifted in economic influence from being an all-powerful hub to being part of a true metropolitan region. Each aspect of this revolution is important in its own right, and when all three are considered together, they tell a fascinating story of a region in transition. The triple revolution has had a profound impact on racial and ethnic attitudes, on the patterns of residential location, and on the distribution of economic gains for workers and their families.

The Demographic Revolution

The demographic revolution refers not only to the truly stunning changes in the region's racial and ethnic composition, but also to a halt in the rapid depopulation of its older cities. In just the last ten years, new immigrant groups have been replacing the out-migrating progeny of previous generations of immigrants, stabilizing population levels. As we shall see in the chapters to come, Boston has always been a city of immigrants with its English, Irish, and Italian roots in the eighteenth and nineteenth centuries. But a new round of immigration that began in the late 1960s, following a major shift in federal immigration policy, is transforming the region again. The city of Boston itself now ranks 7th in the nation in the proportion of new residents who come from abroad. Moreover, between the late 1970s and the late 1980s, the proportion increased enough so that the central city ranked 5th in terms of increased foreign presence. The suburbs ranked 10th.

In 1990, 20 percent of central-city residents were foreign-born—the 10th highest proportion among the top seventy-seven central cities. At nearly 115,000 foreign-born residents, the city of Boston had the 12th highest number of foreign-born residents, despite its relatively small size (Glickman, Lahr, and Wyly 1996).

As a consequence of this recent immigration, the complexion of Greater Boston's population has been changing sharply. Of the 154 cities and towns in the metropolitan region, only one—Boston—had more than a 5 percent minority population as late as 1950 (see map 1.2). In the years between 1950 and 1970, the minority proportion of Boston's population—comprising mainly blacks, Hispanics, and Asians—tripled, to 18 percent. The rest of the region remained mostly white, with the exception of a sprinkling of towns that now housed minority populations of 5 percent or more. These included Cambridge, Chelsea, Norfolk, Carver, and the cluster of towns near the Fort Devens Army Base to the west of Boston in Ayer (see map 1.3). In Norfolk, most of the nonwhite population had little choice about where to live: they were inmates at the state prison. In the small community of Carver in northern Plymouth County, the minority population were those who worked

MAP 1.2   *Percentage Minority Population, 1950*

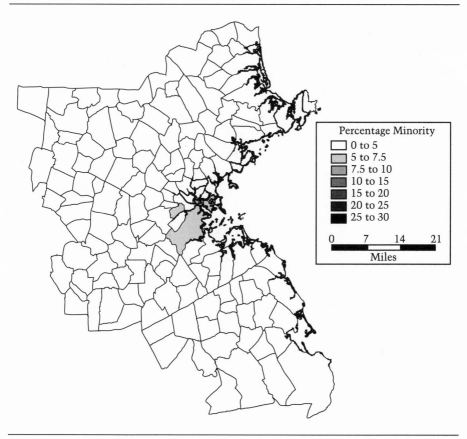

Percentage Minority

☐ 0 to 5
5 to 7.5
7.5 to 10
10 to 15
15 to 20
20 to 25
25 to 30

0   7   14   21
Miles

Source: U.S. Department of Commerce 1952.

9

the cranberry bogs and chose to live there year-round rather than be part of America's migrant farm community. Throughout the entire Greater Boston region, only about 7 percent of the population was minority— and two-thirds of those were black. As late as 1970, the region could still well be considered a white ethnocentric community—with a tiny multicultural island, mostly black, in the region's hub.

The demographic revolution is recent. Between 1970 and 1990, the region's minority population more than doubled, to 14.5 percent. Only half were African American, with the largest minority growth occurring among Hispanics and Asians. Moreover, especially with the geographic dispersion of nonblack minorities, the regional map took on very differ-

MAP 1.3   *Percentage Minority Population, 1970*

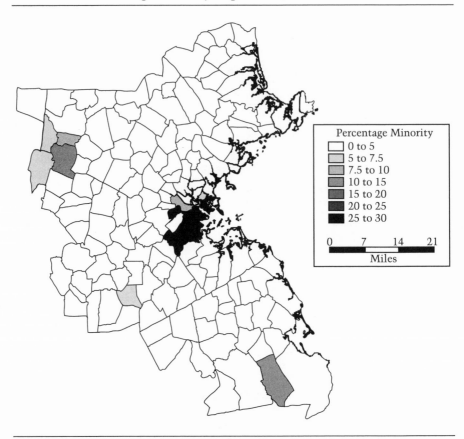

Percentage Minority
☐ 0 to 5
▢ 5 to 7.5
▢ 7.5 to 10
▢ 10 to 15
▢ 15 to 20
▉ 20 to 25
■ 25 to 30

0   7   14   21
Miles

Source: U.S. Department of Commerce 1972.

ent coloration (see map 1.4). By 1990, one-third (fifty-two) of the cities and towns in the Greater Boston region had at least 5 percent minority, with fifteen having better than 10 percent minority and four (Boston, Cambridge, Chelsea, and Lawrence) better than 25 percent. As one indication of the lack of full *racial* heterogeneity, however, only twelve cities and towns had more than 5 percent black populations (see map 1.5). Boston itself was 41 percent minority, while the old white ethnic "Immigrant City" of Lawrence had become a new immigrant city, composed largely of Hispanics. Its minority population exploded from 3,300 in 1970 to almost 32,000 in 1990, of which less than 1,200 were African American. Other cities—including Lowell, Brockton, Randolph, and Lynn—became multicultural with new immigrants from Southeast

MAP 1.4   *Percentage Minority Population, 1990*

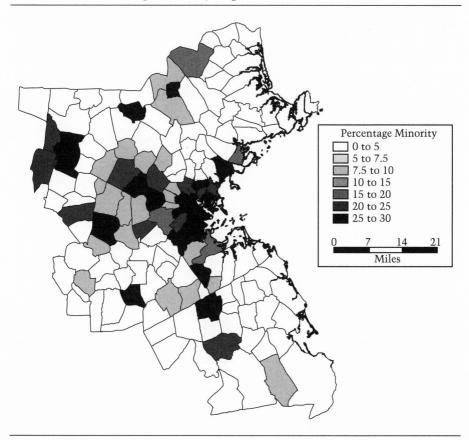

Source: U.S. Department of Commerce 1992.

MAP 1.5   *Percentage Black Population, 1990*

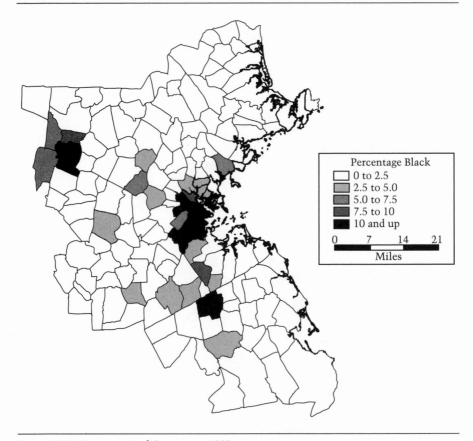

Source: U.S. Department of Commerce 1992.

Asia, Central America, and the Caribbean. (Brockton, Randolph, and Lynn were also gaining in black representation.) Regionwide, the number of minority residents increased by more than two and a half times between 1970 and 1990: from 207,000 to 558,000. Of these, more than three-quarters were nonblack. The region was rapidly becoming multicultural but, except for a handful of communities, not fully racially mixed.

The Industrial Revolution

A key part of this region's triple revolution has been a fundamental restructuring of its industrial and occupational base. In the half-century since World War II, the Boston region has been transformed from a mill-based to a mind-based economy, with new industries that emphasize higher skills and cutting-edge research and technology taking prominence over those that ushered in the Industrial Revolution in Lowell, Lawrence, and other New England mill towns a century or more ago. The growth of services has eclipsed manufacturing growth. The remaining manufacturing activity has shifted from making nondurable goods (such as textiles and shoes) to making durable goods (aircraft engines, missiles, general machinery, and, most important, high-technology office, laboratory, and factory equipment).

Indeed, by 1999, according to a New Economy Index developed by the Progressive Policy Institute in Washington, D.C., Massachusetts ranked no. 1 in the nation's "digital economy." This ranking was based on the state's proportion of "knowledge jobs"; its export orientation; the number of jobs in fast-growing "gazelle" companies (those with a sales growth of 20 percent of more for four straight years); and its capacity for technological innovation, as measured by the number of scientists and engineers, the number of patents issued, industry investment in research and development, and venture capital activity. Its overall ranking placed it above California (number two), Colorado (number three), and Washington (number four) (Atkinson, Court, and Ward, July 1999).

The loss of blue-collar industry and the growing dominance of high technology, financial services, and business consulting have been a familiar story in many parts of the nation, but the New Economy Index demonstrates that these changes are happening more quickly and more thoroughly in Massachusetts than in any other state. Within Massachusetts, the bulk of this activity occurs in the Boston metropolitan area. Nationwide, the proportion of employment in nondurable manufacturing has fallen by half between 1950 and 1990: from 14 to 7 percent. But in the Boston area, in the same period of time, it has fallen by better than three-fourths: from 21 to only 5 percent (U.S. Department of Labor, Bureau of Labor Statistics 1995). In its place, hundreds of thousands of jobs have been created in professional and technology-based industries. Six industrial pillars now undergird the Greater Boston economy: hospitals and health care, higher education, microelectronics, defense, financial services, and construction. Almost one out of five of the region's workers are employed in health or education services alone.

By mid-century, many of the region's manufacturers had already closed or moved to other parts of the country or abroad, yet even then, industrial firms employed nearly one in three of all workers in the region. One in five worked in textile mills and other nondurable industries in 1950, compared with one in seven nationally. But by 1990, just one in twenty Boston-area residents had such jobs, as table 1.1 illustrates. Note that all of the decline in the Boston metropolitan region

TABLE 1.1   *Employment Distribution for Metro Boston and the United States, 1950 and 1990*

	1950		1990	
	Metro Boston	United States	Metro Boston	United States
Manufacturing	32%	30%	17%	18%
Nondurable	21	14	5	7
Durable	12	16	12	11

Source: U.S. Department of Labor 1995.

was in nondurable manufacturing; durable goods industries employed about 12 percent of all of the area's workforce in 1950 and in 1990 as well. To the old durable goods industries, including machine tools, aircraft engines, and other fabricated metal products, the region added computer equipment and other high-tech gear.

An even bigger tale of the area's new economy, however, has been the shift from producing goods to providing services, as table 1.2 depicts. Services as a proportion of total employment have grown faster in Boston than in the United States as a whole. Moreover, there has been a dramatic shift in the nature of service employment. Blue- and pink-collar services, such as repair, private household, and personal services, have given way to white-collar services, including those provided by professionals in such fields as law, medicine, education, and business services, especially those directed toward research and development—as table 1.3 demonstrates. In 1990, 77 percent of all the region's service workers were classified as professional or related employees. Nationwide, the proportion was only 71 percent. This profound upgrading of skill requirements has paid off in terms of higher wages for those with advanced schooling—but resulted in lower earnings for those without. Clearly, Boston has moved more rapidly toward a postindustrial society than the nation as a whole, again with profound implications for the distribution of economic well-being in the region.

TABLE 1.2   *Services as a Proportion of Total Employment, Metro Boston and the United States, 1950 to 1990*

Metro Boston		United States	
1950	1990	1950	1990
21%	39%	21%	34%

Source: U.S. Department of Labor 1995.

TABLE 1.3   Services by Category, Metro Boston and the United
            States, 1950 to 1990

	Metro Boston		United States	
	1950	1990	1950	1990
Professional and related services (for example, health and education)	54%	77%	46%	71%
Business services	6	11	4	10
Repair services	7	2	9	5
Private household services	11	1	16	2
Other personal services	17	6	18	8
Entertainment and recreation services	5	3	6	4
Service sector, total	100	100	100	100

Source: U.S. Department of Labor 1995.
Note: Totals may not add to 100 percent due to rounding.

The Spatial Revolution

The third component of Boston's triple revolution encompasses the
massive decentralization of both residential location and the locus of
business activity. This has required greater commuting not only within
each of the primary metropolitan areas (Boston, Brockton, Lawrence-
Haverhill, Lowell, Salem-Gloucester), but also between these cities, so
that much of eastern Massachusetts can now be conceived of as an economically interrelated unit—not just a patchwork of urban villages,
towns, and cities.

From the 1950s until 1980, both economic activity and population
fled Boston for the suburbs and beyond. From a total of 801,000 in 1950,
Boston saw its population decline to just 560,000 by 1980. Manufacturing moved to the suburbs or out of the region altogether. Retail trade
followed. Only after 1980 did Boston's population stop shrinking—primarily as a result of the continued influx of immigrants who have come
seeking economic opportunity or fleeing political and military repression, and a new wave of mostly young, mostly single professional workers who have moved into the city to take advantage of its social and
cultural amenities.

At the end of World War II, the city of Boston was clearly the hub of
the region in terms of population. Its 801,000 residents in 1950 comprised a full quarter (25.1 percent) of the population of the entire CMSA.
As the CMSA grew during the ensuing four decades and Boston declined, its share of the total region fell to only one-seventh (14.8 percent). The population was spreading north, west, and south—and farther
and farther out as the years went by.

TABLE 1.4   *Population Growth and Decline*
Selected Greater Boston Region Cities and Towns

	1950	1960	1970	1980	1990	Percentage Change 1950 to 1990
Boston	801,444	697,197	641,071	562,994	574,283	−28.3
Cambridge	120,740	107,716	100,361	95,322	94,802	−21.5
Chelsea	38,912	33,749	30,625	25,431	28,710	−26.2
Somerville	102,351	94,697	88,779	77,372	76,210	−25.5
Lynn	99,738	94,478	90,294	78,471	81,245	−18.5
Everett	45,982	43,544	42,485	37,195	35,701	−22.4
Lawrence	80,536	70,933	66,915	63,175	70,207	−12.8
Watertown	37,329	39,092	39,307	34,384	33,284	−10.8
Canton	4,739	12,771	17,100	18,182	18,530	209.1
Randolph	9,982	18,900	27,035	28,218	30,093	201.5
Framingham	28,086	44,526	64,048	65,113	64,989	131.4
Natick	19,838	28,831	31,057	29,461	30,510	53.8

Source: U.S. Department of Commerce 1952, 1962, 1972, 1982, 1992.

Boston's neighboring cities also experienced sharp declines in population (see table 1.4). Between 1950 and 1990, Cambridge's net population declined by 22 percent. Chelsea and Somerville, despite an enormous influx of Hispanics and other immigrants, each saw its net population fall by 26 percent. Lynn and Everett, working-class cities to the north of Boston, lost 19 and 22 percent of their residents, respectively, in the four decades after the war. Lawrence lost 13 percent, while Watertown lost 11 percent. All these cities are older, blue-collar, working-class centers.

At the same time, the nonindustrial suburbs around these cities were gaining population rapidly. The middle-class suburb of Canton to the south of Boston saw its population nearly quadruple, to 17,100, in just twenty years (1950 to 1970) before it ran out of room for more housing. Randolph's population nearly tripled, to 27,000, during the same period. Framingham's population more than doubled, to 64,000. Even before the school desegregation crisis of the 1970s, which has been called a turning point in Boston's demographic shift, the process of urban depopulation had been under way for a generation.

Institutional and Market Forces
Underlying the Triple Revolution

The demographic, industrial, and spatial revolutions in Greater Boston can be seen as stemming from the interplay of both *institutional fac-*

tors—the influence of specific public policy decisions—and more imper-
sonal *market forces*. Figure 1.1 provides a schematic diagram of this set
of relationships.

The demographic revolution that resulted in a shift from a white
ethnocentric-based community to a more multicultural one did not
come about by chance. Rather, it was the end result of explicit policies,
including legislation that altered immigration regulations, judicial decisions regarding school busing, and executive decisions regarding the refugee status of the Vietnamese, Cambodians, and Laotians who had allied themselves with the United States during the Vietnam War. It was
also a product of market forces. High wage levels in the United States
have served as a magnet for many recent emigrants from low-wage developing countries.

FIGURE 1.1   *The Triple Revolution*

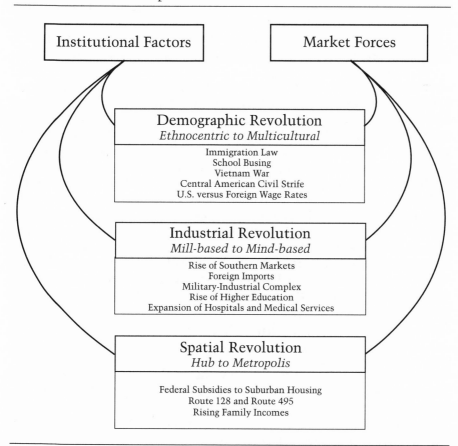

Source: Authors' compilation.

array of government initiatives to promote equality, and identify which of them have widespread support among both whites and minorities and which produce disagreement across the three race-ethnic groups.

Chapter 7 examines residential segregation and compares how GBSS respondents describe their ideal neighborhood, in terms of race and ethnic mix, with the actual neighborhoods in which they live. It examines the extent to which the high degree of racial and ethnic segregation within Greater Boston can be attributed to differences across the race-ethnic groups in housing affordability or in knowledge about specific housing markets across the region.

Chapter 8 is the first of several that examine the Greater Boston labor market. In this chapter, we focus on workers with no more than a high school diploma, a group we expect to be especially vulnerable to labor market distress in a metropolitan economy that has become progressively more knowledge-based. We examine differences in expected annual earnings by gender and by race-ethnicity. We use a set of simulation models, based on econometric analysis, to understand the sources of differences in expected annual earnings and in each of its component parts: labor force participation, the probability of being unemployed, the number of hours worked per week, and the hourly wage rate. We examine the impact of a set of human capital variables (for example, education, age, health, job experience), race and neighborhood, job characteristics (for men), and family structure (for women).

Chapter 9 continues to explore differences between workers by examining how workers get "assigned" to job slots and how differences in human capital (for example, education), cultural capital (for example, mother's education), and social capital (for example, use of networks for job search) account for differences in hourly wages.

Having looked at workers in chapters 8 and 9, we shift our focus to employers in chapter 10. Using a companion survey of employers in the region, we try to gauge the extent to which the differences in labor market outcomes that we noted in the preceding chapters can be attributed to the demand side of the labor market—the decisions made by employers themselves. Finally, in chapter 11, we summarize our analysis and use a "SWOT" analysis to set the stage for policy recommendations that might reduce racial discrimination, reduce housing segregation, and improve labor market outcomes, especially for black and Hispanic workers. The SWOT analysis reviews the region's Strengths, its Weaknesses, the Opportunities before it, and the Threats to its continued prosperity.

We attempt to paint as true a picture of the Greater Boston region as possible. In the end, we see Boston as a renaissance region, one that is again on the move economically and socially. The issue, as always in its history, is when and how its minority population, including recent arrivals, will share in the full fruit of its renaissance.

2

THE DEMOGRAPHIC REVOLUTION: FROM WHITE ETHNOCENTRIC TO MULTICULTURAL BOSTON

NEARLY a century ago, when it was still commonly known for the cod and the baked bean, Boston was largely distinguished by its English, Irish, and Italian roots. It was home to families with names like Adams and Smith, O'Donnell, Murphy, and Dorgan, and the recently arrived Marinos and Toscanos. Other ethnic groups, including a diverse sprinkling of Eastern and Western Europeans and Chinese, came to work in the region's textile, shoe, and watch and clock industries. But the politics and much of the economics of the entire region was dominated by those who came from the British Isles. Newcomers have almost always faced hostilities, and attitudes of one group toward another have ranged from suspicion to hatred.

The demographic, political, and economic structure of the region might have remained stable for generations if not for an important revision in U.S. immigration law in 1965 that resulted in Hispanics becoming a major presence in the region—as well as foreign-born blacks from the Caribbean, and Vietnamese, Laotian, and Cambodian refugees. Today the Boston-area telephone directory contains nearly four columns of Collinses and three of Connollys, and also two of Riveras and nearly four of Nguyens. Racial and ethnic attitudes have been forged by the region's equivocal acceptance of these immigrants.

Successive demographic transformations have made Greater Boston one of the nation's most culturally diverse and colorful regions. But time and time again, immigration has been accompanied by hostilities that affect racial and ethnic attitudes, patterns of residential segregation, and labor market outcomes. In each era, new institutions and strategies arise to attract or repel individual racial and ethnic groups from the central city and to the towns that make up the Greater Boston metropolitan region. The Irish potato famine sent thousands of Irish to Boston. The recruitment efforts of the textile barons of the nineteenth century attracted French Canadians and, in rapid succession, Italians, Russian Jews, Poles, and other Eastern Europeans. Immigrant loom fixers and spinners swelled the size of Lawrence and Lowell. Watchmakers came to Waltham and shoemakers to Brockton. By the late nineteenth century, the new immigrants' children began to influence and control the politics of the region, sharing power with those of English stock who came before them.

A century later, immigration law, the blossoming of high-tech industry, school busing, the Vietnam War, and political struggles in Central America and the Caribbean combined to create the racial and ethnic patterns of today's Boston metropolitan region. Each new wave of immigrants has had to overcome bias and discrimination before gaining its own economic and political standing in Boston's diverse environment. Often, the very fact of resisting discrimination and isolation has been part of the process of building dominant institutions and social niches. Boston's newest arrivals are still trying to gain a foothold in the community's political and economic infrastructure.

The Post–World War II Demographic Revolution

In the second half of the twentieth century, Massachusetts experienced a significant loss in population to Sunbelt states like California, Florida, and Texas. But the losses would have been even greater had not newly arrived immigrants offset part of the net outflow of the native-born, and had they not replenished the population within many of the Commonwealth's cities.

The influx of an entire new wave of immigrants from many parts of the world began in the mid-1960s and continues apace. Simply to serve its expanded clientele, one of the region's largest health maintenance organizations, Harvard-Vanguard Health Associates, uses interpreters who can translate from dozens of foreign languages, including Cantonese, Mandarin, Cape Verdean Creole, Haitian Creole, Khmer, Portuguese, Russian, Spanish, French, and Vietnamese. Not long ago, English, Italian, and French would have served all but a few of their patients.

Statewide, about 12 percent of students in the public schools in 1994 spoke a primary language other than English. These 105,902 students were double the number from just a decade before. The phenomenal increase in the variety of native languages spoken in Greater Boston Metropolitan Area high schools over the last ten years can be seen in the accompanying table, published by the Boston Globe (Lehr 1997).

To see just how recent and rapid the shift to a multicultural society

TABLE 2.1   *Languages Spoken in Selected Greater Boston High Schools*

| | Number of Languages | |
School	1986	1996
Everett High	8	23
Quincy High	8	20
Malden High	17	31
Cambridge Rindge and Latin	46	55
Brookline High	22	33
Waltham High	12	32

Source: Lehr 1997.

has been, one can take the long view going back to the Civil War. Figure 2.1 shows that the city of Boston's minority ranks remained at less than 5 percent of the total population from the end of the Civil War through the end of World War II. The minority population *tripled* between 1950 and 1970 and then *doubled* again in the next twenty years. While the minority population of Boston was overwhelmingly black through 1970, the census for 2000 is expected to show that Hispanics and Asians com-

FIGURE 2.1   *Minority Population, Boston, 1865 to 1990*

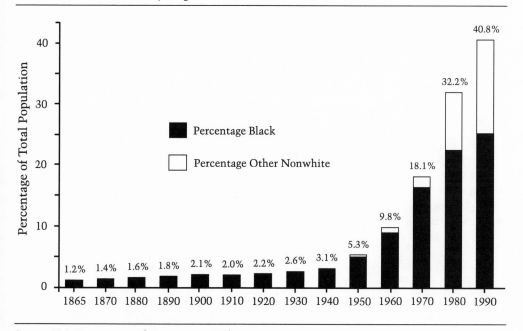

Source: U.S. Department of Commerce 1992b.

bined are as numerous as blacks and that minorities as a group comprise fully half the city's residents.

This shift in the racial and ethnic composition of Boston is not simply, or even primarily, the result of the in-migration of minorities into the city; it has a great deal to do with whites leaving the central city. Between 1950 and 1990, the white population in Boston declined by more than half, from 758,700 to only 338,900. Much of this decline occurred *before* the onset of school busing or the "blockbusting" of white neighborhoods by real estate agents who exploited racial fears to encourage whites to sell their homes. Already by 1970, the white population was down to only 524,000—a loss of nearly a quarter of a million in just two decades. The changing size and composition of Boston's population are demonstrated in table 2.2. Note that the combined white loss in the 1950s and 1960s actually exceeds the loss in the 1970s and 1980s. The lure of the suburbs (and other parts of the country) generated enormous out-migration well before minorities were much of a presence in the city.

TABLE 2.2   *City of Boston Population by Race-Ethnicity, 1950 to 1990*

	1950	1960	1970	1980	1990
White	758,700	622,746	523,581	392,506	360,920
Black	42,744	67,873	104,429	125,983	145,993
American Indian			1,044	1,291	1,865
Asian-Pacific Island			8,442	15,125	30,452
Other[a]			3,575	28,089	35,053
Total	801,444	697,197	641,071	562,994	574,283
Hispanic			17,940	36,010	59,558
Hispanic white				11,790	21,971
Non-Hispanic white	758,700	622,746	523,581	380,716	338,949
Minority (including white Hispanics)	42,744	67,873	116,073	180,530	234,019
Minority as percent of total	5.3%	9.8%	18.1%	32.2%	40.8%
Change		1950 to 1960	1960 to 1970	1970 to 1980	1980 to 1990
Non-Hispanic white		−135,954	−99,165	−142,865	−41,767
Minority (including white Hispanic)		+25,129	+48,200	+64,457	+53,489

Source: The census survey data used here were compiled by the City of Boston, United Community Services (UCS) for the years 1950, 1960, and 1990, and by the Boston Redevelopment Authority (BRA) for the years 1970, 1980, and 1990.
[a]A person is classified by the U.S. Bureau of Census in the "Other" race category when not classifiable in the category of white, black, American Indian, or Asian and Pacific Islander. Hispanic is an *ethnic* subset of the total population and may be a member of any one of the five race categories.

What happened to the city of Boston in the postwar period has its parallels in other parts of the region. An examination of just a few of the surrounding towns and cities provides evidence of these profound changes. The venerable shoe manufacturing city of Brockton had a minority population of just 1 percent in 1950 (see figure 2.2), and less than 5 percent in 1970. Twenty years later—the span of less than a single generation—the proportion had grown to more than 20 percent. Most of Brockton's minority population is black. Likewise, Lowell's population was only 1.2 percent minority as late as 1970. By 1990, its minority ranks had swollen to 22 percent, almost evenly split between Asians and Hispanics (see figure 2.3). An even more astounding change has occurred in Lawrence. Only 1.5 percent minority as late as 1970, by 1990 nearly half of the city's residents were minority, particularly of Hispanic origin (see figure 2.4). It bears repeating from chapter 1 that of the 154 cities and towns in the Greater Boston region, 52 had minority populations of 5 percent or more by 1990 and in another 15, at least 10 percent of the population was composed of blacks, Hispanics, Asians, and Native Americans. Nearly 15 percent of the entire region's population was minority, and that percentage has no doubt continued to grow.

FIGURE 2.2   *Minority Population, Brockton, 1950 to 1990*

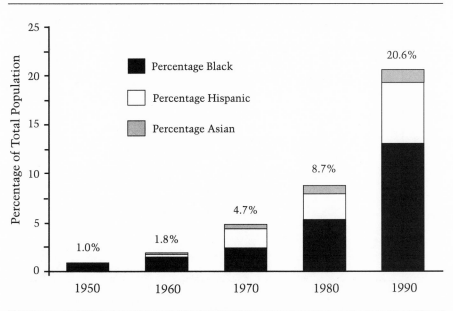

Source: U.S. Department of Commerce 1952, 1962, 1972, 1982, 1993.

FIGURE 2.3   *Minority Population, Lowell, 1950 to 1990*

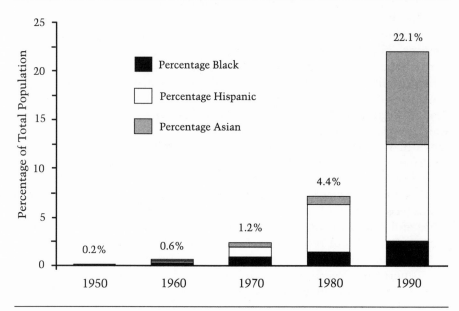

Source: U.S. Department of Commerce 1952, 1962, 1972, 1982, 1993.

FIGURE 2.4   *Minority Population, Lawrence, 1950 to 1990*

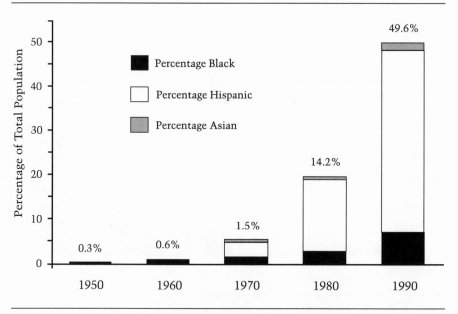

Source: U.S. Department of Commerce 1952, 1962, 1972, 1982, 1993.

The Persistence of Neighborhood Segregation

Although the region is now more diverse, this does not mean that its neighborhoods are integrated by race or ethnicity. The segregation of African Americans is most acute. Within the entire Greater Boston CMSA, blacks are concentrated overwhelmingly in a small number of neighborhoods within the city of Boston. Residents of Boston comprise less than 15 percent of the region's population, but the hub city is home to more than 60 percent of the region's African Americans. (Regionwide, over 75 percent of the black population lives in just four cities: Boston, Cambridge, Brockton, and Lynn.) About one in three (33 percent) Hispanics and one in four (26 percent) Asians in the CMSA live in Boston

FIGURE 2.5   *Black Population as Percentage of Neighborhood, Boston, 1990*

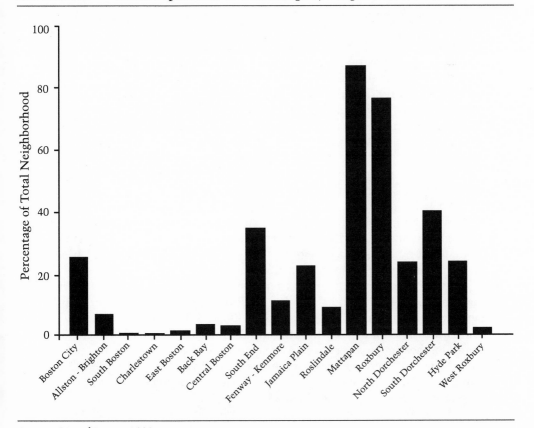

Source: City of Boston 1993.

proper. In contrast, fewer than one in ten (9 percent) of all whites live there.

Neighborhood concentration of African Americans within Boston in 1990 is depicted in figure 2.5. The two inner-city neighborhoods of Roxbury and Mattapan are roughly 80 percent black. At the other end of the segregation spectrum, less than 2 percent of the residents of South Boston, Charlestown, East Boston, and West Roxbury are African Americans. During Boston's school busing crisis, the largest and loudest protests were heard in some of these communities. The legacy of racial antagonism no doubt plays a role in keeping these areas mostly white. This pattern of neighborhood segregation is also found in those communities where blacks have recently arrived. In Brockton, most of the African American families are congregated in just two of the city's eight census tracts.

Latinos and Asians have experienced an easier time integrating neighborhoods in the city of Boston, as a comparison of figure 2.6 with figure 2.5 makes clear. In Boston's working-class community of Allston-Brighton, only 7.3 percent of the population is black—but more than a quarter (27 percent) of the residents are minority. Hispanics also have settled in East Boston, a traditionally lily-white ethnic working-class community. Less than 2 percent of the population is black, yet 24 percent are minority. For the most part, the preponderance of the region's cities and towns with a minority presence of more than 5 percent in 1990 are communities where Hispanics and Asians have settled, not native-born African Americans or (in most cases) black immigrants from the Caribbean.

In Boston, the new immigrants are continuing the next installment in the story of ethnic succession that dates back over a century. From 1880 to 1910, the Irish who moved out of neighborhoods in the North End, West End, and South End were replaced, respectively, by Italians, Jews, and African Americans. The area near downtown that had become Chinatown by 1900 had previously been home to a succession of Irish, Jews, Italians, and Syrians (Conzen and Lewis 1976).

After World War II, many Italian Americans moved from the North End and East Boston northward, to Winthrop, Saugus, Medford, and Lynnfield; Irish Americans from South Boston and Dorchester moved southward, to Quincy, Weymouth, and Braintree; and Jewish Americans from Dorchester, Roxbury, and Mattapan moved westward to Brookline and Newton, and southwestward to Milton, Randolph, Sharon, Stoughton, and Canton (Aucoin 1993). Where they once lived there are now large concentrations of Hispanics in East Boston, large concentrations of Vietnamese in Dorchester, and large concentrations of blacks, including native-born Americans, Haitians, and immigrants from the British West Indies in Roxbury and Mattapan.

FIGURE 2.6   *Minority Population as Percentage of Neighborhood, Boston, 1990*

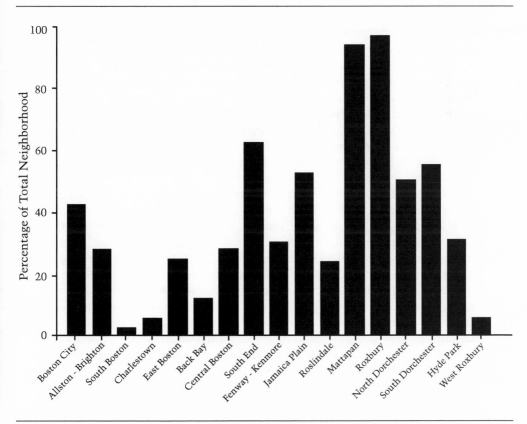

Source: City of Boston 1995.

Immigration Law and the Demographic Revolution

Both the level of immigration and its racial and ethnic composition continue to be heavily influenced by federal immigration law, a factor much in evidence for the better part of the twentieth century. Severe restrictions on immigration had been in place since the 1920s. As a result, Boston remained white ethnocentric for the next forty years. When, in the mid-1960s, Congress amended the McCarran-Walter Act of 1952, it intended to remove discrimination against Southern and Eastern Europeans by eliminating the national-origins quotas that had favored Great Britain, Germany, and Ireland. It placed new emphasis on family unification, with the expectation that this would favor immigrants from countries that had already attracted substantial immigration to the United States—that is, European nations. The 1965 law also established quotas limiting the total volume of immigration.

As the immigration expert David Reimers (1983) argues, other features of the Hart-Celler Act of 1965 led to the unintended consequence of increasing immigration from Third World countries. Under McCarran-Walter, British colonies like Jamaica and Trinidad and Tobago had an annual immigration quota of 100. These quotas remained in place even after the former colonies had gained their independence. When Hart-Celler removed the quotas, far more immigrants than anticipated came to the United States from these former colonies, partly because Great Britain restricted its own immigration at about the same time. The Hart-Celler Act placed a quota on migration from the Western Hemisphere where none had existed previously, but U.S. presidents were given the power to admit unlimited numbers of refugees. The law also allowed immediate family members of U.S. citizens (spouses, parents, minor children) to be admitted outside of quotas, while other family unification categories (such as spouses and children of resident aliens, and brothers and sisters of U.S. citizens) were still included in the quota.

While initially much of the Asian immigration after 1965 filled occupational shortages for doctors, nurses, scientists, and engineers, these new immigrants were now able to make use of the family unification provisions. After the war in Southeast Asia ended, many Indochinese— Vietnamese, Cambodians, Laotians—were allowed to enter as nonquota refugees. In 1980, the law was liberalized again to allow those already in the U.S. on a temporary basis to request asylum, and most of these requests were from citizens of Third World nations.

In addition to the stream of legal immigrants, large numbers of immigrants arrived illegally. The 1965 Immigration Act was passed at about the same time that the Bracero program, allowing the entrance of temporary workers from Mexico, was terminated. The Bracero program had been in effect from 1942 to 1964. Reimers argues that many of these workers continued to do illegally what they could no longer do legally. In 1986, Congress passed a law granting amnesty to illegal aliens who had entered the United States before 1982.

The new arrivals to the Greater Boston Metropolitan Area differ from each other on a host of dimensions. Most are immigrants, whether legal or illegal, but those coming from Puerto Rico are U.S. citizens. Many do not speak or read English, but it is the primary language of those from Ireland and the British West Indies. Most are people of color, but those from Ireland and the former Soviet Union are white. Refugees have come from both the Western Hemisphere (Cubans, Haitians) and the Eastern Hemisphere (Vietnam, Laos, Cambodia, and the former Soviet Union).

Some immigrants are essentially on their own once they arrive, while others receive substantial support from native-born Americans who share their heritage. A 1997 *Boston Globe* article about support from the Combined Jewish Philanthropies for former Soviet Jews notes that "newly arrived immigrants can expect help finding, paying for, and furnishing apartments, aid with vocational training and job-hunting, and money for day school. Almost all immigrants are matched with counselors who help steer them through the maze of American social-service programs, and they are given initial membership at local Jewish Community Centers" (Lehigh 1997). The article goes on to observe that under these relatively favorable circumstances, "still it can be a very difficult transition."

It is even harder for others. While newly arrived Russian Jews and Irish can be absorbed within long-established communities, the same has not been true for recent Hispanic, Asian, and black arrivals. Only at the end of the twentieth century did these communities develop social and economic networks for newcomers.

Hispanic Arrivals

The first Latinos to come to Boston were labor recruits. Just as nineteenth-century Massachusetts mill owners had recruited Yankee farm girls and families from rural French Canada as mill hands, and skilled workers from the British Isles as weavers, so did twentieth-century Massachusetts employers use recruitment to solve the recurrent problem of labor shortage. The earliest streams of Hispanic migration from Puerto Rico and from Colombia can be traced to this same phenomenon.

In the case of Puerto Ricans, agricultural workers were the first to be recruited to work in Massachusetts, just after World War II, harvesting tobacco, cranberries, apples, and vegetables (Borges-Mendez 1994). Part of the process involved formal arrangements between the Migration Division of the Department of Labor of the Commonwealth of Puerto Rico and the Massachusetts Department of Employment Security. Massachusetts farmers augmented the supply by paying their Puerto Rican employees ten dollars for each new worker they recruited and by providing plane fare to the island for their own employees to persuade other Puerto Rican workers to come to Massachusetts (Uriarte 1992). Some of the workers from this agricultural migration stayed behind, though scholars dispute whether they represented a significant number (Piore 1976). Nevertheless, some of the earliest Puerto Rican families in Lawrence appear to have originated from this agricultural flow (Borges-Mendez 1994).

When Lowell manufacturers began to experience labor shortages in the 1950s and 1960s, they also turned to recruitment. As Ramon Borges-Mendez notes:

> Textile and shoe mill owners openly recruited in Puerto Rico through local newspapers. The direct recruitment by firms which owned plants in Puerto Rico and in Lowell brought many Puerto Rican families to Lowell. Many of the first Puerto Rican families in Lowell were originally from the inland towns of Comerio and Barranquitas, Puerto Rico, where actually some Lowell-based manufacturing firms had plants as well. Angel Bermudez, whose family moved to Lowell, although not directly from Puerto Rico, in the early 1960's explains: "the mill owners would recruit in *El Mundo* [a newspaper in Puerto Rico]. . . . And there was a conscious effort in the late 1950's and 1960's to fill job slots in the mills, in remaining textile and shoe operations. . . . Gray Shoe [in Lowell] was White Shoe in Puerto Rico. . . . You know, there was a White Shoe company branch in Comerio, PR." [1994, 115]

The initial Puerto Rican population in Lowell was recruited mainly from the island. But by the mid-1970s, subsequent groups of Puerto Ricans were more likely to come to Lowell from other northeastern U.S. cities like Newark, Boston, Springfield, Hartford, and especially New York City (Borges-Mendez 1994). While we cannot fully explain this secondary migration phenomenon, it should be noted that it coincided with the inauguration of a process that raised the minimum wage in Puerto Rico to the U.S. level, reducing employment and raising unemployment rates on the island (Borjas 1996). For those wanting to leave New York, the option of returning to the island may have looked substantially less attractive after 1974, and Lowell may have seemed more attractive, at least in relative terms. One Lowell company, Joan Fabrics, transferred Puerto Rican workers from their New Jersey mills to Lowell when the New Jersey mills closed (Glaessel-Brown 1991).

Lowell's first Colombians also came to the United States through employer recruitment. Initially, a textile company with a plant in Colombia brought a small number of loom fixers from that country to their Rhode Island headquarters mill in 1963. Then, a firm in New York City recruited twenty loom fixers from Medellin in 1969 to work in their Connecticut and New Hampshire mills. When these factories closed, several of the loom fixers went to mills in New Hampshire, Rhode Island, and New York. One went to Lowell to seek employment at the Wannalancit Mill. Here is the recollection of the mill owner, Ted Larter:

> Oh Christ, it must have been 1970. Can't remember, somewhere in there. He was legal. His name was Mario. I'll never forget the guy as long as I live. He drove up in a car, he spoke English, he asked me if I needed a

Draper loom fixer. And I said, "Buddy, I'll give you a kiss if you know how to fix a Draper loom." He says, "Let me show you." He . . . puts on a set of coveralls, takes his tool box out, walks out in the mill, and shows me that this man knows what he's doing. I said, "Jesus Christ, you've got a job." He said, "Would you like some more Colombian people?" I said, "I sure as hell would." [Glaessel-Brown 1991, 353]

In the ensuing years, Mario brought additional Colombian skilled textile workers to Wannalancit, and he accompanied Ted Larter on a recruiting trip to Medellin.

Such recruiting continued for a brief number of years. In the mid-1970s, however, immigration regulations no longer allowed H2 visas for manufacturing. These visas permitted employers like Ted Larter to hire foreign workers if there was a shortage in the occupation that could not be filled by American citizens. Under the new regulations, it was no longer legal to bring workers to meet emergency labor needs. They came anyway, and for a while the regulations were not strictly enforced. Larter was forced to let these workers go, however, when U.S. immigration officials required adherence to the law in 1979. Deprived of these skilled workers, the Wannalancit Mill closed in 1980 (Glaessel-Brown 1991). It was a pattern that occurred among many other manufacturing businesses in the period.

While it lasted, the Colombian connection had been mutually beneficial. The workers learned skills through training programs operated by both the Colombian government and the companies. Although these workers gave up job security and social benefits in Medellin, higher pay in Lowell attracted them to the United States. For Larter, the presence of a trained and reliable group of skilled workers was crucial to his ability to fill contracts on time (Glaessel-Brown 1991).

One might wonder how it is possible for an industry in decline, such as textile production, to face a shortage of workers and a need for foreign migrant labor. The paradox is solved if we recognize that the industry's decline was a long-run phenomenon—long enough to span a generation or more—and there were periods of brief renaissance in the sector. Thus, as Michael Piore points out,

In the Boston area, undocumented Latin American workers are moving into the jobs once held by Italians, French Canadians, and other older immigrant groups in shoes, textiles, leather tanning, and the like. Employers are quite explicit about the fact that the new migration is necessitated by a labor shortage and attribute the labor shortage to the refusal of the children of older migrant groups to move into their parents' jobs. But it is clear from the comments, not only of employers but also of the workers themselves, that it is not simply, and possibly not primarily, the attitudes of the younger workers that are at issue. Apparently the parental generation looks back upon its own employment experience as humiliating and degrading. They see it justified only by the social advancement of their families; for their children to move into the very jobs that they saw as an instrument of escape would belie the meaning of the parents' work life, and there is thus tremendous parental pressure upon children to refuse the work. . . . As one young worker explained: "That job would kill my grandmother. Even if I wanted to take it, I would never be able to explain it to her. When I came home, she would smell [the chemical dye], and it wouldn't matter how much they paid *me* to do it." [1979, 79–80]

For new immigrants, however, these very same jobs provided a level of pay and benefits not known in the countries from which they came.

The story for other immigrants has less to do with market forces and economic opportunity and more to do with political repression back home. Beginning in the mid-1960s, political instability caused many Dominicans to leave their country. Although many came to Massachusetts legally, a substantial number were unable to get visas and arrived outside the law, via Puerto Rico and New York. Large Dominican communities now live in Boston and Lawrence (Uriarte 1992; Borges-Mendez 1994). Similarly, political and economic instability in Central America during the 1980s caused migration from El Salvador, Nicaragua, Honduras, and Guatemala to the Boston Metropolitan Area. By the early 1990s, these workers became the mainstay of the remaining nondurable manufacturing sector in the Greater Boston region. Hence, the position once held by the Irish and French Canadians in the textile industry is today held not by whites, blacks, or Asians, but by Hispanics.

Besides jobs in manufacturing, Hispanic immigrants have traditionally found work in small ethnic shops in their own neighborhoods. With the recent establishment of large, white-owned supermarkets in a number of Latino neighborhoods—communities once spurned by such chains—there is the fear that many of these small shops will be run out of business. This still may occur, but there are reasons to believe many of these shops will continue to survive, serving at least new immigrants to the region. The *bodega*—the small grocery store in Latino neighborhoods—survives as a place for neighborhood socializing despite the advent of supermarket chains that can offer lower prices and larger selections (Valdes 1997).

These sorts of informal community resources reinforce the role of other social networks, including the networks people use to find jobs. Immigrants, and particularly Hispanics, tend to rely on the dense social networks within their own neighborhoods. A 1972 survey found that in the greater Boston metropolitan area, 57 percent of the Puerto Rican household heads had used personal contacts to find their present jobs, while only 15 percent of black household heads used that method. The proportions for Irish, Italian, and Greek households were 34 percent, 44 percent, and 42 percent, respectively (Action for Boston Community Development and United Community Services of Greater Boston 1972). The Hispanic network in the textile industry is typical of this behavior, as is employment in the bodega and other small-scale retail trade and service enterprises. By the late 1980s, this was true of janitorial services in downtown Boston office buildings. Hispanic crew leaders operating vans recruit day labor in Latino neighborhoods each afternoon and deliver them to an array of downtown building sites (La Plaza 1991). Blacks might have done this work a generation ago; now it is primarily the work of a network of immigrant Hispanics.

Asian Arrivals

The first group of Chinese emigrants to Massachusetts were used as strikebreakers in the late nineteenth century. The C. T. Sampson shoe factory in North Adams recruited seventy-five Chinese laborers from California to replace their striking workers. These new recruits were hired on three-year contracts, and when the contracts expired, they moved 140 miles across the state to Boston. They were joined there by other Chinese immigrants who had left California to escape virulent discrimination (Chu 1987).

Because of federal legislation excluding most immigration from Asia, through the first half of the twentieth century the Chinese population in Boston was overwhelmingly composed of single men. They came for work, but were unable to bring their wives or other family members. That did not change until passage of the War Brides Act of 1945. And substantial immigration of Chinese, largely precluded by the Chinese Exclusion Act of 1882, did not occur until the immigration reform of 1965 (Sagara and Kiang 1993). Most of those who did come settled in Boston's Chinatown.

Despite the fact that post–World War II urban redevelopment, highway construction, and the expansion of Tufts-New England Medical Center encroached on Chinatown's boundaries and reduced its housing supply, the community continues to be an important staging area for new arrivals. It has a massive rate of residential overcrowding (defined as more than one person per room). In 1980, 36.7 percent of the population in Chinatown lived in overcrowded conditions, compared with only 4.2 percent of the population of the city of Boston as a whole (Sagara and Kiang 1993).

Many of the men who live in Chinatown find employment in Chinese restaurants, both within Chinatown and in the suburbs. Shuttle vans routinely pick up workers in Chinatown and deliver them to suburban Chinese restaurants at the far edges of the metropolitan area (Dracut, Tewksbury, Raynham, Brockton) and beyond (towns in New Hampshire and even in Woonsocket, Rhode Island) (Ribadeneira 1997).

Many Chinese immigrant women find work in the garment industry, which can be a boon to their families. Unionized shops generally offer health insurance benefits to their employees, a greatly valued benefit, since the restaurant-worker husbands of female garment workers generally do not receive health insurance from their employers. Indeed, the recent decline in employment in the inner-city garment industry has raised some serious concerns about access to health insurance coverage among immigrant Chinese households (Sagara and Kiang 1993).

A vastly different social status accompanies post-1965 Asian immigrant populations. Many immigrants from India and Korea are highly educated, and arrived under the skills preference provisions of the 1965 immigration law to take professional jobs in high technology, engineering, and medical fields. Those arriving from Vietnam and Cambodia came as refugees after 1975, often with little schooling and limited skills. Many of those who came as children have been the first in their families to go to high school. As such, the Asian population in Boston today has a bimodal distribution of education, with one group among the best educated in the entire state and another having the least formal schooling of any ethnic or racial group in the region.

A second wave of immigration from Vietnam began in 1979. These immigrants tend to be much poorer, less educated, and more rural than first-wave immigrants. A small group among Vietnamese immigrants are ethnic Chinese, many of whom succeeded as merchants and small shopkeepers both before and after their migration to the United States. Their knowledge of the language and culture of both China and Vietnam makes them a critical link between the two communities. A similar role is played by the small number of ethnic Chinese among Cambodian immigrants (Sagara and Kiang 1993).

Large-scale migration of Cambodians to Massachusetts began in 1981, with many choosing Lowell, which became second only to Long Beach, California, in the size of its Cambodian population. The influx to Lowell was a combination of refugee resettlement from Cambodia and a large stream of secondary migration from other parts of the United States. According to Peter Kiang, a leading Asian scholar at the University of Massachusetts, Boston, a combination of factors made Lowell attractive to Cambodians: "Many settled in Lowell because of the city's well-publicized economic health and availability of jobs. Some were drawn by the establishment of one of the few Cambodian Buddhist temples in the country in the mid-1980s. Others came because family members or friends were already established there. Still others came simply because they heard that Lowell was a place where Cambodians live" (Kiang 1993, 55) The Wang Computer Company, one of the early leaders in electronic calculators and then computers, became a leading employer of many refugees.

With the newest wave of Asian immigrants, Boston's Chinatown itself has changed. It is no longer the only regional destination for new Asian immigrants, and many of its former residents have moved to other areas. Now there is, in addition to the Chinese, a large representation of Vietnamese, along with a smaller presence of Thai, Japanese, Cambodians, and Laotians. Chinatown has become a crossroads for Asians throughout the Boston metropolitan area, while remaining an economic and political hub for the broader Asian community.

With the new immigrants, Tom L. Chung (1995) has argued that there are three distinct archetypes of settlement in which Greater Boston Asian Americans reside. One archetype is represented by the "new immigrant" enclaves, including the Boston neighborhood of Dorchester, and the cities of Lowell, Chelsea, and Lynn, where the population is low-income, often transient, and less likely to contain complete family units. In these communities, one will find significant clusters of Vietnamese and Cambodians. Another is the "one-step-up" communities, like Quincy, Malden, and Somerville. Residents of these enclaves have typically resided in the United States for several years, live in large families that pool income across several wage earners in order to afford to buy a home, and value easy access to Chinatown. Finally, the "suburban" Asian enclaves in towns like Lexington, Newton, and Brookline are home to highly educated professionals and successful entrepreneurs. The three largest Asian groups in Lexington are Chinese, Indian, and Korean. Together, Boston and the nine other municipalities named here as enclaves account for about half of the Commonwealth's Asian American population (Chung 1995).

Recent Black Arrivals

Hispanics and Asians are not the only major newcomers to Greater Boston. In the period after World War II, many northern U.S. cities experienced substantial in-migration of blacks from the South. While central cities like Chicago, Detroit, and Cleveland were less than 10 percent black in 1940, the combination of black inflow into these cities and white outflow to the suburban communities surrounding them made each of these cities over 30 percent black by 1970 (see table 2.3). Boston's population had a much smaller proportion of blacks in 1940, and

TABLE 2.3   *Black Population as Percentage of Total Central City Population, 1940 to 1970, Selected Major Northern Cities*

Year	Boston	New York	Chicago	Philadelphia	Detroit	Cleveland
1940	3.1%	6.1%	8.2%	13.0%	9.2%	9.6%
1950	5.0	9.5	13.6	18.2	16.2	15.2
1960	9.1	14.0	22.9	26.4	28.9	28.6
1970	16.3	21.2	32.7	33.5	43.7	38.3

Source: Thernstrom 1973, 179.

despite the growth in black population over the next thirty years, it still had less than half the proportion of blacks as Chicago, Philadelphia, Detroit, or Cleveland (Thernstrom 1973).

Of blacks living in Boston in 1970, only half (49 percent) had been born in Massachusetts. Another 29 percent had been born in the U.S. South, and 16 percent had been born elsewhere in the U.S. Only 6 percent were foreign-born (Thernstrom 1973). In the next twenty-five years, however, much of the growth in the Greater Boston Metropolitan Area's black population was the result of immigration from Haiti and the British West Indies (Jamaica, Trinidad, Barbados, and Montserrat). This makes Boston's black population quite different from that in most America cities—nearly 40 percent are foreign-born.

According to a recent *Boston Globe Magazine* article, Boston has the third largest settlement of Haitians in the United States, after Miami and New York (Radin 1996). They arrived in three distinct waves. The first to leave Haiti dates back to the 1960s, in the early days of the brutal dictatorship of Francois "Papa Doc" Duvalier. Those who left at that time tended to be highly educated professionals seeking the excellent educational opportunities in the Boston area (Radin 1996). By the early 1970s, Jean-Claude "Baby Doc" Duvalier had inherited the dictatorship from his father, and a combination of political repression and disastrous economic policies fueled the second wave of migration out of Haiti. The third wave followed the military coup overthrowing the elected government of Jean-Bertrand Aristide in 1991. This latest wave includes many with peasant backgrounds and many who arrived illegally. They are too recent to have been enumerated in the 1990 census, and it is difficult to get accurate figures. Estimates of the Haitian population in Massachusetts currently range from at least 70,000 to more than 120,000, including Haitian immigrants and their American-born children (Radin 1996).

When the immigration reforms of 1965 lifted the annual quota of 100 people from each of the former British colonies, immigration from the British West Indies increased sharply. Much of the flow to Boston was secondary migration. According to Violet Johnson,

> Although Boston received a sizable portion of the post-1965 arrivals, the official statistics do not adequately reflect this trend because most of the immigrants gave New York, their first U.S. port of disembarkation, as their destination. Community data clearly indicate that many West Indians now living in Boston moved there from other cities of the East Coast, such as Providence, Rhode Island; Hartford, Connecticut; Miami, Florida; and especially New York City. [Johnson 1995]

One of the attractions of Boston is the availability of jobs in the health care industry, where many British West Indians work as nurses' aides, orderlies, lab technicians, medical records clerks, nurses, and housekeepers (Johnson 1995). Many Haitian immigrants also find employment in this sector (Radin 1996).

Although the black population of Massachusetts is concentrated in Boston, Cambridge, and Springfield, suburban communities within the Route 128 perimeter have seen a 63.5 percent increase in their black population, and a 9.2 percent decrease in their white population between 1980 and 1990. However, since the black suburban population in 1980 was so tiny, this large increase involves absolute numbers that are still relatively small. Indeed, in 1990, blacks accounted for only 5 percent of these suburbs' population (Chiu 1997a). Now most of the Haitian population lives in the Mattapan section of Boston, or in working-class areas of Cambridge, Somerville, and Brockton. Those Haitians who have achieved some measure of economic success are more likely to live in the moderate-income suburban community of Randolph, south of Boston (Radin 1996).

One important new area of settlement for blacks in the Greater Boston Metropolitan Area is the city of Brockton, south of Boston. As early as 1900, there were nearly 600 blacks in Brockton, many of whom worked as gardeners, coachmen, janitors, housekeepers, or laborers (Carroll 1989). In 1950, Brockton's population was only about 1 percent black. By 1990, however, it had increased to 13 percent black; an additional 6.3 percent were Hispanic, and there were substantial numbers of Asians as well (Nealon 1991). According to Bruce Hughes, an economic development specialist with the Old Colony Planning Council who was interviewed for this project, blacks and other minorities have moved to Brockton because of the availability of jobs, affordable rental housing, and a good public bus system. Although shoe manufacturing is almost entirely gone from Brockton, some garment industry manufacturing remains. The largest employer in the area is Chadwick's of Boston, a retailer of women's clothing through catalog sales. It has a large minority workforce and is accessible by public transportation.

Beside its employment opportunities, Brockton offers relatively affordable housing close to Boston. Forty-three percent of Brockton's housing stock is rental housing; 12 percent of the housing stock is subsidized. Real estate firms in Brockton advertise in Boston's black media, including the *Bay State Banner*, touting low crime and affordable housing.

With a large and growing minority population, Brockton is facing issues that cities like Boston faced decades ago. In 1992, black clergy and community leaders met with the Commonwealth's attorney general to complain about police brutality and racial insensitivity among police officers; in 1995, Brockton passed a school desegregation plan in response to the failure of four of its schools to meet the Commonwealth's racial imbalance law (Hart 1992; Reid 1995). Still, what Brockton faced in 1995 bears only a faint resemblance to what Boston confronted back in the early 1970s.

Busing and School Desegregation: Tumult in the City

Despite the fact that Boston has historically had a small black population compared with other major northern cities, it was the locale of one of the most dramatic of the northern school desegregation stories. The crisis over school desegregation was arguably the city's most wrenching experience of the late twentieth century.

While busing cannot explain the huge migration of white families out of Boston during the 1950s and 1960s, it is crucial for understanding the development of racial attitudes during the 1970s and after. For months on end, busing was the lead story of every local newscast. The race and class antagonisms that were expressed affected not only those neighborhoods where the buses rolled, but the entire region. Boston is now a city whose overall population is only about 50 percent minority, but whose public school population is 85 percent minority. This aspect of demographic change—namely, the discrepancy in the age distribution of the white population compared with that of minorities—has its origins in the busing crisis.

When the Supreme Court struck down systems of formal school segregation in the 1954 *Brown v. Board of Education of Topeka, Kansas* case, it left untouched the question of segregation that arose in the absence of legal enforcement. In many northern cities like Boston, de facto segregation resulted from deeply entrenched patterns of housing segregation (Hochschild 1984; Orfield and Eaton 1996).

Massachusetts claims the distinction of being the only state that has attempted to outlaw de facto segregation within its schools. Its Racial Imbalance Act of 1965 declared it illegal for any school to be more than 50 percent black. At the time, the act had practical meaning for only three jurisdictions within the Commonwealth: Boston, Cambridge, and Springfield, the only cities with sizable enough black populations to make it possible to have schools that were racially unbalanced, as the term was defined by the law. This definition, of course, did not affect suburban communities, whose school systems were almost exclusively white.

Even before the law was enacted, an advisory committee to the State Education Commissioner recommended that racial imbalance in Boston could be corrected by changes in the open enrollment program, the strategic siting of new school buildings, the closing of some school buildings, and limited use of busing. The Boston School Committee, then an elected body, resisted these remedies for years. By 1971, the State Board of Education decided to freeze $200 million in funds for new construction and to withdraw $14 million in state aid, saying that the School Committee had "taken official action to increase and encourage racial isolation" (Lukas 1985, 218). Later that year, the Boston School Committee and the State Board of Education were embroiled in a court battle in the state Superior Court.

When the NAACP filed suit against the Boston School Committee in Federal District Court in 1972, in the case of *Morgan v. Hennigan*, it argued that school segregation in Boston was not merely the result of housing segregation, but that the Boston School Committee had deliberately followed policies that discriminated against black schoolchildren—that is, that the segregation existing in Boston schools was indeed de jure. Thus, the two cases proceeded almost simultaneously, the state case arguing that the School Committee had violated state law by failing to correct de facto segregation and the federal case arguing that the School Committee had violated *Brown* with long-standing practices that amounted to de jure segregation. In the federal case, plaintiffs' lawyers argued that the School Committee had practiced intentional discrimination through a host of methods, which Lucas lists as "optional attendance zones, manipulated district lines, differential grade structures, open enrollment, feeder patterns, site selection policies, portable classrooms, and various pupil assignment practices" (Lukas 1985, 236).

In 1973, the state's Supreme Judicial Court ordered the State Education Department to prepare a plan to correct the racial imbalance in

Boston's schools. On June 21, 1974, Federal Judge W. Arthur Garrity found the School Department guilty of de jure segregation and ordered the State Education Department plan implemented when schools reopened in September. The new plan called for the extensive use of busing between hostile communities, including South Boston and Roxbury. Outraged by the court's order or frightened by its implications, many white families withdrew their children from Boston's public schools and enrolled them in private and parochial schools. Some who could afford to move picked up and relocated to suburban school jurisdictions. The racial climate in the city degenerated rapidly. Whites who did not flee to the suburbs helped elect school committee members prone to intemperate and baldly racist comments. One of the new school committee members, Pixie Palladino, referred to blacks as "jungle bunnies" and "pickaninnies." Another, John Kerrigan, described a black television network news correspondent as "one generation away from swinging in the trees" (in Lukas 1985, 137–38). Emblematic of the hardening of racial attitudes in Boston's white working-class communities was the Pulitzer Prize–winning photograph taken at an antibusing rally in 1976, in which angry white youths wield an American flag to attack a lone, well-dressed black man (Lukas 1985).

Much of the working-class Irish anger was directed at the more prosperous and privileged Irish who supported school desegregation but did not have to endure it themselves. Anthony Lukas describes the busing crisis as "a family feud between the Irish who had made it and the Irish who hadn't" (Lukas 1985, 246). Picketers demonstrated outside Judge Garrity's Wellesley home; Senator Ted Kennedy was pelted with tomatoes for his support of school desegregation.

Experts on school desegregation such as Jennifer Hochschild (1984) and Gary Orfield et al. (1996) have argued that the most successful plans are those that include the entire metropolitan area. Such plans are more common in the South, in places where school districts are countywide, in a county large enough to embrace both the central city and its suburbs. In the North, it is more common for school districts to be coterminous with municipal boundaries.

Rulings by the U.S. Supreme Court assured that this school district pattern would drive a sharp wedge between Boston's schools and those beyond the city's borders. In *Milliken I* (*Milliken v. Bradley* 1974), the Court ruled against integration plans that would cross central-city school district boundaries unless it could be shown that suburban jurisdictions or state action contributed to de jure segregation within the central city. The immediate impact of *Milliken I* was to overturn lower court rulings that would have required a metropolitan-wide school desegregation plan for Detroit and its suburbs. In a follow-up decision in

1977, the Supreme Court ruled in *Milliken II* that a state could be required to pay for educational programs to compensate for segregation. This was a monetary remedy for the overwhelmingly black Detroit school system, where integration was impossible in the absence of a solution for the whole metropolitan area (Orfield 1996).

Milliken made it far more difficult to implement metropolitan plans for desegregation, though various federal district courts found grounds to mandate city-suburban desegregation in Louisville, Wilmington, and Indianapolis (Orfield et al. 1996, 13). In Boston, the legal case against segregation was brought against the actions of the Boston School Committee, not suburban jurisdictions or the Commonwealth itself. As a result, only those whites who continued to live in the city saw their children bused to accomplish the court's intent of integrating the region's schools. Ethnic whites, who for years suffered from isolation and inadequate spending on education and other social needs, bore the brunt of a wider and deeper challenge.

Thus, the tumultuous earthquake that shattered Boston's surface once again came down to the fault lines of race and class. Ron Formisano, another chronicler of the school desegregation saga, writes: "If there is anything to the analogy that sees busing as 'the Viet Nam of the seventies,' it lies in the fact that once again poor blacks and lower-class whites were the foot soldiers for a war initiated and pursued by liberal elites, and most of the affluent and college educated were exempt" (Formisano 1991, 225). The era of school desegregation in Boston officially ended on July 14, 1999, when the School Committee voted in favor of the superintendent's recommendation to remove race as a factor in assigning students to schools (Zernike and Vigue 1999). The superintendent's decision was prompted by legal advice presented to the Boston School Committee contending that continued use of racial preferences would almost surely involve a costly and losing court battle, given the Supreme Court's revised stand on affirmative action.

Race and Ethnicity: Beyond the Public Schools

The questions of race, ethnicity, and social class go well beyond the public schools, of course. Here's how one writer describes the city: "In Boston, movie theaters cater to black crowds or white crowds. Restaurants rarely attract racially mixed gatherings, although there's a sprinkling of South End places that manage. At Red Sox games you can spot more blacks on the playing field than in the stands. Same thing at the Garden when the Bruins play. The Celts are marginally better. Boston is two separate cities, one black, one white" (Barnes 1995, 209).

Given this description, is it any wonder that some black leaders in the 1980s decided it might be a good idea to make the metaphor a political reality, and to create two separate cities? The frustrations of dealing with a city government perceived to be unresponsive to the needs of its black citizens was one of the motivating forces behind a campaign in black neighborhoods to create a separate jurisdiction, named in honor of the South African leaders Nelson and Winnie Mandela. In the context of the booming Boston economy of the early 1980s, black residential areas like Roxbury had the potential to be prime real estate, and the fear was that once again, residents would lose control over the land they occupied, and once again, an area ripe for redevelopment would mean displacement of the African Americans who lived there. The nonbinding referendum to establish Mandela was on the November 1986 ballot in those wards of the city that would have contained the proposed new jurisdiction. Opponents outspent proponents 2 to 1, with 90 percent of the opposition funding coming from white individuals and corporations. Although the proposal was defeated 3 to 1, it gave the issue of who controls economic development, and especially who controls the land, much attention (Kenney 1987; Kennedy, Gaston, and Tilly 1990).

In the aftermath of the defeat of the Mandela referendum, there were attempts on behalf of both black and white leaders to improve the racial climate in the city. But in October 1989, a single incident would do much to reopen old wounds. Boston and the nation were shocked by reports of a callous crime: it had been reported that a pregnant woman had been shot dead, and her husband seriously wounded, by a black man who had jumped into their car to rob them of money and jewelry as the white suburban couple was driving home from their childbirth preparation class at Brigham and Women's Hospital in Boston. Details given by the husband, Charles Stuart, indicated that the black man had ordered them to drive to a nearby public housing project, where he made his escape.

It was the nightmare version of the suburban paranoia that causes many white suburban residents of the metropolitan area to avoid the city, despite the fact that Boston has a relatively low crime rate. In response, Boston police conducted an intensive search in the Mission Hill public housing project, seeking a rather vaguely described black man in a jogging suit, of medium height and build. It turned out that the perpetrator was none other than the husband himself, who had taken out substantial insurance policies on his wife in a coldly calculated scheme, a crucial part of which was to blame it all on a marauding black man, that quintessential symbol of white suburban fear. The tragedy is that he was so willingly believed. As Joe Sharkey points out in his book on the subject: "From the moment he had decided to kill his wife and try to get away with it, Chuck had sensed that the time was right. From cynical street-smart cops to hard-nosed editors on assignment desks, from the townhouses of Cambridge to the triple-deckers of Chelsea and the cottages of the North Shore, white people in the metropolitan area were primed to give automatic credence not only to the plausibility of Chuck's story but also to its absolute inevitability" (1991, 135).

The incident severely damaged race relations. In their zeal to find a suspect in a sensational case attracting nationwide media attention, the Boston police desperately searched the area around Mission Hill: "black males were strip-searched on the streets of Mission Hill. A man who looked the wrong way at a cop who stopped him soon found himself against a wall with his pants down at his knees—often as his girlfriend or even children stood looking on. Nothing that was done on Mission Hill in the aftermath of the Stuart shootings caused the outrage that this did. It was worse than a beating. It was the ultimate sign of disrespect, and a generation of black males from the Mission Hill Projects will never forget it." (Sharkey 1991, 149)

Struggles over political and economic power and basic issues of respect have not been limited to black-white relations. Ethnic and racial antagonisms in Lawrence, Boston, and Lowell have involved clashes between whites and members of various new immigrant groups. In August 1984, two days of rioting broke out in Lawrence, beginning with a name-calling incident that pitted Latinos against French Canadians, both groups living in poor-quality public and private housing near the bottom of Tower Hill (Schinto 1995).

In 1985, an incident of police brutality against Long Guang Huang, a recent Chinese immigrant, galvanized the Chinatown area of Boston into protest and eventual victory. As Doris Chu points out: "The police beating of Long Guang Huang came at a time when anti-Asian violence was raging. During the summer of 1985 alone, a Vietnamese family was attacked in South Boston, a Cambodian household was attacked in East Boston, fourteen Cambodian families were burned out of their apartment building in Revere by arson, a Cambodian was beaten to death in Medford, and numerous other cases of racial violence against Asian Americans were reported and unreported throughout the Commonwealth" (Chu 1987, 73).

In 1987, tensions in Lowell arose over the failure of the public schools to accommodate a large influx of non-English-speaking Latino and Southeast Asian children. When their parents filed a lawsuit against the public schools, they were met with substantial anti-immigrant sentiment and calls for an English-only municipal policy. Under pressure, the Lowell School Committee adopted a controversial desegregation plan in June 1987: "Fueled by English-only rhetoric, anti-immigrant sentiment escalated throughout the summer and climaxed in September with the drowning of Vandy Phorng, a thirteen-year-old Cambodian boy who was thrown into one of the canals by an eleven-year-old white boy who called him racist names. The white child's father was an outspoken advocate for English-only in Lowell" (Kiang 1993, 56). In November 1989, voters in Lowell approved an English-only nonbinding referendum by a margin of 72 percent to 28 percent (Kiang 1993). Thus, white-Hispanic and white-Asian conflicts added new chapters to the long history of racial and ethnic antagonism in Greater Boston.

Access to Decent Housing and Schools

Racial antagonism and discrimination, of course, can take much more subtle forms. In 1989, the Boston Federal Reserve Bank found that predominantly minority neighborhoods were not being treated equitably by Boston-area lenders. The study found that the ratio of mortgage loans to potentially mortgageable homes was 24 percent higher in white areas than in minority areas, after controlling for nonracial differences such as family income and wealth, housing value and age, vacancy rates, and new housing construction. Members of the newly created Community Investment Coalition used these findings to launch a $400 million, five-year effort by Boston banks to expand their lending in underserved areas and provide more ATMs and other services and amenities (Squires 1994).

A limitation of the 1989 study is that while it pointed to unequal treatment of places, data gathered under the 1975 federal Home Mortgage Disclosure Act (HMDA) could not provide information regarding bias toward individuals of different racial groups. To fill this need, Representative Joseph Kennedy III of Boston succeeded in 1990 in getting HMDA to require data collection on mortgage loan and application rates by race, gender, and income. A subsequent Federal Reserve Study of Boston-area lending using 1990 HMDA data found that 30 percent of black and Hispanic mortgage applicants were turned down, compared with 11 percent of whites. The ambitious study polled 131 of the area's most active mortgage lenders, examining a sample of about 3,000 applicants of various races. While economic variables such as credit history, ratios of debt to income, and other factors explained some of the variation, it was found that if minority applicants had the same economic characteristics as whites, their denial rate still stood at 17 percent versus the 11 percent for whites (Browne and Tootel 1995). The study highlighted the importance of the subjective dimension in lending decisions—the degree of judgment exercised by loan officers in applying secondary market guidelines.

To the credit of the area's banking industry, there have been definite signs of improvement. From 1990 to 1993, denial rates for black and Hispanic households in the city of Boston were halved, and most of this improvement was the result of changes in performance by Boston's largest banks (Campen 1995). A follow-up study showed that denial rates in Boston were substantially below nationwide denial rates for whites as well as for blacks and Hispanics, but that while denial rates for black households in Boston fell continuously between 1990 and 1995, denial rates for Hispanic households began to rise in 1995 (Campen 1996).

The interplay of market and institutional forces has been exhibited in the housing market in still another way. In 1994, Massachusetts voters approved a state referendum to end rent control in the last three jurisdictions where it still existed: Boston, Brookline, and Cambridge. Opponents of rent control had contended that the policy was poorly targeted, citing accounts of controlled units held by students, higher-income professionals, and even elected officials. The end of rent control led to an almost immediate sharp increase in rents. A recent study of the Cambridge rental market finds that median monthly payments for formerly rent-controlled units rose 85 percent, and as a result younger, wealthier, and better-educated tenants are now displacing former residents (Babson 1998). In Boston, evictions following vacancy decontrol increased by 17 percent, with just under one-third of all evictions in 1996 occurring in rent-controlled units.

Unfortunately, for those who were unable to afford the substantial increases in rent, there were few openings elsewhere in the immediate area, with vacancy rates at 0.5 percent and long waiting lists for public housing. Ironically, the ending of rent control may have led to increased integration in nearby working-class communities, where at least some minority families sought more affordable housing.

What adds to the problem is that suburban resistance to affordable housing is still strong, particularly in the richer suburbs more distant from Boston. For example, despite state law that sets a goal of 10 percent affordable housing in each community, it took the town of Dover thirty years to approve its first affordable housing initiative—six units of housing for the elderly (Curran 1997). So the opportunity to find housing in many of Boston's suburbs is severely limited for families of modest income, especially for those who are nonwhite.

Demographic Change and the Future

The Greater Boston Metropolitan Area is in the midst of a remarkable demographic revolution thirty years in the making and still very much in progress. Old hostilities based on religious differences have given way to newer suspicions and resentments based on race and class. In this new and dramatically restructured economy, the newcomers to the region are seeking a way to earn a living and to provide decent housing and good-quality education for themselves and their families. In many ways, this is an old story. For the better part of two centuries, virtually all the new arrivals to Boston have faced challenges in the workplace, in the schools, and in the political arena as a result of deep-seated ethnic and class antagonism. Racial and class attitudes provided a critical element in the opportunity nexus that restricted the residential choice and labor market mobility for the Irish who came in the middle of the nineteenth century. It was necessary to overcome discrimination and prejudice in order for them to gain access to decent jobs and decent housing.

How will those at the bottom of the income ladder at the beginning of the twenty-first century fare, especially immigrants and people of color, many of whom have come with little education and few financial resources? What are their chances of joining the social, political, and economic mainstream, as immigrant groups before them have? How long will it take? This will depend, in part, on whether racial and ethnic antagonisms can be overcome.

It will also depend on the market—on whether the regional economy will provide sufficient opportunity for all workers in Greater Boston to obtain good jobs at good pay. This, in turn, depends a great deal on whether the new industries that comprise the region's economic base will provide good job opportunities for the region's newcomers and those who are well down in the job queue in the local labor market. Understanding the nature and extent of the region's industrial revolution therefore becomes critical to considering the opportunity nexus faced by Boston's new diverse, multicultural workforce.

3

THE INDUSTRIAL REVOLUTION: FROM MILL-BASED TO MIND-BASED INDUSTRIES

THE SINGLE most important factor affecting a household's economic well-being is its relation to the labor market. After all, with the exception of the very rich, the very poor, and the retired, the majority of most families' income emanates from earnings, not from income-generating assets or transfer payments. Annual earnings for a family depend on a wide range of factors: the number of individuals within the household who work; how much each worker earns per hour; how steady is his or her employment; and whether the worker can find full- or part-time work.

To a greater or lesser extent, these labor market phenomena are related to the skills and talents workers bring to the workplace. But how they actually fare in the market depends on the type, strength, and viability of the industries that dominate a regional economy. During the 1950s and 1960s, for example, even workers with modest skills prospered in cities like Detroit because of the high-wage jobs, replete with a profusion of employee benefits, offered by the auto industry or won by their union. At the same time, workers with no less skill would be impoverished in some New England company towns where the local textile mill or shoe factory had shut down operations.

Moreover, virtually every region's industrial structure changes and evolves over time in response to a wide array of institutional factors and market forces. As some sectors grow in importance while others decline, there will be a concomitant shift in the labor market opportunities facing each household. Some will see their skills outmoded, while others will find their skills in great demand. Hence, to understand the labor market opportunities open to the households within a metropolitan area, we must understand the region's industrial structure and how it has changed over time.

As noted in the previous chapter, the industrial revolution of the nineteenth century created a huge demand for unskilled and semiskilled workers to tend the machinery of the textile mills and shoe factories. Boston-area employers solved their labor shortage problems by actively recruiting workers from the agricultural hinterlands of New England initially, and then from French Canada and Europe. Until the early 1920s, the doors of the country were thrown open to bring in successive waves of immigrants to serve as the nation's factory workforce.

Throughout the twentieth century, Greater Boston experienced a wrenching change in its industrial base. Only within the past twenty-five years has the area tasted the fruits of the process that the great economic historian Joseph Schumpeter called "creative destruction," whereby new growth and prosperity depend on the previous era's obsolescence. Old capital, he argued, must be abandoned to provide the resources for new industrial pursuits. This always involves a painful disruption in the lives of some workers as it provides new opportunities for others.

A nearly inevitable aspect of creative destruction during the past half century has been the declining demand for traditional low-skilled factory workers. New industries generally require a workforce more skilled than the old one, with employees more used to working with their minds than the sweat of their brows. These industries, including high-tech hardware and software, higher education, health care, and financial services, rely on legions of professional workers. But they depend on low-skilled workers as well. High-tech needs assembly workers; higher education needs groundskeepers and cafeteria workers; hospitals need orderlies; and financial services located in downtown office buildings need their suites cleaned by janitors. The problem in any local economy for individual firms is finding the right number of workers with the right skills to fill the number and types of jobs offered. The problem for individual workers is to acquire the right skills to get a job that provides reasonably good wages, reasonably steady work, and the chance for promotion. When the industrial structure of a region is changing rapidly, both firms and workers can find themselves challenged by the process of creative destruction—by institutional factors and market forces often outside their control. This is the case in Boston as it continues its high-tech industrial revolution.

Greater Boston's Changing Economic Base

No metropolitan area is entirely self-sufficient, in the sense of being able to produce within its boundaries all the goods and services its residents want to consume. There are, for example, no automobile assembly lines currently in operation in the Greater Boston Metropolitan Area—although Henry Ford operated an assembly line on the banks of the Charles River in Cambridge from 1917 to the early 1950s and General Motors assembled Chevrolets in Framingham until the early 1980s. Since there is no longer a Model T to buy from Ford or a Chevy Lumina from GM, Greater Boston residents who wish to buy new cars must "import" them from outside the metropolitan area. And to "import" desired goods and services from outside the region, they must produce something they can "export"—that is, sell to the rest of the world outside Greater Boston—in return. This is the central premise of *economic base theory*, which argues that an area's ability to export products beyond its boundaries is crucial, both because the income from exports can pay for imports and because income flowing into the area from exports can recirculate and support public- and private-sector services, from garbage collection to dry cleaning. If the demand for an area's export goods should fall, the ability to import goods will be compromised, and the wherewithal to support public and private local services will begin to disappear (Heilbrun 1987). When this happens, a region sees its prosperity vanish.

In the late nineteenth century, when the price of silver was high, many silver mining towns in Colorado grew to great prosperity. When the price of silver fell, most of them became ghost towns. A few received a mid-twentieth-century new lease on life as tourist destinations. Why were these mining towns economically viable for only a few years, while Greater Boston has been viable for over 350? Indeed, why didn't Greater Boston turn into a ghost town with the collapse of shipping and whaling in the early nineteenth century, or the decline of textiles and shoes in the early twentieth?

What matters over the long run is an area's ability to invent or attract new export bases as the old ones decline. Success here is largely a matter of the quantity and quality of an area's productive resources. Whereas the mining towns' productive resources consisted almost entirely of the silver deposits lying underground, Greater Boston has been able to offer a variety of productive resources that have made it a place from which new firms and industries can emerge. Still, Boston has had periods in which its old industries were drying up well before new ones arose. During these periods, Boston saw its economic ranking among cities fall precipitously.

The physical features of the region played a prominent role in the development of its early export success: a deep harbor for the shipping industry and proximity to fishing and whaling grounds, and fast-flowing rivers with steep fall lines for the water-powered textile mills. As natural resources faded in importance because of revolutions in transportation and communication, features of human creation became more important—including a skilled and educated labor force and a spirit of entrepreneurship.

In examining this shift in the Greater Boston Metropolitan Area economic base, one can find themes of profound change as well as of continuity. Changes that have occurred include the shift from manufacturing to services, the shift within manufacturing from nondurable goods to durable goods, and the shift in business location from a highly concentrated central city to a more dispersed variety of suburban locations.

The most visible evidence of continuity appears in the adaptive reuse of the built environment. Quincy Market, for example, which opened on the Boston docks in 1827 during the heyday of ocean shipping and subsequently fell into partial disuse, reopened 150 years later as one of the first "festival marketplaces" in the United States. The Assabet Mill in Maynard was once the world's largest woolen factory (Mullin, Armstrong, and Kavanagh 1986); it went on to house the Digital Equipment Corporation. The canals and locks that once controlled the water flow into the Lowell Mills now carry boatloads of tourists, who come to see a bygone era recreated for them. Another example of continuity is in the area's use of labor: continued reliance on a skilled and versatile labor force, a higher proportion of female workers than almost all other regions, and heavy use of immigrant labor.

The American Industrial Revolution

Perhaps the most important of the themes of continuity in the region is the prevalence of innovation, both technical and organizational. As the journalist Neal Peirce writes,

> The textile industry was in fact New England's first high technology industry. It had its genesis in 1790 in a daring act of industrial espionage by young British immigrant, Samuel Slater, who brought to America, in his head, the secret designs of the first power looms ever made. Slater's technology was then exploited by shrewd Yankee businessmen, largely out of capital generated by New England's seafaring successes, and by utilizing the power from the region's abundant rivers. From the technology applied in textiles, machinery could be developed for the shoe, leather, paper, and . . . machine tool industries which followed. [Peirce 1981, 111]

As Peirce observes, each wave of innovation leaves an invaluable "residue" of finance, skilled labor, cheap but reusable old buildings, and educational institutions created with money donated by the magnates of earlier industries. Thus, early in the nineteenth century, the fortunes made in shipping and commerce were being used to finance a new endeavor: the production of cloth in factories. To the west of Boston, the city of Waltham preceded Lowell and Lawrence as a site for textile production, the Boston Manufacturing Company having started there in 1813. The Lowell mills began when the Merrimack Manufacturing Company was formed in 1822, and for a century after, Lowell dominated cotton textile production and deserved its nickname of the Spindle City. The town of Lawrence was created by the Essex Company in 1845 (Federal Writers' Project 1937).

The mills themselves, initially dependent on water power, needed to be located at the fall lines of fast-moving rivers. The mills built at Lowell, for example, were at the confluence of the Concord and the Merrimack. Still, the finance capital, and the families that provided the finance capital, were located in Boston proper. The textile industry continued to grow throughout the nineteenth century, and as it expanded, its labor force shifted from Yankee farm girls to immigrant men, women, and children. While Yankee farm girls constituted a large majority of New England textile workers in 1850, they accounted for only 11 percent of the textile workforce by 1900 (Dublin 1994). Immigrants, in fact, were the real basic raw material of the textile mills. As Oscar Handlin writes, "in the two decades after 1845 the Irish energized all aspects of industrial development in Boston by holding out to investors magnificent opportunities for profits from cheap labor" (Handlin 1959, 74).

Other cities in eastern Massachusetts became early sites for shoe production. By 1836, Haverhill, to the north of Boston, had more than two dozen shoe factories. Shoemaking in Lynn extends back to the craft workers of the eighteenth century, the predecessors of the nineteenth-century factory workers. During the Civil War, Brockton, to the south of Boston, would become the largest shoe manufacturing city in the country, the result of contracts from the U.S. government to produce boots for the Union Army (Federal Writers' Project 1937). Brockton's peak shoe production occurred more than a century ago, in 1899. The industry suffered a long decline in the twentieth century, as other centers of shoe production grew in the Mississippi Valley and elsewhere and internal organizational problems stymied the industry's ability to adapt to change. That much of Brockton's twentieth-century economic problems stemmed from overreliance on a single industry is reflected on the title page of a 1947 report to the city by the noted economic consultant Homer Hoyt, which reads: "there was a fair city that lived in a shoe" (in Carroll 1989).

With its expanding manufacturing sector and vibrant construction industry needed to build the mills and the housing for its workers, it is not surprising that Boston became a center for union organizing. By the end of the nineteenth century, the American Federation of Labor (AFL) had become the dominant labor organization nationally, and many of the trades within the construction industry had organized themselves into AFL-affiliated craft unions. In Boston, these unions were dominated by the Irish, and became another vehicle for delivering some measure of economic security, as well as political support, for Irish politicians such as James Michael Curley. As early as 1910, 21.1 percent of Boston's workforce was unionized. In Lynn, site of a dramatic strike among workers in the shoe industry a half-century earlier, 25.5 percent of the workforce was unionized. And in Brockton, unions were so successful that nearly 60 percent of the workforce was unionized, either in the Boot and Shoe Workers union or other AFL unions (Juravich, Hartford, and Green 1996). Unionization brought wage gains, restrictions on child labor, and safer working conditions.

The New England economy did well during World War I, with high wartime demand for textiles, garments, and shoes. After the end of the war, however, its economy fell on bad times. The textile industry declined dramatically after 1924, the result of mill owners' decisions to build their new plants in the South, while phasing out the older plants in the North. Rationalization of production allowed them to make use of a cheaper, less skilled, and less militant labor force. In the shoe industry, plant closings were more often the result of "runaway shops"— equipment was actually loaded onto trucks to move from one location to another (Harrison 1984). Even before the rest of the country experienced the high unemployment rates of the Great Depression, unemployment in New England ranged between 12 and 15 percent (Miller 1974).

The area that now comprises Greater Boston contains many municipalities with formidable independent industrial histories. The 1937 *WPA Guide to Massachusetts* (Federal Writers' Project 1937) provides sketches of these municipalities as they existed in the period just prior to World War II, and it is from these wonderfully written sketches that the following descriptions are drawn. Table 3.1 lists the population of these communities as tabulated by the WPA Guide, using the 1935 state census.

Immediately to the north of the city, Boston's industrial neighbors include Cambridge, Somerville, and Chelsea. While Cambridge's image to the outside world may be based on Harvard and MIT, there is another Cambridge, the industrial city the WPA Guide refers to as the "Unknown City." In 1937, the value of goods manufactured in Cambridge ranked third in New England, behind only Boston and Providence. In Somerville, industrial development began with the opening of the Middlesex Canal in 1803. By 1937, major industries included meat-packing

TABLE 3.1   *Population of Selected Industrial Municipalities*
             in Eastern Massachusetts, 1935

Boston	781,188
Brockton	62,407
Cambridge	118,075
Chelsea	42,673
Haverhill	49,516
Lawrence	86,785
Lowell	100,114
Lynn	102,320
Quincy	76,909
Somerville	100,773
Waltham	40,557

Source: Federal Writers' Project *1937.*

plants and slaughterhouses, bakeries, confectioners, foundries, and machine shops. Although Chelsea had been a summer resort in the nineteenth century, the advent of reliable steam ferry service transformed it into a manufacturing and shipping community by the turn of the century.

Farther to the north, Haverhill and Lynn were early manufacturing sites. Haverhill's products included boxes, paper, foodstuffs, and brooms, in addition to textiles and shoes. Alongside the shoe industry in Lynn, the General Electric plants located there would make GE the largest single employer in the Commonwealth on the eve of World War II. It would become one of the primary producers of piston aircraft engines during the war, and later one of the nation's premier producers of jet engines for small aircraft and helicopters. Woolen mills were still the primary source of employment in Lawrence, but other industries had also settled there, including paper and soap. To the south, Boston's immediate neighbor, Quincy, was the site of enormous quarries that were providing granite for buildings and bridges all along the East Coast by the late eighteenth century. Its history of shipbuilding began in the late nineteenth century and continued until the 1980s. To the west is Waltham, which the WPA Guide called the City of Five-Score Industries because of its diverse manufacturing base. Its most famous was the Waltham Watch Company, established in 1854.

Each of these cities and industries would be hard hit by the establishment of competing firms in other regions of the country and then pounded by the Great Depression. When the writer Louis Adamic visited New England in 1930, he was struck by the terrible poverty, hunger, and despair caused by the massive unemployment that had by then been prevalent for several years even before the 1929 stock market crash.

Places like Lowell, Lawrence, and Haverhill had experienced dramatic losses in population during the 1920s. In shoe towns like Lynn and Brockton, Adamic estimates that about two-thirds of the industry's workers had no work at all, not even on a part-time basis.

Once the United States geared up for wartime production, however, and companies won government contracts, employment in the textile and shoe towns picked up. The exceptions were companies producing women's shoes: they used a process different from that used in the production of men's shoes and could not easily make the conversion to manufacturing footwear for soldiers. In Lowell, many of these companies closed when their workers were attracted to the better wages in existing factories with wartime contracts and in the new factories that were opening up or expanding: Remington Arms, General Electric, and U.S. Rubber (Miller 1988).

While the city of Boston did not suffer the large population decline that befell Lowell, Lawrence, and Haverhill during the 1920s, its population grew very slowly during that decade and declined during the next. Boston's population grew again during the war (Thernstrom 1973). World War II represented both a bridge to a new era and a temporary interruption of industrial decline. Manufacturing temporarily rose from 42 percent to 45 percent of Massachusetts employment. War production restored full employment to the mills, at least through 1943. But, even before Germany and Japan surrendered to Allied troops, these towns experienced a decline in employment. Outlying areas such as Brockton and Lowell were especially hard hit. Over one in four workers was out of work in some communities, such as Lawrence (Eisenmenger 1967).

The steady loss of work in the region's core industries exacted high human costs. Boston-area textile wages, which had been 52 percent higher than those elsewhere in the United States in 1926, were forced down after the war by high unemployment and the migration of jobs (Krushnic 1974). In response, many workers and their families, particularly younger people, fled the region, while others were forced to accept work in lower-paying occupations. Relatively few—3 percent, by one estimate—made the transition to high-technology industries. The early electronics firms along Route 128 were able to draw some of their production recruits from traditional mill and metal-working industries, mostly women who had been doing precision work in companies like the Waltham Watch Company (Krushnic 1974).

In many ways, the decline of the mill economy of textiles, footwear, and related machine tools acted as a crucible for the region's "restructuring," creating a pliant and lower-cost labor force, disciplined by unemployment and declining unionization (Harrison 1984). The New England region as a whole had 357 textile establishments in 1919, 259 in

1929, and 161 in 1939 (Harrison 1984). These and other maturing indus-tries were lured south by lower labor costs, tax advantages, and other inducements, including lower rates of unionization. Market changes also played a role in industrial decline: rising demand for cheaper, mass-produced cotton apparel, and subsequently for synthetics, advantaged other regions. The adoption of central heating reduced the demand for heavy woolen clothing.

Financial inertia also played a role. Descendants of New England's "money men," who had become fabulously rich during the boom years of clipper ships and cotton spinning, grew complacent in the twentieth century, declining to invest heavily in new enterprises or in upgrading old ones (Adams 1977). The region's industrial facilities and equipment came to be seen as increasingly obsolescent. Government investment in the infrastructure of competing regions' economies, particularly in the Sunbelt during World War II, contributed to New England's and Boston's industrial decline as well (Harrison 1984). The claim has been made that Lowell's and Lawrence's heavy reliance on the textile industry and fail-ure to broaden their economic bases were partly the result of mill owners' using their economic and political power to deter the entry of new industries that might compete for the same labor force (Miller 1988; Schinto 1995).

For twenty-five years, until the late 1970s, it appeared that the de-cline would continue as traditional goods-producing economic activity continued to shift to other parts of the country and, increasingly, abroad. Yet, with the growth of high-tech industry, the health care and higher-education sectors, and financial services, the region began its phoenix-like renaissance.

The Beginning of the Late-Twentieth-Century Industrial Revival

In the postwar decades, the world of the mills and allied machine shops gave way to something new. Nonmanufacturing industries—including trade, finance, transportation, and services of all kinds—became much more prominent as places of employment throughout the country. In no place was this more true than in Greater Boston. Within manufacturing, durable goods industries—primarily the making of various kinds of ma-chinery—took precedence over nondurables. The occupational mix within the growing sectors of manufacturing, including office machin-ery and transportation equipment, became less blue-collar, with rising proportions of professional, managerial, and technical employment. The skill level of blue-collar jobs in these fields rose as well, with a corre-sponding drop in low-skilled manufacturing jobs. Very low-skilled (and low-paying) work mushroomed in other fields, however, servicing the new professional-based economy.

Boston once again became a hotbed of innovation. Some of the post–World War II inventions created in the region include the computer architecture designed by the region's big four high-tech companies of the 1970s and early 1980s—Digital Equipment, Data General, Prime, and Wang—and the microwave oven, developed by Raytheon. Other innovations that have emerged from the Boston metropolitan area have had a profound impact on the way we organize economic life. These include the industrial park, the venture capital market, circumferential, limited-access highways like Route 128, and the fully enclosed shopping mall. Perhaps the most important organizational change, however, was the relationship that developed among research universities (notably MIT), the federal government, and industry. High technology—and the wider "new economy" of knowledge-based goods and services—would be unthinkable without this nexus, which has its roots in World War II but has older antecedents in New England history as well.

Postwar economic development in Greater Boston is typically told as a story of high technology. This is only part of the tale. The dominant trend in metro Boston actually has been the area's transformation into a service economy, with manufacturing a smaller, though important, portion of the region's total product and employment. High technology itself is dominated by service employment, housed in research and development corporations, and in engineering and consulting firms. Even at the height of the so-called Massachusetts Miracle, in 1986, only one in ten jobs statewide was in high technology (Rosegrant and Lampe 1992) and only one in fifteen was specifically in high-tech manufacturing (Dukakis and Kanter 1988).

Well before the "miracle" decade, the Boston region had been firmly established as a service exporter, based on its institutions of higher learning, hospitals, and allied health services. Now the demand for those services was expanding rapidly. A 1976 report found that the Boston metro area "exports proportionately more of the services it generates than any other large metropolitan area": 29 percent (Carlaw 1976, 12). Higher education and its world-renowned hospitals bring in students and patients from around the country and around the world, producing export revenue—income flowing into Greater Boston from outside the region.

Professional services, including legal, architectural, and engineering, and business services, including advertising and consulting, swelled the ranks of white-collar employment and filled the office towers that were added in profusion to Boston's skyline beginning in the late 1970s. Government also grew as an employer, with Boston itself housing not only its own City Hall, but the state capital and the New England regional headquarters of the federal government. The creation of a special Government Center in Boston assured that billions of dollars of economic activity would not be scattered across the state and region. No other city has such a wide range of government employment concentrated in such a way as to drive the whole regional economy.

Government and the Renaissance of Boston's Industrial Base

The region's profitable links among private industry, academia, and federal funding date back to the mid-nineteenth century. In 1861, the brothers William and Henry Barton, both scientists, realized their dream of a first-class school dedicated to the "practical arts" when the state approved the charter for the Massachusetts Institute of Technology (MIT), first located in Boston's Back Bay. Initial funding came from educational, business, and professional leaders of Boston, but the school received a crucial boost when President Abraham Lincoln signed the Morrill Act into law the following year. The act granted large tracts of land to states to subsidize colleges supporting agriculture and the "mechanic arts." It gave substantial support for incorporating science and engineering into university curricula; besides MIT and the state university's first campus in Amherst, these years also saw the creation of industry-focused institutions such as Northeastern University, the Wentworth Institute of Technology, and the Lowell Technical Institute (now the University of Massachusetts, Lowell) (Rosegrant and Lampe 1992).

From the outset, MIT sought close links to industry, placing students in real-world as well as classroom settings, and encouraging close consulting relationships with the business world. Numerous business leaders were educated there; the future chief executives of General Motors, General Electric, DuPont, and Goodyear were all classmates in the 1920s. One student who never graduated, but who blazed a trail for many others in the region's development, was a young chemist named Arthur D. Little, who established the world's first industrial consulting firm in 1886 on Milk Street in Boston. ADL would in time become consultants to such regional and national giants as United Shoe Machinery, General Chemical Corporation, and International Paper. The world-famous consulting company also set up, in 1911, General Motors' first materials-testing laboratory. ADL's work helped prove the worth of industrial research. During this time, the firm joined MIT in moving across the Charles River to a section of Cambridge that would later be dubbed Research Row. Eighty years later, the number of management consultants in Massachusetts would swell to 11,000, as this industry gained prominence in the new global economy (Rosegrant and Lampe 1992; Kahn 1986; Porter 1991).

Research laboratories also grew. Bell Laboratories evolved from the work of Alexander Graham Bell, who utilized free access to MIT's research facilities to perfect the telephone in 1876, and soon placed the first "long-distance" telephone call, from Boston to his Cambridge laboratories. General Electric—a merger of Lynn electrical companies and Edison's Schenectady works—established the state's largest industrial facility in the former shoemaking center just north of Boston. GE also created the first industrial laboratory, oriented primarily to basic scientific research. This represented a departure from the electrical giant's past strategies of development via the buying up of inventors' patents or acquiring smaller companies. GE was also a pioneer in MIT's cooperative education program, created in 1917, which would eventually embrace most of the state and nation's premier high-technology firms (Rosegrant and Lampe 1992; Krushnic 1974).

Perhaps the most fruitful collaborator between industry and MIT was electrical engineering professor Vannevar Bush, who helped found in 1922 the American Appliance Company—initially a maker of refrigerators in Cambridge's Kendall Square. The fledgling company soon changed its name to Raytheon and began producing radio tubes, as well as plowing an unprecedented amount of the small firm's funds into basic and applied research. It soon built an extensive collaborative and consulting relationship with MIT. The Boston magnate Charles Francis Adams, who became chairman of Raytheon, would later report that these cooperative links had been critical to the firm's survival (Rosegrant and Lampe 1992; Saxenian 1994; Scott 1974).

The easy working relationships between academic scientists and industrial engineers would prove to be critical to another kind of partnership, which Bush was also central in promoting. On the eve of America's entry into World War II, Bush employed his considerable clout with academics, businessmen, and politicians to convince President Franklin Delano Roosevelt to establish the National Defense Research Committee (NDRC). The researchers mobilized by Bush would report directly to FDR, achieving an "end run" around the military bureaucracies and funneling millions of dollars in research contracts to Boston-area universities—with MIT reaping the lion's share. During the war, its faculty received seventy-five contracts, totaling $117 million for research and development of radar and sonar and a host of other sophisticated technologies.

Bush headed the NDRC's sponsor agency, the newly formed Office of Scientific Research and Development. In Anna Saxenian's words, his work with OSRD "revolutionized the relationship between science and government by funding universities rather than government labs to pursue basic military research" (Saxenian 1994, 13). It also vastly expanded small companies such as Raytheon and large research-based firms such as GE, Bell Labs, and Westinghouse. The wartime experience would enable Raytheon and similar organizations to bid successfully for huge defense contracts to develop missile-guidance systems in the decades to come. All of this would presage Boston's late-twentieth-century industrial revolution.

Another product of these efforts was MIT's Radiation Laboratory (Rad Lab), the first "large scale interdisciplinary R&D organization at a U.S. university" (Saxenian 1994, 14). Its four thousand employees included over a thousand scientists and engineers, many of whom would work in private industry—or found their own firms—after the war. The state's and the region's postwar renaissance, particularly in the field of high technology, was in large part the product of this collaboration. The military and, later, the space program were avid and continuing consumers of the area's burgeoning expertise in all things technical. As a result, the region became a powerful magnet for technology and science professionals. A poll commissioned in the 1950s by Clevite, an early denizen of Route 128, found that scientists ranked the Boston area second only to San Francisco as their most preferred place to live (Krushnic 1974).

Federal largesse fed the economy in civilian areas as well, with each new agency stamped from the original mold of OSRD. These would include the National Science Foundation (another Vannevar Bush creation), the National Institutes of Health, the Atomic Energy Commission, and later the Departments of Energy and Transportation, and NASA. The region's medical research complex, aided by NIH and NSF, among others, has in recent years incubated entire industries, including biotechnology and medical instrumentation, much as defense research spawned electronics and computing machinery in prior decades. By the 1970s, the medical sector was New England's largest employer, with its world-class teaching hospitals and research facilities concentrated in Boston.

Pent-up postwar demand for consumer products helped feed the new electronics boom, as did the cold war, especially with the rush to develop advanced air defense systems. At the request of the armed forces, MIT created the Lincoln Laboratory to develop long-range radar, radio communications, and digital computing, and later spun off another laboratory, the quasi-public MITRE Corporation. Modern computers can be traced in part to Project Whirlwind and related efforts by MIT's Jay Forrester and colleagues at other schools to calculate massive amounts of military data quickly. The navy nearly pulled the plug on the project until the Russian atom bomb and the Korean War restored interest in it (Warsh 1986). In similar fashion, the Soviet's launch of Sputnik propelled MIT's Instrumentation Lab to develop space guidance systems.

Legions of spinoffs emerged from these laboratories. Founders of these firms, in turn, created their own startups, often tapping similar pools of research contracts. By the early 1960s, Raytheon—itself an MIT spinoff, in a sense—had spun off nearly 150 companies. "Like a biblical patriarch," in Russell Adams's phrase, MIT begot untold generations of companies, by some estimates over four hundred in Massachusetts alone (Adams 1977). ITEK spun off from Boston University, while Harvard's An Wang would found his own minicomputer dynasty. Perhaps the best-known spinoff firm was started by Lincoln Lab's Kenneth Olsen, a graduate student of Jay Forrester, who co-founded Digital Equipment Corporation in 1957. The legacy continued as Digital's Edson de Castro departed ten years later to found Data General, which would spawn Apollo Computer, in turn sparking nine other computer firms (Rosegrant and Lampe 1992).

The benefits of government spending went far beyond the GEs, Raytheons, and Digital Corporations. The research complex that was constructed during World War II rested not only on academic and government institutions but also on an industrial infrastructure of machine shops and other suppliers that had initially developed to support textile, footwear, and other traditional industries (Krushnic 1974). New generations of tooling firms, many with old-time roots, evolved to service succeeding clusters of high technology firms in assorted industries.

Still another industry critical to high-tech's success, and itself a product of the Boston region, has been financial services. The development of venture capital funds for new high-risk startups can be traced to the Boston machine tool executive and Federal Reserve Board member Ralph Flanders, who sought a means to finance new, research-based companies that might develop peaceful applications for war-created technologies. He also saw in the stagnant pools of Boston's textile fortunes, which were held primarily in insurance companies and trust funds, untapped opportunities for capital investment. To channel these funds, Flanders argued for "a development corporation financed in large measure by these two groups of institutions, under the directorship and management of the most capable men available in the fields of business and technology" (quoted in Adams 1977, 280).

Backed by partners in business, academia, and banking, Flanders founded American Research and Development (ARD) in 1946, under the leadership of General George Doriot, a Harvard Business School professor. Early investments were made in electronics startups founded by

MIT faculty and staff, though MIT eventually curtailed its financial relationship with ARD (Saxenian 1994). ARD would later provide startup capital of $70,000 to Olsen's Digital Equipment Corporation, an investment that would grow in value to over $300 million by 1966, when DEC went public. The First National Bank of Boston (now BankBoston and soon likely to be part of the regional banking powerhouse, Fleet Financial) also guided wealthy investors to high-tech entrepreneurs, and formed the nation's first Small Business Investment Corporation (SBIC) in 1958. The bank also set the precedent of accepting federal R&D commitments as collateral for loans to startups (Lampe 1988). ARD and First National employees would go on to "spin off" their own venture funds as well (Saxenian 1994).

The mutual fund industry was spawned in the mid-1920s by Massachusetts Financial Services, Inc.—now MFS. By the end of the century, this entirely new industry begun in Boston would control $5 trillion in investment funds. Fidelity, Puritan, Putnam Investments, and Keystone would be added to the long list of global financial companies operating from headquarters in downtown Boston. Employment in this industry would explode in the 1980s and 1990s as stock and mutual fund ownership expanded to much of the middle class.

The Decline of Defense, Economic Malaise, and Economic Recovery

In the 1960s, federal defense spending comprised 65 percent of the state's high technology expenditure (Dukakis and Kanter 1988). This dependence was widely noted and lauded at the time, but it would become a serious problem when spending on both Vietnam and the space program began to wind down at the end of the decade (Arthur D. Little, Inc. 1970). Between 1970 and 1972, thirty thousand jobs were lost in the region's high-technology industry, with Raytheon alone shedding ten thousand employees—40 percent of its workforce (Saxenian 1994).

These defense-related losses were compounded in 1973, when President Richard M. Nixon—some say avenging his loss in the Bay State to George McGovern—closed Charlestown Navy Yard, which had employed over five thousand workers in the early 1970s, down from a peak of fourteen thousand in the previous decade (Hill 1996; Arthur D. Little, Inc. 1970; Warsh 1986). More than fifty high-technology manufacturing plants also closed during these years, while nondurable goods manufacturing continued its slow decay (Lampe 1988). By mid-decade some were calling New England the "new Appalachia, " as unemployment rates topped 11 percent and Massachusetts ranked at the bottom of major industrialized states in per capita income (Dukakis and Kanter 1988). A decade later, less than a quarter of high-technology work would be defense-related, but no one could deny that a significant portion of the Massachusetts Miracle employment growth had been attributable to defense.[1]

To fill the gaping hole in the economy left by declining government spending in the region, private markets for high-tech products would be needed. This became obvious as the regional recession of the mid-1970s deepened. Many of the surviving technology firms were forced to seek commercial markets when the relative protection of government-sponsored work collapsed. These markets in turn were shaped by new technological advances: innovations in performance and capacity that drove the size and cost of computers down to a level that small and mid-sized business users could afford. DEC had already made history with its Programmed Data Processer (PDP-8), a minicomputer that outperformed its rivals, despite its incredibly low $20,000 price tag. Later generations would rival mainframe computers at a fraction of their cost and size. DEC so revolutionized the computer mainframe market that it would grow to become second only to IBM in computer sales and employment (Saxenian 1994).

The industry that grew up around minicomputers would signal the second act of the region's postwar development, as electronics had represented the first. By 1980, Massachusetts would capture 70 percent of the burgeoning computer industry, which would be dominated by DEC, Data General, Prime, Wang, and a handful of other minicomputer makers. Suppliers of electronic components and accessories would also expand rapidly in these years, as would a raft of supporting business and professional services, including software design, computer and data processing, management consulting, advertising, and public relations. These services were spurred by new technological innovations which, in turn, boosted the computer industry even more. They would also generate a greater share of employment growth, disproportionately in the highly educated, professional, and technical ranks—40 percent in both computer and management services (Dorfman 1988; Kuhn 1982; Browne 1988).

The area's economic revival can also be tied to corporate actions and labor conditions that provided the image of a "good business climate," in Bennett Harrison's words. These included the weakening of unions, as traditional sectors declined; the establishment of less unionized sectors, as high technology manufacturing and business and personal services grew; the depressing of wage demands, as successive recessions and high unemployment dampened militance; and rising proportions of women, youth, and immigrants in the workforce, who tended to be more flexible with regard to wages and working conditions

(Harrison 1989; Krushnic 1974). High-tech executives organized to counter the state's "Taxachusetts" image, creating the Massachusetts High Tech Council (MHTC) in the late 1970s, primarily to lobby for lower tax rates and related pro-business policies.

The Occupational Transformation

We have already described the massive *industrial* shift, from manufacturing to services, and within manufacturing, from nondurable to durable goods. Changes in *occupation* paint a similar portrait: the move from a lower-skill, mill-based economy to one based on higher skills and high technology. At mid-century, a worker in the Boston region was nearly as likely to wear a blue collar as a white one. By 1990, the ratio of white- to blue-collar employment was more than 3 to 1 (see table 3.2). The balance of employment is pink-collar—mainly clerical work—which has remained a near constant share of employment in the region and the country over the past forty years.

Professional and technical fields have led all other occupations in growth in the post–World War II period. Over one-third of the new employment generated since 1950 has been in these occupations; one in four of all employees today hold such jobs. Executive and managerial positions represent the second largest group in terms of the employment growth rate. This group has expanded by more than tenfold since 1950; those who hold these top-level jobs now comprise about one in six workers in the region. The growth of higher-skilled occupations has been accompanied by a drastic decline in lower-skilled work, particularly the type of semiskilled trades that characterized the textile mills and other blue-collar employers. Table 3.3 illustrates this transition.

In 1950, only a little better than one-fifth of the Boston metro labor force was employed as professional, technical, executive, or managerial workers. By 1990, the proportion had nearly doubled, to 39 percent. Pre-

TABLE 3.2   *White-Collar Versus Blue-Collar Employment, Metro*
            Boston and the United States, 1950 and 1990

	Metro Boston		United States	
	1950	1990	1950	1990
White-collar	47%	69%	47%	60%
Blue-collar	42	19	42	27

Source: U.S. Department of Labor 1995.

TABLE 3.3   *Occupational Distribution: Metro Boston and the*
             United States 1950 Versus 1990

	Metro Boston		United States	
	1950	1990	1950	1990
Professional-technical	12%	23%	9%	18%
Executive-managerial	10	16	17	13
Clerical-administrative	17	18	13	17
Sales occupations	8	12	7	12
Precision production-crafts	15	9	15	12
Operatives-assemblers-laborers	27	10	27	15
Service occupations	11	12	11	14

Source: U.S. Department of Labor 1995.

cisely the opposite had happened to the relative size of the lower-skilled blue-collar and service occupations: they fell from 38 percent of the total labor force in 1950 to just 22 percent by 1990. This great shift in occupations is dramatically evident in Figure 3.1. In 1950, there were 221 sales and clerical workers and 233 semiskilled and unskilled blue-collar workers per 100 professional and technical workers. By 1990, the ratios were down to 126 and 41, respectively. Clearly, this shift has major implications for what skills one needs to succeed in the Greater Boston labor market. During boom times, there may be enough jobs to keep less educated and less skilled workers employed, but if and when Boston's economy slows down, the occupational twist away from blue-collar work and unskilled work in general may pose a serious challenge.

Preserving and Expanding Greater Boston's Economic Base

Efforts to stem the tide of inner-city plant closings and to retain manufacturing within the old industrial cities are on the agenda of many of the area's municipalities, along with efforts to court new industries outside manufacturing. To provide jobs in Boston's inner city, both the Stride Rite Shoe Manufacturing Corporation and the Digital Equipment Corporation (DEC) built neighboring light industrial facilities in Roxbury's Crosstown area in the late 1970s. Great fanfare greeted these plant openings with the hope that such commitments to the inner city would pave the way for additional companies to set up shop in this once-spurned area of the city. This would not come to pass. Worse yet, in a grim coincidence, both companies announced the closing of these landmark facilities on the very same day, in December 1992. The announce-

FIGURE 3.1   *Number of Employees per 100 Professional and Technical Workers, Metro Boston*

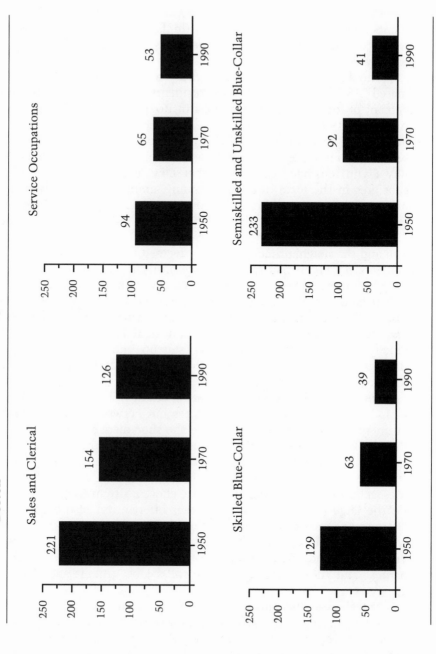

Source: U.S. Department of Labor 1995.

ments shocked the community, particularly given the widely heralded reputation for socially conscious business practices on the part of both employers.

The dual closings cost the Roxbury neighborhood 340 jobs, an estimated 215 of them held by local residents. The job loss represented 17 percent of total manufacturing jobs in Roxbury (Boston Redevelopment Authority 1993). City officials were angered by the closures and the breaking of an implicit social contract between business and its public benefactors. In a press conference soon after the announcements, Mayor Ray Flynn reminded the media that DEC had received $7 million in subsidies in the form of bond financing, grants, tax incentives, and reduced rent since it had broken ground in 1978 at the site. "Two hundred families have been given a terrible Christmas gift by Digital," he added. "In the final analysis, the company got what they could get from the city and the neighborhood and then decided to get out" (Biddle and Hyatt 1992, 1). Flynn had tried unsuccessfully to convince DEC to retain its jobs in the inner-city facility, but the computer maker concluded that it could obtain needed cables less expensively by purchasing them from outside vendors rather than manufacturing them. The former DEC plant now houses the Boston Technological Development Center, an "incubator" facility for nurturing startup and young biotechnology firms, as well as employers that offer job opportunities to area residents (City of Boston 1995).

For its part, Stride Rite's relocation out of Roxbury was the object of a bidding war not only between states but between city and state government. While Boston tried to woo the shoe distribution facility to the former Boston State Hospital site in Mattapan or the former Readville railyards in Hyde Park, Governor William F. Weld urged the company to consider the soon-to-be-closed military base, Fort Devens, in central Massachusetts. In the end, Stride Rite chose a site in Kentucky, not only for the large financial subsidies it was offered, but also because of the latter state's proximity to its western markets (Biddle 1993, 57).[2] Meanwhile, city officials suggested darkly that state decision makers were viewed by Stride Rite's leaders as "exclusively chasing biotech companies" and "not interested in blue collar jobs" (Biddle and Hyatt 1992, 1).

Lowell was also the site for dramatic plant closings in the 1990s. Wang Laboratories, Inc., relocated its assembly plants and corporate offices to Lowell in 1976 and, in a decade of stupendous growth, became Lowell's largest employer, with a 1986 payroll of $114 million. What followed, however, were several years of equally precipitous decline, with the firm filing for bankruptcy in 1992 (Kiang 1993). Old-line firms were closing, too. In 1997, the Borden Foods Corporation announced that it would close the venerable Prince pasta plant, which employed about four hundred workers, most of whom were immigrants from Portugal and Laos (Reidy 1997a). The pasta plant ceased production, but a group called the Boston Macaroni Company—composed of investors, the plant's union, and former plant managers—made plans to buy the facility (but not the Prince brand name, which Borden refused to sell) and reopen it. Ultimately the plans failed, and Borden agreed to sell the plant to Joan Fabrics for use as a textile warehouse (Reidy 1997b).

Amid all the sad stories of corporation CEOs choosing to leave Massachusetts cities, one happy story involves the commitment of Aaron Feuerstein, the owner of Malden Mills (whose textile products include the popular Polartec fleece fabric), to rebuild his plant on-site in Lawrence after it was destroyed by a devastating fire in 1995. Feuerstein received nationwide recognition, including a seat next to Hillary Clinton during her husband's 1997 State of the Union message, for choosing to reinvest in Lawrence when he had other options (Powers 1997, 41). Hundreds of jobs, most held by Hispanic workers, were saved in the process.

Boston has made an explicit (although, as can be seen in the Digital and Stride Rite cases, not always successful) effort to retain, attract, and develop manufacturing within the city through its Economic Development and Industrial Corporation (EDIC), established by Mayor Kevin White in 1971. Its early accomplishments included the acquisition on favorable terms of vast tracts of former military facilities and Massachusetts Port Authority land in South Boston, and establishment of nonprofit development entities that could provide industrial firms with financial assistance. It also gained attention by assisting the Hood Dairy in staying in Charlestown, and working with Chinatown organizations to stem the loss of garment industry jobs. (The eventual loss of much of this employment testifies to the difficult odds faced by EDIC and similar agencies.) As a quasi-public entity, EDIC was empowered to take land by eminent domain, issue taxable and tax-exempt revenue bonds, buy and sell property, and otherwise act as a banker, broker, and developer of industrial land (Boston Redevelopment Authority, Economic Development and Industrial Corporation, n.d.). It also operates the Boston Technical Center, a private, nonprofit trade and business school.

The primary inducements employed by EDIC to cultivate blue-collar jobs are cheap land and low-interest financing for firms' capital needs. Its industrial parks include South Boston's Marine Industrial Park, Roxbury's Crosstown Industrial Park, and Dorchester's Alsen-Mapes. The South Boston facility, EDIC's largest, encompasses nearly

200 acres and houses about 200 companies employing 3,500 people. More recently, the agency has been absorbed into a larger superagency for zoning, planning, and economic development, encompassing the Boston Redevelopment Authority. The city even briefly considered the sale of EDIC's successful Boston Marine Industrial Park to the private sector in order to reap increased property tax revenue (Boston Redevelopment Authority, Economic Development and Industrial Corporation, n.d.).

Several Massachusetts cities have attempted to broaden their economic base to include a variety of industries outside manufacturing. Some have considered the standard and now-familiar, if questionable, panaceas of casino gambling, major league sports stadiums, and convention centers. Others, like Lynn, have turned to new immigrant businesses to renew their ailing downtowns. A new $2 million facility on Union Street, which houses the Community Minority Cultural Center and the Business and Cultural Opportunity Center, has been opened with the hope that it can help transform a downtown district blighted by boarded-up buildings into a hub of ethnic entrepreneurship (McCabe 1997). Chelsea, Lowell, and Lawrence are seeing similar changes, with significant Hispanic ownership of retail shops in Chelsea and Lawrence, and significant Southeast Asian ownership in Lowell (McCabe 1997).

The city of Lowell has received much recognition for its Lowell Plan, which the late Senator Paul Tsongas, a Lowell native, helped create in 1979. It is a partnership between the public and private sectors that guides economic development. According to the journalist John Powers, the Lowell Plan is one important reason why Lowell has had more success in recovering from economic hardship than has its neighbor, Lawrence. Another reason is that Lowell has a vision for itself: "So Lowell knows what it wants and what it has to have to be successful in the 21st century—a city with a balance of knowledge-based and manufacturing jobs and a downtown attractive enough that its people don't have to go elsewhere to buy a book, eat dinner, see a play, or watch a hockey game" (Powers 1997, 44). Recently, the Wannalancit Mill buildings and the Prince pasta plant have both undergone extensive renovations to house the industries of a new era, including a video-editing software firm (Bushnell 1999).

Thus, we have found that in the period since the end of World War II, Greater Boston has witnessed severe decline in the industries that had been its legacy since the nineteenth century. However, like the proverbial phoenix rising from the ashes, the area has been able to transform its inheritance—the quantity and quality of productive resources that were a by-product of its previous era of economic prosperity—into a postindustrial mind-based economy of high technology and services. This has had, as we shall see, a profound effect on the labor market prospects of the region's new immigrants, as well as those whose ancestors came to the area decades or even centuries ago.

4

THE SPATIAL REVOLUTION: FROM HUB TO METROPOLIS

FROM the top floor of Boston's tallest skyscraper, I. M. Pei's John Hancock Building, one can view both the tiny area that comprised colonial Boston and the broad sweep of settlement that comprises Greater Boston today. While every metropolitan area can tell a story of outward expansion from an original core city, the Greater Boston story is unique in some important respects. Its spatial revolution sets the stage for understanding residential segregation by income and by race, just as its demographic and industrial revolutions provide the backdrop for understanding racial and ethnic attitudes and labor market outcomes. The spatial revolution affects not only the relocation of households but the relocation of business. Where people live and where they work are two crucial elements in the opportunity nexus of a region.

Like the demographic and industry revolutions, spatial change is a product of both institutional and market forces. Federal, state, and local government housing and transportation policies have a profound effect on the value of land and its use. The siting of subway stops in the city and the placement of highways and their on/off ramps in the suburbs create new centers for community and commercial activity. Market forces enter the picture as changes in income and wealth make it possible for families to invest in new housing and move to new locations. A booming economy can provide the incentive for firms to convert abandoned lofts in the city into office space and abandoned mills in surrounding towns into corporate headquarters.

Over the past twenty years, all this has been happening in Boston and the larger metropolitan region surrounding it. The result has been a profound alteration in the housing and employment opportunities open to workers and their families. The spatial distribution of housing has changed, along with the spatial distribution of business enterprise.

Any realtor will tell you that "location, location, location" are the three most important factors in determining the value of a piece of real estate. Two homes identical in every other respect will sell for very different prices depending on the desirability of their community's amenities. Moreover, the value of particular locations changes over time, as the stately housing of one era may filter down to lower-income occupants, or the shabby rooming houses of another period gentrify into condominiums for young urban professionals. Greater Boston has seen both patterns in abundance. The same is true of industrial and commercial properties.

In his 1992 book, *Edge City: Life on the New Frontier*, the journalist Joel Garreau describes the phenomenon in which sleepy little villages thirty or forty miles from the downtowns of large cities have become major centers of economic activity. While Greater Boston has its share of "edge cities," like Framingham and Burlington, the pattern of outward expansion there is more complex than elsewhere. As economic activity spilled over Boston's boundaries, it filled in the spaces between already-existing cities that were important sites of production in their own right. Greater Boston's spatial transformation has intersected with its demographic and industrial transformations to produce a unique set of problems and opportunities for the region.

Spatial Change in Nineteenth-Century Boston

The hub of the eastern Massachusetts region has always been Boston, even when other towns (like New Bedford) were richer. In the aftermath of the War of 1812, Boston experienced population growth of nearly 3 percent a year. Geographically, the small, crowded peninsula could not offer much vacant land for new enterprise. Residences and business establishments were jumbled together, as were the elegant homes of the wealthy and the modest homes of the poor (O'Connor 1991; Warner 1962; Edel, Sclar, and Luria 1984).

After 1830, the city's population started to grow even more quickly, and the small peninsula hemmed in by water was in desperate need of more space. The development of railroads in the 1830s helped solve the space problem, by making commuting from the suburbs a feasible option, at least for the wealthy, and also transporting the huge amounts of earth that were necessary for large-scale landfill operations needed to establish new wharves in this sea-based commercial city and to create the South End in the 1850s and the Back Bay in the 1860s (Whitehill 1968). Because of the early rail transport to communities beyond Boston's borders, the area contains some of the nation's oldest suburbs. The early development of Newton as a suburb may be traced to the opening of the Boston and Worcester Railroad in 1834; three railroads served Boston and its environs as early as 1850 (Edel, Sclar, and Luria 1984). A hundred years later, the automobile, an interstate highway running into the heart of the city, and circumferential highways skirting Boston provided the means for another, more powerful centripetal migration from the central city.

Beyond the "streetcar suburbs" such as Roxbury and Jamaica Plain—formerly independent villages that were incorporated into the city of Boston itself—outlying towns such as Medford were transformed from summer estates for the wealthy to workaday communities for the "middling" classes, as electric railways (and, later, the automobile) made them accessible to commuters (Warner 1962; Jackson 1985). Wealthier commuters moved to farther removed locations, such as Lincoln and Concord, and communities located on Boston's edges became blue-collar suburbs that grew as Boston's trade and textile-based economy stagnated.[1] Towns like Belmont were settled by wealthy taxpayers and real estate speculators who sought to "create a residential enclave free from the costs of services for other classes of citizens" (Edel, Sclar, and Luria 1984, 232). By the late nineteenth century, the area experienced phenomenal geographic expansion, but as economic activity spilled beyond city limits, municipal boundaries would no longer expand to encompass the new growth.

For nearly a decade after the Civil War, the municipal boundaries of Boston had grown through annexation: Roxbury was annexed in 1868, Dorchester in 1870, and Charlestown, Brighton, and West Roxbury in 1873. The town of Brookline resisted annexation in 1873. It was large and prosperous enough to have its own municipal waterworks. The establishment of metropolitan districts in 1885 extended that kind of independence to smaller suburban jurisdictions (Warner 1962). These districts were a rational response to problems that needed coordination beyond the level of local government, but they also shifted the balance of power among Boston, other local governments, and the state government. Suburbs were no longer forced into being annexed by Boston simply to gain access to a safe and reliable water supply (Edel, Sclar, and Luria 1984).

Decentralization in the Late Nineteenth and Early Twentieth Centuries

If we define *decentralization* as a slower rate of population growth inside the central city, compared with the growth rate of the surrounding suburbs (Heilbrun 1987), that process was already under way in Boston by 1890—a full century ago (Thernstrom 1973). In contrast, for the United States as a whole, central cities were still growing faster than their surrounding suburbs until 1920 (Heilbrun 1987). Although Hyde Park was finally annexed to Boston in 1912, the annexation process in Boston was substantially over by 1873, and the city of Boston's share of the metropolitan population fell continuously, from nearly half (46 percent) in 1880 to little more than a third (35 percent) in 1940 (Thernstrom 1973). The end of annexation created a Boston metropolitan area in which the central city comprised an unusually small proportion of the population and land area, compared with other metropolitan areas throughout the nation.

It also created an opportunity for the more privileged Bostonians to insulate their residences from the disamenities of the late-nineteenth-century industrial city. Oscar Handlin observes that in the aftermath of the Civil War, "Depressed by the ugliness of industrialization and by the vulgarity of its new wealth, the proper Bostonians wished to think of themselves as an aristocratic elite rooted in the country, after the English model. They moved out to the rural suburbs of Brookline and Milton and resisted proposals to annex those towns to Boston. They sent their children to private schools and found self-contained satisfaction in their gentlemen's clubs" (Handlin 1959, 221). The spatial divide between classes hardly began with school busing in the 1970s; it was under way a hundred years earlier.

To their credit, the Brahmins continued the tradition of philanthropy established by the previous generation of mercantile wealth, whose contributions founded the Boston Athenaeum, Massachusetts General Hospital, McLean Hospital, and The Perkins School for the Blind in the early part of the nineteenth century. Their late-nineteenth institutions include the Boston Symphony Orchestra, the Boston Public Library, the Museum of Fine Arts, the Lowell Institute, and the Massachusetts Institute of Technology. They did not found Harvard, which had been established in the seventeenth century, but they supported it mightily (Adams 1977). Thus, they continued to direct the educational and cultural life of the area, even while insulating their families from the poverty and grit of its everyday rhythms.

The decentralization begun before the turn of the twentieth century has never really stopped. To some extent, this pattern is similar to that of other metropolitan areas. However, unlike the case in other cities, where suburban expansion spread out over farmland and sleepy villages, in the Boston metropolitan area, suburban growth occurred in the interstices between long-established municipalities that were already significant loci of industrial activity. As Boston's suburbs expanded, they filled in the spaces between the old manufacturing cities that had been economically independent entities in the nineteenth century—creating a dense web of urban "villages" networked together by mass transit and highways. This spatial reorganization was accompanied by an increase in residential segregation by income and race.

From 1890 to 1940, the area within a ring four to nine miles away from the center of Boston grew the fastest. In part, this growth was due to the advent of trucking, which allowed the creation of industrial sub-urbs and their concomitant stock of working-class housing (Edel, Sclar, and Luria 1984). Thus, as the suburban ring grew, it became ever more differentiated, and segregation by income increased. At the same time, racial segregation within the central city of Boston was reinforced by the policies of the Boston Housing Authority (BHA). When the BHA began to build subsidized housing in the 1930s, it segregated all black tenants into one project in the South End; none were placed in Irish-dominated South Boston or in other white areas of the city, like Charlestown. Its policy of deliberate racial segregation remained in place until the 1960s (Lukas 1985).

The Post–World War II Spatial Revolution

World War II and its aftermath would bring another round of astounding spatial change to the area. The postwar decline of central cities and the concomitant explosive growth of suburbs across the United States have been well documented by such historians as Kenneth T. Jackson (1985) and a group of urban economists including James Heilbrun (1987). This dramatic decentralization may be seen as the consequence of market forces, often ratified by explicit government policy. For business firms, market forces include changes in technology—for example, the use of assembly-line production and forklift trucks that make single-story fa-cilities preferable to multistory lofts; single-story facilities require more land area, so many manufacturing and warehousing firms sought outly-ing areas, where land was less expensive. For households, market forces refer to the combination of widespread preferences for low-density neighborhoods of single-family homes plus the ability to realize those preferences as real incomes rose during the postwar era, which propelled many families toward the "crabgrass frontier" of the suburbs, with sin-gle-family homes with lawns to mow (Jackson 1985; Heilbrun 1987). In addition to the attractiveness of the suburbs, business firms and some households were also motivated by the desire to leave central cities that were perceived as having high crime rates, strong trade unions, road congestion, high tax burdens, and growing numbers of blacks.

Explicit policies enacted by the federal government provided incentives that fueled the growth of suburbs at the expense of central cities. The Federal Housing Administration (FHA) brought homeownership within the range of a large group of moderate-income households that would otherwise not have been able to afford it. By insuring mortgages against default, the FHA guaranteed that banks could make these loans risk-free. In return, it required that banks offer better terms than in their conventional mortgages: lower down payments and longer payback periods.

Part of the requirement for eligibility was that structures meet minimum construction standards established by the FHA. In practice, it was easier to meet these standards through new construction than through renovation of existing housing. Similarly, the program was administered to favor single-family over multiple-family structures. The result was that the bulk of FHA insurance was written for newly constructed single-family homes in the suburbs (Jackson 1985).

Federal policies also reinforced local factors working to make Boston's suburbs economically and racially homogeneous. In 1938, the FHA's Underwriting Manual asserted that "if a neighborhood is to retain stability, it is necessary that properties shall continue to be occupied by the same social and racial classes. A change in social or racial occupancy generally contributes to instability or a decline in values" (quoted in Squires 1994, 53). To maintain racial segregation, the agency encouraged the use of racially restrictive covenants in sales contracts and deeds involving mortgage insurance. Its instructions for avoiding "infiltration" of "inharmonious racial or national groups" were maintained officially until 1948, when they were ruled unenforceable by the Supreme Court. But the FHA continued to "redline," or refuse mortgage insurance to minority-dominated inner-city areas, until 1965 (Colman 1975).

Explicitly racialist federal policies were complemented by local public- and private-sector actions. These include deliberate racial "steering" by real estate brokers and other discriminatory practices, as well as zoning, land use, and subdivision policies that limited densities and use categories, while expanding frontage and setback requirements. Many suburban communities in the Boston area also fiercely resisted efforts to develop denser and/or subsidized housing, and continue to do so to this day.

A second policy of the federal government aiding suburban growth at the expense of central cities was the mortgage interest–deduction provision of the federal personal income tax code. This provision subsidized homeowners but not renters, with the greatest subsidies going to those in the highest income tax brackets. Before the advent of the condominium in the 1970s, apartment living was synonymous with rental tenure, while those occupying single-family homes tended to be owners.

Hence, the occupants of urban housing generally did not benefit from the home mortgage deduction, while suburbanites reaped billions in tax savings from homeownership. By providing an economic reward for homeownership, these provisions of tax law provided an additional inducement for households to leave central-city apartments and move to suburban single-family homes (Heilbrun 1987).

Finally, the subsidization of highway construction through the National Defense Highway Act of 1956—which created the 41,000-mile interstate highway system—encouraged automobile use at the expense of public transportation. There was no federal funding of mass transit prior to the 1970s. As business firms and households relocated to the suburbs, retail trade followed in their wake, as did the back-office functions of many white-collar industries like finance and insurance.

For about a century, employment was organized around Boston as a trade, financial, and distributive hub, with various mill towns, located near water power, situated along the fringe of the region in Lowell, Lawrence, Brockton, and similar communities. Railroad lines ran like spokes of a wheel to connect these manufacturing centers to the hub and to one another. In the postwar pattern of development, according to the economist Heinz Muehlmann, the new science- and technology-based industries clustered not around natural resources but around centers of education, fanning out rapidly beyond the old city boundaries. This required a "realignment," in Muehlmann's words, of both public and private services, and rerouted workers, both blue-collar and white-, to America's first edge city: the arc defined by Route 128. Later, Route 495 became the location of edge city development farther from Boston (Muehlmann et al. 1970). The new high-tech industries also fostered considerable new employment and rebuilding in the region's urban core, particularly in East Cambridge near MIT.

Turf Battles and the Reconfiguration of Space Inside the City of Boston

Some of the most dramatic events in post–World War II Greater Boston involve battles over turf. Struggles over who would control the land and how the land would be used had important implications not only for how land parcels would be reconfigured, but also for labor market outcomes, patterns of residential location, and even the racial and ethnic attitudes of the region's residents.

Between 1914 and 1949, when James Michael Curley's personalized style of ethnic and class politics dominated Boston, the business and financial elite withdrew from making investments in a Boston they viewed as hostile to their interests. Although general economic conditions during the Depression years caused hard times for many U.S. cities, Boston faced harder times than most, given that its decline had begun in the 1920s. Politics did not favor the city either.

While the New Deal infused public spending to compensate for the dearth of private spending in many cities, Boston did not receive its proportionate share of federal largesse. Curley feuded with other Democrats at the local, state, and federal levels, including President Roosevelt. Emblematic of their troubled relationship was that Curley, having been the first big city mayor to endorse Roosevelt for president, aspired to become secretary of the navy in the Roosevelt cabinet. Roosevelt, instead, offered him the ambassadorship to Poland, a post the mayor declined. It has been estimated that the result of Curley's feuds "cost the city as many as 10,000 CWA [Community Works Administration] jobs, the benefit of any PWA [Public Works Administration] money until 1935, a serious delay in the start-up of [local projects of] the WPA [Works Progress Administration], and a year-long delay in the payment of unemployment compensation provided by the Social Security Act of 1935" (Kennedy 1992, 146). And during World War II, when other cities were becoming "arsenals of democracy," Boston's economy did not rebound very much, despite the temporary boost experienced by its manufacturing industries.

After reaching its peak population of 801,444 in 1950, the city of Boston would lose over 100,000 people in the ensuing decade and suffer additional losses throughout the 1960s and 1970s. Meanwhile, its suburbs continued to experience at least some population growth, with the fastest growth occurring at the edges of the metropolitan area (Edel, Sklar, and Luria 1984). Against this backdrop of severe economic and demographic decline the post–World War II turf battles were fought.

Urban Renewal

Federally sponsored urban renewal was initiated with Title I of the U.S. Housing Act of 1949. This legislation empowered local housing authorities, and later quasi-public bodies such as the Boston Redevelopment Authority (BRA), to purchase land via eminent domain, relocate residents and businesses, and clear large tracts for new development. While its original language emphasized creation of better housing opportunities in declining areas, its implementation was driven by the belief that revitalization demanded replacement of "blighted" areas by higher-value homes and businesses that would draw middle- and upper-income residents and shoppers. It was later supplemented in Massachusetts by the state legislature's passage of Chapter 121A, which expanded the BRA's urban renewal powers.

Private and public advocates of urban renewal made their case by presenting urban neighborhoods as diseased tissue or blighted wastelands that required clearance, but residents of the first area to face urban renewal in Boston—those who lived in the "New York Streets" area of the South End—looked at their neighborhood in different terms. Descriptions by the Greater Boston Chamber of Commerce and by the activist Mel King, whose childhood home was uprooted in the South End, suggest this contrast vividly. In the chamber's words:

> The New York Streets was the City's first effort to assemble enough land for private industry to build efficient, modern structures. It represents the thinking which characterized the inception of renewal throughout the country. . . . Industry could not afford to buy numerous parcels, clear them all and still construct a factory on which investment capital could derive a profit. This undertaking is proof that renewal can serve as a vehicle for private industrial and commercial development. This is the classic partnership of city officials and private interests aimed at improving the economic base of the city. [Quoted in King 1981, 20]

And in Mel King's:

> Up and down Harrison Avenue there were shops and stores of all descriptions and families who lived over them in apartments upstairs. On the corner of Seneca and Harrison there was an Armenian store with olives in barrels out front, and a fish market next door. The next block down on the corner of Oneida was Leo Giuffre's bakery, I think. There was a synagogue on Oswego.
>
> On Seneca Street, where I lived with my parents, there were also Irish, Portuguese, Albanians, Greeks, Lithuanians, Armenians, Jews, Filipinos, Chinese and a few (very few) Yankees. Across the tracks were Syrians and Lebanese. . . . Although our buildings were pretty well sorted out by color and ethnic background, the street belonged to all of us. [King 1981, 20–21]

The removal of the New York Streets residents was complete by 1957; by April 1958, the city gave eviction notices to their counterparts in the West End. This 23-acre area, sandwiched between Beacon Hill, the Charles River, and old Scollay Square (now Government Center), had been an immigrant center (and the target of renewal plans) for much of the century.[2] By 1950, a population that once topped 23,000 was about half that size; by 1958, it had dwindled to 7,000, as rumors of the wrecking ball drove many more away (Kennedy 1992). Nearly half of this population was Italian. In contrast to official characterizations of their enclave as a slum, Herbert Gans recognized the vitality and resilience of this colorful community, while acknowledging such problems as substandard housing and social ills.

Gans and later researchers, including the urban planner Chester Hartman, marshaled evidence contradicting the city's delineation of the neighborhood as a slum. They found that the level of substandard dwelling units was far lower than official reports, and that a part of the deterioration after 1951 was traceable to landlords avoiding repairs after announcements about slum clearance. Buildings that were poorly maintained from the outside often concealed well-kept apartments, recently modernized or improved by their inhabitants (Gans 1962). The planners' characterization of the West End social milieu as "pathological" masked its high levels of stability, attachment to place and "highly developed informal social control," in Jane Jacobs's words (Jacobs 1961, 272; Gans 1962).

Nonetheless, virtually all of elite Boston fell in line behind the West End demolition plan: politicians, priests, newspaper editors, developers. A front-page columnist in the *Herald* praised the plan for replacing the "cesspool" and "slum area" with modern housing, parking areas, and gardens. The *Boston Globe* promised that successful conversion of the West End from "dilapidation to delight" would spark the revitalization of all of Boston (O'Connor 1992). At BRA hearings and other forums, the community opposed the plan, but it lacked the resources and self-confidence to fight City Hall effectively. Members of the Save the West End Committee protested, and a few youth engaged in half-hearted sabotage of construction equipment, but according to Lawrence Kennedy, "members of the BRA board assumed that the project had gone too far to stop" (Kennedy 1992, 164). Many residents simply didn't believe that the plans were more than rumors. In a little over eighteen months after evacuation notices were given, however, all 2,700 households were gone, and every building save Massachusetts General Hospital, two churches, and the historic Harrison Gray Otis house had been razed.

Though the project was originally touted as a mixed-income development open to former West Enders, virtually every unit constructed was a luxury rental. The city also made very few provisions for relocating residents and businesses, assuming that 60 percent of the residents would move into public housing units, while the remainder could easily find decent and affordable housing in the city's private market. As Gans observes, only about 10 percent actually moved into public housing. Most were unwilling to move into the projects, both because of their negative image and because they were unwilling to be split off from friends, relatives, and other members of their peer and ethnic groups. Relocation planners "failed to see the ties that existed between families," and imposed their own standards of what was appropriate housing (Gans 1962, 323). Later research found that a majority of West Enders, who dispersed to points throughout the Boston region, experienced significant depression, grief, and helplessness in the process. Many were immigrants and/or elderly. An elderly Jewish woman from Russia "described the process as though the Cossacks had come riding into her neighborhood" (O'Connor 1993, 139).

In Gans's account, few in the West End conceived of themselves as "West Enders" prior to the neighborhood's destruction, aligning themselves instead with smaller sections of the community, or with family and immediate peer group. After the diaspora of urban renewal, former residents became notably cohesive, keeping the community spirit alive through newsletters, reunions, and other means. More than thirty years after the destruction of the West End, former residents were finally given the opportunity to give at least limited physical form to their virtual community through the construction of West End Place: 183 units of mixed-income housing on the one remaining undeveloped parcel of the renewal area. Forty-three apartments, all bearing subsidies for low- to moderate-income households, were set aside for former West Enders. Adjacent to the cooperative housing complex, which was developed by the archdiocese of Boston, will eventually be a museum housing West End memorabilia, news clippings, and other documents of the neighborhood and its destruction (Dreier 1995).

Although the New York Streets and West End urban renewal projects were intended to improve the city's fiscal health, Boston had the lowest bond rating of any major U.S. city at the end of the 1950s. With the city on the brink of bankruptcy, members of its banking and financial elite began to meet informally, forming a coordinating committee that would ultimately cooperate with municipal government to help guide the city back to prosperity. The hostility toward municipal government that was a hallmark of the Curley years and persisted through the administration of John Hynes, Curley's successor, was replaced by more cordial relations with John Collins, who became mayor in 1960. The coordinating committee itself was often referred to as The Vault, because they met in a basement boardroom of the Boston Safe Deposit & Trust Company (Adams 1977).

When John Collins became mayor, he hired Edward Logue, who had received much acclaim for his urban renewal work in New Haven, to head the Boston Redevelopment Authority. Collins and Logue embarked on an ambitious plan for revitalizing the city, and in the course of bringing the stalled Prudential Center project to fruition, the BRA was given greater power over comprehensive planning within the city. The state legislation that gave the Prudential Insurance Company the tax break it demanded for building its new skyscraper in the Back Bay also gave the BRA unprecedented power to plan and implement redevelopment in Boston. Under Logue's leadership, Boston became the fourth largest recipient of federal funds for urban renewal during the 1960s, helped no doubt by Boston's own John F. Kennedy being in the White House (Kennedy 1992). The erection of the Prudential Center itself would foster the renaissance of the South End and Back Bay, with a rejuvenated retail district stretching along Boylston Street and neighboring Newbury Street.

With this new relationship to the federal government and to its own business and financial elite, and with community resistance not yet effective, Boston proceeded through the early 1960s to reconfigure itself. One hallmark of this reconfiguration was the massive Government Center project, which obliterated the seedy entertainment district of Scollay Square.

Scollay Square was not a residential district, and the Government Center urban renewal project proceeded without opposition. However, when the BRA tried to implement the rest of its ambitious plans for redevelopment—it has been estimated that at the time, one-fourth of the city's land area and almost half of its population were inside designated renewal areas (Kennedy 1992)—the bitter legacy of the West End came home to roost. A $30 million renewal plan for South Boston, an Irish working-class area, called for the demolition of 22 percent of the area's housing units as well as several of its pre-1900 public schools and touted assistance for local businesses and homeowners. Suspicious South Boston residents, however, fearing that these ambitious plans would disrupt their old neighborhood and displace old-time residents, as they had seen happen in the West End, used their political power to stop the BRA cold (O'Connor 1993, 215).

Similar community resistance faced the BRA when it tried to implement its plans for Charlestown, another working-class Irish enclave, and the North Harvard Street area of Allston-Brighton, a working-class area near the Harvard Business School. In Charlestown, Logue and the BRA had the full support of the Catholic Church, including Cardinal Cushing and Monsignor Frank Lally, editor of the archdiocese's newspaper, who had been named to the BRA board by Mayor Hynes and appointed chairman of the board by Mayor Collins. Logue also had the support of the local Catholic clergy. Nevertheless, local residents resisted for over two years before a badly divided community ultimately gave its approval to the project in 1965 (O'Connor 1993).

In the North Harvard Street project, the plan was to clear a 10-acre working-class neighborhood to make way for construction of luxury housing. The neighborhood resisted from the time of the initial announcement in 1961 until the last residents were forcibly evicted in 1969. Ultimately, the site was cleared, but as a result of the negative publicity, in the end it was used for moderate-income housing (O'Connor 1993).

In these battles between the neighborhoods and the BRA, the dividing lines were drawn differently from where they had been since the turn of the century. No longer was it a clear-cut matter of the upper-class-Yankee-Protestant-financial-power arrayed against the working-class-Irish-Catholic-municipal-political-power. In Charlestown, the residents were fighting an Irish mayor, an Irish head of the BRA, and the Irish hierarchy of their church. Moreover, détente between the Brahmin financial establishment and the Irish municipal political establishment had proceeded to the point where Collins not only met regularly with The Vault, but also became, in 1964, the first twentieth-century mayor of Boston to receive an honorary degree from Harvard University (O'Connor 1993).

In a foreshadowing of the tumultuous events that would occur when Boston faced its crisis over school desegregation in the following decade, O'Connor comes to the following conclusion regarding the urban renewal struggles of the 1960s: "Although Collins, Logue, and the BRA eventually succeeded in getting most of their projects through, the result was a growing and bitter antagonism between the Irish-Catholic residents of the ethnic neighborhoods and the Irish-Catholic politicians who ran the city government" (O'Connor 1995, 237). This antagonism continues to this day, notably in struggles over the development of the waterfront area of South Boston. Ever since the destruction of the West End and school desegregation, community groups in the city have galvanized over issues closely related to turf.

Highways

While some Boston neighborhoods were fighting the city and its plans for urban renewal, other Boston and Cambridge neighborhoods battled the state and its plans for new highways. Proposals for an Inner Belt highway circling through Cambridge, Brookline, and Boston had existed since 1948, but became financially possible only after the National Defense Highway Act of 1956 provided 90 percent federal funding for such projects. In addition to the proposed Inner Belt, plans for the construction of I-95, the interstate that would run from Maine to Florida, called for a Southwest Corridor Expressway link with the Inner Belt that would run right through the middle of the inner city, cutting through Roxbury and Jamaica Plain.

Opposition to the Inner Belt's Cambridge spur delayed implementation of the project. Residents of the Jamaica Plain section of Boston were at first resigned to the Southwest Corridor, and initially organized over such questions as whether the community should insist that the roadway be depressed below street level. But organizing in Cambridge spread to other communities. Eventually, a broad coalition of community groups representing all of the Inner Belt and Southwest Expressway communities, and cutting across lines of race, class, and ethnicity, exerted enough pressure to halt the plan. An article in the *Boston Globe* explained the huge significance of this victory: "a number of poor and working-class people, aided by underpaid, committed professionals, built a strategic alliance responsible for fundamentally reorienting the transportation policy of the Commonwealth of Massachusetts" (Lupo et al. 1971). Although the land in the Southwest Corridor had already been cleared by the time Governor Frank Sargent announced a moratorium on the project in 1970, the proposed highways were dead, and the land would instead be used for public rail lines and linear parkland (Kennedy 1992).

Space and Race

Black groups were part of the antihighway coalition, but much of the story of community resistance in the 1950s and early 1960s was about white working-class neighborhoods. By the late 1960s, conflicts between the city government and its neighborhoods, or between one neighborhood and another, often included a racial dimension. This was not an entirely new phenomenon, since racial antipathy between the Irish and the blacks dated back to the antebellum era. But in a decade that saw dramatic battles over civil rights and the emergence of black leaders like Martin Luther King, Jr., and Malcolm X, Boston's black community—5 percent of the city's population in 1950, 9.1 percent in 1960, and 16.3 percent in 1970 (Thernstrom 1973)—asserted itself more dramatically. In assessing the impact of the rebuilding process in Boston from 1950 to 1970, O'Connor concludes that it "changed the major force dividing the two Bostons from religion and ethnicity to race and class. . . . There were still two Bostons, but from now on the inhabitants were separated by the size of their wallets and the color of their skins" (O'Connor 1993, 295–96).

Resistance to top-down urban renewal spread from white neighborhoods to Hispanic and black communities within the city. In the late 1960s, a group of Puerto Ricans in the Columbus Avenue section of the South End successfully resisted the destruction of their neighborhood. The BRA had planned a community center for the site, which would have required displacing the predominantly Puerto Rican residents of the area. The battle consumed several years, but the result was the creation of "Villa Victoria," an 844-unit complex which combines family, senior, and single rental apartments and townhouses with commercial development and public spaces. Inquilinos Boricuas en Accion (IBA), the organization born out of this struggle, gradually developed into one of the largest Latino community development corporations in the United States (Uriarte 1992, 15).

A few weeks after the assassination of Martin Luther King, Jr., in April 1968, and in reaction against city policies that were displacing low-income residents of the South End to make the area more attractive to higher-income households, community activists pitched tents on a parcel of land to protest the bulldozing of the property. The site had served as housing for 100 families before it was bulldozed by the BRA, but was now used as a parking lot. The occupation became known as Tent City, and its aim was to stop the displacement of people of color from the South End, to build new low-income housing, and to create "an elected urban renewal committee which would allow for community control of urban renewal plans" (King 1981, 112). Two decades later, a mixed-income housing development was finally built on the Tent City site (Kennedy 1992).

In light of the Tent City demonstration, it is ironic that black leaders in Roxbury had welcomed the BRA and its model of redevelopment earlier in the decade. The Washington Park Urban Renewal project became the first major residential project undertaken by Logue's BRA. Guided by the Housing Act of 1954, which shifted the emphasis of urban renewal from total clearance to a combination of selected clearance along with rehabilitation of the existing housing stock, the boundaries of the project encompassed an area that had been 70 percent white in 1950, but was 70 percent black by 1960 (Kennedy 1992). The project's area encompassed two very different communities. According to data from the 1960 census of housing, the area north of Townsend Street contained a disproportionately high number of dilapidated units; below Townsend Street (that is, the area adjacent to the northern edge of Franklin Park), housing quality was higher. In fact, in one of the three renewal area census tracts below Townsend Street, housing quality was better than it was for the city as a whole: 89 percent of the units there were sound, compared with 79 percent sound units for the city as a whole (Huff 1966).

The project can be viewed as an attempt to stabilize a middle-income black community from the encroaching decay that was occurring to its north, as low-income blacks crowded into the area after their displacement from other neighborhoods. Yet the project itself did nothing to relieve the severe housing shortage within the black community per se: it called for the relocation of 1,639 families and 603 individuals; it provided for the replacement of 1,300 units of low and moderate income housing and 200 replacement units of public housing for the elderly, but no new housing (Huff 1966). Since the project placed an emphasis on rehabilitation, with only 25 percent of the 502 acres to be cleared, the rest to be improved (Kennedy 1992), special financing was needed to bring the units into compliance with building codes. A group of Boston banks agreed to make loans available within the renewal area. This was the origin of the Boston Banks Urban Renewal Group (B-BURG).

B-BURG funds were supposed to be made available to blacks who had been excluded from conventional mortgage sources. However, while the consortium's pool reached several million dollars in the early 1960s, little publicity attended the program and few buyers were directed to the new mortgage source (Levine and Harmon 1992, 109). In the wake of the King assassination, Mayor Kevin White's fledgling administration met with the city's leading bankers to reinvigorate the moribund program. By mid-May 1968, Mayor White was able to announce that a consortium of twenty-two savings banks and life insurance companies would make $50 million available for mortgages to support low-income homeownership (Levine and Harmon 1992).

As the program was implemented, it was limited to black families, and it was available only for homes within a specific boundary—roughly encompassing the area known as Mattapan, a heavily Jewish area on the southeastern side of Franklin Park. In a perversion of the more familiar practice of redlining (in which banks circle an area on a map and refuse to make loans within it), this time the area inside the circle was the *only* place in which loans would be made. In drawing the B-BURG boundary, the banks unleashed the tremendous power of greed and cynicism. Conditions were ripe for blockbusting, and many realtors set up shop to destabilize the neighborhood for hefty profits, encouraging panic selling by whites and then reselling at inflated prices to blacks who had no other options. They were assisted in their endeavors by some dishonest Federal Housing Administration (FHA) inspectors who, for a price, would falsely certify dilapidated housing as being in good condition. The banks found profitable opportunities in destabilizing the area: it had been so stable beforehand that many of the mortgages had been paid off, while others were old mortgages at low interest rates. Moreover, the banks' activities were risk-free: if the new owners defaulted, the banks were guaranteed repayment of their loans, and the foreclosures became the responsibility of the FHA (Levine and Harmon 1992).

By 1970, 19,107 blacks lived in Mattapan, mostly as a result of the B-BURG program; only 473 blacks had lived there in 1960 (Levine and Harmon 1992, 209). Visions of establishing a stable community of low-income black homeowners proved illusory, however:

> In the early 1970s, more than 70 percent of B-BURG-assisted homeowners were unable to keep up their mortgage payments, because those payments

far exceeded their earning power or because they were faced with repair costs about which the FHA appraisers and the loan officers had failed to warn them. The banks foreclosed on more than a thousand single-family homes and multiunit dwellings in the area. The local HUD Office took over these houses after paying the banks full compensation for their lost loan moneys. HUD was ill equipped to manage this real estate. Some feeble efforts were made to repair, rent, or even auction off some of the houses, but these efforts themselves became the source of new charges of corruption against federal government officials. The solution of choice for beleaguered bureaucrats became condemnation—whatever the actual condition of the house. [Levine and Harmon 1992, 332]

One important aspect of the Mattapan blockbusting story is that the formerly white neighborhood had been occupied overwhelmingly by Jewish families, many of whom were working-class and/or elderly. In the chaos that followed the frenzied real estate speculation and profiteering, relations between the Jewish and black communities deteriorated. Hillel Levine, a sociologist, and Lawrence Harmon, a journalist, argue that Mattapan had been chosen in part because resistance to blacks there would be significantly less vehement than in the Irish or Italian sections of Boston. But in the aftermath of the artificially rapid change, Jews left as crime and vandalism increased, and blacks who could not leave were angry at being abandoned.

While Levine and Harmon point out the cynicism of the realtors, FHA inspectors, and banks that profited from the turmoil that engulfed Mattapan, they also assign blame to the leaders of the Jewish community in metropolitan Boston, who chose to attend to the desires of their more prosperous suburban groups, while ignoring the needs of the city dwellers. According to Levine and Harmon, decisions made in the 1950s to relocate community institutions such as a flagship temple and religious school hastened the suburbanization of the Boston Jewish community, ultimately leaving behind in the city a powerless and vulnerable remnant population.

This interpretation is disputed by the political scientist Gerald Gamm, who points out that the Jewish population of the Roxbury-Dorchester area had already declined from 70,000 in 1950 to 47,000 in 1960. He argues that "by 1968, when the mortgage program began, the area's Jewish neighborhoods were already in their last stages of disintegration. At root, the Jewish exodus was caused by socioeconomic mobility" (Gamm 1995, 155).

While the Jewish migration from Mattapan was well under way before B-BURG and would likely have continued even in the absence of the program, other aspects of the story are not so clear. From the initial 1968 meeting with the White administration, the B-BURG banks were adamant about refusing to make these loans available for houses in the suburbs. Ultimately, the banks unilaterally decided that these loans would not be available in most parts of the city, either. While the fact that loans were available only inside the B-BURG line was withheld from the general public, that information "was known to FHA officials, Boston Redevelopment Authority officials, and leaders in both the black and Jewish communities" (Levine and Harmon 1992, 323), who chose to comply with the banks' terms rather than challenge them. With few other places in the city open to them, black families flocked to the banks for B-BURG mortgage money and moved into Mattapan. Whites fled in a panic. Perhaps no place in the country would see a quicker racial transformation of an entire neighborhood.

Both the old and the new residents of Mattapan were made worse off by the B-BURG fiasco. In some sense, both groups were betrayed not only by those who profited at their expense, but by the leaders of their own communities. Like O'Connor, Levine and Harmon see the new battle lines drawn on class and race, rather than between ethnic groups. They see in the story of Mattapan a foreshadowing of the intra-ethnic class conflict that would erupt around school desegregation.

The reconfiguration of space inside the city of Boston exacerbated class tensions and racial animosity, and reinforced residential segregation on the bases of income and race. Outside the city of Boston, the spatial revolution produced suburbs that also reinforced residential segregation.

Route 128 and the Reconfiguration of Space in the Suburban Ring

The completion of Route 128, the Massachusetts Turnpike, and the Central Artery, as well as improvement of the radial roads linking them to one another and to Boston, would foster enormous suburban growth, as would the demographics of the baby boom and the "white flight" from the central city. Passage of the 1956 Interstate Highway Act added federal impetus to the road-building visions initiated in Boston's 1948 Master Highway Plan. A report by the Central Transportation Planning Staff describes the effects of federally funded highway building:

> These roads provided good access to uncrowded, undeveloped and inexpensive land, and those people who wished to move out of the urban core flocked to the suburbs. With relatively few cars on the road, suburban dwellers could have the best of all worlds: a job in the city, an inexpensive house with plenty of space in a non-urban neighborhood, and an easy commute in between. [Falbel and Hamel 1989, 27]

As Boston and the region's blue-collar cities (Lawrence, Lowell, Brockton) hemorrhaged population, the outlying suburbs accounted for nearly all the growth occurring between 1950 and 1970. The thirty towns and cities along Route 128 swelled with over a quarter of a million new people—an increase of more than 50 percent (Zaleski 1985). Particular towns along the route grew at even faster rates during this two-decade period, including Burlington (by 272 percent) and Sudbury (by nearly 200 percent) (MCAD 1974). These population shifts were followed in turn by large retail developments and service industries. Framingham's Shoppers' World was an early avatar of the now familiar suburban shopping mall and allied developments that anchor expressways and interchanges across the country. Boston's share of the region's retail employment and sales correspondingly declined.

The expansion of research firms and other technology-based employment in the region changed the residential profile in many communities. A 1957 study of Lexington noted that about one in five employed residents worked as operatives or service workers in 1950; one in three of those moving to the Route 128 suburb in the next six years were professional or technical workers. Rising land values, tax rates, and housing prices made the wealthier suburbs even more exclusive (MCAD 1974; MIT 1958). At the same time, rapid development changed the physical character of many of these communities. Once rural locations sprouted strip malls, office parks, and condominium developments to serve those who work in them. Again, these developments have occurred in the interstices between long-established cities and towns.

The history of Route 128 is fascinating in its own right, given that it would have such a profound impact on the entire nature of the Greater Boston metropolitan area. Creation of a widened, limited access roadway to bypass Boston and suburban town centers was discussed as early as 1930, when Robert Whitten, writing for the Boston Planning Board, predicted that congested roadways would soon bear double the traffic: "There should be a series of roads leading in a genuinely circumferential direction around the main business center at intervals of one to three miles" (Whitten 1930, 11). His strategy followed the proposal of the regional planner Barton Mackaye, who called for a bypass highway ringing Boston, making the whole metropolitan area accessible and easing traffic. Mackaye hoped the road would link together a "Bay Circuit" of small cities limited in size by open spaces or "green belts." As the urbanist Lewis Mumford has noted, much of Mackaye's vision was lost once it was translated by highway engineers, whose primary concern was moving residents and commerce efficiently from point A to point B (Jones, n.d.).

Though some work was completed on Route 128 before 1941, the war would postpone all versions of highway construction until 1948. By 1951, when construction was completed on a four-lane, 22-mile section linking Wakefield to Wellesley, critical views such as Mumford's were distinctly in the minority. As Adams notes, completion of Route 128 and the rapid expansion of high technology "coincided with such artful symmetry that the Miracle Highway seemed almost foreordained" (Adams 1977, 287)

The highway, 65 miles in total length, provided rapid access to low-priced land located in attractive suburbs within twenty minutes of MIT and Harvard, a boon for the new technology firms. Its role in industrial development, however, was entirely unplanned. The road's original charter was to "provide ready access to the north and south shore recreational and residential areas for traffic from the Metropolitan area and Western sections of the state" (Rosegrant and Lampe 1992). As it happened, however, its undeveloped tracts developed quickly over the following decades; in six years, the former pig and poultry farms along the corridor were replaced by industrial, commercial, and residential development valued at more than half a billion dollars, and a widening of the road was already under way (Krushnic 1974). As early as 1957, 140 companies occupied sites along the beltway; ten years later, there were 729, and by 1973, over 1,200, employing more than 80,000 people (Mass. Commerce and Development 1973). The 128 corridor became home to branches of national corporations, including Sylvania, RCA, and Honeywell, and to technology startups, as well as research laboratories, including Lincoln Labs and MITRE (Saxenian 1994). Numerous distribution, professional service, and traditional manufacturing firms also relocated to Route 128, most of them departing from cramped quarters in Boston or Cambridge. Two-thirds of the relocated firms had previously been within 2.5 miles of Boston's statehouse; 96 percent had been within a 4.5-mile radius (MIT 1958).

A good number of urban core residents did not relocate to the new sites—either because they lacked access to automobiles or because they did not wish to commute that distance. Studies for the Boston Federal Reserve Bank in 1957 and 1961 showed that firms with high levels of female staff, as well as those with high levels of unskilled and/or part-time workers, reported higher rates of "lost" workers upon relocation (Burtt 1961).

The exodus of jobs to the suburbs was facilitated by a companion invention to circumferential highways: the landscaped, suburban industrial park. This concept was promoted aggressively by a young developer, Gerald Blakely, who joined the old money management firm, Cabot, Cabot and Forbes (CC&F) in 1947. The son of an MIT professor, Blakely envisioned "garden type industrial parks" in a bucolic, campuslike setting as the best way to capitalize on the new industries that prized access to MIT. Also critical to his vision was the "packaging": developers would provide construction, land assembly, commercial approvals, financing and continuing services, and in some cases even build an access road (Rosegrant and Lampe 1992). This left little for firms to do except move in and begin production. Still, Blakely had to overcome considerable skepticism among Boston's conservative money men, as well as initial resistance from the suburban towns where CC&F began assembling land before Route 128 had been completed. However, on his second appeal to the town of Needham, which included an aggressive advertising campaign, Blakely won zoning approval for the New England Industrial Center, the prototype of industrial park land use along the highway (Massachusetts Commission Against Discrimination 1974). Town governments in Lexington, Waltham, and others on the route would soon follow suit, altering their zoning to woo industry, in the hope of vastly expanding their tax base and considerably elevating the value of nearby residential property (MIT 1958).

Blakely's firm became the premier developer of Route 128, responsible for 85 percent of the industrial land and sixteen industrial parks along the highway. As traffic (and industrial tenants) began to congest the region in the late 1950s, CC&F and other business interests prodded for a second beltway farther from the city, which was to be the 88-mile expanse of Route 495, linking Salisbury on the north to Foxboro on the south. With 90 percent of its funding covered by the federal Highway Trust Fund for interstate roads, Route 495 was completed in 1969, and CC&F was again the major developer of industrial property (Adams 1977; Krushnic 1974). CC&F gave "specific form to the pattern of land use" in the suburban region, in Krushnic's words (Krushnic 1974, 10). Blakely himself reaped a fortune for his efforts, eventually buying out the Cabots and Forbes to become sole owner of the firm. The "new" industrial revolution was well under way with an entirely new spatial dimension in its wake.

Between 1972 and 1990, total private-sector employment in the Boston CMSA increased by 39 percent, to 1.8 million jobs—a rate nearly five times as high as Boston as a whole. In 1972, nearly a third (31.5 percent) of total private-sector employment was in Boston. Only two decades later, as table 4.1 demonstrates, less than a quarter (24.5 percent) of the region's workforce was employed in the city.

Total manufacturing employment declined by 44 percent between 1972 and 1990 in the city, while in the balance of the CMSA it actually increased. As a result, Boston's share of manufacturing employment declined from 15.8 percent to only 9 percent of the CMSA total. Indeed, all the cities and towns closest to the central city lost manufacturing jobs

TABLE 4.1   *Private-Sector Employment, 1972 and 1990*

	City of Boston		Boston CMSA		Boston as Percentage of CMSA	
	1972	1990	1972	1990	1972	1990
Total private	405,560	438,300	1,286,552	1,792,284	31.5%	24.5%
Manufacturing	55,792	31,459	353,683	340,775	15.8	9.2
Trade	105,807	74,831	362,190	469,752	29.2	15.9
Finance, insurance, and real estate	65,953	76,437	99,160	161,124	66.5	47.4
Services	119,925	211,160	308,153	651,668	38.9	32.4

Source: Commonwealth of Massachusetts 1999.

as these moved out to the area between the Route 128 and Route 495 circumferential highways. Cambridge's manufacturing sector declined from over 19,000 jobs to fewer than 7,500. Other cities and towns losing large numbers of durable and nondurable manufacturing jobs were Waltham, Lynn, Quincy, and Lawrence. Map 4.1 shows this pattern clearly, with manufacturing growth concentrated northwest of the city in towns like Chelmsford, Billerica, Wilmington, Bedford, Sudbury, and Marlborough.

Even more dramatic has been the spatial reorganization of retail and wholesale trade. Wholesale trade went in search of less expensive ware-house space, while retail trade moved to the suburbs, where the population was growing fastest. Boston lost more than 30,000 of these jobs in the two decades before 1990, and the balance of the region saw its trade employment explode. In 1972, nearly 30 percent of all trade jobs were in Boston; by 1990, only a little more than 15 percent remained. The balance of the CMSA saw its retail and wholesale trade employment climb by more than 50 percent in less than twenty years, with the fastest-growing suburbs registering 70 percent or more growth (see map 4.2).

Finance, Insurance, and Real Estate (FIRE) decentralized as well, as the population relocated outside Boston and as it became easier to move "back office" functions away from a firm's headquarters. Nevertheless, Boston retained nearly half the jobs in this sector, as the banking, insurance, and mutual fund industries continued to expand downtown. The city is still the hub of financial transactions in the entire region. Most of the growth outside the central city represents the relocation of back office functions as well as the presence of real estate offices, local consumer bank branches, and local insurance agencies—the consumer end of the financial transactions industry (see map 4.3).

MAP 4.1   *Change in Manufacturing Employment, 1972 to 1990*

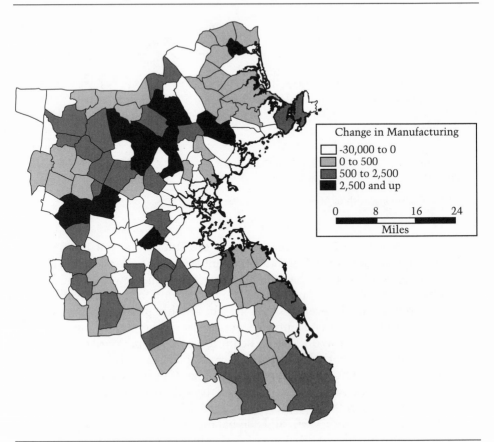

Source: Commonwealth of Massachusetts 1999.

There are two other sectors where Boston has prospered. Service employment has grown rapidly, particularly as a result of the expansion of hospitals and other medical institutions in the city. Between 1972 and 1990, central-city private-service employment nearly doubled, to 211,000 workers. Indeed, by 1990, nearly half (48 percent) of Boston's private-sector employment was in services. Its share of total regional employment remained at close to one-third (32.4 percent), down a bit from the 38.9 percent it had in 1972.

As noted in the last chapter, Boston is also unique in being a government "capital" not only for the city but for the state and the entire New England region. As such, for the Boston CMSA as a whole, government at all levels was responsible for over a quarter of a million jobs

MAP 4.2   *Percentage Change in Wholesale and Retail Trade*
          Employment, 1972 to 1990

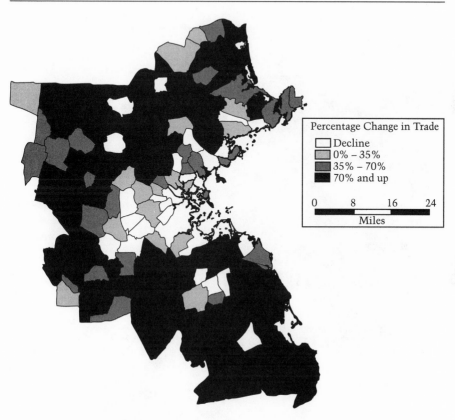

Source: Commonwealth of Massachusetts 1999.

(265,400) in 1990. More than one in eight regional workers was a government employee. Boston itself was home to nearly 100,000 of those public-sector jobs, more than 37 percent of the CMSA total. Indeed, nearly three-fifths of the city's employment is now located in just two sectors: the public sector and private-sector service employment.

The strength of these sectors has kept the city of Boston from becoming a "jobless" hub, despite the fact that manufacturing, trade, and FIRE employment has dispersed throughout the metropolis. In other cities, researchers have found a "spatial mismatch" between where workers live and where jobs are located (Kasarda 1988; Wilson 1987, 1996). This spatial mismatch leads to low rates of labor force participation, high rates of unemployment, and large earnings gaps between

MAP 4.3   *Percentage Change in Finance, Insurance, and Real
Estate Employment, 1972 to 1990*

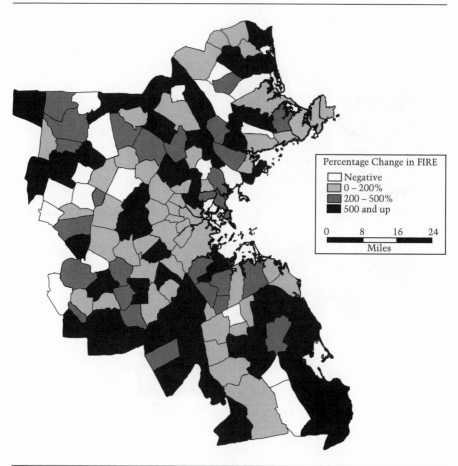

Source: Commonwealth of Massachusetts 1999.

those who have access to suburban jobs and those trapped in the central
city.

   While overall employment is down from its peak of 562,000 in
1988, Boston still boasts nearly 540,000 jobs (in 1997), about the same as
in 1986. Indeed, there are nearly 1.9 jobs in the city per labor force par-
ticipant in the city's population (Division of Employment and Training
1999a). This ratio is as high as anytime in the last decade. If all of Boston's labor force were constrained to working in the city itself, Boston

would still need to import nearly a quarter of a million workers from the suburban ring to fill all its jobs. As is, with many city residents able and willing to work outside the city itself, the number of commuters into the city each day must exceed this number substantially in order to staff Boston's workplaces.

Some of these commuters travel long distances to get to their jobs downtown. Examining a new townhouse development in a wooded section of Grafton, fully 42 miles from Boston, Joel Garreau likens this residential pattern to "tenements turned on their side" or "worker housing" for the information age (Garreau 1992). Unlike the conventional spacious suburbs of the past, these developments are sometimes packed densely together. A two-earner professional couple interviewed by Garreau could afford nothing closer to Boston, where zoning in most suburban towns dictates far lower densities but untouchable prices for many working families. The "large lot" ordinances—or, less politely, "snob zoning"—date back in some cases to the 1950s, according to a report titled "Route 128: The Road to Segregation." In the author's account:

The more affluent towns near the road responded to the possibility of in-migration by enacting large-lot zoning ordinances. This had an additional effect on the already rising land values. Towns like Lincoln and Weston, threatened with a massive in-rush for single-family housing on their graceful stretches of farmland, were among the first to protect themselves in this way. For other towns like Waltham, 128 answered the need for an improved tax base, and they set about zoning for industry; some towns, including Lexington, did both almost simultaneously. [MCAD 1974, 39]

Even towns that were willing to accept higher population densities found that rising land costs made home building for low- and moderate-income residents prohibitive without considerable subsidies. Little or no public housing went up in Route 128 localities during the first decades after its construction (MCAD 1974). The resulting "jobs/housing imbalance" combined to push lower-income industrial and service workers farther away from their place of work, while "redistributing the low income workers into low income communities" (MCAD 1974, 41). The movement of lower-skill work in manufacturing, warehousing, and similar blue-collar activities to suburban sites was even more damaging to those remaining in the central city, who were disproportionately poor, less educated, and of minority backgrounds. These workers were also less likely to own or have access to a vehicle.

In 1969, Brookline state representative Martin Linksy drafted "anti–

snob zoning" legislation in an effort to overcome such resistance. The bill was driven in part by the climate of desegregation; activists and legislators felt strongly that Boston alone should not shoulder the burden of social change. Advocates also sought to fill the gap left by the federal government's refusal to take a strong stand on integrating the suburbs. Early in the Nixon administration, HUD Secretary George Romney threatened to withhold government services from towns recalcitrant in easing zoning restrictions—helping proponents win acceptance of affordable housing in Stoughton, for instance. Soon after, President Nixon reversed course, stating that he would not use federal funds as leverage to bring "forced integration" to the suburbs (Herbers 1974).

The Linsky bill established a target of 10 percent affordable housing in each community, defined as such by the presence of public subsidies. It placed the burden on town officials to show legitimate purposes for refusing affordable housing. It provided state officials and developers with the power to pressure towns to relax zoning laws that restricted affordable housing creation. Specifically, the governor may deny state funds for such services as parks and street work. A few towns, such as Boxford and Weston, have simply turned down such support rather than accept the bill's requirements (Canellos 1989a).

A *Boston Globe* report twenty years after the bill's passage found it to be ineffective in meeting its goals. A scant 1.43 percent of family housing units in Boston's suburbs were subsidized in 1989; just 28 of the state's 351 localities had met the 10 percent target. Of the suburban units, twice as many are set aside for elderly and disabled renters as for low-income families (Canellos 1989b). Moreover, many communities give preference to their own residents, making these units unavailable to people in the central city who might wish to relocate.

With housing shortages aggravated by growth and housing prices pushed up by speculation in the 1980s, few communities were willing to add significantly to their stock of affordable housing. Some communities "discovered" environmental obstacles or historic structures when called to defend their resistance to affordable housing developments. (In Stoneham, for instance, residents went so far as to offer Polaroid prints of "endangered salamanders" allegedly living on a proposed housing site) (Canellos 1989a). More typically, towns complained that new and denser housing would result in increased traffic, service burdens, and stress on infrastructure, as well as violating historical norms of local control dating back to the origins of town meeting government.

Class and racial objections were more veiled. A few communities, including Newton, have made important strides in creating a more inclusive housing market. The situation in most of the suburbs remains more restrictive, however. As a result, many municipal workers, ranging from firefighters to teachers, some who even grew up in a given town, cannot afford the housing prices in the town where they work.

The Uneasy Relationship Between Boston and Its Suburbs

Boston and the communities that surround it maintain an uneasy relationship. The region's hub and the state capital, Boston remains a crucial employer as well as a retail, commercial, and cultural center for the metropolitan area and beyond. It contributes a disproportionate amount of wealth to the metropolitan economy, although its share has declined over time (Brown 1982). Yet Boston—and a few other urban communities, including Cambridge, Chelsea, Lawrence, and Lowell—also house higher proportions of the region's poorest residents, and face significant fiscal burdens in servicing these populations, as well as providing for the wealthier daytime population of commuters whose tax dollars flow to other, often distant, places.

With job and housing disparities have come fiscal disparities. Perhaps the most basic reason for this is the fact that cities, unlike people or businesses, cannot move to seek more profitable opportunities. Over the past four decades, Boston has added considerably to its tax base, but demands to provide services to people and businesses have grown as well. At the same time, it has lost substantial tax-paying population and employment to the suburbs (and to newer metropolitan areas in the South and West), while a larger proportion of the remaining residents are poorer. At several points in the postwar decades, the city has faced outright fiscal crisis. In 1959, the city had the lowest bond rating of any city with a population of over 500,000; this nadir was the culmination of years of economic decline and disinvestment in the built environment. More recently, the miracle years of the 1980s actually began with public revenues so low that the city temporarily froze all capital improvements and drastically cut back expenditures in public safety, public works, recreation, and other areas. Property tax reductions in the wake of Proposition 2½ and a court case (*Tregor v. City of Boston*) mandating rebates to commercial owners contributed to Boston's fiscal crisis (Brown 1982).

Boston's fiscal problems, however, have even deeper and older roots. Public finance in any American city is complicated by the unusual degree of decentralization in American federalism, and the greater degree of responsibility (and burdens) expected of local governments for policy making, financing, and implementation of public activities. Fiscal stress is heightened by the fragmentation among individual municipalities, which often results in considerable duplication of services and infra-structure, and a lack of coordination and burden-sharing on a regional level. The combination of fragmentation and decentralization makes urban governments more vulnerable to demands by business interests for public investments, tax subsidies, and other supports, while making them reluctant to raise taxes to support social services and other public goods (Ehrlich 1987).

The form of local government peculiar to New England reinforces these problems. Where the county provides many broad government functions in other U.S. regions, here its role is largely residual. The legacy of town meetings and home rule provide an unusually high degree of local government discretion—and a strong resistance to interlocal cooperation. With no provision for unincorporated villages, fiscal tensions between portions of communities were resolved historically by "the creation of more and more, smaller and smaller, autonomous units of government" (Edel et al. 1984)

As noted in an earlier chapter, for a brief period in the nineteenth century (1868 to 1873), the city of Boston and a few abutting towns tried the opposite strategy—annexation—to relieve fiscal problems. Brookline's refusal of annexation, combined with the Depression of the 1870s, ended this era abruptly. From here on out, except for the annexation of Hyde Park in 1912, Boston would remain within its borders and its suburbs would be free from responsibility for the city's social needs, while benefiting from the downtown as a place of employment and entertainment.

Boston's fiscal situation was shaped profoundly by the timing of annexation and its conclusion. This becomes clear when the metropolitan area is compared to other urban regions in the United States. By being limited in its geographic growth, Boston's physical area and population was eventually dwarfed by the wider metropolitan area. In contrast, cities such as Houston, Albuquerque, and Columbus have grown in population—and tax base—"through the aggressive annexation of surrounding areas," according to David Rusk, former mayor of Albuquerque. Some have also expanded through development of vacant or lower-density tracts within the city's borders (Rusk 1995). In Rusk's terms, central cities that are "elastic," or have the political tools and geographic good fortune to expand, are advantaged over older cities that are inelastic, or fully hemmed in. While elastic cities "capture" suburban growth, inelastic cities "contribute" to it:

> Inelastic cities could not grow either through in-fill or annexation. They could not compete with new suburbs in offering the desired suburban life-style model for family life. Incapable of capturing a share of suburban-type

development, inelastic cities have actually contributed White, middle class families to the new suburbs. In recent years . . . a rapidly growing Black middle class has moved to the suburbs as well. [Rusk 1995, 20]

Rusk also finds that metropolitan areas with inelastic cities are more segregated than their counterparts who were able to continue annexing and/or developing vacant areas. In a series of paired comparisons, this relationship held true whether the pair were in the same or in dissimilar regions of the country. He also demonstrated that more fragmented metropolitan regions were more racially segregated than those areas with "geographically large, multipowered governments and more unified school systems" (Rusk 1995, 34). Finally, less elastic cities were found to have much higher income gaps with their metropolitan region than their elastic counterparts. Other research corroborates Rusk's work. It has been found, for instance, that the metropolitan areas with the widest disparities between central city and suburb had lower rates of economic growth and prosperity, and that declining cities can lead to declining regions (cited in Squires 1994).

While the contrast between Boston and its surrounding area may not be as stark and unidimensional as in other metropolitan areas, where "city" is synonymous with "poor and minority" and "surrounding area" is synonymous with "prosperous and white," it is nevertheless true that Boston and the other industrial cities in the metropolitan area bear a disproportionate share of the area's problems. Moreover, their inability to annex wealthier jurisdictions or to form a viable regional governing body means that they are particularly ill equipped to deal with those problems.

Spatial Change in the Twenty-First Century

As spatial change has altered the relationship between the 154 municipalities that comprise Greater Boston, another item on the area's agenda involves regional cooperation on issues of transportation and planning. State officials have pinned much of the region's future on so-called mega-projects: vast public works aimed at reshaping the area's physical fabric and strengthening its economic base. Chief among them are the reconstruction of the Central Artery and the recently completed third harbor tunnel. The Artery project will depress an elevated section of Interstate 93 that for decades isolated the North End and the city's waterfront from the rest of the city. Landscaped green spaces and pedestrian ways will replace concrete overpasses in a section between North and South Station. The new Ted Williams tunnel supplements the two existing tunnels between Boston and East Boston's Logan airport.

Artery improvements aim for a better urban aesthetic by reknitting portions of the city sundered by the elevated roadway. In addition, the new Central Street Surface Plan, approved by a coalition of business, environmental, and community groups in March 1996, calls for a "broad, tree lined boulevard with wide, grassy parcels of land along the middle of the road" and accommodations for bicyclists and walkers as well as vehicle traffic (Chacon 1996a). The proposal cuts the number of lanes of traffic in the surface roadway in the artery's State Street section from twelve to six, and recognizes "pedestrian movement . . . as the primary mode of transportation in the urban core" (Move Massachusetts 2000, 1995) Community protests, as well as a threatened lawsuit by the Conservation Law Foundation, led to a reduction in parking and turning lanes, freeway ramps, and other features that would have taken away from the aesthetic of the new Boston downtown project. Overall, according to Mayor Menino, the project's goal is "to reconnect the city to the waterfront while keeping it open for people to move in and out of the area" (quoted in Chacon 1996a, 23).

An equally important goal of the artery, tunnel, and other megaprojects is economic improvement. The primary economic benefit will be in jobs created and improved travel time, with secondary benefits in retail sales and improved tourist access to downtown, once the disruptive construction period is over. The most optimistic estimates project creation of 15,000 jobs during construction (Sum and Harrington 1994). The original price tag for the combined artery-tunnel project was set at about $2.5 billion, with completion originally expected by the year 2000. While the tunnel is complete, the roadway depression has repeatedly faced delays and huge budgetary over-runs, the latter in part reflecting environmental remediation and other design shifts to assuage affected communities. By 1996, the best cost estimates for the project put the price tag at more than $10 billion (Altshuler and Luberoff 1996). In April 2000, the estimate rose to almost $14 billion, and it came along with the warning that costs could jump higher before the project is completed in 2005 (Palmer 2000), making this by far the most costly road project in the history of the world.

While the central artery-third harbor tunnel project is expected to facilitate the flow of automobile and truck traffic in the twenty-first century, existing public transportation routes are still based on travel patterns that began to be outdated nearly a half-century ago. When downtown Boston was the hub of employment, retailing, and other activities, a pattern of radial roads and transit routes, or "spokes," connecting outlying residents to the city center made sense. Today, however, urban job opportunities, as well as visits to doctors, to cultural events, and to a myriad of other destinations are as likely to be in locations such as the Longwood Medical Area or East Cambridge as they are to be downtown. This has made commuting a more awkward and time-consuming affair for many, often involving a trip into downtown on one subway line, and outward again on another. The Urban Ring is a proposal for a mixed-mode system of bus and trolley routes—and possibly boat and electric rail routes as well—that would loop from Logan Airport, through Chelsea, Everett, Somerville, Cambridge, the Fenway, Brookline, Roxbury, and down to Columbia Point-University of Massachusetts, linking urban dwellers to research, medical, and manufacturing jobs as well as health services, banks, and retail centers. The hope is that the proposed public transit route would revitalize now-underutilized areas such as Roxbury's Crosstown area, Cambridge's North Point, and the current industrial sections of East and South Boston (Campbell 1994). It is a vision of a "market route" that would spawn new commercial and industrial investment, much as Route 128 has done in the suburbs, while creating more public spaces, including plazas and walkways. Planners also hope to balance some glaring inequities along the way. They note, for example, the proximity of some of the world's leading medical institutions to residential areas with infant mortality levels rivaling those in the Third World (Lakshmanan 1993).

Current interest in the Urban Ring dates to 1992, when M. David Lee, a Boston architect appalled at the inequities revealed by the 1992 riots in Los Angeles, pointed to the isolation faced by neighborhoods much closer to home. Support for the concept has since spread to government representatives, local businesses, and officials in the large institutions along the route, including the city's leading hospitals and MIT. A planner for the Medical Area Service Consortium (MASCO) noted that about 40 percent of the 27,000 jobs in the Longwood Medical area are held by residents of Boston, Chelsea, Dorchester, and Mattapan, but many of them face horrendous commutes because of the lack of good circular public transit routes (Campbell 1994). An aide to Mayor Menino saw work on the Urban Ring as a symbol of new regional cooperation, of mayors and town managers "pooling resources, trying to get some clout through working together" (Lupo 1995a). For now, the Massachusetts Bay Transportation Authority has simply added some express bus routes linking several points along the proposed route, including Kendall Square, the Medical Area, and Roxbury. Transportation planners expect that fulfillment of their vision will come piecemeal, through evaluation of the best routes and encouragement of public and private transit along them (Campbell 1994).

A critical challenge facing metropolitan Boston as it enters the new century is the achievement of regionwide cooperation on such issues as economic development, infrastructure, and environmental quality. One approach to these problems is suggested by MetroPlan 2000, a strategy for growth management advanced by the Metropolitan Area Planning Council (MAPC). When the MAPC mounted its MetroPlan effort in 1987, it did so "in recognition of the mixed impacts of widespread low density development in the region"—in today's parlance, suburban sprawl (MAPC 1994, I-3). The plan's prescription is for more concentrated development that "encourages and enhances transit use, ride sharing and pedestrian traffic" while reducing "pressure to develop open space and environmentally sensitive lands" (MAPC 1994, I-3).

In addition to broad regional planning recommendations, MetroPlan sets out action recommendations in such areas as housing, transportation, land use, economic development, and water resources, orienting them to distinct conditions in the MAPC's seven subregions. Its overarching concept is that of the "urban service boundary," which stipulates that new growth should be spatially limited, as far as possible, to areas served by existing infrastructure. This concept was first adopted by the Twin Cities Metro Council in Minnesota in the early 1980s. The plan draws further geographic distinctions between the "urban core" (Boston, Cambridge, and nearby communities served by rapid transit); the "multi-service area," outside the urban core but served by public sewerage; and "suburban-rural" areas lacking public sewer service. Areas with environmentally sensitive open spaces and similar land resources are also designated.

MAPC's plan was approved in 1991, and it has continued to seek member community endorsement in subsequent years. Its strength is its close mesh between economic and environmental criteria; its weakness, which extends to the regional body as a whole, is the near total absence of political and financial enforcement mechanisms for attaining the plan's goals. One promising development in this area is that new powers have been granted to "metropolitan planning organizations" (MPOs) under the 1991 federal Intermodal Surface Transportation Efficiency Act (ISTEA). Under ISTEA, MPOs are given broad discretion "to allocate lump-sum federal funds among road, bridge and transit projects." David Rusk envisions that ISTEA can be "an important building block towards regional integration" (1995, 120). Whether MetroPlan 2000 or similar efforts will be advanced by this and other shifts in federal-local relationships remains an open question.

While the process of decentralization in the decades following World War II applies to Boston as it does to many U.S. metropolitan areas, there are aspects of the process that are unique to Boston. Compared to other metropolitan areas, the central city of Boston is a tiny portion of the whole, both in land area and in population. Because of the interstitial growth in which decentralization spread between existing industrial cities in the area, there is probably less spatial mismatch between inner-city workers and the location of jobs in Boston than anywhere else in the United States, and greater heterogeneity of communities across the area. While the image of "chocolate city, vanilla suburbs" may be an apt description of Detroit or Newark, it is not a good fit for spatially diverse, multicultural Boston. Moreover, because annexation came to a halt so early in the region's development, there are over 150 separate municipalities within the region, with great disparities of income and race among them and precious little in the form of regional cooperation.

Thus, the Greater Boston Metropolitan Area finds itself in the midst of a still-unfolding story of demographic change, industrial change, and spatial change as it begins the twenty-first century. It is against this backdrop that our findings regarding ethnic and racial attitudes, housing market outcomes, and labor market outcomes must be understood.

5

WHO WE ARE: HOW FAMILIES FARE IN GREATER BOSTON TODAY

AN IMPORTANT starting point for any discussion of a place is to find out who lives there. Since this research is especially aimed at understanding those characteristics of households and individuals that affect the opportunity nexus, and in particular how that nexus differs for non-Hispanic black, Hispanic, and non-Hispanic white families, the baseline information presented here compares these three race-ethnic groups on a variety of indicators of economic well-being. "Who are we?" varies enormously, depending on whether "we" refers to blacks, Hispanics, or whites.

Who Are "We" If We Are Black?

More than a third of Boston-area blacks are immigrants, making this community far different from black communities in many other major U.S. metropolitan areas, where the black population is often a greater presence and where they are overwhelmingly American-born. Thus, a substantial portion of the blacks in the region are here by choice and have come here relatively recently.

Among households with children, blacks are about twice as likely as whites or Hispanics to be single parents (mostly single mothers). This carries important implications for the income and employment prospects facing these women, as we shall see in later chapters. While blacks do not have the same amount of education as whites within this highly educated metropolis, over 40 percent have more than a high school education and another third are high school graduates. They are therefore, on average, much better educated than the Hispanics who live there. The vast majority of black households live in what are still segregated communities where the majority of their neighbors are black or, increasingly, Hispanic.

Black households have incomes that average only two-thirds that of whites and have only a tiny amount of net assets exclusive of housing value—on the order of $500. Moreover, they are far less likely than whites or Hispanics to be homeowners. Among those who do own homes, only a few own them outright. About a quarter of all black households live in public housing, with fully half of single-parent black households living there.

Twenty-three percent of black men work in the professions, but only a minuscule proportion are found in executive or managerial occupations. Many are in service occupations, especially protective services, where they work as security guards or night watchmen. Black women work in service, clerical, and sales occupations; foreign-born black women are especially likely to be in service occupations, many working in hospitals and nursing homes or as home health aides.

Who Are "We" If We Are Hispanic?

The 4 percent of Greater Boston households that are Hispanic are the most likely to be recent arrivals to the area, with about four-fifths born in Puerto Rico or other parts of Latin America. They are the youngest of the race-ethnic groups, and most are still in their childbearing and child-rearing years. Over 85 percent of Hispanic households have children under eighteen, a far higher proportion than among whites or blacks. Hispanics are the least well educated of the race-ethnic groups; an enormous number (58 percent) have not completed high school.

While over one-third live in majority-minority neighborhoods, Hispanics are less segregated than blacks, despite the fact that they have lower incomes. Race, therefore, is a much more powerful factor than ethnicity when it comes to housing (and, as we shall see later, in the labor market). The poorest of the groups at present, Hispanic households receive only 55 percent as much income as whites. With such low incomes, a high proportion are eligible for and receive public assistance of one kind or another. A quarter of all Hispanic households report receiving AFDC, while more than a third receive food stamps. The typical Hispanic household is in debt, in addition to the mortgage debt many hold. Part of this may be explained by the fact that they are overwhelmingly young families with children. Taking homeownership into account, 42 percent are homeowners, but less than 1 percent own their homes free and clear. A disproportionate number of Hispanic households live in public housing: more than two out of five (43 percent), and nearly half (47 percent) of the single-parent households.

Hispanic men are highly concentrated in less-skilled service, factory operative, and laborer occupations; 10 percent are in the executive-managerial category, but many of these are small-scale proprietors within ethnic enclaves. Hispanic women are clustered in the category of machine operators and have become the backbone of the factory work-force in textile cities like Lawrence. As long as these jobs continue to be available, they will provide steady work for those with limited educa-tion and limited English-language skills.

Who Are "We" If We Are White?

What can we say about the overwhelming majority of families in the region, the 89 percent of all households in Greater Boston who are non-Hispanic white? For one, this population tends to be older and nearly all U.S.-born. Three-fifths of the households have not had children or are now empty-nesters. Educational attainment is high, with about a quar-ter holding four-year college degrees and another 13 percent achieving some form of postbaccalaureate graduate or professional education.

They live almost exclusively in white neighborhoods. Less than 1 percent live in majority-minority neighborhoods. Whites have the high-est household incomes—an average of nearly $49,000. One-third receive at least some income from Social Security, Supplemental Security In-come, or other pensions.

Unlike blacks and Hispanics, they have financial assets—averaging $17,000 per family—beyond the equity in their homes. This asset gap between whites and minorities is widened when home values are taken into account, because whites are more likely to be homeowners and to own their homes free and clear.

White men are heavily concentrated in the more highly skilled and better-paid occupational categories: they are executives and managers, professionals, sales representatives in wholesale trade, or craft workers. In comparing the occupation distribution of foreign-born white men with all white men, it is noteworthy that a far higher proportion of the foreign-born are in a very highly skilled category, such as professional specialties, or a very low-skilled category, like laborer. This is a reflec-tion of the bimodal educational distribution of the foreign-born immi-grants to Greater Boston. Similarly, white women tend to work as pro-fessional or clerical workers, but foreign-born white women have a greater proportion in professional specialties and also a greater propor-tion in service and factory operative jobs.

The Basis for These Findings

This description of "who we are" and the analysis of racial attitudes, residential segregation, and labor market outcomes in later chapters is based on the Greater Boston Social Survey (GBSS) sample of 1,820

Greater Boston adults, age twenty-one and over, who were interviewed in 1993 and 1994. To obtain a large enough sample of black and Hispanic households for the purpose of detailed analysis, the original GBSS survey called for extensive oversampling of minority households so that we would end up with close to 600 interviews with black families, 600 with Hispanic households, and the remaining 600 with nonblack, non-Hispanic, mostly white families. The final sample was weighted by 1990 census figures on age, gender, race, and ethnicity so that estimates using the sample would be representative of the entire region's population. An appendix to this chapter provides detailed information on the methodology used to collect the GBSS data.

To maximize the chances of obtaining 600 interviews with each race-ethnic group, samples were drawn from five selected geographic strata based on 1990 U.S. census block group data:

1. higher-income white: > 50 percent white and < 20 percent in poverty
2. lower income white: > 50 percent white and >= 20 percent in poverty
3. Hispanic: > 50 percent Hispanic (any race)
4. black: > 50 percent black
5. mixed: no racial-ethnic majority

Within selected areas matching these strata definitions, we ultimately chose a sample of 3,732 addresses, from which an adult aged twenty-one or older was randomly selected for interview with the core household interview schedule.[1]

As it turned out, even *we* underestimated the explosive pace of the demographic revolution in the region. Despite our attempt at securing 600 interviews each with black, Hispanic, and white households, the sampling strata we used based on 1990 census data skewed our final sample away from black families and toward Hispanic households. By the period from 1993 to 1994, so many Hispanics had moved into what had been predominantly black neighborhoods that by the time our survey went into the field, our sampling strategy proved inadequate. We fell 135 interviews shy of our target for black respondents, while obtaining interviews with 101 more Hispanic households than originally intended. The final counts for the GBSS sample are found in table 5.1.

Table 5.2 indicates the difference between what we expected the race-ethnic composition would be in each stratum, based on the 1990 census, and the actual observed percentage when the GBSS went into the field just three years later.

We expected to find that 96.1 percent of the households in the

TABLE 5.1   *The Final GBSS Sample*

Household n = 1,820	Non-Hispanic Whites n = 589		Non-Hispanic Blacks n = 465		Hispanic n = 701		Asian n = 38		Other n = 27	
	Male	Female	Male	Female	Male	Female	Male	Female	Male	Female
Age										
Twenty-one to twenty-four	24	18	10	28	27	72	3	6	1	2
Twenty-five to thirty-four	75	85	36	90	63	180	12	6	2	7
Thirty-five to sixty-four	121	144	95	150	103	229	5	6	6	7
Sixty-five and over	50	72	18	38	7	20	0	0	1	1
Total	270	319	159	306	200	501	20	18	10	17

Source: Greater Boston Social Survey 1995.

TABLE 5.2   *Estimated and Observed Percentage of Households in Each Race-Ethnic Category by Sample Stratum*

Stratum	Percentage White		Percentage Black		Percentage Hispanic[a]	
	Estimated	Observed	Estimated	Observed	Estimated	Observed
>50 percent white, < 20 percent poverty	96.1	92.7	1.4	1.7	1.7	3.0
>50 percent white, >=20 percent poverty	83.0	71.4	6.4	8.1	10.4	13.0
>50 percent Hispanic[a]	42.7	20.7	14.3	8.9	71.9	67.8
>50 percent black	9.8	9.1	83.1	69.8	10.3	17.3
Mixed, no racial-ethnic majority	24.4	38.0	16.1	26.0	12.5	28.0

Source: Greater Boston Social Survey 1995.

[a]Note that the census rates (estimated rates) allow Hispanics to be any race, while the observed rates assume exclusive classification. Therefore, the census estimated rates for the Hispanic stratum can add to more than 100 percent. The observed rows do not add to 100 percent due to the Asian and other category.

higher-income white stratum would be white. In fact, by the period of 1993 to 1994, the actual proportion of our final sample from that stratum was only 92.7 percent white. Instead of 1.4 percent black, we found a few more such households, 1.7 percent. We expected that 1.7 percent of the households in this higher-income stratum would be Hispanic; 3 percent were.

But what was particularly stunning was the demographic shift in the black stratum—neighborhoods where we expected to find mostly black families. Based on the 1990 census, we expected that 83.1 percent of the households in this stratum would be black and only 10.3 percent Hispanic. We found that less than 70 percent were black and better than 17 percent were Hispanic. Asians have also moved into these neighborhoods.

Who We Are

The GBSS provides a rich array of data, permitting a more refined analysis of the basic demographics of the Greater Boston region. Variations in the distribution of family structures, age, family income, sources of income, assets and wealth, homeownership, education, residential location, and occupational attachment paint a picture of continuing gaps in the opportunity nexus.

Race-Ethnicity and Family Type

Despite the demographic revolution, the weighted GBSS sample (in accordance with the 1990 census) suggests that the Greater Boston area as a whole was still predominantly white (89 percent) in 1994, with a minority population of blacks (5 percent), Hispanics (4 percent), and Asians (2 percent). Even with the high rate of immigration into the region and the growth of minorities in many previously all-white communities, the minority presence in the region still trails the U.S. rate as well as that of the Northeast region as a whole (the six New England states plus New York, New Jersey, and Pennsylvania). Blacks are much more prevalent in the southern states and in the Midwest industrial region. Hispanics are found in much greater numbers in the Southwest and Western states, as well as in New York and in Florida. In 1997, blacks comprised 12.1 percent of the U.S. population, while Hispanics and Asians made up 10.3 percent and 3.8 percent, respectively. Even in 1990, the black population of the Northeastern states as a whole comprised 10.3 percent of the total population, double the proportion in the Greater Boston metropolitan region. Still, as we noted in the history section on immigration, the *growth* in the Hispanic and Asian populations in Greater Boston has been especially rapid. By the time we have Census 2000 data, we expect to see a region even more multicultural and diverse.

The internal structure of households in the region differs sharply across racial and ethnic groups (see table 5.3). In part, this is due to differences in the age structure of each group. Hispanics in the region are much younger, on average, than blacks or whites, and are more

TABLE 5.3   *Family Type Distribution by Race and Ethnicity*

Family Type	Black	Hispanic	White
Multi-adult with children	31%	68%	32%
Multi-adult with no children	16	8	39
Single adult with children	18	17	7
Single male adult with children	1	2	1
Single female adult with children	18	15	6
Single adult with no children	35	7	22
Single male adult with no children	25	2	7
Single female adult with no children	10	4	15

Source: Greater Boston Social Survey 1995.

TABLE 5.4   *Distribution of Family Type for Those Families with Children*

Family Type	All	Black	Hispanic	White
Multi-adult with children	80%	63%	80%	82%
Single adult with children	20	37	20	18

Source: Greater Boston Social Survey 1995.

likely to be in their childbearing and child-raising years. More than three-fifths of the white households in the region (61 percent) are childless, as are 51 percent of black households. Some of these are younger families who have not had children yet, others are empty-nesters, and some are households containing only a single individual. In contrast, only 15 percent of Hispanic households have no children in them.[2] These differences in family structure have important implications for differences in household income with respect both to levels and sources.

Looking only at families with children, table 5.4 illustrates the proportion that are multi-adult and the proportion that are single adult. Twenty percent of all families with children are headed by a single adult, while the remaining 80 percent are multi-adult families. This proportion is essentially the same for Hispanics and whites, but not for blacks. Black families with children are twice as likely as Hispanic and white households to be headed by a single adult (37 percent as opposed to 20 percent and 18 percent, respectively). This clearly will have implications for who faces employment and income problems and who most likely will rely, at least periodically, on traditional welfare programs and food stamps.

Age Distributions

The age distributions by gender, race, and ethnicity are shown in figures 5.1 and 5.2. Disparities in the age structure can be expected to influence racial and ethnic attitudes, patterns of residential locations, and especially labor market outcomes. Note that more than half of Hispanic men and women in the Greater Boston region are younger than thirty-five, while only about a third of whites are this young. At the other end of the age span, over a quarter of white men and about a third of white women are over fifty-five, while the corresponding proportions for Hispanics are 11 and 14 percent, respectively. The black age distribution falls in between that of whites and Hispanics.

FIGURE 5.1   *Male Age Distribution by Race and Ethnicity*

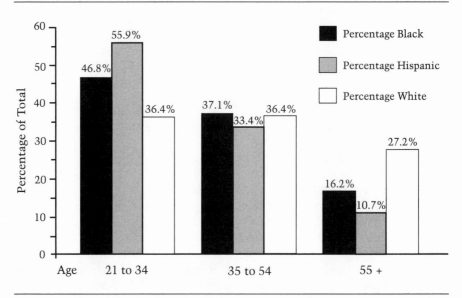

Source: Greater Boston Social Survey 1995.

FIGURE 5.2   *Female Age Distribution by Race and Ethnicity*

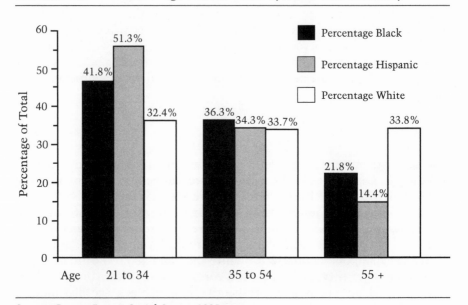

Source: Greater Boston Social Survey 1995.

As we will find when we analyze the labor market, age does explain a significant amount of the difference in average earnings between Hispanics, on the one hand, and whites and blacks, on the other. The typical Hispanic in Boston is still moving up the "age-earnings" trajectory, while many white and black workers have already arrived at or near their peak earnings potential. This should be expected to affect wages across race and ethnic groups, and family incomes as well.

Family Income

Since income is the primary determinant of a family's ability to meet and satisfy its basic needs, one extremely important measure of economic well-being for individual race-ethnic groups is average family income. According to the GBSS, mean family income across all households in the Greater Boston area was $46,781 (in 1994 dollars). Hispanic families had the lowest income of the three populations ($26,710), while white families topped the distribution (at $48,609).[3] Black families enjoyed incomes some $5,000 higher than Hispanics—but, at $31,209, trailed their white counterparts by more than $17,000. Hence, Hispanic family income averages only 55 percent of non-Hispanic white income, while blacks earn 64 percent of that of white households.[4] Median family incomes were considerably lower than the means, as is normally the case because of extreme (high) values for a few families. However, the income rankings are identical.

While the gaps are large, the level of income is reasonably high compared with the United States as a whole. In 1993, the median household income for all U.S. households was $31,241 (U.S. Census Bureau 1997). The median for the typical Greater Boston household, at $37,500 according to the GBSS, was a full 20 percent higher. The typical white household in Greater Boston (with a median income of $42,500) enjoyed an annual income more than a third (36 percent) higher. But black and Hispanic households did not even reach the national median. At $27,500, the median black household in Boston fell 11 percent below the national standard. Hispanics, at $22,500, trailed the typical U.S. family by 28 percent (see figure 5.3).

Some of the large gaps in family income are explained by differences in household composition, as well as the age of family breadwinners (see table 5.5). *Regardless* of race and ethnicity, single-parent families have incomes that average only 37 to 48 percent of multi-adult families with children.[5] Part of this no doubt reflects the number of breadwinners each household contains; part can be explained by the gender of the household head, with most of the single-parent families headed by a woman. Another portion of the explanation for these large gaps can be found in

FIGURE 5.3   *Mean and Median Family Income by Race and*
            Ethnicity

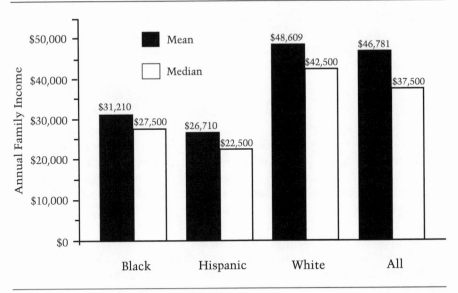

Source: Greater Boston Social Survey 1995.

educational and occupational differences across the race-ethnic groups,
topics we discuss later in this chapter.

Sources of Income in the Greater Boston Region

Most income is generated from wages, but for individual subpopula-
tions, nonwage income sources—including Social Security, Aid to Families with Dependent Children (AFDC), food stamps, unemployment

TABLE 5.5   *Mean Family Income Multi- Versus Single-Adult*
            Families with Children (Nonelderly Adults, Age
            Twenty-One to Sixty-Five)

	Multi-Adult	Single-Adult
All	$53,924	$19,790
Black	35,931	17,394
Hispanic	31,637	12,099
White	57,295	20,976

Source: Greater Boston Social Survey 1995.

benefits, and Supplemental Security Income (SSI)—are significant contributors to overall family resources. Whether a family receives income from any number of sources differs largely by age, race, and ethnicity.

Overall, only 37 percent of all households in Greater Boston have family incomes composed exclusively of wage earnings. Another 30 percent report sources of income from wages plus at least one nonwage income source. The remaining third of the population relies exclusively on nonwage sources. Half of these households (16 percent) depend on pensions and Social Security for their entire income. Figure 5.4 depicts this breakdown of income sources for all households in the region.

If we exclude the elderly (age sixty-five and over), still only about half (47 percent) of all households rely on wages alone, while another 10 percent live off wages plus unemployment benefits (see figure 5.5). That still leaves more than two out of five nonelderly families who rely on something other than wages and/or unemployment benefits to make ends meet. For most of these families earnings are combined with SSI, workers' compensation, disability pay, or child support.

Who receives what form of income also has a strong racial and ethnic dimension. Table 5.6 answers the question, "What proportion of those receiving a particular type of nonwage income are of a given race-ethnic background?" In general, we see that payments from Social Security, SSI, unemployment insurance, workers' compensation, and court-

FIGURE 5.4   *Sources of Income—All Households*
             Percentage Households by Income Source

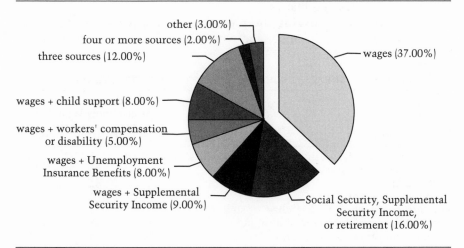

Source: Greater Boston Social Survey 1995.

FIGURE 5.5   *Sources of Income—Nonelders*
Percentage Households by Income Source

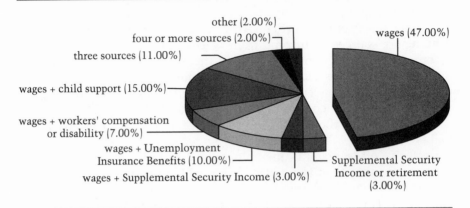

other (2.00%)
four or more sources (2.00%)
three sources (11.00%)
wages + child support (15.00%)
wages + workers' compensation or disability (7.00%)
wages + Unemployment Insurance Benefits (10.00%)
wages + Supplemental Security Income (3.00%)
wages (47.00%)
Supplemental Security Income or retirement (3.00%)

Source: Greater Boston Social Survey 1995.

ordered child support and alimony go overwhelmingly to white families. More specifically, at least 90 percent of the households receiving these income sources are white families—about the same as the 89 percent share of whites in the Greater Boston population. Virtually all the unemployment benefits and workers' compensation go to white families. By contrast, a disproportionate share of AFDC and food stamp recipients are black and Hispanic: approximately half the recipients of these forms of public assistance are white families; the remaining half is divided between Hispanics and blacks.

In addition to analyzing the *proportion of nonwage income recipients* who are black, Hispanic, and white, it is also possible to compare

TABLE 5.6   *Nonwage Income Sources by Race and Ethnicity*

| Income Source | Percentage of Recipient Households Who Are | | |
	Black	Hispanic	White
Social Security, SSI, or other retirement benefits	3	1	95
AFDC or other welfare	18	25	55
Food Stamps	21	32	45
Unemployment Insurance	2	1	97
Workers' compensation, disability, or sick pay	2	1	97
Court-ordered child support or alimony	4	3	93
Money from others outside home	3	4	91

Source: Greater Boston Social Survey 1995.

TABLE 5.7   *Proportion of Race-Ethnic Families Receiving Nonwage Income Sources*

Income Source	Percentage of Households Who Receive Income from This Source		
	Black	Hispanic	White
Social Security, SSI, or other retirement benefits	22	10	34
AFDC or other welfare	13	25	2
Food Stamps	18	37	2
Unemployment insurance	5	4	14
Workers' compensation, disability, or sick pay	5	3	13
Court-ordered child support or alimony	4	3	4
Money from others outside home	8	12	12

Source: Greater Boston Social Survey 1995.

and contrast *the actual proportions of racial and ethnic populations* who receive such assistance. Table 5.7 answers the question, "What proportion of a particular race-ethnic group received a particular nonwage income source?" Proportionately, more whites received Social Security or SSI than did blacks or Hispanics, reflecting the fact that they are a somewhat older population. Indeed, while a third of all white families received Social Security or other retirement benefits, only a fifth of black families and a tenth of Hispanic families did. Likewise, white families were three times more likely to be recipients of unemployment benefits than either blacks or Hispanics, and at least twice as likely to receive workers' compensation or disability pay.

Just the opposite was the case when it came to receipt of AFDC, other forms of cash welfare assistance, and food stamps. According to the GBSS data, a full quarter of Hispanic families received AFDC or other welfare, while more than a third (37 percent) received food stamps. The rate of AFDC and food stamp receipt among black families was only half the Hispanic rate (13 percent and 18 percent, respectively). Only 2 percent of white families received either. Given that these welfare programs are income-contingent—and given the relative income levels of racial and ethnic groups in Boston—it is not surprising that nonwage income sources would be distributed this way.

Assets and Wealth

Differences in average *income* tell only part of the well-being story. Another compelling measure is average *net assets*. This measure is calculated by taking gross family assets (excluding housing values) and sub-tracting gross family debt (excluding housing values), and then averaging across each race-ethnic group. While family income is a useful measure of what a family can generally afford to spend during a given year, net assets tell us something about how much a family has had to go into debt in the past in order to sustain itself and how much it has been able to save in order to provide for retirement, for bad times, or for invest-ment in education or in starting up a small business.

The GBSS indicates that race-ethnic differences in mean family net assets are enormous, swamping even the sizable differences we found in family incomes (see figure 5.6). Whites averaged nearly $17,000 in mean net assets, nearly *thirty times* the $583 figure for black families. His-panics, on average, are deeply in debt. Their net asset position exceeds minus $4,300. These differences, while seeming extreme, are in remark able agreement with the national statistics on wealth compiled by Melvin Oliver and Thomas Shapiro (1995). They find, like we do, a ra-cial gap in wealth that leaves the typical black family with practically no family wealth to speak of.

FIGURE 5.6   *Average Family Net Assets by Race and Ethnicity*

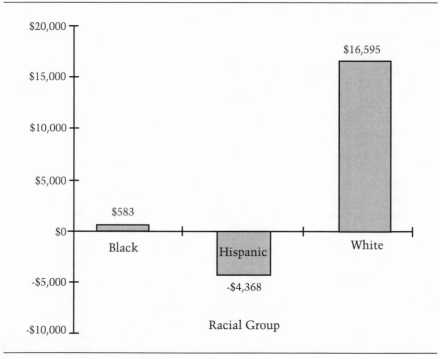

Source: Greater Boston Social Survey 1995.

Such extreme differences in net asset position could be due to many factors. One of the most important is simply the age of the adults in the family. Younger families generally have had little time to build up assets and often have gone into debt in order to outfit a home, acquire a car, or pay for education expenses. Older families have had the time to accumulate savings and prepare for retirement, although their actual circumstances may or may not have allowed them to do so. Since the adults in white families in the Greater Boston region are generally older than those in black families, while those in Hispanic families are the youngest, a part (perhaps a large part) of the race-ethnic differences in net assets might be attributable to this factor alone.

But the three segments in figure 5.7 suggest that even after controlling for age, the extreme gaps in family wealth remain. As expected, younger families (adults aged twenty-one to thirty-four) had few assets. The mean net wealth of younger white families was only $1,351. However, white families, on average, were the only families not in debt. Black families averaged over $1,600 in net debt, while Hispanic families averaged over $5,600 in net debt.

Families with adults in prime age (age thirty-five to fifty-four) already show signs of building up some net assets (or reducing net debt). But the gaps by race and ethnic group are very wide. White families now have over $15,000 in net assets compared with only $2,000 for black families. Hispanic families have reduced their indebtedness, but still find themselves nearly $4,000 in debt.

Finally, we would expect older families (with adults age fifty-five and over) to have the highest net asset positions. This is true for white families, who now average nearly $35,000 in net wealth. But it is not true for black or Hispanic families. Older black families average only about $1,000 in net assets, while older Hispanic families are still nearly $2,500 in debt. Obviously, the opportunities for asset accumulation vary dramatically by race and ethnicity, even after controlling for age. Part of this may be the legacy of the historic gaps in earnings and incomes. With higher incomes, it has been easier for white households to save. Whites may also have benefited, to some extent, from inheritance. Given past discrimination, the parents of the current generation of blacks in Boston likely had such low incomes that they were able to pass on practically nothing to their children. White families, on average, were able to provide their children with more of a grub stake. Moreover, many, if not most, Hispanic immigrants brought with them few assets when they came to the United States and, given their low earnings, have not had much opportunity to save once they arrived. In any case, such a lack of wealth on top of low incomes surely limits the ability of families to weather downturns in the economy and invest in themselves or their children.

FIGURE 5.7   *Average Family Net Assets by Race, Ethnicity, and Age*

Respondents Aged Twenty-One to Thirty-Four

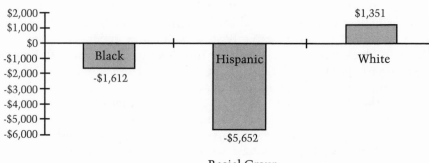

Respondents Aged Thirty-Five to Fifty-Four

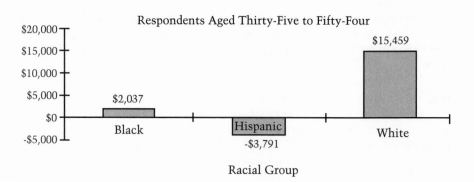

Respondents Aged Fifty-Five and Over

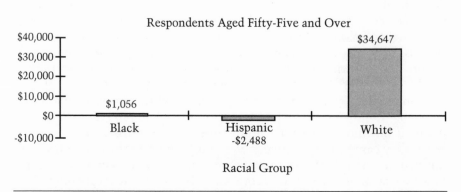

Source: Greater Boston Social Survey 1995.

Housing in Boston:
Who Rents, Who Owns?

The most important asset that most families in the United States have is their own home. Nearly 65 percent of all American families own their own homes—if not outright, then at least with the help of a mortgage. In the Boston metropolitan area, the overall average is somewhat lower. According to the GBSS, 55 percent of households are homeowners, while 45 percent rent the dwellings in which they live. Like income and wealth, however, homeownership varies dramatically by race and ethnicity, as well as by family-household composition and age of the household head. With nearly two-thirds owning their own homes, whites are one-third more likely than Hispanics to be homeowners (42 percent), while blacks—even though they have higher incomes and wealth than Hispanics—have the lowest homeownership rate by far (24 percent) (see table 5.8). This may also help explain the high indebtedness of Latino families. With homeownership high on their list of assets to acquire, even with their low average income, buying furniture and household appliances could account for the "negative" household asset positions we noted earlier. A closer look at homeownership with mortgage debt status by race and ethnic background reflects this as well. Fewer than 1 percent of Hispanic homeowners own their homes free and clear, while 37 percent of whites do (see figure 5.8).

Public Housing

Of all families surveyed, 11 percent reside in public housing. Hispanic families have by far the largest proportion residing in such dwellings: 43 percent.[6] Nearly a quarter of black families (24 percent) also live there, while only 7 percent of whites do (see figure 5.9). Since public housing residency is available only to households with low income, it is no surprise that single adults with children are the most likely to reside there. At 26 percent, this is a significantly higher proportion than the 6 per-

TABLE 5.8   *Home Ownership by Race and Ethnicity*

	Percentage Who Own	Percentage Who Rent
All households	55	45
Black	24	76
Hispanic	42	58
White	64	36

Source: Greater Boston Social Survey 1995.

FIGURE 5.8   *Homeownership Status by Race-Ethnicity*
                Who Owns Free and Clear?

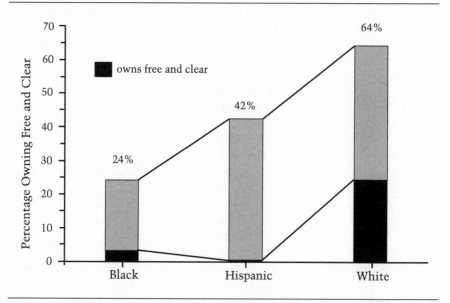

Source: Greater Boston Social Survey 1995.

FIGURE 5.9   *Public Housing by Race-Ethnicity*

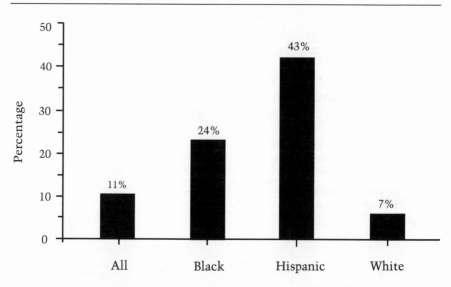

Source: Greater Boston Social Survey 1995.

cent of multi-adult families with children living in public housing. The second highest concentration rate is found among single adults with no children. These tend to be elderly people living on small fixed incomes.

Among single parents, there is a slightly higher concentration of blacks in public housing than Hispanics—despite the fact that Hispanics, across all family types, have a higher concentration living in public housing. Fifty-one percent of black single guardians, 47 percent of Hispanics, and 20 percent of white single parents live in public housing in Greater Boston (see figure 5.10).

FIGURE 5.10   *Concentration in Public Housing by Family Type and Race*

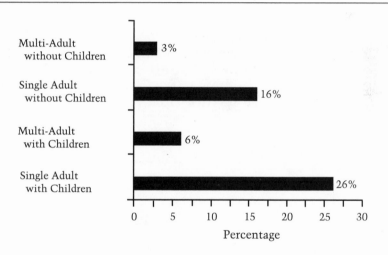

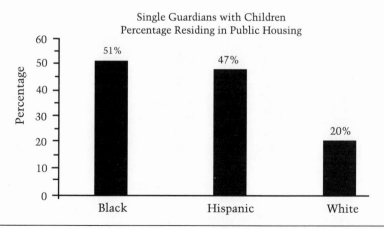

Source: Greater Boston Social Survey 1995.

127

Education

Differences in earnings, incomes, assets, homeownership, and the probability of living in public housing are, by all accounts, at least partly related to education. According to the GBSS, only about 7 percent of white adults have not completed high school. This compares with nearly a quarter of blacks (24 percent) and three-fifths (58 percent) of Hispanics. At the other end of the education spectrum, 37 percent of whites have a college degree or schooling beyond the undergraduate degree, while only 15 percent of blacks have this much education and only 6 percent of Hispanics do. If we were to consider modal education levels in the region, Hispanics have not completed high school, while blacks are primarily high school and community college graduates. The modal white adult in the Greater Boston region has completed university or postgraduate training (see figure 5.11). These differences—and their potential implications—are enormous.

A quite different, and fascinating, pattern emerges when we analyze education by nativity. As figure 5.12 clearly indicates, the schooling distribution of foreign-born residents of the Greater Boston region is bimodal. One could draw an inverted U on the graph to trace out the

FIGURE 5.11   *Years of Education*

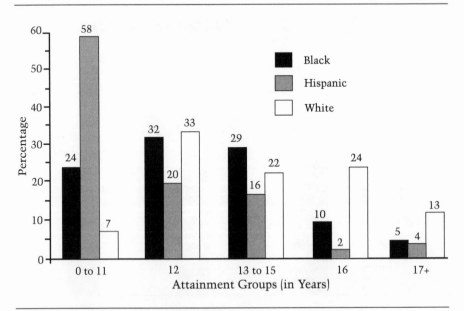

Source: Greater Boston Social Survey 1995.

FIGURE 5.12   *Years of Education, Native-Born Versus Foreign-Born*

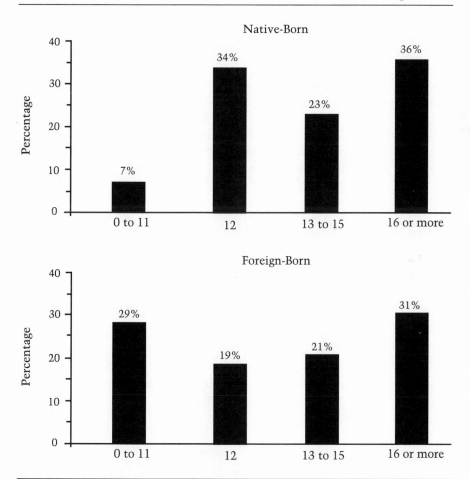

Native-Born

Foreign-Born

Source: Greater Boston Social Survey 1995.

progression of attainment associated with native-born residents, while a V better describes the schooling distribution of the foreign-born. Although nearly 30 percent of all foreign-born did not complete high school, about the same proportion (31 percent) have graduated from college or gone beyond the undergraduate degree. This is almost as high as the 36 percent of native-born who have had this much education.

Such an education distribution among the foreign-born is most likely unique to the Greater Boston region. With its high concentration of colleges and universities—and its abundance of high-tech firms—

Boston attracts a large contingent of well-educated and well-trained immigrants, some of whom arrived initially as students. At the other end of the education spectrum, however, it has attracted a significant number of political and economic refugees from Central America, Haiti, the Dominican Republic, and Southeast Asia—where education levels tend to be extremely low. Given this bimodal distribution, one would not expect a simple relationship between nativity and income. Indeed, as we shall demonstrate later in this book, the variable "foreign-born," taken by itself, explains virtually none of the difference in labor market outcomes. The bimodal education distribution explains why.

Nativity for each race-ethnic group is shown in figure 5.13.[7] As expected, an overwhelming proportion (81 percent) of the Hispanic population has emigrated from abroad (or migrated from Puerto Rico). More surprising, as noted in an earlier chapter, is the high proportion of blacks in the region who are immigrants to the United States. According to the GBSS data, over a third (35 percent) of the blacks living

FIGURE 5.13   *Percentage Foreign-Born Population by Race and Ethnicity*

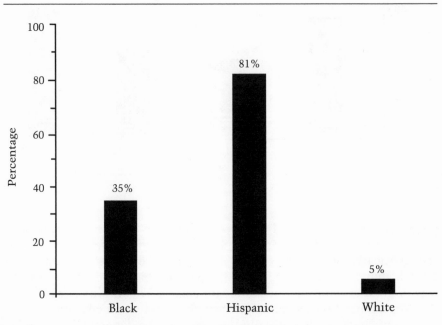

Source: Greater Boston Social Survey 1995.

in the Greater Boston region have come here from such countries as Haiti, Jamaica, and the rest of the British West Indies, as well as from various African nations.

Residential Location

Despite the growing multiculturalism of the overall metropolitan area, a high degree of residential segregation still structures everyday life, particularly for black and white families. A huge percentage (70 percent) of blacks are found in neighborhoods where the majority of residents are black themselves, and only 1 percent of whites live outside white neighborhoods (see table 5.9). Hispanics live in the most integrated neighborhoods, with only 38 percent living in communities where blacks and Hispanics comprise more than half the residents. Thus we can see that although segregation remains very high, Hispanics have had an easier time than blacks integrating into white communities—often despite a language barrier and the fact that Hispanic incomes and net assets are lower than those of blacks. Foreign-born blacks are somewhat *less* likely to be living in minority communities. Native-born Hispanics are more likely to be living in integrated communities, suggesting that second-generation Latinos are more likely to leave the local barrios for neighborhoods that are predominantly white.

Why these segregation patterns persist is a matter of great controversy. Clearly, in the past, explicit mortgage lending and real estate practices were instrumental in dividing neighborhoods and communities along racial and ethnic lines. This was true for the Irish more than a century ago and for blacks as late as the early 1970s. But there is also

TABLE 5.9   *Percentage of Individuals Living in Majority-Minority Neighborhoods*[a]

Group	All	Black	Hispanic	White
All	6	70	38	1
Males	6	73	40	1
Females	6	68	37	0
Foreign-born	20	64	40	1
U.S.-born	4	74	31	0

Source: Greater Boston Social Survey 1995.
[a]A majority-minority neighborhood is a census block that has more than 50 percent black or more than 50 percent Hispanic residents.

the possibility that segregation simply reflects differences in income and social class, with richer whites able to escape the inner city much more readily than blacks or recent immigrants. Then, too, there is the possibility that the persistent segregation we find at least partly reflects consumer "tastes"—on the part of both whites and blacks. Few blacks may choose to live in communities that are overwhelmingly white, even if whites are hospitable and neighborhood amenities are better there. A sense of community may not rest on race alone, but race is nonetheless a factor in choosing where to live—as religion or ethnicity has been for centuries. We will explore this issue at greater length later in this book.

Whether voluntary or not, housing segregation may have a direct impact on earnings and incomes, although deciphering the direction of causation is difficult. To the extent that blacks are "trapped" in the inner city while many jobs have moved to the suburbs suggests the possibility of a spatial mismatch between where people live and where they can find work. Alternatively, poor job prospects may mean that families are unable to afford to live in suburban neighborhoods, creating a Catch-22: to get a good job, you need to live in the suburbs; to live in the suburbs, you need to have a good job. In any case, where you live and what credentials you bring to the labor market help determine where you fit into the occupational distribution in a regional economy.

Occupational Attachment

The landscape of occupations revealed by the GBSS suggests uneven terrain. Boston area residents occupy sharply different occupational niches, depending on their race, ethnicity, and gender. To some extent, variations in work patterns are also evident between native-born and foreign-born residents.

Today, Greater Boston can be defined as a white-collar region with an unusually high level of skilled and credentialed workers. This high-skill bias represents a sea change from the region's blue-collar past. As we noted earlier, it is part of a drastic shift from a mill-based to a mind-based economy, from work with the hands requiring physical strength or dexterity to work with ideas, information, and people. The magnitude of this reversal is startling. At mid-century, slightly less than half the region's workers worked in white-collar fields, while nearly as many (42 percent) worked in lower-skilled blue-collar occupations. Today, the ratio of white- to blue-collar jobs is greater than 3 to 1.

In chapter 3, we were able to trace the changes in the number and nature of jobs in the region using state employment data. Here we can

use the GBSS to probe deeper into the occupational distribution by gender, race, and nativity, thus providing more detail on who is working
where in Greater Boston.

Male Occupations by Race
and Ethnicity

Not surprisingly, given their average educational achievement and their
long-term social dominance in the region, white men are overwhelmingly concentrated in high-skilled white-collar fields, with professional and managerial occupations predominating (see table 5.10).
More than two-fifths (40.5 percent) of white men in the region work in
such jobs, about equally divided between executives and managers, on
the one hand, and professionals, on the other. Another one in six (15.9
percent) white men work in sales occupations, many in financial services and other highly paid retail positions. Skilled blue-collar work,

TABLE 5.10   *Male Occupation by Race and Ethnicity*

Occupation	Black Male Distribution	Hispanic Male Distribution	White Male Distribution
Executive, administrative, and managerial occupations	1.4%	10.6%	**20.2%**
Professional specialty occupations	**23.1**	0.8	**20.3**
Technical and related support occupations	3.0	0.0	2.8
Sales occupations	7.0	1.1	**15.9**
Administrative support occupations	10.7	10.0	6.2
Private household occupations	0.0	0.0	0.0
Protective service occupations	**11.9**	1.2	3.4
Service occupations	**15.3**	**19.6**	3.5
Farming, forestry, and fishing occupations	3.2	0.7	1.0
Precision production, craft, and repair occupations	7.6	12.6	12.8
Machine operators, assemblers, and inspectors	2.7	**22.6**	2.6
Transportation and material-moving occupations	6.3	7.2	9.1
Handlers, equipment cleaners, helpers, and laborers	7.8	**13.7**	2.3

Source: Greater Boston Social Survey 1995.
Note: The three most common occupations for each group appear in boldface.

such as carpentry or other trades, remains a stronghold of white males as well: more than one in eight (12.8 percent) works in precision production, craft, or repair positions. Much smaller percentages are employed in less-skilled blue-collar trades, in transportation, machine operation, or laboring occupations.

Black men, by contrast, are almost invisible in Greater Boston's executive suites. Barely more than one out of a hundred holds an executive or managerial job. They are, however, strongly represented in the professional specialties, with almost one in four so employed. This broad occupation group includes, among others, medical technicians, teachers, and social workers. Black men are also concentrated in service occupations: over 27 percent are found there. They are more likely than any other group to work in protective services, a category that includes security guards and night watchmen—indeed, more than one in nine (11.9 percent) are found in this field alone. Blue-collar work occupies the remainder, with more in laboring positions and fewer in skilled craft work than among white men.

Blue-collar and service occupations overwhelmingly predominate for Hispanic men, with better than half (56 percent) in occupations such as machine operation, transportation and laboring, and precision production. Another one in five (19.6 percent) is employed in a service occupation. Their heavy concentration in production trades recalls the region's workforce at mid-century, when manual or mill-based occupations predominated for most men (and many women as well). It also suggests the strong concentration of Hispanics in such cities as Lawrence, where there is still a remnant of textile and similar nondurable goods production.

In addition to their strong representation in lower-skilled manual and service work, Latino men in the Boston region are also found, unlike blacks, in executive and managerial occupations. Over one in ten works in such a position. This can be explained by the fact that this occupational category includes proprietors, and among Hispanic ranks are numerous Caribbean and Central American immigrants who have established small businesses such as bodegas and taxi companies in Boston, Lawrence, and other Latino outposts in the region: they are not executives in downtown office towers, but owners and managers of ethnic firms in local neighborhoods.

Female Occupations by Race and Ethnicity

White women in Boston are most heavily concentrated in professional specialty occupations, outdistancing every other racial and gender group in this category (see table 5.11). Among their numbers are a few scientists and architects, but many more teachers and nurses. All together, nearly three out of ten (29.2 percent) white women work in the professions. Smaller proportions (about one in five) work in administrative support positions, with another 17 percent in sales and 14 percent in service occupations. Very few white women (under 5 percent) work in blue-collar jobs, and they are almost entirely absent from work in protective services.

In contrast to whites, black females are concentrated in administrative support positions and service occupations. Fully half (53.6 percent) of this group are found in these occupations, which range from execu-

TABLE 5.11   *Female Occupation by Race and Ethnicity*

Occupation	Black Female Distribution	Hispanic Female Distribution	White Female Distribution
Executive, administrative, and managerial occupations	7.5%	0.8%	7.1%
Professional specialty occupations	8.5	**15.6**	**29.2**
Technical and related support occupations	1.9	0.1	5.2
Sales occupations	**15.8**	8.7	16.9
Administrative support occupations	**23.2**	15.0	**20.1**
Private household occupations	0.7	0.2	0.3
Protective service occupations	1.4	0.0	0.0
Service occupations	**30.4**	**17.9**	**13.6**
Farming, forestry, and fishing occupations	0.0	0.1	1.5
Precision production, craft, and repair occupations	0.4	0.3	3.3
Machine operators, assemblers, and inspectors	4.7	**41.0**	1.7
Transportation and material-moving occupations	4.6	0.1	1.3
Handlers, equipment cleaners, helpers, and laborers	0.9	0.3	0.0

Source: Greater Boston Social Survey 1995.
Note: The three most common occupations for each group appear in boldface.

tive assistants and data entry clerks to waitresses, orderlies, and house-keepers. Another one in six works in sales positions. Women of color are underrepresented in the professions, however. Barely eight black women out of a hundred are so employed, far less than black men (23 percent), or white women (29 percent). Relatively few work in blue-collar trades (about one in ten), with most concentrated in machine operation, assembly, and transportation work.

Latina workers occupy a niche traditionally held by immigrant women of earlier generations who found work in the region's factories. Instead of operating looms at Lawrence's American Woolen Company, they may now be producing synthetic PolarTec fleece at Malden Mills. Over 40 percent of Hispanic women in the Greater Boston region work as machine operators, assemblers, and inspectors, while almost none are employed in skilled production or craft positions. Among less educated workers, the niche that Hispanic women have obtained in manufacturing-based occupations is critical, as we shall discuss in later chapters, for giving them an edge in annual earnings relative to black women. Production work provides them higher hourly earnings, more hours of work per week, and more annual income than African American women with limited education, who tend to be more prevalent in service occupations, which pay lower wages and often offer only part-time hours.

Some Latinas have begun to attain white-collar positions. Better than three out of ten work in professional or administrative support occupations (30.6 percent), with their ranks evenly split between these two types of work. An additional 18 percent are employed in service occupations, with smaller proportions in sales work. Under 1 percent have attained executive or managerial roles.

Occupations by Nativity

As immigrants have come to Boston, their occupational distribution has become curiously bimodal, reflecting their bimodal education level (see table 5.12). While well-educated immigrants specialize above all in professional and technical positions—with one-third (33.9 percent) of all immigrants working in these highly skilled occupations—newcomers also make up the ranks of the region's lowest-skilled positions. Over one in six (17.3 percent) works in a service occupation, so that newcomers are twice as likely as native workers to be employed in such positions and about three times as likely to work as technicians. They are underrepresented in managerial and executive ranks, relative to natives, with about 10 percent so employed, compared with 15 percent of native-born workers. Relatively few immigrants (4 percent) are occupied in sales po-

TABLE 5.12   *Occupation by Nativity*

Occupation	Native-Born Distribution	Foreign-Born Distribution
Executive, administrative, and managerial occupations	**14.8%**	9.5%
Professional specialty occupations	**22.9**	**23.5**
Technical and related support occupations	3.7	10.4
Sales occupations	**16.3**	3.9
Administrative support occupations	13.4	12.3
Private household occupations	0.0	1.2
Protective service ccupations	2.0	0.2
Service occupations	8.6	**17.3**
Farming, forestry, and fishing occupations	1.3	0.1
Precision production, craft, and repair occupations	8.1	4.9
Machine operators, assemblers, and inspectors	2.1	**11.1**
Transportation and material-moving occupations	5.4	1.8
Handlers, equipment cleaners, helpers, and laborers	1.3	3.6

Source: Greater Boston Social Survey 1995.
Note: The three most common occupations for each group appear in boldface.

sitions. Many sales jobs, particularly those in wholesale trade, require sophisticated customer contact. This may put immigrants with limited English-language ability at a disadvantage. In contrast, immigrants are prominent in semiskilled blue-collar jobs, such as machine operation and assembly, where communication skills are less critical. Newcomers are five times as likely as natives to be employed as assemblers, handlers, and laborers.

Male Occupations by Nativity and Race

Still more detail on the occupational landscape of Greater Boston can be obtained by disaggregating the GBSS data by gender, race, and nativity. For example, white immigrant males are heavily concentrated in professional and technical occupations, where over 80 percent work. In contrast, blacks are fairly evenly distributed among professional specialties, service occupations, and administrative support. Hispanic immigrant males are highly concentrated in the blue-collar and service occupations, with over two-thirds (68 percent) employed in these fields. Despite their general concentration in blue-collar work, foreign-born His-

TABLE 5.13   *Foreign-Born Males: Occupation by Race and*
Ethnicity

Occupation	Black Male Distribution	Hispanic Male Distribution	White Male Distribution
Executive, administrative, and managerial occupations	0.0%	**14.8**%	0.5%
Professional specialty occupations	**20.1**	1.1	**62.4**
Technical and related support occupations	1.2	0.0	**19.8**
Sales occupations	12.7	1.5	0.0
Administrative support occupations	**17.1**	12.6	0.2
Private household occupations	0.0	0.0	0.0
Protective service occupations	3.8	1.3	0.3
Service occupations	**18.2**	**27.1**	0.0
Farming, forestry, and fishing occupations	0.0	0.8	0.0
Precision production, craft, and repair occupations	11.8	7.4	3.8
Machine operators, assemblers, and inspectors	1.3	**14.7**	3.2
Transportation and material-moving occupations	4.4	10.0	0.0
Handlers, equipment cleaners, helpers, and laborers	9.5	8.8	**9.9**

Source: Greater Boston Social Survey 1995.
Note: The three most common occupations for each group appear in boldface.

panic men are also more likely than either white or black immigrant males to be in executive or managerial positions (15 percent). Again, this mostly represents managers and proprietors of small neighborhood businesses—often catering to the Spanish-speaking community (see table 5.13).

Female Occupations by Nativity and Race

Female immigrants hold lower-skilled and lower-status positions than those of their male counterparts. Immigrant women are also heavily concentrated in machine operation, assembly, and inspection positions and administrative support. While they are less likely to work in professional and executive positions than native-born women, over one in six female newcomers is in the professional specialties. Black immigrant

TABLE 5.14   *Foreign-Born Females: Occupation by Race and Ethnicity*

Occupation	Black Female Distribution	Hispanic Female Distribution	White Female Distribution
Executive, administrative, and managerial occupations	2.7%	0.1%	1.0%
Professional specialty occupations	7.5	**17.7**	**34.2**
Technical and related support occupations	0.0	0.2	0.0
Sales occupations	**18.9**	5.6	4.5
Administrative support occupations	**8.6**	14.2	3.1
Private household occupations	2.3	0.2	6.8
Protective service occupations	0.0	0.0	0.0
Service occupations	**57.1**	**14.6**	**30.8**
Farming, forestry, and fishing occupations	0.0	0.1	0.0
Precision production, craft, and repair occupations	0.0	0.4	0.0
Machine operators, assemblers, and inspectors	2.5	**46.5**	**19.8**
Transportation and material-moving occupations	0.6	0.1	0.0
Handlers, equipment cleaners, helpers, and laborers	0.0	0.3	0.0

Source: Greater Boston Social Survey 1995.
Note: The three most common occupations for each group appear in boldface.

women are highly concentrated in service occupations (57 percent), with a smaller proportion employed in sales positions. Close to half of all Hispanic female immigrants operate machines or assemble goods, while 18 percent work in professional specialty occupations. White female immigrants, who are a small proportion of the sampled group, are about evenly divided between professional and service occupations (see table 5.14).

Not only is Boston divided into racial (and, to some extent, ethnic) neighborhoods, but the occupational landscape of the region is also divided into racial, ethnic, and gender niches. This segmentation may play an important role when we turn our attention to trying to explain the differences in family incomes that we encountered at the beginning of this chapter.

Conclusion

Despite the progress the region has made in providing homes to new families, the old pattern of having to fight for a place at the social and economic table, so prevalent for early immigrants to the region, still persists for those who have come here during the past quarter-century and for those who may have been here for generations, but bear the consequences of being black. We find deep divisions in the opportunity nexus *across* race-ethnic groups. How this actually plays out in terms of racial and ethnic attitudes, in decisions over housing choices, and in the determinants of success and failure in the local labor market will be explored in the following chapters.

Appendix: The Greater Boston Social Survey
Sample Design

The Greater Boston Social Survey (GBSS) was designed with the help of colleagues in three other cities and with foundation support from the Ford Foundation and Russell Sage Foundation. Working in accord with study teams in Los Angeles, Detroit, and Atlanta, where similar surveys were to be conducted, we developed a standardized sampling procedure, beginning in 1992. In Boston, this would ultimately yield a sample of 1,820 adults age twenty-one and over. To ensure adequate samples of minority and low-income households, we used a multistage area probability sample frame of households in the Massachusetts portion of the Greater Boston Consolidated Metropolitan Statistical Area (CMSA), with clusters of housing units drawn disproportionately from areas with concentrated minority-ethnic and poverty populations.

The Boston CMSA includes the Boston, Brockton, Lawrence-Haverhill, Lowell, and Salem-Gloucester Primary Metropolitan Statistical Areas. Other Massachusetts cities encompassed within this area include Cambridge, Chelsea, Framingham, Lynn, Somerville, Quincy, and Waltham. The Nashua, New Hampshire, metropolitan area is also included in the CMSA, but is not included within the scope of this study. At the county level, the area included in the study encompasses all or part of the following Massachusetts counties: Bristol, Essex, Middlesex, Norfolk, Plymouth, Suffolk, and Worcester. All together there are 154 cities and towns in the Massachusetts portion of the CMSA.

Interviewing was conducted by the staff of the University of Massachusetts Center for Survey Research (CSR) between May 1993 and November 1994. Interviewers were assigned sampled housing units to visit for the purpose of ascertaining eligibility and for conducting in-person interviews. At each assigned unit, they determined the number of resident adults twenty-one or older. If there was more than one eligible adult, they used systematic selection procedures to yield a probability sample of respondents. Interviews were completed in English (n = 1,399) and Spanish (n = 421); all field materials were translated using independent forward-backward translation to assure validity of the translation. Respondents were paid a $5.00 incentive for a completed interview.[8]

Interviewing assignments were made to maximize the likelihood of agreement between the race of the interviewer and the race of the respondent.[9] However, limited availability of experienced minority interviewers made race-matching extremely difficult, and we met with only moderate success. Despite continuous and thorough recruitment, the pool of minority interviewers was too small and turnover was too high. Interviewer-respondent race-matching occurred at the following rates:

- 92 percent of non-Hispanic white respondents were interviewed by a white interviewer; about half the remaining whites were interviewed by a black interviewer;
- 49 percent of non-Hispanic black respondents were interviewed by a black interviewer; about 48 percent were interviewed by a white interviewer;
- 55 percent of Hispanic respondents were interviewed by a Hispanic interviewer; about 40 percent were interviewed by a white interviewer.

In the end, with repeated trips to sample households, the CSR team was able to compile a reasonably good response rate, given the difficulty of tracking down a substantial number of families with limited income and assets. The final estimated response rates by race-ethnicity were: non-Hispanic white (66 percent); non-Hispanic black (66 percent); and Hispanic (74 percent)[10]

The resulting sample is complex and requires weighting for proper analysis. Most survey items were designed to yield estimates of people's characteristics. Some information provided by respondents may be used to generate estimates of household characteristics—including household income, assets, and debt—requiring a household weight. We computed basic person and household weights that have been adjusted to compensate for nonresponse, so that weighted counts of persons by age-sex-race reflect the proportionate distribution of the adult population of the study area, as established in the 1990 census, and households follow the proportionate race distribution.

The Survey Instrument

Research team members from Boston, Detroit, Atlanta, and Los Angeles met repeatedly to develop a unified survey instrument. The teams included economists, sociologists, geographers, psychologists, anthropologists, and survey design specialists. It is fair to say there may have been too many cooks. Each group had a list of questions long enough to thoroughly exhaust an interviewer and his or her respondent. In the end, it was necessary to pare down the questionnaire so that it could be completed in approximately ninety minutes. Still, more than 600 questions were included in the final GBSS survey.

From the beginning of the research process, it was agreed that three central topics would be covered in the survey: racial attitudes, residential location, and labor market outcomes. In the end, the instrument included nine sections:

    I.   Residence and Housing
   II.   Attitudes About Current Neighborhood
  III.   Demographics and Household Composition
   IV.   Attitudes About Racial-Ethnic Groups
    V.   Family Background, Education, and Training
   VI.   Labor Force Participation, Employment, and Earnings
  VII.   Attitudes About Residential Location
 VIII.   Social Networks
   IX.   Interviewer Observations Regarding Respondent

The set of questions provided information not only about the demographic and economic status of the 1,820 respondents and their families, but also about their attitudes regarding race, ethnicity, quality of neighborhood, quality of jobs, and opportunities for residential mobility. In order to economize on interview time, parts of the survey instrument used randomized "split ballots," where part of the black sample, for example, would be asked for their attitudes toward Hispanics while another part of the black sample would be quizzed about their attitudes toward Asians or whites. Kish tables were used to ensure randomized split forms.

The interview data were coded, entered, and cleaned by the CSR staff. Further recoding was carried out by the analysis team. The team did not attempt to impute values for missing data.[11]

6

WHAT DO BOSTON-AREA RESIDENTS THINK OF ONE ANOTHER?

B oston's history, like that of many other cities, has a legacy of racial and ethnic division. Especially in the decades after World War II, blacks and whites were at odds over neighborhoods, schools, jobs, and politics. An environment of conflict and distrust influenced racial identity and often hardened one group's view of another.

In recent years, however, Boston has gone through dramatic change, as we saw in chapter 3. Since the 1970s, the metropolitan area has developed a more diverse racial and ethnic mix. The Hispanic population has surged, as refugees have fled Central America and Puerto Ricans have come to the mainland. Asians are more likely to reside well beyond their traditional enclave in Chinatown, with Vietnamese clustering in Dorchester and Cambodians in Lowell. Caribbean immigrants have added to Boston's black population. Many of the new arrivals have settled in areas that had once been reserved for whites. This fact, as well as the foreign-born status of these new residents, imposes new challenges for many residents of the metropolitan region whose virtually all-white neighborhoods are closer to areas where the proportion of racial minorities has increased significantly.

This new diversity has no doubt influenced people's ideas about race and ethnicity. The Greater Boston Social Survey (GBSS) tried to capture some of those attitudes. We wanted to know how the various groups viewed themselves and one another and to assess the current perception of discrimination in the workplace, so as to gauge opinions about policies that might be used to rectify it. We were curious about whether women saw things differently from men. Our concern with these issues stems from the considerable body of prior studies showing wide gaps between whites and nonwhites in perceptions of how much discrimination is experienced by nonwhites,[1] and in the factors that different groups think are important in causing group inequality in access to good jobs and good neighborhoods and in outcomes of labor market processes (Kluegel 1990; Schuman, Steeh and Bobo 1985).

These differing perceptions are compounded by whites' persistent reference to negative stereotypes of blacks, Hispanics, and Asians (Bobo and Kluegel 1991; Smith 1991). Previous research has suggested that adherence to overgeneralized and often erroneous attributions reduces support by whites for government intervention specifically designed to help minority group members achieve economic and social success (Bobo and Kluegel 1991). More generally, considerable social science evidence has accumulated to support the notion that the attitudes of individuals are correlated with their behavior (Zimbardo and Leippe 1991). Indeed, research confirms that negative stereotypes influence employers' hiring decisions (Kirschenman and Neckerman 1991).

Understanding racial attitudes is an important element in considering group dynamics in the region. Groups of individuals holding similar attitudes may be expected to draw on their beliefs in their reactions to events, in shaping group goals, or, as has already been suggested, in supporting housing, education, or workplace policies that are targeted for the benefit of other groups. Our findings, quite frankly, are often ambiguous, and sometimes hard to interpret. We found ample evidence of continuing prejudice and discrimination, yet we also found that a substantial number of blacks and Hispanics feel unconstrained by their race or ethnicity. We found broad support for some measures to address discrimination, but conflicting views about affirmative action in the labor market. We found that men and women usually have similar views about race and discrimination, except that women think discrimination is a much bigger problem for themselves than men think it is for women.

This study also breaks new ground in its effort to assess the views not only of whites but also of blacks and Hispanics about race and ethnicity. Most previous national surveys have interviewed whites only. A few surveys have asked blacks about their perceptions of themselves, or about the way they believe they are perceived by whites. But most have ignored the attitudes of blacks toward other groups, and most have also ignored the views of Hispanics or Asians. Indeed, a 1997 Gallup poll on racial attitudes focused strictly on blacks and whites (Holmes 1997); Latino respondents were made to identify with one race or the other.

In our survey, all respondents were asked whether they were of Spanish or Hispanic origin, and they were asked to identify the racial group that best described them. When respondents said they were of Spanish or Hispanic origin, they were classified as Hispanic, regardless of whether they were white or black. Thus throughout this book the term *whites* refers to non-Hispanic whites and *blacks* to non-Hispanic blacks. In line with the immigration trends already discussed, among Hispanics, about half said they were Puerto Rican, nearly a third were Dominican, and the rest were mostly Cuban, Salvadoran, Guatemalan, or Nicaraguan. We were unable to interview a significant number of Asians, so while we occasionally consider how Asians are viewed by other groups, we cannot report on the views of Asians themselves.

The Importance of Race and Ethnicity

Respondents' answers to the survey are considered in terms of their self-attributed ethnicity and race. To begin with, we were curious about the extent to which individuals believed their fates were tied to the position of their racial or ethnic group. We asked blacks and Hispanics: *Do you think what happens generally to (black-Hispanic) people in this country will have something to do with what happens in your life?* (If yes) *Will it affect you a lot, some, or not very much?*

A clear majority of each group responded *some* or *a lot* (see table 6.1). Still, a substantial number said *no* or *not very much*: 37 percent of blacks and 41 percent of Hispanics. Among blacks and Hispanics alike, women were more likely to say no, as were immigrants, the elderly, and those living in relatively poor neighborhoods.

We then asked respondents to characterize racial and ethnic groups along a number of lines. The survey used a stereotype trait-rating measure to overcome potential limitations of traditional survey questions that allowed respondents only "yes/no" or "agree/disagree" options when asked to endorse or reject negative stereotypes of members of other groups. The measures we used had been tested before their use in our survey to ensure that respondents were willing to perform the task, respondents did not consistently bias their answers in socially

TABLE 6.1   *Identity and Destiny*

How Respondents Think Their Own Lives Will Be Affected by What Happens to Their Racial or Ethnic Group

	Type of Respondent	
	Black	Hispanic
Percentage who think they will be affected		
not at all	31	29
not very much	6	12
some	30	36
a lot	34	23

Source: Greater Boston Social Survey 1995.

desirable ways, responses about individual traits related to each other in an internally consistent fashion, and the responses were related to variables usually understood to correlate with indicators of prejudice, such as education, age, and political ideology (Bobo, Johnson, and Oliver 1992).

Respondents were given the following instructions:

> Now I have some questions about different groups in our (U.S.) society. I'm going to show you a seven-point scale on which the characteristics of people in a group can be rated. In the first statement a score of 1 means that you think almost all of the people in that group are "rich." A score of 7 means that you think almost everyone in the group is "poor." A score of 4 means you think that the group is not towards one end or the other, and of course you may choose any number in between that comes closest to where you think people in the group stand.

In addition to thinking of the groups as rich or poor, respondents were asked to place the groups on scales contrasting the following additional traits:

- unintelligent or intelligent,
- prefer to be self-supporting or prefer to live off welfare,
- easy to get along with or hard to get along with,
- speak English well or speak English poorly,
- involved in drugs and gangs or not involved in drugs and gangs,
- treat members of other groups equally or discriminate against members of other groups.

The scores for the ends of the scale were alternated to reduce respondent bias toward a particular scale value. We also sought to determine whether images of the groups were associated with gender. (Images common in today's media and mass culture frequently portray gang members as young black males and welfare recipients as black females.) To do this, we randomly assigned respondents the task of rating the group as a whole (whites, blacks, Hispanics, and Asians), rating males in each group, or rating females in each group.

Respondents were free to decline to rate a group on a particular trait. Overall, however, respondents offered judgments quite readily. Only 4.5 percent of white and black respondents and 8.3 percent of Hispanics declined to give a rating on one or more questions. Whites and blacks alike most readily rated their own group. Whites, blacks, and

TABLE 6.2   *Racial and Ethnic Perceptions and Stereotypes*

	Type of Respondent		
Rich Versus Poor	White	Black	Hispanic
Percentage of respondents who think their own group tends to be poor	7	64	62
Percentage of respondents who gave other group lower rating than own group Other group			
White	n.a.	7	6
Black	80	n.a.	26
Hispanic	85	18	n.a.
Asian	64	10	18

Source: Greater Boston Social Survey 1995.

Hispanics all were reluctant to judge Asians. Hispanics were less comfortable rating blacks than rating themselves or whites.

Tables 6.2 through 6.8 provide the basic data for this analysis. For example, table 6.2 shows that 7 percent of whites rated their own group as tending to be poor, compared with 64 percent of blacks and 62 percent of Hispanics. The remaining rows of each panel show the percentage of respondents rating members of other groups *more negatively* than they rated members of their own group. For example, Table 6.2 shows that 80 percent of whites rated blacks more negatively than whites on the rich-poor scale, while only 7 percent of blacks rated whites

TABLE 6.2   *Racial and Ethnic Perceptions and Stereotypes*

	Type of Respondent		
Intelligent Versus Unintelligent	White	Black	Hispanic
Percentage of respondents who think their own group tends to be unintelligent	8	11	15
Percentage of respondents who gave other group lower rating than own group Other group			
White	n.a.	21	11
Black	45	n.a.	38
Hispanic	49	24	n.a.
Asian	20	23	29

Source: Greater Boston Social Survey 1995.

TABLE 6.4   Racial and Ethnic Perceptions and Stereotypes

Self-Supporting Versus Live Off Welfare	Type of Respondent		
	White	Black	Hispanic
Percentage of respondents who think their own group tends to live off welfare	7	43	49
Percentage of respondents who gave other group lower rating than own group Other group			
White	n.a.	16	20
Black	64	n.a.	27
Hispanic	62	18	n.a.
Asian	36	11	13

Source: Greater Boston Social Survey 1995.

more negatively than blacks. In this particular case, perceptions appear to reflect reality.

How Groups See Themselves and Others

The results of our survey indicate that whites generally perceive themselves in a positive light. Fewer than 10 percent saw their group as tending to be poor, unintelligent, preferring welfare, hard to get along with, or speaking English poorly. As many as 25 percent, however, thought

TABLE 6.5   Racial and Ethnic Perceptions and Stereotypes

Easy to Get Along With Versus Hard to Get Along With	Type of Respondent		
	White	Black	Hispanic
Percentage of respondents who think their own group tends to be hard to get along with	5	20	20
Percentage of respondents who gave other group lower rating than own group Other group			
White	n.a.	35	37
Black	39	n.a.	69
Hispanic	44	18	n.a.
Asian	32	39	51

Source: Greater Boston Social Survey 1995.

TABLE 6.6   *Racial and Ethnic Perceptions and Stereotypes*

Speaks English Well Versus Speaks English Poorly	Type of Respondent		
	White	Black	Hispanic
Percentage of respondents who think their own group tends to speak English poorly	10	24	42
Percentage of respondents who gave other group lower rating than own group			
Other group			
White	n.a.	6	2
Black	64	n.a.	22
Hispanic	86	68	n.a.
Asian	77	67	21

Source: Greater Boston Social Survey 1995.

whites tend to be involved with gangs and drugs, and fully *half* said whites tend to discriminate.

Blacks and Hispanics had much in common in their self-perceptions. More than 60 percent of each group said their own group tends to be poor. Forty-three percent of blacks and 49 percent of Hispanics said their own group prefers welfare over work. Nearly 40 percent of both groups perceived their groups as tending to be involved in drugs and gangs. On a positive note, both groups rated themselves favorably on the questions of intelligence and getting along with others.

TABLE 6.7   *Racial and Ethnic Perceptions and Stereotypes*

Not Involved with Drugs or Gangs Versus Involved with Drugs or Gangs	Type of Respondent		
	White	Black	Hispanic
Percentage of respondents who think their own group tends to be involved with drugs or gangs	25	37	37
Percentage of respondents who gave other group lower rating than own group			
Other group			
White	n.a.	24	30
Black	62	n.a.	32
Hispanic	58	7	n.a.
Asian	38	24	33

Source: Greater Boston Social Survey 1995.

TABLE 6.8   Racial and Ethnic Perceptions and Stereotypes

Tends Not to Discriminate Versus Tends to Discriminate	Type of Respondent		
	White	Black	Hispanic
Percentage of respondents who think their own group tends to discriminate	51	43	39
Percentage of respondents who gave other group lower rating than own group Other group			
White	n.a.	46	63
Black	29	n.a.	47
Hispanic	28	19	n.a.
Asian	22	46	37

Source: Greater Boston Social Survey 1995.

The survey results are perhaps most revealing when one compares the way respondents see their own group to the way they see others, or the way others see them. Whites consistently gave the other groups lower ratings than themselves, except on one count: discrimination. Among blacks and Hispanics, characteristics that they were unlikely to attribute to their own group (for example, being unintelligent and tending to be hard to get along with) were more readily attributed to other groups.

While it is easy to dismiss the significance of these results by taking the position that to some degree, so-called negative ratings may reflect the simple facts of life: blacks and Hispanics *do* experience more poverty than whites, for instance; whites on the whole may have more fluency in English than Hispanics and Asians; the tendency to consistently, negatively characterize groups as a whole on traits that may reflect individuals' desirability as neighbors and employees, or that suggest that social welfare policies are implicitly racial, surely colors public discourse about urban inequality.

The views of whites clearly reflect some negative stereotypes. Nearly half gave their own group better ratings on intelligence than they gave blacks and Hispanics, and about a third said blacks and Hispanics were harder to get along with than whites. On all traits except English ability, Asians got better ratings from whites than did blacks and Hispanics.

Most blacks and Hispanics viewed whites at least as favorably as they viewed themselves on the questions of poverty, welfare, English, drugs or gangs, and intelligence. But blacks and Hispanics alike took whites to task most for being difficult to get along with and for tending to discriminate: more than a third of blacks and Hispanics rated whites lower than themselves on getting along; nearly half of blacks and a majority of Hispanics rated whites lower than themselves on discrimination.

Blacks and Hispanics

Though blacks and Hispanics were quite similar in their views of whites and in their self-perceptions, their views of each other were less parallel. In general, the majority of Hispanics rated blacks at least as favorably as their own group, and blacks did the same for Hispanics. Nonetheless, Hispanics were more critical of blacks than vice versa. Almost half of Hispanics said blacks were more likely than their own group to discriminate, for instance, while only 19 percent of blacks said Hispanics were more likely than themselves to discriminate. Similarly, 38 percent of Hispanics rated blacks lower on intelligence, while only 24 percent of blacks rated Hispanics lower. On one count, getting along, a majority of Hispanics rated blacks lower than themselves.

Discrimination in the Workplace

Whites perceive their own group as tending to discriminate against other groups, and drew the most criticism from blacks and Hispanics for discrimination and difficulty in getting along. These perceptions may reflect a history of racial conflict, but our survey indicated that they also follow from personal experience. We asked respondents four questions about their own experience of discrimination on the job. The results are found in table 6.9. We asked first: *During the past year (or last year you worked), did your supervisor or boss ever use racial slurs?* The slurs did not have to be directed specifically at the respondent or the respondent's group. Twelve percent of Hispanics and 10 percent of blacks responded yes.

Then we asked: *During the past year (or last year you worked), were you discriminated against at your work because of your race-ethnicity?* Fifteen percent of both blacks and Hispanics said yes. Next we asked: *Have you ever felt at any time in the past that others at your place of employment got promotions or pay raises faster than you did because of your race or ethnicity?* Twenty percent of blacks and 13 percent of Hispanics said yes. Then we asked: *Do you think a job was ever denied to you because of race or ethnicity?* More than a third of blacks and a fourth of Hispanics said yes.

By contrast, responses to the same questions indicate that very few whites thought they had suffered from discrimination. Four percent said

TABLE 6.9   Workplace Discrimination

	Type of Respondent		
	White	Black	Hispanic
Percentage of respondents who have experienced			
Boss's use of racial slurs	14	10	12
General discrimination	4	15	15
Denial of pay or promotion	5	20	12
Denial of a job	7	36	26
Percentage who have experienced			
None of the above incidents	75	56	62
One of the above	21	23	16
Two of the above	2	12	13
Three of the above	1	6	8
All of the above	0	3	1

Source: Greater Boston Social Survey 1995.
Note: Use of racial slurs refers to witnessing such slurs; they need not have been targeted against the individual or his or her group.

they had experienced discrimination in the past year. Five percent thought promotions or pay raises had been hindered for this reason. Seven percent thought that at some time a job had been denied them. A higher number—14 percent—said their bosses had used racial slurs, but it's reasonable to assume that these slurs were directed largely against other groups.

Separately, the four questions we asked focus on distinct aspects of racially targeted treatment in the workplace, and suggest that no particular form of discrimination is highly prevalent. What, then, accounts for the widespread perception that whites tend to discriminate against members of other groups—reported by both whites and nonwhites in the trait-rating portion of the interview? The answer may lie in considering the likelihood of members of different groups to experience multiple forms of negative treatment. When we looked at the responses to all four questions simultaneously, we found that 75 percent of whites report no experience of these discriminatory behaviors, but this was only the case for 55 percent of blacks and 62 percent of Hispanics. Certainly, broadening the scope of our questions to other spheres of activity, such as education, housing, treatment by store clerks, or access to public recreation facilities, would have reduced the fraction of each group who had never experienced discrimination, but it is still unlikely that whites would have experienced more than nonwhites.

Negative stereotyping and negative trait-rating of each group by members of other groups create barriers to interracial and interethnic contact, but it is actual discrimination in education, housing, employment, and other spheres of social participation—both perceived and real—that has become the wedge issue splintering the American community. The problem of discrimination is widely acknowledged but, as additional evidence from our data indicates, there are distinctive group differences in the perceived severity of discrimination's consequences for the respondent's own group and for other groups. We asked: *In general, how much discrimination is there that hurts the chances of Hispanics to get good-paying jobs? Do you think there is a lot, some, only a little, or none at all?* We repeated the questions in reference to blacks, whites, Asians, and women. The results are found in figure 6.1.

Asked about blacks, a majority of blacks and Hispanics thought there was a lot of discrimination that hurt blacks' chances, and virtually none thought blacks were completely free of discrimination. Only about a quarter of whites thought blacks suffered a lot of discrimination. Still, only 6 percent saw no discrimination at all.

Asked about Hispanics, blacks and Hispanics alike thought that Hispanics suffered somewhat less discrimination than blacks. In both groups, 40 percent said Hispanics faced a lot of discrimination, although again, almost no one thought Hispanics were completely free from it. Whites perceived Hispanics to fare about the same as blacks.

Few respondents thought whites faced a lot of discrimination, although whites thought their situation was tougher than blacks or Hispanics thought it was. About 6 percent of whites thought their group suffered a lot of discrimination; 4 percent of blacks and 3 percent of Hispanics thought so.

Regarding women, about 25 percent of Hispanics and 28 percent of blacks thought women faced a lot of discrimination. Only about half as many whites thought so. Among all groups surveyed, views about Asians were remarkably similar to views about women.

We separated male and female responses to all the questions about discrimination and found that they were almost always similar. The exception was regarding discrimination against women, which women thought was worse than men did.

Addressing Inequality

Just as whites stand apart in their perceptions of discrimination, they are divided from other groups in their opinions of what to do about it. We asked opinions about two types of policies to address inequality: training and education, and job preferences. We posed the questions carefully to avoid loaded terms that pervade public debate about race, such as *racism, discrimination,* or *government involvement.* We asked:

FIGURE 6.1   *Perception of Discrimination Against Groups in Getting Good-Paying Jobs*

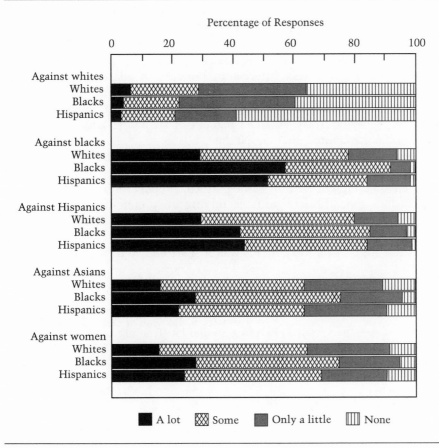

Source: Greater Boston Social Survey 1995.

Now I have some questions about what you think about the fairness of certain policies. Some people feel that because of past disadvantages there are some groups in society that should receive special job training and educational assistance. Others say that it is unfair to give these groups special job training and educational assistance. What about you? Do you strongly favor, favor, neither favor nor oppose, oppose, or strongly oppose special job training and educational assistance for women?

We then asked the same questions about blacks, Hispanics, and Asians. We also asked: "*Some people feel that because of past disadvantages, there are some groups in society that should be given preference in hir-*

ing and promotion. Others say that it is unfair to give these groups special preferences. What about you?" Again we asked about women, blacks, Hispanics, and Asians as well.

Throughout, we found strong support for training and education (see table 6.10). A majority of each group surveyed favored such assistance to blacks, Hispanics, Asians, and women alike. Still, just as whites viewed discrimination as less of a problem than did other groups, whites also showed less interest in policies to address the problem. Fifty-five to 70 percent of whites favored training and education, depending on the group to be targeted and whether men or women were responding; by contrast, 70 to 83 percent of Hispanics and 75 to 90 percent of blacks favored such assistance.

In sharp contrast, preferences in hiring and promotion received far less support than training and education. Only 11 to 20 percent of whites favored job preferences. This same pattern, support for broadening opportunity but opposition to policies relying on preferential selections or quotas, is found in national opinion studies as well (Bobo and Smith 1994). While blacks and Hispanics favored education over job preferences too, their support for job policies was still strong: 50 to 60 percent.

TABLE 6.10   *Policies to Address Discrimination*

	Percentage of Respondents Favoring or Strongly Favoring Special Job Training and Education for			
	Blacks	Hispanics	Asians	Women
Type of respondent				
White male	59	58	55	55
White female	70	64	61	72
Black male	88	89	75	88
Black female	90	81	78	83
Hispanic male	81	83	80	83
Hispanic female	74	75	72	71
	Percentage of Respondents Favoring or Strongly Favoring Job Preferences for			
	Blacks	Hispanics	Asians	Women
Type of respondent				
White male	18	19	17	20
White female	13	13	11	21
Black male	57	51	47	52
Black female	59	53	46	54
Hispanic male	47	51	47	50
Hispanic female	55	57	55	61

Source: Greater Boston Social Survey 1995.

Taken together, do the responses about discrimination shed any light on current debates about affirmative action and enforcement of civil rights? The implications seem to be mixed. While the nation may have made progress over the past thirty years in achieving racial and ethnic equality, the survey confirms that there is still a long way to go. All groups see discrimination as pervasive, and the majority in each group favors some political response. On the other hand, whites are less interested in corrective action than other groups. It is not certain whether respondents interpret "preference in hiring and promotion" to be the same as "affirmative action." But if this is the case, it looks as if the current backlash against affirmative action has broad support. Indeed, if this is true in Boston, a city many would consider liberal, we can assume it is at least as strong a sentiment elsewhere.

Intergroup Competition

Group identification is clearly important. It is associated with notions of common fate, negative characterizations of outgroup members, and perceptions of discrimination. And it divides the residents of Greater Boston when they are asked about policies to deal with perceived discrimination. As whites are still numerically dominant, it seems crucial to try to account for their lack of support for affirmative action or other race-targeted programs. Studies of minority-group relations have long suggested that the motivation to discriminate may be grounded partly in the perception that one group's gain is another's loss (for example, Blalock 1967). We asked respondents whether they saw themselves in direct competition with other groups, economically as well as politically:

> Please tell me whether you strongly agree, generally agree, neither agree nor disagree, generally disagree, or strongly disagree with these statements:
>
> - *More good jobs for Asians/blacks/Hispanics means fewer good jobs for whites/blacks/Hispanics* (respondent's own group).
>
> - *The more influence Asians/blacks/Hispanics have in local politics, the less influence whites/blacks/Hispanics* (respondent's own group) *will have in local politics.*

In each case, we asked the respondents to compare their group to just one of the other groups, assigning the other group at random.

Twenty to 40 percent of respondents viewed the success of other groups as detrimental to their own group (see table 6.11). The greatest apprehension was among blacks with regard to Asians: 38 percent of blacks felt their jobs were at stake, and 34 percent felt they stood to lose

TABLE 6.11   *Competition for Jobs and Political Power*

	Other Group						
	Asian			Black		Hispanic	
	Type of Respondent			Type of Respondent		Type of Respondent	
	White	Black	Hispanic	White	Hispanic	White	Black
Share of Respondents Who Think More Good Jobs for Another Group Means Fewer Good Jobs for Own Group							
Percentage who							
Strongly agree	11	20	10	7	8	9	13
Generally agree	16	17	15	13	10	22	18
Neither agree nor disagree	29	21	31	30	43	25	21
Generally disagree	27	25	21	28	29	30	27
Strongly disagree	17	16	24	22	9	14	21
Share of Respondents Who Think More Political Influence for Another Group Means Less Influence for Own Group							
Percentage who							
Strongly agree	4	19	12	3	5	8	10
Generally agree	16	15	20	9	13	23	10
Neither agree nor disagree	29	26	27	25	45	20	28
Generally disagree	31	21	27	37	22	35	26
Strongly disagree	21	19	14	26	16	14	26

Source: Greater Boston Social Survey 1995.

political influence. Blacks and Hispanics both perceived more threat from Asians than from each other when it came to jobs or politics. Whites were more apprehensive about Asian or Hispanic success than about black success: 32 percent worried about job competition from Hispanics, 27 percent from Asians, and 20 percent from blacks.

Respondents consistently felt most threatened by groups whose numbers are growing the fastest in the region. Between 1980 and 1990, the black population of Boston grew by 16 percent and the Hispanic population by 65 percent; the Asian population doubled. Meanwhile, the city's white population declined by 8 percent. Changes across the metropolitan area as a whole are somewhat less dramatic, but again, certain satellite cities have experienced changes at least as dramatic as those of the city of Boston, and the dispersion of these changes across these submetropolitan nodes places many white suburban and small-city residents in closer proximity to significant numbers of minorities than ever before.

The importance of minority population growth surfaced again when we surveyed respondents' views about immigration (see figure 6.2). We asked:

- *If immigration to this country continues at the present rate, how much political influence do you believe people like you (respondent's group) will have? Do you believe it will be much more political influence than you have now, some but not a lot more, no more or less than now, less than now, or a lot less influence than now?*

FIGURE 6.2   *Perceived Group Competition, "Negative" Impact of Immigration*

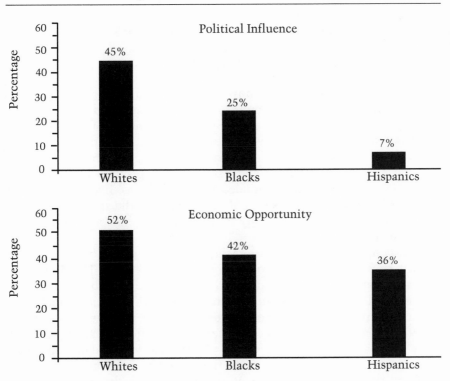

Source: Greater Boston Social Survey 1995.

- *What about economic opportunity? If immigration to this country continues at the present rate, do you believe people like you (respondent's group) will probably have much more economic opportunity than now, some but not a lot more, no more or less than now, less than now, or a lot less opportunity than now?*

All groups felt they had more at stake economically than politically. Whites by far felt they stood to lose the most on both fronts. Forty-five percent said that continuing immigration would mean less or a lot less political influence for them; 52 percent said it would mean less or a lot less economic opportunity.

Among blacks, 25 percent said they would have less or a lot less political influence, and 42 percent said they would have less or a lot less economic opportunity. Hispanics had very little concern about loss of political influence. Only 7 percent said they would have less or a lot less influence. But 36 percent said they would have less or a lot less economic opportunity.

How Attitudes About One's Community Differ by Race and Ethnicity

Beyond attempts to ascertain how racial and ethnic groups felt about each other, we also probed about how each group rated the neighborhoods in which they lived. The GBSS asked respondents a range of questions on this topic. City services such as street cleaning and garbage collection were rated, along with general housing and property upkeep, and the prevalence of crime and vandalism in respondents' neighborhoods. Further, residents responded to questions asking them to rank such neighborhood services as police protection, the quality of public schools, neighborhood retail outlets, and access to banks or savings and loan institutions.

Responses varied across the racial and ethnic populations surveyed, and the results are a mixture of both good and bad news. The good news is that a vast majority of residents across the metropolitan area were pleased with their neighborhoods. In response to questions about the quality of city services, 88 percent of blacks, 85 percent of Hispanics, and 97 percent of whites rated city services excellent or good (see table 6.12). Even in neighborhoods where the majority of residents are black or Hispanic, a large majority rated their neighborhood city services as satisfactory or better. Indeed, over 85 percent of blacks, Hispanics, and whites living in these majority nonwhite neighborhoods rated these city services either excellent or good (see table 6.13).

TABLE 6.12   *Satisfaction with Neighborhood and Services—All*
              Neighborhoods

Percentage Satisfied with (a Positive Ranking)[a]	Black	Hispanic	White
City services	88	85	97
Property upkeep	77	80	93
Crime and vandalism	67	69	94
Police protection	38	62	84
Public schools	38	71	70
Neighborhood shopping	50	79	78
Banks-lending	59	82	88

Source: Greater Boston Social Survey 1995.
[a]A "positive ranking" or "satisfied," as used here, indicates respondents offered the highest or next-to-highest ranking choice for the question asked of them. Thus, for questions that offered "excellent," "good," "fair," or "poor" as choices for respondents' opinions about a service, this chart tallied as "satisfied" those who responded "excellent" or "good"; for questions that were asked in the negative, where respondents were offered the choice of "always," "often," "sometimes," or "never" (that a service is a problem), this chart tallied as "satisfied" those who responded "sometimes" or "never."

Similarly, more than three-quarters of residents reported that they found the quality of property upkeep in their neighborhoods to be excellent or good. This was as true in black and Hispanic neighborhoods as in the region as a whole.

But on other measures, there are clear differences between how blacks, Hispanics, and whites feel about the quality of their neighborhoods. A third of blacks and Hispanics found their neighborhood's record on crime and vandalism to be only fair or poor. In contrast, only about 6 percent of whites rated their neighborhood's record on crime

TABLE 6.13   *Satisfaction with Neighborhood Services—Minority*
              Neighborhoods

Percentage Satisfied with	Black	Hispanic	White
City services	87	87	89
Property upkeep	78	75	67
Crime and vandalism	65	62	56
Police protection	67	45	57
Public schools	36	63	43
Neighborhood shopping	47	71	45
Banks-lending	57	76	70

Source: Greater Boston Social Survey 1995.
Note: This chart shows results only from those respondents who live in the study's "minority neighborhoods," which include census blocks where over 50 percent of residents are black or Hispanic.

and vandalism fair or poor—and these were mostly whites living in predominantly black and Hispanic neighborhoods.

The quality of neighborhood shopping and access to banks and lending institutions is also rated differently by blacks, Hispanics, and whites in the Greater Boston region. Only half of all blacks rated the retail outlets in their neighborhoods as excellent or good, while nearly four-fifths of both Hispanics and whites did. Over 40 percent of blacks rated access to banks and lending institutions unsatisfactorily, while more than four-fifths of Hispanics and whites rated these institutions as excellent or good.

By far, the largest difference by race and ethnicity was found when examining opinions about police protection and public schools. Blacks exhibited significant dissatisfaction—only 38 percent said they were satisfied with these two services. By contrast, 62 percent of Hispanics and 84 percent of whites were satisfied with police protection in their neighborhoods. About 70 percent of both Hispanics and whites were satisfied with their public schools.

In questioning Hispanics and whites living in majority-black or Hispanic neighborhoods, we find some consistency with the opinions held by blacks—who are overwhelmingly likely to live in majority-black neighborhoods. For example, over half (55 percent) of Hispanics living in majority-minority neighborhoods rate their police protection as only fair or poor (see figure 6.3). (Indeed, blacks in these neighborhoods have a better opinion of the police.) Even 43 percent of whites in majority-

FIGURE 6.3   *Satisfaction with Police Protection*

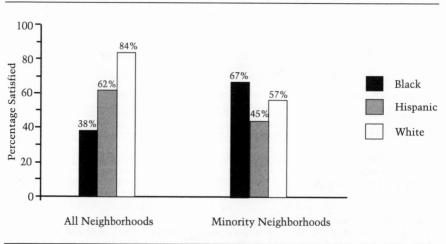

Source: Greater Boston Social Survey 1995.

minority neighborhoods rate police protection as unsatisfactory. Similarly, only 43 percent of white residents in these neighborhoods and only 36 percent of black residents rate their public schools as excellent or good.

Overall, then, while city services and property upkeep are rated reasonably highly nearly universally, the gap in opinions regarding police protection and public schools is enormous.

Conclusion

The picture that emerges from our interviews with residents of the metropolitan area is one of significantly different perceptions of group position and group destiny. White, black, and Hispanic respondents displayed distinctive group differences in identity, out-group perception, and experience of discrimination. Against this background, respondents in the different racial groups perceived different threats and opportunities, as measured by expectations about job opportunities, political influence, and the impact of immigration. The net impact of such experience and expectations on explanations of inequality is also reflected in differential support for policies— training versus hiring preferences for minorities and women.

Racial attitudes carry over into the perception and reality about the neighborhoods where each group lives. While Boston-area communities are reasonably well appreciated by all groups, inner-city neighborhoods are ranked as having much poorer schools, unsatisfactory police protection, and less access to good retail outlets and banking institutions. This is all part of the opportunity nexus of racial attitudes, residential segregation, and labor market outcomes we have discussed at length in this book.

Admittedly, the Greater Boston Social Survey is tricky to interpret. Much depends on whether one sees the glass as half empty or half full. On the one hand, we see much evidence of attitudes that might fuel racial and ethnic conflict. Large numbers of blacks and Hispanics feel they have been subjected to discrimination. We asked only about workplace discrimination; had we asked about other areas, such as housing or education, the numbers of aggrieved likely would have been much higher. Clearly, discrimination is a much bigger problem in the eyes of blacks and Hispanics than in the eyes of whites.

On the other hand, large numbers of whites acknowledge discrimination as a problem that requires some kind of response. Half believe that their group tends to discriminate, and the majority favor special job training and educational assistance to rectify past injustice. While a substantial share of all groups feel they may lose out from the economic and political success of other groups, the majority of each group said they did not feel threatened. And as blacks and Hispanics grow in number, their increased clout may help them to win more equality. However, as the next chapter shows, the spatial distribution of minority populations and the residential preferences of metropolitan residents virtually assure that these issues will play out in a distinctive subset of the region's municipalities.

7

RESIDENTIAL PREFERENCES
AND SEGREGATION

I N THE last chapter, we considered prevailing racial and ethnic attitudes in Greater Boston. The analysis suggested that the region faces
a great challenge, to the extent that a significant proportion of each
racial and ethnic group perceives its own economic and political future
as part of a zero-sum game. Whites worry that economic gains by blacks
through affirmative action hiring might come at their expense. Many of
those who already live in the area, regardless of skin color or country of
origin, fear that further immigration to Greater Boston would threaten
their own job security. Success and failure in the labor market are commonly viewed through the lens of what is good for one's own racial or
ethnic group.

In this chapter, we extend the analysis to the next step in the opportunity nexus, focusing attention on where people live in the region and
why. We use the Greater Boston Social Survey (GBSS), complemented by
an analysis of existing census data, to demonstrate that the racial and
ethnic composition of Greater Boston communities is an important factor reinforcing a polarized view of group destiny.

The economic and social fortunes of the city of Boston and the
other cities and towns in the metropolitan area have long been inter-
twined. While many of these communities are themselves nodes of significant economic activity and offer unique cultural and recreational
amenities, they also provide the hub city with a substantial portion of
its labor force. Conversely, these same cities and towns provide Boston-
based workers with an array of residential options. The problem is that
the array is much more limited for some groups than for others. While
trends in population growth and composition indicate an increasing minority presence throughout much of the Boston region, the data also
confirm the continuation of long-term trends in residential segregation.

In virtually every case, the places where we see this segregation are
communities that have experienced long-term economic decline and lit-

tle overall white population growth between 1980 and 1990. Hispanics and Asians are partially ghettoized in the city of Boston and in its less prosperous satellite cities and towns. But, overall, blacks are the most segregated group in the region.

The groundwork for further racial divisions within the Greater Boston region is already in place. Even where expenditures for housing across all groups is similar, our survey data show that all racial groups perceive the financial resources of blacks and Hispanics as inadequate to allow them into more desirable areas.

Furthermore, these data suggest that group self-perceptions of affordability and desirability would also place different groups in separate communities. The growth of racially identifiable communities generates assumptions regarding the openness of different areas to other groups. It also affects the attractiveness of these communities to investment, job growth, and economic opportunity; or, conversely, it increases their exposure to disinvestment, employment losses, and economic hardship. Laid upon the foundation of historic racial divisions and conflict, and in a climate characterized by perceptions of increasing economic insecurity, residents otherwise open to integration may come to fear it. Such fears may encourage institutional practices that foreclose the possibility of greater residential integration, as sellers, brokers, and lenders steer home seekers through the myriad set of market alternatives. These are the processes that have given America its racial ghettos (Massey and Denton 1993). In addition, our data point to at least some resistance to integration among *all* groups. The task of fully explaining the sources of this resistance remains for future research, but the racial and ethnic attitudes we noted in the last chapter surely are one key reason.

The regionwide scope of our study causes us greater pessimism about the prospects for residential integration than if we had limited the focus to the city of Boston. The perceptions of our respondents describe processes affecting residential location decisions as they play out in the 154 separate towns and cities of the Greater Boston area. Strategies to encourage residential integration must therefore encompass an even larger multitude of statutory agents and secondary stakeholders than would be the case in a single municipality. Without regionwide action of both public and private agents, divergent group perceptions and ongoing racial stereotyping may fuel the continued presence of "American Apartheid" in Greater Boston.

Residential Segregation

The work described here closely parallels studies completed by Reynolds Farley et al. (1993) for Detroit, and by Camille Zubrinsky and Lawrence Bobo in Los Angeles (1996). First, using data from the *1990*

Census of Population and Housing, we describe the extent of racial residential segregation and the cost of rental and owner-occupied housing for various groups living in the Greater Boston community. Then, using data from the GBSS, we examine racial and ethnic differences in knowledge relating to the perception of the housing market, perceived institutional barriers in obtaining housing, and group preferences regarding alternative neighborhoods. We could not ask survey respondents about every area in the region, nor did we think we would learn much by asking respondents to generalize about the entire region. Instead the survey was designed to focus on the desirability of five specific communities in Greater Boston distinguished by class and racial concentration, affordability, and openness to integration. Analysis of these questions is used to establish the extent of group differences in *perceptions* of residential areas.

Our analysis then goes on to explore how differences in attitudes among racial groups help explain residential housing patterns, including group preferences for neighborhoods with a particular racial makeup. This relies on an analysis of a "showcard" procedure first used in studies of residential segregation in Detroit, in which respondents rated the attractiveness of neighborhoods that varied in racial composition (Farley et al. 1978). We revised this survey protocol, incorporating a split-ballot experimental design to allow measurement of intergroup perceptions of Hispanics and Asians, as well as African Americans and whites. This refinement and expansion of Farley's method permits our analysis to encompass multiracial views of residential location, not just black-white differences.

As noted in chapter 1, black-white residential segregation in Greater Boston, while on the decline, is still highly prevalent. This has also been somewhat true for Hispanic-white and Asian-white segregation in the 1970s and 1980s (Massey and Denton 1987).

Many measures of segregation are available (for example, White 1986; Massey and Denton 1988), but we conduct this analysis using the two that are most common: the *index of dissimilarity,* indicating the proportion of a minority population who would have to move to produce an even distribution of the group across all areas; and the *isolation index,* which measures the probability of contact among group members within an area.

These measures have most frequently been computed for census tracts across an entire metropolitan area. However, given the numerous, autonomous communities in the Greater Boston region, restricting this analysis to a comparison of census tracts across the entire metropolitan area would obscure important data on how segregation varies among cities and towns. Therefore, we computed each segregation measure at the municipal (city-town) level for blacks, Asians, and Hispanics. Rather than having a single value of segregation for the region, as is typically reported in research on residential segregation (for example, Farley and Frey 1994), we report on the extent of segregation in each town and city. The results, not surprisingly, show that segregation exists in suburbia as well as in the central city, and affects all racial groups. But perhaps more important, the analysis shows that racial residential segregation across Boston-area communities is associated with class stratification (Logan and Alba 1993) and with income inequality. That is, the historic inequality of community resources, uneven opportunities for good housing and employment, and overall quality of life across the cities and towns in the Greater Boston labor market is highly correlated with its racial and ethnic composition. Areas with higher levels of minorities and higher levels of segregation are almost always likely to be worse off economically and to be perceived more negatively as places to live or work. It is unlikely that this phenomenon is accidental.

Table 7.1 shows the index of dissimilarity and the isolation index for the Boston CMSA in 1990 and the group of forty-six cities and towns with populations of at least 25,000 within the region. These measures are based on the census determination of the race of the head of each household. For external comparison, we also include black-white measures for the United States. What the U.S. figures show is that 28 percent of the blacks in the nation as a whole would have to relocate to other states for the distribution of blacks across states to match the

TABLE 7.1   *Indices of Segregation for Greater Boston Area and the United States, Various Levels of Geography, 1990*

United States (Black-White)	Index of Dissimilarity		Isolation Index	
Between states	.28		.17	
Between counties	.46		.26	
Between cities (> 25,000 pop.)	.49		.35	
Boston CMSA	all	>25,000		
Between Towns	(n = 154)	(n = 46)	all	>25,000
Black-white	.60	.55	.15	.16
Black-Asian	.41	.39		
Black-Hispanic	.38	.38		
Asian-white	.38	.31	.04	.04
Hispanic-white	.49	.41	.10	.11
Hispanic-Asian	.32	.30		
Hispanic-non-Hispanic	.46	.37		

Source: Greater Boston Social Survey 1995.
Note: Values for United States taken from Massey and Hajnal 1995.

distribution of whites. Seventeen percent would have to move across state lines to have a chance of living in areas populated by groups other than their own racial or ethnic group.

The amount of segregation and isolation is higher at the county and city level. Nearly half of all blacks would have to move to other cities to achieve perfect racial balance across cities. Massey and Hajnal (1995) show that this pattern, in which segregation between cities is greater than between states, emerged from a nearly century-long transition that began when large numbers of black families began to move North to take advantage of employment opportunities in the burgeoning northern manufacturing centers. But when they moved, they ended up isolated in urban ghettos. This trend ensured that, statistically, white contact with blacks would be minimized, even though whites in the North would now live in much closer proximity to black families.

Black-white separation across towns and cities in the Boston region is somewhat higher than the national average. And it is substantially higher than the segregation of other groups (Hispanics and Asians) from whites, or of blacks from these ethnic groups. Sixty percent of black families would have to move to other cities and towns within the region to have racial balance. Only 49 percent of Hispanics and only 32 percent of Asians, would have to do this. Considering only Boston-area communities with populations of 25,000 or more, there is slightly less segregation of each group, indicating that the higher segregation levels for the overall CMSA are caused by the absence of minorities in smaller communities. The forty-six largest municipalities in the region contain about 68 percent of the overall CMSA population, but account for 95 percent of the non-Hispanic black population, 94 percent of the Hispanic population, and 88 percent of the Asian population. The isolation index shows the same pattern.

Table 7.2 shows each index computed for each of the cities and towns in the Boston region with populations of 25,000 or more. The indexes are computed for block groups, which are smaller areas than standard census tracts. This produces higher (though possibly more unstable) estimates of segregation and isolation, since an individual census tract could have families from various racial groups, but segregated within particular block groups. However, the smaller block group areas are a more appropriate level of analysis in communities where the size of the overall minority population is relatively small. The cities are listed in order from largest to smallest population. Half the cities have a black-white segregation index of .21 or higher, Hispanic-white segregation of .17 or higher, and Asian-white segregation of .19 or higher. The isolation indices tend to be quite low, but the exceptions show that significant isolation occurs in different places for different groups. For

TABLE 7.2   *Indices of Segregation for Greater Boston Cities and Towns, 1990*

Population	Percentage Households			Index of Dissimilarity (Segregation from Whites, Between Tracts)			Isolation Index		
Greater Boston, Cities and Towns > 25,000	Black	Hispanic	Asian	B	H	A	B	H	A
Boston (574,283)	20.1	8.1	4.1	.75	.52	.44	.61	.17	.18
Lowell (103,439)	1.9	8.4	6.6	.27	.42	.34	.03	.15	.11
Cambridge (95,802)	10.9	4.8	5.4	.43	.33	.30	.20	.07	.09
Brockton (92,788)	10.2	5.1	1.1	.24	.31	.21	.13	.07	.01
Quincy (84,985)	1.0	1.2	4.0	.22	.17	.25	.01	.01	.06
Newton (82,585)	1.6	1.3	3.2	.16	.12	.14	.02	.01	.04
Lynn (81,245)	5.6	6.7	1.8	.38	.38	.40	.06	.11	.03
Somerville (76,210)	4.2	4.5	2.9	.20	.21	.14	.05	.05	.03
Lawrence (70,207)	1.5	32.3	1.2	.22	.39	.31	.02	.44	.02
Framingham (64,989)	3.1	6.3	2.4	.21	.42	.14	.04	.14	.03
Waltham (57,878)	2.3	4.1	2.6	.18	.23	.11	.03	.05	.03
Medford (57,407)	3.5	1.4	1.4	.52	.11	.17	.20	.02	.02
Brookline (54,718)	2.2	2.2	6.1	.19	.13	.13	.03	.02	.07
Weymouth (54,063)	1.0	0.9	0.6	.35	.21	.22	.02	.01	.01
Malden (53,884)	3.9	2.1	3.6	.23	.13	.17	.05	.02	.04
Haverhill (51,418)	1.4	3.7	0.6	.22	.42	.23	.02	.08	.01
Peabody (47,039)	0.7	2.5	0.7	.20	.47	.21	.01	.06	.01
Plymouth (45,608)	1.2	0.7	0.4	.22	.15	.17	.02	.01	.01
Arlington (44,630)	1.1	1.3	2.5	.12	.14	.11	.01	.01	.03
Revere (42,786)	1.2	3.0	2.0	.24	.27	.53	.02	.04	.06
Methuen (39,990)	0.6	3.9	0.9	.26	.55	.19	.01	.16	.01
Beverly (38,195)	0.7	0.9	0.6	.25	.21	.20	.01	.01	.01
Salem (38,091)	1.1	4.5	1.0	.12	.40	.29	.01	.13	.02
Billerica (37,609)	0.8	0.7	1.3	.11	.21	.19	.01	.01	.02
Woburn (35,943)	1.1	1.9	1.2	.08	.20	.12	.01	.02	.01
Everett (35,701)	3.0	2.8	1.2	.11	.15	.21	.03	.03	.01
Braintree (33,836)	0.6	0.7	1.1	.19	.15	.08	.01	.01	.01
Watertown (33,284)	1.0	1.6	1.9	.16	.08	.09	.01	.02	.02
Chelmsford (32,388	0.4	0.8	2.5	.09	.04	.04	.01	.01	.02
Marlborough (31,813)	1.6	3.2	1.6	.08	.14	.21	.02	.04	.02
Natick (30,510)	1.9	1.4	1.8	.28	.17	.27	.02	.02	.02
Randolph (30,093)	6.9	1.4	3.8	.12	.08	.06	.07	.01	.04
Andover (29,151)	0.9	1.2	2.8	.23	.13	.23	.01	.01	.04
Lexington (28,974)	1.0	1.0	4.9	.18	.10	.11	.01	.01	.05
Gloucester (28,716)	0.2	0.8	0.1	.17	.20	.26	.01	.01	.01
Chelsea (28,710)	3.9	22.7	3.0	.17	.40	.23	.04	.32	.03
Norwood (28,700)	1.4	0.9	1.1	.31	.15	.26	.02	.01	.01
Melrose (28,150)	0.6	0.6	0.9	.30	.07	.23	.01	.01	.01
Needham (27,557)	0.5	0.7	1.5	.29	.11	.15	.01	.01	.02
Tewksbury (27,266)	0.9	0.8	1.1	.12	.14	.11	.01	.01	.01

TABLE 7.2   *Continued*

Greater Boston, Cities and Towns > 25,000				Index of Dissimilarity (Segregation from Whites, Between Tracts)			Isolation Index	
	Percentage Households								
Population	Black	Hispanic	Asian	B	H	A	B	H	A
Stoughton (26,777)	3.4	1.6	0.8	.12	.10	.15	.04	.02	.01
Wellesley (26,615)	1.0	1.1	1.8	.24	.05	.05	.01	.01	.02
Milton (25,725)	3.9	0.7	0.9	.46	.29	.16	.08	.01	.01
Dracut (25,594)	0.6	0.7	1.0	.18	.08	.20	.01	.01	.01
Saugus (25,549)	0.5	0.8	0.6	.08	.09	.17	.01	.01	.01
Milford (25,355)	1.0	3.2	0.9	.15	.27	.10	.01	.05	.01

Note: Differences in percent minority in this table from proportions indicated in chapter 3 and in table 6.10 are due to the fact that this table reports on *households,* while other tables report on individuals. Since minority households tend to be younger and larger than white households (and may be composed more often of multiple families), the minority proportion of households will be lower than the minority proportion of individuals.

black families, by far the highest levels of segregation and isolation are observed in the city of Boston. Relatively high levels are also apparent in the cities of Cambridge, Lynn, Medford, and Milton. This is probably not an indication that integration is more successful within most of the other cities. Rather, within many of the suburban communities, blacks are too few in number to be isolated within their own neighborhoods, but instead are spread throughout white neighborhoods. In the five cities listed, enough blacks are present for largely black neighborhoods to exist.

At the national level, black segregation from whites is typically higher than Hispanic or Asian segregation, but this pattern is frequently broken within Greater Boston. Hispanic-white segregation exceeds black-white segregation in nearly half the communities, including Lowell, Brockton, Lawrence, Framingham, Haverhill, Peabody, Methuen, Revere, Salem, Somerville, Salem, and Waltham. These are generally communities with enough Hispanics to have something approaching a barrio, but not enough blacks to have an Afican American ghetto. Asian-white segregation also exceeds black-white segregation in many places. The cities and towns in which Hispanic-white and Asian-white segregation exceeds black-white segregation include Chelsea, Everett, Gloucester, Lowell, Lawrence, Lynn, Haverhill, Peabody, Quincy, Revere, and Salem. All are communities that have experienced rapid immigration of Asians, making it possible to have small Asian enclaves within them.

TABLE 7.3   *Median Household Income, 1989, Boston CMSA*

	CMSA	Boston	Outside Boston
Overall	$40,276	$31,389	$45,621
White households	$41,651	$33,725	$45,819
Black households	$26,099	$24,036	$36,802
Hispanic households	$21,860	$19,257	$31,958

Source: U.S. Department of Commerce 1990, tables 3 (61), 6 (355), 7 (384), and 10 (470).

One simple reason for this high degree of segregation could be differences in household income. Higher-income families can leave the central city for more affluent suburbs; low-income minorities are trapped inside the city. The income data are consistent with this explanation. Table 7.3 shows the median household income by race and location within the Boston Consolidated Metropolitan Statistical Area (CMSA)—the largest part of the Greater Boston region, as we have defined it. Clearly, central-city residents are less well off than their suburban counterparts. Hispanics living in Boston itself have incomes that average only a little more than 40 percent ($19,257 versus $45,819) that of whites living outside the central city. Blacks do a little better, averaging 52 percent of the mean white income. Similar and even more extreme differences hold for per capita income, across different types of families, and for households with different levels of labor force participation (see U.S. Bureau of the Census 1993, table 46).

Additional Reasons for the Segregation Pattern

Severe as these average income differences appear, it is nonetheless likely that they only partially account for the observed degree of residential segregation. In fact, demographic studies of the nation's large metropolitan areas, including Boston, have shown that segregation by race persists even when different racial groups have similar incomes (Farley and Allen 1987, 149; Farley, Danziger, and Holzer, 2000; Massey and Denton 1993, 86). Moreover, if income differences were the sole cause of housing segregation, we would expect minorities to be spending less on housing than whites. But figures 7.1 through 7.4 show that monthly housing costs across race-ethnic groups do not vary anywhere near as much as income. Figure 7.1, for example, demonstrates that the pattern of monthly rents paid by Boston region residents was remarkably similar across race and ethnic groups in 1990. Sixty percent of black families paid $500 or more in rent, compared with 70 percent of

FIGURE 7.1   *Monthly Rent, Renter-Occupied Units, Boston CMSA,*
              1990

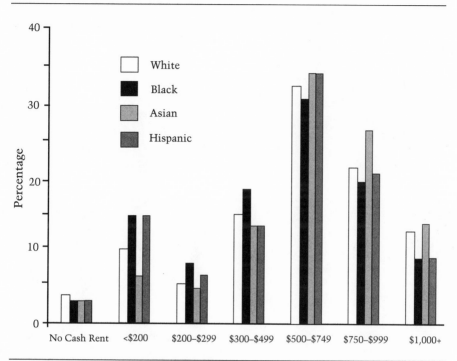

Source: Greater Boston Social Survey 1995.

whites. Figure 7.2 demonstrates that while rents were generally higher
outside the city of Boston, a majority of black families (53 percent) in
the hub city spent $500 or more on monthly rent. This group spent
more than did one-third of the whites who lived in the suburbs. A similar conclusion for the homeowning population follows from figure 7.3,
which compares the profile of costs for black homeowners with that of
other race-ethnic groups. Figure 7.4 compares black mortgage costs in
Boston proper with white mortgage costs in the balance of the CMSA.

In this light, we can see that many minority households could afford to rent in any area of Greater Boston, and were carrying monthly
housing costs comparable to many white renters and homeowners. Because expenditures for housing vary so little across these racial groups,
affordability cannot solely explain the persistent, high levels of segregation existing in metropolitan Boston.

To explore other explanations, we turn to data from the GBSS sur-

FIGURE 7.2   *Black Housing Costs in Boston versus White Costs Out of Boston, Renters, 1990*

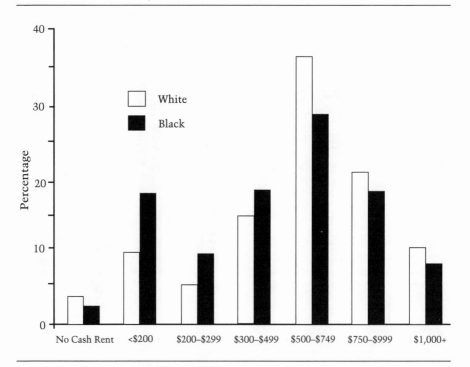

Source: Greater Boston Social Survey 1995.

vey. Following methodology developed by Farley et al. (1978, 1993) in the Detroit Area Study, we asked the residents we surveyed what they knew of housing costs and affordability in specific communities across the metropolitan area, in order to determine whether whites, blacks, and Hispanics have similar information about the housing market. Because there are 154 separate incorporated communities in the Greater Boston area, any given respondent was unlikely to have reliable information about the housing market in general, or to have much need for such information. But it is useful to see whether, on average, these groups differed systematically in their knowledge and perception of distinctive communities within the metropolitan area. The communities we asked respondents about are Cambridge, Newton, South Boston, Lowell, and Brockton. They were not chosen at random and are somewhat larger than the typical community in the metropolitan area. They were chosen because they were likely to be known to most respondents and typify different aspects of the housing market: proximity to Boston,

FIGURE 7.3   *Monthly Mortgage and Selected Costs, Owner-Occupied Units with Mortgage, 1990*

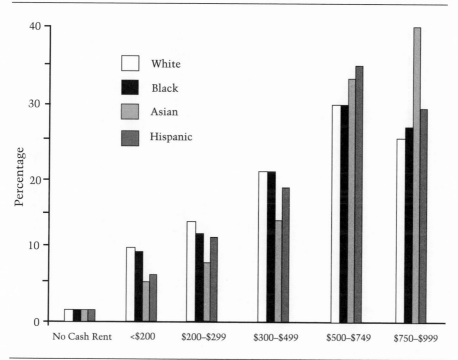

Source: Greater Boston Social Survey 1995.

prevalence of homeownership, and experience of population and economic change.

Cambridge   Located two miles west of central Boston, across the Charles River, Cambridge is known for its unique cultural and economic mix. It is the home of Harvard University and the Massachusetts Institute of Technology, so one-quarter of the population is in college and one-sixth is employed in higher education. Even though it is famous for its two world-renowned universities, Cambridge remains largely a working-class community, with its great number of three-deckers—the quintessential form of New England workers' housing. Cambridge experienced little growth in its total population between 1980 and 1990, yet its African American, Hispanic, and Asian populations grew significantly. In 1990, its residents were 14 percent black, 7 percent Hispanic, and 8 percent Asian. Overall employment grew from the mid-1980s to the present, despite the loss of nearly 5,500 manufacturing jobs. Wages

FIGURE 7.4   *Black Housing Costs in Boston Versus White Costs Out of Boston, Owners, 1990*

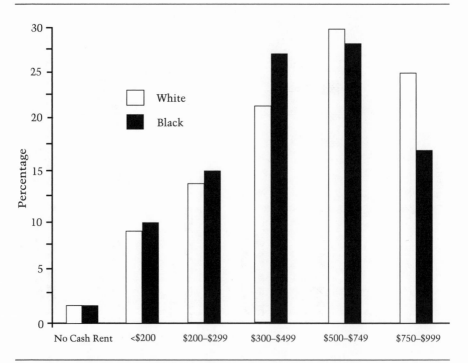

Source: Greater Boston Social Survey 1995.

increased over the decade at a rate above that for the overall CMSA. Median household income was $33,100, with 11 percent of the population living in poverty. Detached single-family housing is scarce in Cambridge, about 12 percent of all units. Median housing values are reasonably high, however, because of the large proportion of three-deckers supplying shelter for three families.

Newton   Located six miles west of central Boston and known as the Garden City, Newton enjoys a reputation for attractive neighborhoods, well-run government, and an excellent school system. It is, for the most part, a thoroughly middle-class inner suburb. The population declined slightly between 1980 and 1990, and remained overwhelmingly white (91 percent). Employment declined as well, but wage growth was better than in the CMSA as a whole. Median income in 1990 was high ($59,719) and poverty was low (4 percent). About 60 percent of dwelling units in Newton are detached single-family homes.

South Boston   South Boston is immediately adjacent to downtown Boston, separated by a small inland channel. The overall city population grew slightly from 1980 to 1990, while employment declined slightly, especially in manufacturing. The net decline masks an employment boom between 1985 and 1989, a decline between 1989 and 1992, and a slight recovery between 1992 and 1994. Housing in South Boston is relatively affordable, and the public enjoys direct access to large swaths of beach and parkland along Massachusetts Bay. This community is stereotypically referred to as Boston's most stable, homogeneous neighborhood, its most Irish neighborhood, its most xenophobic neighborhood, and to its detractors home to "bigots and Philistines" (*Boston Globe* 1993a). Its infamy has been sustained by its violent reaction to the court-ordered busing of minority students to South Boston High in the mid-1970s, more recent racial conflict among students (*Boston Globe* 1993b), racial harassment and attacks at public housing projects (*Boston Globe* 1990, 1994a, 1994b, 1994c, 1994d, 1996), and disputes over the right of Irish gay and lesbian organizations to participate in the traditional St. Patrick's Day parade (*Boston Globe* 1995; *Boston Herald* 1994). Its population in 1990 was nearly all white (97 percent).

Lowell   An old manufacturing center, Massachusetts' fourth largest city is located twenty-five miles north of Boston, near the intersection of three interstate highways (Routes 95, 495, and 3). It also is served by the Massachusetts Bay Transportation Authority (MBTA) commuter rail, which allows residents to reach North Station in Boston in about 40 minutes. Lowell has experienced an enormous erosion in its economic base, as total employment declined 46 percent between 1985 and 1994, from 45,400 to 32,400. This decrease has been steady and primarily a function of the disappearance of manufacturing jobs. Wage growth lags well behind the overall average for Greater Boston. Despite the worsening employment situation, Lowell has actually experienced population growth of about 12 percent. An important source of the growth in the 1980s was a large influx of Cambodian refugees, as noted in chapter 2. The 1990 population was 2 percent black, 10 percent Hispanic, and 11 percent Asian. Median income was $29,351, with about 18 percent of the population living below the poverty line. About a third of dwelling units are detached single-family homes with housing values that are quite reasonable for the Greater Boston region. Lowell is several miles west of Lawrence, where the population is over 40 percent Hispanic.

Brockton   A diverse urban area located twenty miles south of Boston, Brockton prides itself on its industrial history, especially as a center of shoe manufacturing. The city experienced a small decline in population in the 1980s, even as the combined black, Hispanic, and Asian population doubled. In 1990, 13 percent of the population was black, 6 percent Hispanic, and 2 percent Asian. Employment declined between 1985 and 1994, and wage growth was about the same as for the overall CMSA. In 1990, median household income was $31,712, with 14 percent of the population in poverty. Housing in Brockton is also reasonably afford-able, and the area has a reputation for being open to black families. De-tached single units make up about half (46 percent) the housing stock.

Knowledge of Housing Costs

We assess the respondents' knowledge of housing costs in the selected Boston area communities in table 7.4. When the Massachusetts econ-omy was hit by the recession from 1990 to 1991, housing values, which had been inflating rapidly in many local communities, fell substantially. By 1994, when the GBSS was conducted, values in some areas were in-creasing again—as they had during most of the 1980s. However, this was not true in either Lowell or Brockton, communities that had seen relatively large increases in their minority populations and continuing declines in employment. Because of the rapid changes in rent levels and housing prices, we would not have been surprised to find that many respondents to the GBSS survey had poor knowledge of housing values at the time of the interview. To take account of this, the right-hand columns in the table 7.4 show the percentage of respondents in each racial group who correctly placed the cost of housing in a given commu-nity within a home cost bracket that includes either the actual 1990 or 1992 median house value in that community. This accepts quite a bit of error, since the real-estate industry estimate of median value of units sold in 1990 is significantly lower than the census estimate.

Even under this generous definition of accuracy, no group of respon-dents demonstrated a good working knowledge of costs in any of the communities they were asked about. The proportion of African Ameri-can respondents giving accurate estimates for Cambridge and Newton was very low, moderate for South Boston and Lowell, and best for Brockton. Black respondents who gave incorrect cost estimates were more likely to provide low estimates for Cambridge, Newton, and South Boston, and high estimates for Lowell and Brockton. Hispanics' price assessments were nearly always the most inaccurate, although they did better for the two communities in which they could most likely afford a home: Lowell and Brockton. Hispanic respondents who gave incorrect estimates were more likely to provide low estimates for all areas. As a group, whites gave consistently more accurate estimates, perhaps re-flecting their higher rate of homeownership and self-interest in the mar-ket value of their homes. But at their best, only about two-thirds of

TABLE 7.4 Population Characteristics of Boston and Selected Housing Search Areas (1990 Census) Estimated Cost of Homes by Race of Respondent, and Ratio of Estimate to Actual Race of Respondent

Area	1990 Population	Percentage			Median Home Value, Owner-Occupied Units, 1990 Census	Median Sales Price 1992	Percentage of GBSS Respondents Estimating Costs Consistent with 1990 to 1992 Actual Costs		
		Black	Hispanic (Any Race)	Asian			Black	Hispanic	White
Boston (city)	574,283	25.6	10.8	5.3	$161,400	$118,000	n.a.	n.a.	n.a.
Boston (CMSA)	3,871,968	6.0	4.7	3.0	$179,300	n.a.	n.a.	n.a.	n.a.
Cambridge	95,802	13.5	6.8	8.4	$263,800	$175,000	40	30	64
Newton	82,585	2.1	2.0	4.5	$293,400	$248,500	40	21	60
South Boston	26,264	1.0	1.0	1.0	$137,500	n.a.	52	56	60
Lowell	103,439	2.4	10.1	11.1	$131,100	$ 86,000	54	58	66
Brockton	92,788	13.0	6.3	1.7	$131,700	$ 88,000	64	55	64

Source: Commonwealth of Massachusetts, Executive Office of Communities and Development—Community Profiles Website (www.magnet.state.ma.us/eocd/eocd/iprofile).

white respondents gave accurate estimates. White respondents tended to err by giving low estimates for Cambridge, Newton, and South Boston and high estimates for Lowell and Brockton.

What is most important, however, is that the accuracy of housing cost estimates of the three race-ethnic groups did not differ dramatically. For Brockton, for example, equal percentages of blacks and whites gave accurate estimates of house values in that city. Only 8 percent more whites than blacks gave accurate assessments of the housing prices in South Boston, a community that few blacks have ever visited, let alone lived in. Hence, it would be erroneous to assert that the knowledge of any single group is vastly superior to the others. As such, there is little to suggest that inaccurate information contributes significantly to residential segregation.

Perceptions of Affordability

The census data reveal that many minority-group households have the financial capacity to reside in almost any sector of the Greater Boston housing market. The costs of homeownership vary widely across the market and among the areas we asked about, but rental costs vary somewhat less. In 1990, median rents and vacancy rates for the communities we asked about were: Cambridge, $483 (3 percent); Newton, $809 (3 percent); Boston, $546 (8 percent); Lowell, $494 (10 percent); and Brockton, $491 (9 percent) (U.S. Bureau of the Census, 1990). Thus, except for Newton, the median rents varied by no more than 13 percent across these communities. Group differences in *perceptions* of housing affordability, regardless of their accuracy, are potentially important factors in explaining residential segregation, either because minority homebuyers may limit their search for affordable housing, or they may experience statistical discrimination because of negative stereotypes held by white homeowners or real estate agents.

Hence, to examine group differences in perceptions of affordability, survey respondents were asked how many black, Hispanic, or Asian families could afford to live in each community: almost all, many, about half, a few, or just about none. Respondents were asked about all five communities, but to minimize their burden, they were asked only about one of the minority groups. The group that a respondent was asked to rate was randomly assigned under a split-ballot experimental design (Schuman and Bobo 1988).

Table 7.5 shows the percentage of respondents rating half or more of each group as able to afford housing in each area. For example, the cell for "Cambridge" and "black families" reveals that 77 percent of black respondents felt half or more black families could afford to live in Cam-

TABLE 7.5   *Split-Ballot Experiment Measuring Perceptions of Group's Ability to Afford Housing in Selected Boston-Area Communities for Blacks, Hispanics, and Asians*

| | Percentage Reporting at Least Half of their Group's Families Can Afford to Live in Area | | | | | | | | |
| | Black Families | | | Hispanic Families | | | Asian Families | | |
Respondent's Race >	Black	Hispanic	White	Black	Hispanic	White	Black	Hispanic	White
Cambridge	77	65	49	60	60	37	61	59	61
Newton	25	17	13	23	29	11	46	53	36
South Boston	66	55	70	56	36	63	55	53	82
Lowell	65	58	83	61	74	75	68	77	84
Brockton	92	74	79	75	67	82	81	71	79

Source: Greater Boston Social Survey 1995.
Note: Percentages are based on weighted observations and include respondents who indicated they "didn't know."

bridge, compared with only 65 percent of Hispanic respondents and 49 percent of white respondents. For Newton, only 25 percent of black respondents felt half or more black families could afford housing there, compared with 17 percent of Hispanic respondents and 13 percent of white respondents. When asked about the ability of Hispanic families to afford housing in these areas, 60 percent of black respondents felt half or more Hispanic families could afford housing in Cambridge, and 23 percent felt this was so for Newton. Equal or higher proportions of Hispanic respondents rated these areas as affordable for Hispanic families, while white respondents reported less confidence in the financial capabilities of blacks and Hispanics to live in either area. Whites reported more confidence in Asians' ability to afford housing in these areas than for either blacks or Hispanics. Black and Hispanic respondents did not perceive Asians to be as well off as white respondents, rating them similar to their own group in Cambridge, but more able than blacks or Hispanics to afford Newton.

In extending the analysis to all five areas, it appears that all groups' perceptions are moderately conditioned by variations in the price of owning a home. Housing is seen as least affordable for all groups in Newton and most affordable in Lowell and Brockton. Black respondents tend to rate black families' capacity higher than they are rated by other groups, but, interestingly, Hispanics are not as likely to do this. Whites perceive Asians, blacks, and Hispanics to be similarly positioned for the Lowell and Brockton housing markets.

181

Blacks' and Hispanics' perceptions of their own and other groups' ability to afford housing across the metropolitan area appear to be in line with their financial capability and market price variation. These groups correctly perceive that large fractions of minority groups can afford to live in the five communities. In three of the communities—Cambridge, Lowell, and Brockton—minorities are represented in numbers consistent with their proportion in the overall population in the metropolitan area, although they are subject to moderate levels of segregation (see table 7.2). In Newton and especially South Boston they are not. As has been noted for comparable areas in Detroit (Farley 1978; Holzer et al., forthcoming), the absence of minorities in these areas cannot be explained by their actual financial limitations or by beliefs held among these groups that they cannot afford to live there.

Perceived Hostility of Whites

Financial capacity by itself cannot enable residential mobility and greater integration if minorities perceive new areas as less desirable or more hostile than where they currently live. To test these factors, we assessed whether respondents perceived the five selected communities as "desirable." We asked them to rate each area as "very desirable," "somewhat desirable," "somewhat undesirable," or "very undesirable," and to say whether they thought a black, Hispanic, or Asian family moving to the area would be welcome, or if the people already living there would be "upset."

Table 7.6 shows that black respondents thought Cambridge and Newton were the most desirable of the communities, Lowell and Brockton somewhat less desirable, and South Boston distinctly undesirable. Hispanic responses were much less favorable toward Cambridge, Newton, and Brockton, but similar to blacks for Lowell. Hispanics were slightly more likely to exhibit favorable attitudes toward South Boston as a place to live, but three-fourths still reported it as an undesirable location.

Whites see these communities somewhat differently. Newton is rated as "somewhat" or "very" desirable by proportionately as many whites as minority respondents, but all the other communities are rated less well, with the exception of South Boston. A majority of white respondents (58 percent) see Cambridge as desirable, but only about a quarter of respondents felt South Boston, Lowell, or Brockton were desirable.

Although their levels of affinity for these communities differ, both whites and nonwhites tend to view the more affluent communities more favorably. Respondents who said an area was undesirable were

TABLE 7.6 Perceived Desirability and Split-Ballot Experiment Measuring Perceptions of Receptivity of Whites to Minority Families in Selected Boston-Area Communities

| | Percentage Reporting Area is Somewhat or Very Desirable | | | Percentage Reporting that Whites Would Be Upset if a Family of Another Group Moved into Area | | | | | | | | |
| | | | | Black Family | | | Hispanic Family | | | Asian Family | | |
Respondent's Race >	Black	Hispanic	White	Black	Hispanic	White	Black	Hispanic	White	Black	Hispanic	White
Cambridge	79	48	58	13	25	36	21	27	30	24	36	16
Newton	75	37	75	53	50	62	60	41	67	40	35	43
South Boston	15	26	26	83	66	67	69	46	63	70	51	47
Lowell	43	45	27	17	8	15	28	5	13	19	17	17
Brockton	45	32	23	9	7	26	8	7	12	13	13	20

Note: Percentages are based on weighted observations and include respondents who indicated they "didn't know." Hispanic responses on the desirability question are dominated by don't knows; if analysis is limited to those with non-don't know responses, the ratings of blacks and Hispanics are very similar, with the exception of South Boston, which Hispanics are more likely to rate as desirable.

asked to indicate why they thought so. Those responses (not shown) indicate that racial issues—that is, concerns about prejudice, discrimination, or dislike for the ethnic or racial makeup of the area—rarely concerned respondents who felt that Cambridge or Newton was undesirable. Rather, respondents expressed concerns about crime or safety in Cambridge, and thought locating in Newton would be inconvenient because of their work location or lack of public transportation. Concern with crime and safety were also mentioned by the overwhelming majority of respondents who rated Lowell and Brockton as undesirable. Racial issues were not frequently mentioned in relation to these places by either black or Hispanic respondents, but did surface more frequently in whites' responses. Finally, when giving reasons for finding South Boston undesirable, blacks overwhelmingly cited concerns about prejudice and discrimination, and many were also concerned about crime and safety. Among Hispanics who rated the area as undesirable, crime and safety were mentioned with slightly greater frequency than racial issues. Still, both issues were noted by a clear majority of Hispanic respondents who felt South Boston was an undesirable place to live. White respondents had more varied reasons for finding the area undesirable, but the most frequently cited reasons again included crime and safety concerns and concerns about prejudice and discrimination.

For respondents who described particular areas as undesirable, their perception that the movement of minority families into these communities would upset whites can be taken as an indicator of concern about racial prejudice. The right-hand panel of table 7.6 shows that fewer respondents thought minority families would upset whites already residing in Brockton, Lowell, or Cambridge than in Newton and South Boston. Across the five sample communities, black and Hispanic respondents were less likely than whites to perceive that black families would be unwelcome, with the notable exception of South Boston. By contrast, black and Hispanic respondents were generally more likely than white respondents to perceive that Asian families would be unwelcome in these communities. Interestingly, Hispanic respondents were less likely than either black or white respondents to perceive that Hispanic families would be unwelcome.

The contrasts in table 7.6 invite speculation regarding why respondents think whites would be upset if minorities were to move into these areas, save for South Boston, which is widely understood to be hostile to outsiders, especially nonwhites. It is possible, for example, that economic concerns dominate overt racial concerns. This might be inferred from the survey data showing that white respondents perceive little difference in the feelings of whites toward any of the minority groups in the lower-income communities of Lowell and Brockton, but that Asians would upset whites *less* than Hispanics or blacks in Cambridge or Newton. Likewise, few blacks or Hispanics reported that Newton was undesirable, and racial issues were seldom mentioned by those who did see this Boston suburb as undesirable. Yet the majority of black respondents feel whites would be upset if a black or Hispanic family moved into Newton. These patterns are consistent with what we found in table 7.5, concerning perceptions of the ability of minorities to afford housing in the different areas. Such perceptions can be barriers to greater integration, affecting the behavior of minority homeseekers.

Perceived Institutional Barriers to Good Housing Opportunities for Minorities

Perceptions about how existing residents would treat minorities who tried to settle in their neighborhoods could influence residential housing patterns. Another factor involves the role of housing market intermediaries, including real estate agents and mortgage bankers. A substantial gap exists between black and nonblack respondents in their perceptions of how market actors influence housing outcomes for minorities. Survey respondents were asked whether they thought minorities missed out on good housing opportunities in the Boston area "very often," "sometimes," "rarely," or "almost never"—for reasons relating to white homesellers, real estate agents, lenders and banks, affordability, and because they lacked good information (the question stems are listed in table 7.7). The split-ballot method was used to allow comparison of the responses of blacks, Hispanics, and whites on questions regarding the treatment of blacks, Hispanics, and Asians.

Most black respondents said that white owners and lenders discriminate against blacks, and 47 percent thought that the same was true for white real estate agents. Relatively small percentages of whites (from 16 to 28 percent) perceived that these three types of actors discriminate against blacks or Hispanics. Hispanic respondents perceived discrimination against blacks at about the same rates as did whites. These results are more specific than the generalized perceptions of discrimination reported in the previous chapter, but are generally consistent in reflecting the gap in attitudes.

As in the Detroit (Farley et al. 1993, 19–20, Farley, Danziger, and Holzer 2000) and Los Angeles (Zubrinsky and Bobo 1996) studies, table 7.7 suggests that whites are more likely to believe that individual white homeowners discriminate against minorities than they are to believe that institutional agents discriminate. For example, 28 percent of whites felt blacks miss out on good housing "very often" because white owners

TABLE 7.7   *Split-Ballot Experiment Measuring Perceptions of Group's Exposure to Institutional Barriers to Good Housing Opportunities in the Boston Area*

Respondent's Race >	Percentage Reporting that Other Groups Miss Out on Good Housing for Given Reasons Very Often								
	Black Families			Hispanic Families			Asian Families		
	Black	Hispanic	White	Black	Hispanic	White	Black	Hispanic	White
Because white owners will not rent or sell to them	59	21	28	48	36	40	28	23	19
Because real estate agents will not show, sell, or rent to them	47	9	17	23	16	20	12	14	2
Because banks and lenders will not lend money to them to purchase a home	64	18	16	52	22	18	14	10	3
Because they can't afford good housing	32	14	25	20	40	27	19	15	17
Because they lack information about where to find good housing	34	26	17	30	21	23	35	19	10

Source: Greater Boston Social Survey 1995.
Note: Percentages are based on weighted observations.

will not rent or sell to black families, while only 17 percent felt this happened because real estate agents would not show, sell, or rent to black families. And only one in six white respondents felt blacks suffered in the housing market because banks and lenders would not lend money to black families to purchase a home.

Black respondents were much less likely to believe that they missed out on good housing because of an inability to afford it or a lack of information about housing options. They were much more likely to blame discrimination. Both whites and Hispanics, on the other hand, gave about the same importance to affordability and information as to discrimination.

Regarding the role housing market actors play in Hispanic housing outcomes, blacks continued to see discrimination at much higher rates than did either Hispanics or whites (the latter two groups again had perceptions of discrimination consistent with each other). For example, 52 percent of blacks said banks will very often not lend to Hispanics, while only 22 percent of Hispanics and 18 percent of whites thought that this was the case. Both blacks and Hispanics perceived fairly low rates of discrimination against Asians, with whites perceiving even lower rates. Hence, blacks feel that they are not the only ones who have borne the brunt of housing market discrimination—something Hispanics and Asians are less likely to recognize or experience.

The perception of blacks regarding their own status in the housing market is corroborated by Federal Reserve Bank studies of minority access to mortgages. Data from a comprehensive study of lenders, conducted by the Bank's Boston office, show that high-income blacks in Boston were more likely to be turned down when seeking loans than low-income whites (Munnell et al. 1996).

Neighborhood Racial Composition and Residential Preferences

The analysis so far suggests that minorities' perception of negative attitudes by whites might limit their consideration of alternative residential areas, and that minorities would receive different treatment in the housing market. These two factors working in tandem surely could explain a least some of the residential segregation pattern we find in Greater Boston. Nonetheless, some would assert that these factors are relatively unimportant contributors to residential segregation, and that the primary determinant of racial separation in the housing market is the preference for same-race neighbors (see Clark 1986, 1988, 1991, 1992; Thernstrom and Thernstrom 1997, 225–30). Data on the desirability of alternative neighborhoods, shown previously in table 7.6, suggest that all groups are strongly motivated by quality of life issues. Nearly everyone, regardless of race or ethnic origin, preferred more affluent areas and found undesirable those that were thought to have higher crime rates or racial prejudice.

But it is possible that each group has a desire to live in communities where they were not the only white, black, Hispanic, or Asian. To test this, we explored the impact of neighborhood racial composition on residential preferences, using an extension of the method developed in the Detroit Area Study (Farley et al. 1978, 1993) and elaborated for use in the Multi-City Study of Urban Inequality (Zubrinsky and Bobo 1996). In these studies, respondents were asked about their comfort with neighborhood alternatives that ranged from a configuration where the respondent lived in an all-same-race neighborhood to one where the respondent would have few or no same-race neighbors. The protocol varied slightly for white and nonwhite respondents, as we will describe, and the split-ballot technique was used to allow us to assess how the preferences of whites, blacks, and Hispanics varied in response to situations where their neighbors were either white, black, Hispanic, or Asian. While asking for reactions to one group at a time may seem simplistic and superficial, we note that this has never been done before in either this or a more complicated fashion. All prior surveys have only asked blacks and whites about each other, and no such survey results are previously available for Boston.

The protocol for soliciting white responses is found in the five diagrams of neighborhoods shown in the left-hand column of figure 7.5. Respondents were asked to imagine that they lived in a neighborhood that looked like the first card, an all-white neighborhood with fifteen homes and the respondent living in the center house. He or she was then shown the second card, which indicated that one minority family had moved into the neighborhood. The respondent was asked how comfortable he or she would feel in this situation: "very comfortable," "somewhat comfortable," "somewhat uncomfortable," or "very uncomfortable." The race of the hypothetical minority household was either black, Hispanic, or Asian and was determined under the split-ballot assignment. It was held constant throughout the remainder of the exercise. Respondents who said they would be somewhat or very comfortable with the situation were shown the next card, indicating three minority neighbors, or a neighborhood that was 20 percent minority. The interviewer continued with the series until the respondent indicated a level of discomfort, or until the fifth card was shown, a scenario in which the neighborhood was 53 percent nonwhite.

At the point in the series where the respondent indicated discomfort, the interviewer asked if the respondent would try to move out of the neighborhood. If the respondent indicated that he or she would stay, the interviewer would show the next card in the series and ask if the respondent would move then, continuing until either the respondent indicated he would move or the end of the series was reached. No neighborhoods can remain stable and integrated if whites begin moving out and are never willing to move into an integrated neighborhood. So, as the final step in the exercise, the white respondent was asked to imagine a different situation where he or she was looking for a place to move, then asked to indicate whether he or she would eschew moving into any of the five neighborhoods represented by the cards.

FIGURE 7.5 *Show Card Alternatives for Study of Residential Preferences*

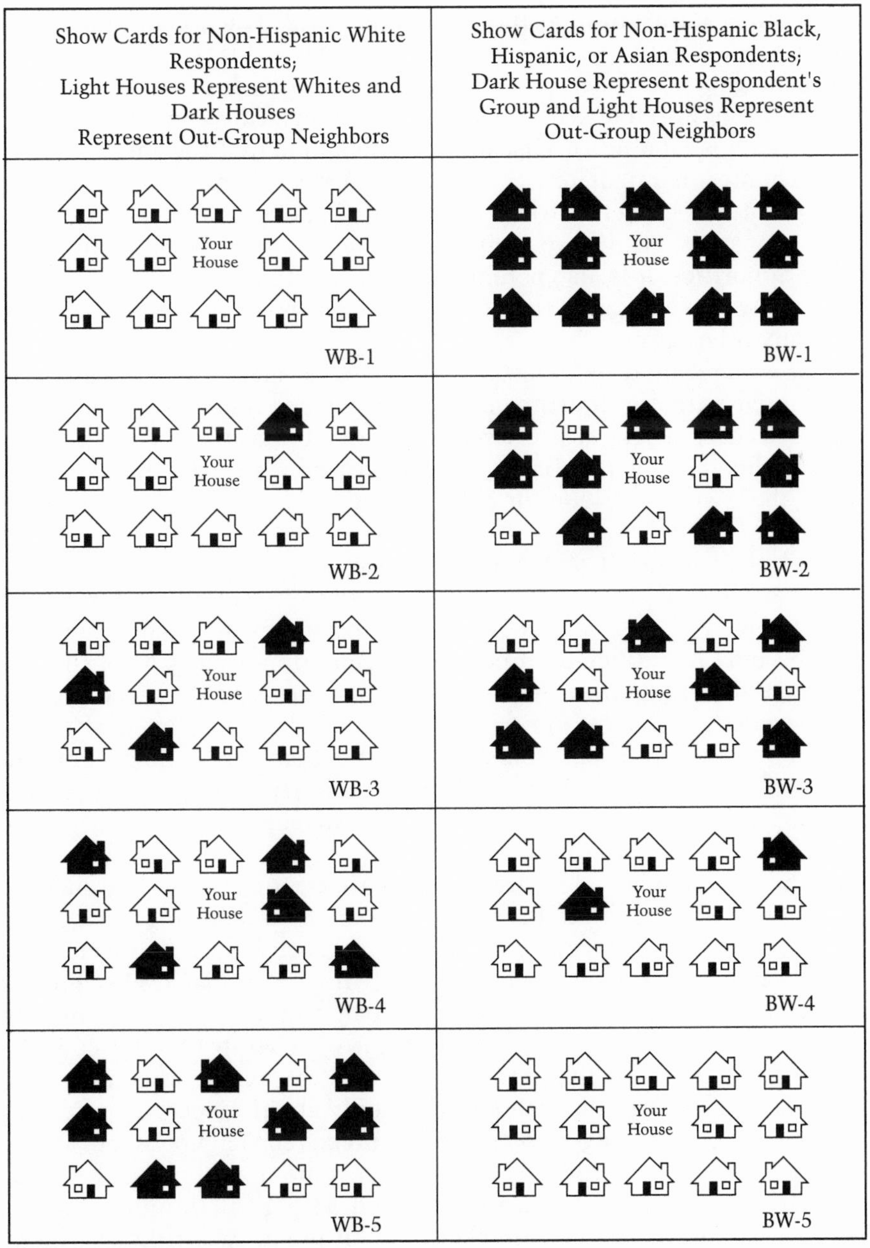
Show Cards for Non-Hispanic White Respondents; Light Houses Represent Whites and Dark Houses Represent Out-Group Neighbors
Show Cards for Non-Hispanic Black, Hispanic, or Asian Respondents; Dark House Represent Respondent's Group and Light Houses Represent Out-Group Neighbors
Your House
WB-1
BW-1
WB-2
BW-2
WB-3
BW-3
WB-4
BW-4
WB-5
BW-5

Source: Greater Boston Social Survey 1995.

White Preferences

The reactions of white respondents to these different scenarios are shown in figure 7.6. A smaller percentage of whites said they would feel comfortable with minimal integration (card #2) when confronted with Hispanic neighbors (88 percent) as compared to black (97 percent) or Asian neighbors (95 percent). The percentage of whites who said they would be comfortable with slightly more integration (card #3) dropped for all groups, and again Hispanic neighbors elicited the most discomfort. This result might reflect the fact that many whites living outside Boston have relatively little contact with blacks or Asians, but more with Hispanics, who have dispersed throughout the region more than other minorities. It is also potentially problematic for the region's future because the overall growth rate of the Hispanic population is higher than any other group.

The aggregate level of discomfort increases sharply when whites are confronted with the fourth scenario (33 percent nonwhite). Under the fifth scenario, where white families represent only 47 percent of the neighborhood, only two-fifths (40 percent) of white respondents indicated they would be comfortable with that many black or Hispanic neighbors.

White resistance to integration of their neighborhoods provides only a partial view of the role of white behaviors in producing residential segregation. Whether whites are willing to remain in neighborhoods as they become more racially mixed is a second important part of the picture. The data in figure 7.6 show that few whites said they would move if Hispanics or Asians moved into the neighborhood, even after the number of nonwhite neighbors was greater than white neighbors. But over a quarter of respondents said they would try to move if the neighborhood became a third black, and over 40 percent said they would move if blacks became the majority.

The last element of white behavior that contributes to residential segregation is the choice that whites make when selecting a neighborhood to move into. The percentage of whites saying they would consider moving into the various neighborhoods (with either black, Hispanic, or Asian neighbors, according to the split-ballot assignment) is shown in the right-hand column of figure 7.6. Nearly all whites would consider moving into the all-white neighborhood and the neighborhood containing only one minority household, while only about 40 percent said they would consider moving into the most integrated neighborhood, where whites represent just under half (47 percent) the households. The intermediate options, 20 percent minority and 33 percent minority, would not receive consideration from about one-fifth and two-fifths of whites,

FIGURE 7.6   Attractiveness of Neighborhoods of Varying Racial Composition to White Respondents

Show Cards for Non-Hispanic White Respondents; Light Houses Represent Whites and Dark Houses Represent Out-Group Neighbors	Percentage of White Respondents Who Would Feel Somewhat or Very Comfortable with (Black/Hispanic/Asian) Neighbors	Percentage of White Respondents Who Would Try to Move out of Each Neighborhood	Percentage of White Respondents Who Would Consider Moving into Each Neighborhood
 WB-1	—	—	99/97/97
 WB-2	97/88/95	1/4/0	97/90/97
 WB-3	84/74/91	6/6/2	82/81/94
 WB-4	63/62/83	28/11/5	59/57/61
 WB-5	40/41/61	42/9/11	39/41/38

Source: Greater Boston Social Survey 1995.

respectively. At the level of 20 percent minority neighbors, there is a somewhat greater preference to have Asian neighbors, but this preference disappears when the percentage of minority households is higher (cards #4 and #5).

Nonwhite Preferences

What are the residential preferences of blacks and Hispanics? Are they similar to those of whites, or more favorable toward integration? Figure 7.7 summarizes the attractiveness of various neighborhoods to blacks and Hispanics. The data reveal that blacks and Hispanics prefer neighborhoods where they constitute a plurality of all families living there. Yet, few are unwilling to move into neighborhoods where they are not the majority group, as long as they have some same-race neighbors (card #4). Neither blacks nor Hispanics are very likely to prefer situations in which they are isolated (card #5), but their unwillingness to move into such neighborhoods is driven partly by the race of their other-race neighbors. Ironically, the *lowest* level of unwillingness to pioneer in all other-race neighborhoods occurs when the new neighborhood is all-white, the group from which both blacks and Hispanics are most segregated. Recent research has documented the psychic costs that blacks feel they will endure if forced to live in all-white areas where they are not welcome (Feagin and Sikes 1994). But these psychological costs are offset by the perceived advantages enjoyed by living in white neighborhoods in terms of the quality of services and schools. The majority of black respondents rated the third neighborhood option—the most balanced neighborhood, where blacks live in eight households and nonblacks live in seven—as their first choice. Almost half rated the second neighborhood, containing eleven black households and four nonblack households, as their second choice. The proportion of respondents rating these two neighborhoods first or second was not strongly related to the race of other-race neighbors. Virtually no black respondents said they were unwilling to move into these neighborhoods. Only about one in eleven (9 percent) black respondents rated the all-black neighborhood as their first choice when the alternative was a neighborhood composed of whites or Asians. This preference for living in an all-black neighborhood rises to 23 percent, however, when the alternative is to have a large number of Hispanic neighbors. On the other hand, the neighborhood containing only three black families (card #4) was the first choice of only 8 percent of black respondents. Fewer than 1 in 20 respondents rated the all other-race neighborhood (card #5) as their first choice, and the majority of respondents said they would not be willing to move into the neighborhood. While the antipathy of blacks for all other-race neigh-

FIGURE 7.7   Attractiveness of Neighborhoods of Varying Racial Compositions to Nonwhite Respondents

Show Cards for Non-Hispanic Black, Hispanic, or Asian Respondents; Dark Houses Represent Respondent's Group and Light Houses Represent Out-Group Neighbors	Percentage of Black Respondents Rating (White/Hispanic/Asian) Neighborhood First, Second	Percentage Not Willing to Move into (White/Hispanic/Asian) Neighborhood	Percentage of Hispanic Respondents Rating (White/Black/Asian) Neighborhood First, Second	Percentage Not Willing to Move into (White/Black/Asian) Neighborhood
 BW-1	15/23/9 8/5/9	37/40/29	13/28/19 3/24/3	37/20/37
 BW-2	19/24/32 48/55/45	2/1/1	19/45/8 50/45/62	2/5/11
 BW-3	53/51/51 21/20/29	0/0/1	47/26/47 35/26/14	2/6/11
 BW-4	8/2/8 21/17/12	5/13/15	19/0/21 10/4/9	5/28/9
 BW-5	5/1/0 2/3/6	59/66/75	2/1/6 2/1/12	54/85/43

Source: Greater Boston Social Survey 1995.

borhoods is clear, it also varies by race of neighbors. Of respondents, 59 percent said they would not move into an all-white neighborhood, 66 percent an all-Hispanic neighborhood, and 75 percent an all-Asian neighborhood. Hence, blacks have a strong preference for living in integrated neighborhoods, but they generally do not want to be integration pioneers.

Hispanic responses are similar to those given by blacks, though not identical, for they reveal a distinctive antipathy toward black neighbors. For example, the neighborhood attracting most first-place ratings from Hispanic respondents (47 percent) was one in which the other-race neighbors were whites or Asians, with a nearly even split between Hispanics, on the one hand, and other-race households, on the other (card #3). But only 26 percent of Hispanic respondents rated this their first-choice neighborhood when their other-race neighbors were black. So Hispanics seem to prefer living in a mixed-race community, as long as the percentage of blacks is small. Like black respondents, very few chose the all other-race neighborhood (card #5) first or second, and this occurred least when the other group was black.

Responses indicating the willingness to move into black-dominated communities reinforce the view that Hispanics are unenthusiastic about sharing neighborhoods with blacks. Almost nine out of ten (85 percent) said they would not move into an all-black neighborhood, whereas only a little more than half (54 percent) said they would not move into an all-white neighborhood, and only four out of ten (43 percent) said they would not move into an all-Asian neighborhood. Yet, as we saw earlier in this book, Hispanics have in fact moved into black-dominated neighborhoods in Greater Boston. These pioneers who have moved into communities like Roxbury, for example, may not have shared the antipathy for blacks that our survey respondents seem to exhibit. And once a Hispanic foothold in a previously black neighborhood has been established, other Hispanics follow. Only a quarter (28 percent) of Hispanic respondents indicated they would not move into a neighborhood as long as it was at least 20 percent Hispanic (card #4), even if the other neighbors were black.

Ideal Multiracial Neighborhoods

The scenarios presented so far did not afford respondents to the Boston survey the opportunity to react to more complex patterns of racial mixing, or to suggest in their own terms an optimal degree and form of integration that accommodates more than two groups simultaneously.

Recent population changes in the Greater Boston area mean that the typical resident is confronted with greater racial diversity than in the past. And all reasonable projections suggest that the future population will contain relatively fewer whites. As a result, the scope of attitude studies concerning segregation must expand. Unfortunately, the existing literature—which focuses on black-white segregation—provides little guidance about how best to explore this issue. Nonetheless, we felt it was important to do so. Following from the showcard exercises, two alternative response tasks were developed to assess multiracial neighborhood preferences. Half the overall sample of respondents was randomly assigned to each response task.

In the first task, respondents were shown a card representing a neighborhood that contained fifteen houses and asked to imagine that they lived in such a neighborhood. The respondent's house was in the middle of the diagram, and the other fourteen houses were identified as two black families, five Hispanic families, two Asian families, and five white families. The position of the houses in the neighborhood is shown in panel a of figure 7.8. As the race of the respondent varied, the overall neighborhood composition varied. Therefore, black respondents were rating a neighborhood with three black families, Hispanic respondents were rating a neighborhood with six Hispanic families, and white respondents were rating a neighborhood with six white families. Thus, respondents were never in the position where their group was more numerous than all other groups combined, yet Hispanics and whites were presented with situations where their group represented a plurality. Respondents were asked to indicate whether they would be "very comfortable," "somewhat comfortable," "somewhat uncomfortable," or "very uncomfortable" in this situation.

The proportion of each group saying they would be somewhat or very comfortable with this diverse community was the following: blacks, 87 percent; Hispanics, 89 percent; whites, 55 percent. Those respondents who said they would be uncomfortable were asked why that was so. The most common reason given was that the area was too racially mixed, but most respondents did not clearly articulate the basis for this concern. Respondents who mentioned specific issues suggested that in such a diverse neighborhood, there might be too much conflict and they feared being in the minority.

We designed an alternative task to measure ideal neighborhood preferences. It allowed respondents to build their own neighborhood by filling a blank showcard, as shown in panel b of figure 7.8, indicating the location and number of same and other-race neighbors. Respondents were asked to imagine an ideal neighborhood that had the ethnic and racial mix with which they would personally feel most comfortable, and then fill in the entire card. Panel b shows the mean number of each group—white, black, Hispanic, and Asian—specified by black, Hispanic,

FIGURE 7.8   *Multi-Ethnic Neighborhood Preferences, Split Ballot Experiment*

Panel A	Panel B

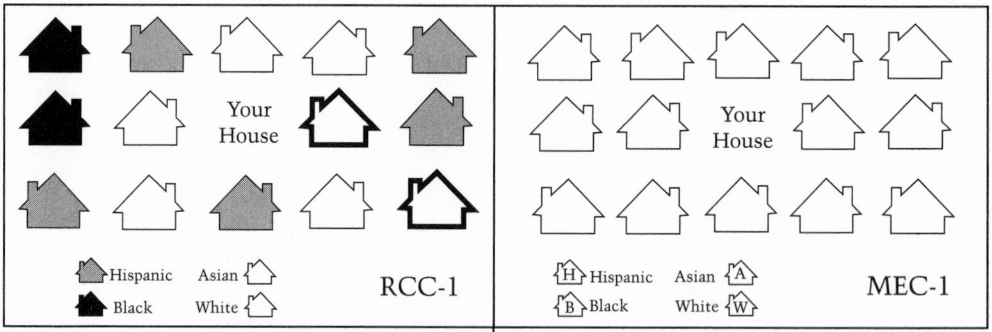

RCC-1 (Panel A legend: Hispanic, Asian, Black, White)

MEC-1 (Panel B legend: H Hispanic, A Asian, B Black, W White)

Percentage of Respondents Who Would Be Very or Somewhat Comfortable in This Neighborhood		Mean Number of (White/Black/Hispanic/Asian) Neighbors in "Ideal" Neighborhood	
Blacks	87	Blacks	3.5 / 4.2 / 2.8 / 2.6
Hispanics	89	Hispanics	3.8 / 2.9 / 4.4 / 2.4
Whites	55	Whites	7.5 / 2.2 . 1.5 / 1.9

Panel C

Percentage of Respondents Who Placed No (Whites/Black/Hispanic/Asian) Neighbors in "Ideal" Neighborhood

Blacks	10.5 / 9.8 / 18.7 / 17.4
Hispanics	9.4 / 11.1 / 4.1 / 16.2
Whites	5.2 / 23.6 / 37.1 / 24.5

and white respondents (possible range = 0 to 14). Each group of respondents exhibits an ethnocentric tendency consistent with their responses to previous questions. The ideal neighborhood for blacks would contain, on average, 4.2 additional blacks, 3.5 whites, 2.8 Hispanics, and 2.6 Asians. For Hispanics, the ideal neighborhood would contain, on average, 4.4 additional Hispanics, 3.8 whites, 2.9 blacks, and 2.4 Asians. The ideal neighborhood for whites contains 7.5 additional whites, 2.2 blacks, 1.5 Hispanics, and 1.9 Asians.

FIGURE 7.9   *Race-Ethnic Composition of "Ideal" Neighborhood*

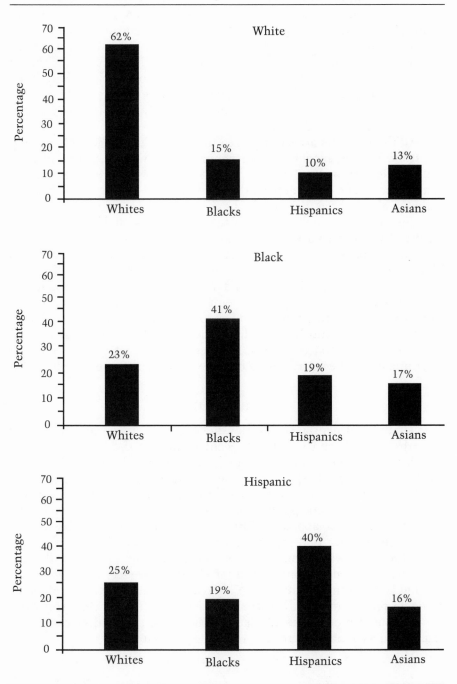

Source: Greater Boston Social Survey 1995.

Panel c illuminates these differences, showing the percentage of respondents who would completely exclude other-group households. Among blacks, about 10 percent of respondents indicated they wanted no whites in their ideal neighborhood, and about 18 percent indicated they wanted no Hispanics or Asians in their neighborhood. The reports of Hispanic respondents are similar with respect to other-race neighbors. Higher percentages of white respondents indicated they would exclude black and Asian (about 24 percent), and especially Hispanic (37 percent) neighbors from their ideal neighborhood.

All these results are summarized in figure 7.9, and they tell a sobering story. Whites, blacks, and Hispanics are all willing to live in integrated neighborhoods. But each group desires a different race-ethnic composition. The ideal neighborhood for whites is one in which they make up about three-fifths of the households, with the other two-fifths distributed about evenly among blacks, Hispanics, and Asians. Blacks want to live in integrated neighborhoods, too. But their ideal neighborhood would have them comprise about two-fifths of the community's households, with the other three-fifths made up of approximately equal numbers of whites, Hispanics, and Asians. Hispanics feel about the same way as blacks, except they want to be the plurality group in the community. Unfortunately, the ideal neighborhood for any one race-ethnic group is incompatible with the ideal for others. This may explain why, even with a concentrated effort to eliminate institutional housing discrimination, the actual levels of segregation remain very high.

Conclusion

This study of residential segregation in Greater Boston conforms closely in both approach and results to recent studies of the Detroit and Los Angeles metropolitan areas. Although at the metropolitan-area level, blacks, Asians, and Hispanics in Greater Boston are not quite as separated from whites as in some other large metropolitan areas, the structure of intergroup perceptions and attitudes contributing to residential segregation is all too apparent. While housing costs are relatively high in the Boston area, we find that minorities could afford to live in a significant number of white communities where rents are no higher than in areas that are predominantly black or Hispanic. Hence, the segregation we find is not primarily related to affordability. Housing discrimination no doubt plays a role in the pattern of residential segregation. However, the individual preferences of blacks, Hispanics, and whites cannot be discounted as a major factor in producing this outcome.

8

THE LABOR MARKET: HOW WORKERS WITH LIMITED SCHOOLING ARE FARING IN GREATER BOSTON

W E ARE now prepared to ask how the triple revolution and the opportunity nexus have figured in the success or failure of blacks, Hispanics, and whites in the regional labor market. In the complex environment of multicultural Boston, where high-tech is king and the economy is strong; where ethnic and racial identities remain powerful; where the spatial distribution of economic activity is constantly shifting; and where the political context is always in flux, who is winning in the labor market and why? Is the boom bypassing the inner city, or does Boston buck the emerging trend of the "jobless ghetto"? Hispanics are at the bottom of the labor market heap today, but will they stay there? How are women workers faring in this boom economy, particularly those who are single parents? These issues and others will be addressed in this chapter, with special attention paid to workers who have no more than a high school degree.

How Do Less-Educated Men Fare?

What we shall demonstrate is that the booming labor market found in the Greater Boston metropolitan area makes it possible for black and Hispanic men with limited schooling to participate in the labor force at rates equal to that of white men. Moreover, the probability of working at some time during the year is equally as high. There is, therefore, no jobless ghetto in Boston as might be found in other cities.

Nonetheless, noncollege black men—even after controlling for differences in human capital—earn little more than two-thirds (69 percent) as much as white men. The large gap in expected annual earnings is due to higher unemployment rates and the higher probability of working in part-time jobs with little opportunity for overtime. In contrast, after controlling for human capital, Hispanic men close the annual earnings gap with white men, as they have unemployment rates no higher than white men and apparently are not limited in their ability to obtain jobs that permit many hours of work. Although their median hourly wage rate is only 85 percent as high as that of black men, their expected annual earnings are 16 percent higher—based on working 36 percent more hours a year.

Our findings suggest that annual earnings depend on a whole range of factors, and those important for improving the labor market fortunes of blacks are quite different than those for Hispanics. If we were asked what one set of policies would most improve the lot of Hispanic men with limited schooling, our answer would be more human capital. If asked the same question regarding noncollege black men, we would suggest focusing much more attention on dealing with what appear to be persistent forms of discrimination in the labor market. The discrepancy in their annual earnings is not so much a function of no experience in the labor market or even lower wages when work is found. It is rather the apparent inability to procure the types of employment that provide secure, steady full-time jobs with the opportunity for overtime and moonlighting. Working time has become the key problem for blacks in Boston, not low labor force participation or a total lack of job experience. What Greater Boston appears to have is a mismatch between black workers with work experience needing more work and employers who may not know that there is a ready and willing labor force who could benefit from more job opportunity. Employers' assumptions about black male workers may be based on a false image of the inner city.

How Do Less-Educated Women Fare?

Greater Boston women with a high school diploma or less have a firm attachment to the workforce. Regardless of race or ethnicity, about two-thirds of these women are in the workforce, and similar proportions have recent employment experience. William Julius Wilson's "jobless ghetto" may be an apt description of Chicago, but it does not fit Boston for either men or women. Nevertheless, black women with limited education do face very high unemployment rates and do receive lower hourly wage rates, resulting in annual earnings that are only two-thirds as high as whites'. Hispanic women, on the other hand, tend to work many more hours per year than whites. That helps to counteract their hourly wage disadvantage relative to white women, giving them annual earnings that are only 6 percent less than whites'.

Black women with limited education suffer extraordinarily high unemployment rates, primarily because they are likelier than whites to be single and to have younger children. This also accounts in large part for their relatively low annual earnings.

Although Hispanic women with limited education have a lower unemployment rate than whites, it could be pushed down even further if these women acquired education levels equal to their white counterparts. This would increase their expected hours even more, raising their annual earnings even further. The high concentration of Hispanic women in the manufacturing sector has allowed them to work longer hours per year than whites, and to receive a relatively good hourly wage rate for what is very low educational attainment.

Human capital improvements will bring Hispanic women beyond parity with white women. For black women, the answer lies neither in human capital nor in labor market discrimination or residential segregation per se. For them, family structure seems to be the key factor that keeps them at the bottom of the annual pay structure.

These summaries are based on a detailed analysis of the Greater Boston labor market. To understand how we arrived at these conclusions, it is necessary to probe more deeply into the nature of underlying labor market dynamics. We begin with an examination of the role of earnings in family incomes.

The Role of Earnings in Family Incomes

Families survive by tapping a variety of income sources. Beside wages and salaries, there are dividends, rental income, and capital gains; pensions and Social Security; welfare and unemployment benefits. For some fortunate households, there are lottery winnings and gifts from relatives or friends. But the most important source of income for the vast majority of families comes from paid work. According to 1992 personal income tax returns, more than four-fifths of adjusted gross household income comes in the form of wages and salaries (77.3 percent) and self-employment earnings (4.3 percent).[1] Interest, dividends, rents, royalties, and net capital gains account for another 12 percent. Moreover, since these nonwage sources tend to be concentrated among wealthier families, non-aged lower- and middle-income households get substantially more than four-fifths of their total income from work.[2]

As a consequence, the family incomes we reported back in chapter 5 largely reflect how well their breadwinners are doing in the labor market. That white families in the Greater Boston Social Survey report an average income of a little better than $48,600 while black families have to make ends meet on 36 percent less ($31,210) and Hispanics on 45 percent less ($26,710) has to do with how many workers there are in each family and the extent to which each is successful at finding and retaining a "good" job.

Most studies of the labor market focus attention on hourly wages as the relevant measure of labor market success; a few focus on annual earnings. In the next chapter we examine the Greater Boston labor force as a whole, and we will restrict our investigation to the determinants of hourly wages. In this chapter, however, in order to zero in on the labor market prospects of those workers who are most vulnerable in an increasingly globalized and technologically advanced economy—those with no more than a high school degree—we take a more detailed look at how individual earnings are generated, examining each of the major components of labor market activity: the probability of participating in the labor force; the probability of working throughout the year uninterrupted by unemployment; the number of hours worked during a typical week; and finally hourly wages. From these components, we generate a summary measure of labor market success—the "expected value" of annual earnings—for groups of workers who share such characteristics as race and ethnicity.

We employ this method for two reasons. One is because families live by the year, not the hourly paycheck. The hourly wage is the appropriate measure to study if we are interested in the "price" of labor per se. But by itself, the hourly wage does not supply sufficient information to ascertain a family's standard of living. A $50-an-hour job may be a superb one, *if* it is available full-time throughout the year. If one gets to work only two weeks at such a job and then spends six months looking for more work, the annual earnings associated with this wage will leave a family in poverty. Moreover, it turns out that we can understand the large interracial and interethnic differences in living standards only if we pay close attention to differences in working time as well as differences in pay. How Greater Bostonians survive in this high-cost-of-living metropolitan region depends very much on getting a good job, working at it steadily, and keeping it. We will investigate just how successful various groups in Boston are at doing this.

Important Themes in Understanding Individual Earnings

While workers' annual earnings reflect both the hourly price of their labor and the amount of labor they offer the market, labor economists have paid particular attention to the determinants of hourly wage rates: the price of a given hour of work.

In truth, the price we pay for any good or service—whether it is a grain merchant's bid for #2 winter wheat, an airline's purchase of a jumbo jet, or what an employer pays per hour for a journeyman carpenter or counter help at the local McDonald's—is ultimately determined by supply and demand. But having acknowledged this, it is widely accepted that the pricing of labor is a far more complex matter than that for nearly any other good or service because the "peculiarities" affecting supply and demand in labor markets are so pervasive. These include, but are by no means limited to, various forms of racial, ethnic, and gender discrimination; the problem of limited information about the availability of jobs; the difficulty of uncovering the true "quality" of a potential worker; unequal spatial access to jobs based on residential living patterns; the use of networks by workers in seeking employment, as well as employers in seeking workers; and the impact of such factors as specialized skills (for example, computer knowledge) and union membership. All of these can be shoehorned into the traditional supply-and-demand framework, but in doing so we do not make it any easier to parse out what really determines an individual's wage.

While we cannot do justice to the wide assortment of factors that should be taken into account when attempting to quantify the determinants of earnings, we can briefly list the key elements that social scientists have studied in their search to explain how wages and earnings are determined.

Human Capital

Over the past quarter of a century, most studies of earnings have focused on variables associated with human capital—the level of formal schooling, occupational experience, on-the-job training, vocational education, health status, and migration, to name the most obvious. Assuming away the peculiarities of labor market imperfections (such as discrimination, lack of information), there is even some attempt in this literature to infer the distribution of innate abilities from the distribution of earnings. If two people with the same measured human capital earn very different wage rates, then—in the absence of discrimination and other imperfections—the remaining differences can be attributed to unmeasured differences in ability, motivation, or work effort (Becker 1985).

In virtually all studies of wage determination, years of schooling is found to be positively associated with earnings. The same is true of job experience and health status. Commonly, such human capital models explain somewhere between 20 and 40 percent of the variance in individual earnings. While this might seem low, one needs to recognize that there are literally thousands of factors that can influence wage differences. That just a few can explain as much as two-fifths of the total variation in earnings speaks to the remarkable economy of this single explanation.

In most conventional human capital models, there is a large gap between the wage rates of black and white workers and between the wages of men and women. Some of this gap is normally explained by differences in human capital. Then, using various simulation techniques, the remaining unexplained variance is usually taken to be a measure of "discrimination." Thus, for example, if there remains a statistically significant wage gap between black and white men after controlling for a battery of human capital attributes, the remaining gap—although technically nothing more than unexplained variance or, what is the same, a "residual"—is chalked up to labor market discrimination, which is not and cannot be directly captured in the model.

The practice of using the residual in earnings models as a measure of labor market discrimination has not gone unchallenged. In particular, a number of critics have argued that such variables as "years of education" are a poor proxy for human capital. After all, two workers could have gone to school for the same number of years, with one graduating at the top of the class, the other at the bottom. To suggest that in this case any resulting wage gap is due to labor market "discrimination" clearly seems misguided, especially if the class valedictorian is white and the class laggard black. Part of this wage gap might be related to the greater difficulty blacks face in the labor market, but much and perhaps even all of the gap could be related to differential ability. Conversely, if the class valedictorian is black and the class laggard white and they received the same wages, the absence of a wage gap would mask racial discrimination between individuals with the same years of schooling but different ability.

In a controversial *Atlantic Monthly* article appearing in 1971, Richard Herrnstein argued that the United States was becoming a more meritocratic society. While racial bias had historically played an unconscionable role in limiting black economic opportunity, racial differences now were due less to outright discrimination and more to differential abilities or merit. In particular, Herrnstein argued that test scores were predicting people's life chances better than ever before. In reviewing this and later work, Christopher Jencks and Meredith Phillips summed up the argument succinctly. In the new meritocratic America: " 'Smart' people rose to the top of the economic ladder, while 'dumb' people languished in poverty" (Jencks and Phillips 1996, 2). In 1994, Herrnstein, along with his colleague Charles Murray, revived the meritocratic argument in their book, *The Bell Curve.*

What test scores actually measure is a matter of great dispute. Herrnstein and Murray clearly believe that tests measure "aptitudes" or "abilities"—traits that are normally considered fixed at an early age if not innate, and difficult if not impossible to augment. That individuals test differently reflects differences in the ability to learn new things, presumably an important advantage in an information age. Such a fatalistic view of test scores is challenged by those who argue that tests measure the accumulation of knowledge and skills, some of which are useful in the workplace. In Jencks's and Phillips's words, what counts is "what you know, not how hard you had to work to learn it" (Jencks and Phillips 1996, 4). Instead of "aptitude," test scores really measure "achievement." This optimistic view suggests that while individuals' aptitudes differ, all of us can improve our skills with the help of good schools and solid effort, and that these enhanced skills will pay off in the labor market. This latter view is much closer to the human capital theory, which focuses on the real investments people make in themselves to improve their employment opportunities.

One of the more ambitious attempts at empirically unraveling the forces of aptitude, achievement, and discrimination appears in the work of the Harvard economist Ronald Ferguson (1993; 1995). Using the 1979 *National Longitudinal Survey of Youth* panel data, Ferguson introduced into an hourly earnings model for twenty-three-year-old black and white men their Armed Forces Qualification Test (AFQT) scores for reading and math skills. The question he poses is how much of the increased racial wage gap during the 1980s can be explained by differences in human capital—specifically, level of schooling and tested ability—and how much by discrimination. What he finds is striking. If test scores are *not* included in the model, the black-white wage gap for the nation as a whole during the period from 1986 to 1988 was is in the range of 16 percent. Conventionally, this gap would be interpreted as a measure of labor market discrimination. However, once test scores are added, the gap shrinks to only about 5 percent. Essentially, two-thirds of the apparent discrimination is a reflection of the poorer skills of young black men, as evidenced by test scores (Ferguson 1993, fig. 7).[3] As Ferguson puts it, "averaged across all regions and schooling levels, the residual difference in earnings between young black and white males would have virtually disappeared by the middle of the decade if blacks and whites had equal test scores" (Ferguson 1993, 22).[4] In related research, the Baruch College economics professor June O'Neill, currently director of the Congressional Budget Office, finds that the actual .829 black/white hourly wage ratio for men age twenty-two to twenty-nine rises to .991 when region, schooling, AFQT test scores, and actual work experience are taken into account (O'Neill 1990).

Does this mean that the efforts of the civil rights movement and civil rights legislation have met their goals of a bias-free environment? Is the remaining gap in wages due to differences in aptitude that simply cannot be erased by antidiscrimination policy? Not necessarily. Based on further research, Ferguson finds that test score differences are related to the school resources black and white children are accorded. Fitting data from Texas and Alabama into a specially constructed "educational production function" that makes reading test scores a function of a variety of school inputs, Ferguson has found that the quality of teachers (as measured by their tested ability and years of teaching experience) and class size both influence student test scores (Ferguson 1994, 1995a, 1997). Moreover, he demonstrates that good teachers have a strong predilection to teach in districts where the educational level of adults in the community is high, where schools are integrated rather than all-black, and where teacher salaries are relatively high compared to those in surrounding districts. Hence, "money matters for raising test scores," for this helps attract the best teachers to a given district.

This research helps inform the debate over the impact of achievement versus aptitude. Combining Ferguson's test score studies with his school resource findings, it appears that much of the difference in black/white earnings reflects real differences in tested skills, but that these differences result primarily from inequality in human capital investment, rather than differences in innate aptitude. Near the end of this research, Ferguson concludes that:

> the most important disparities in opportunity may occur before young people even enter the labor market: in the provision of schooling and other resources that influence skill-building and the socialization of youths. These include not only current disparities in the quality of schooling and recreation and discouraging messages from society at large, but also racial inequities in past generations of institutions that prepared parents and grandparents for their roles as teachers and care givers. [Ferguson 1995, 67]

In essence, discrimination is still pervasive in America, but it is situated not so much in the labor market per se as in *all* the institutions that prepare young people to enter the world of work. With returns to education and skill increasing as a result of changes in technology and global interdependence, unequal access to human capital along all its dimensions (schooling, training, family and community socialization, health, job experience) increases in importance.

The Social Environment

The importance of neighborhood and, more generally, the social environment on individual success in the workplace has played a prominent role in sociological accounts of the labor market. One prominent observer working from this perspective, William Julius Wilson, argues that in many central-city black neighborhoods, a majority of the adult population has no connection to the world of work—no current or recent job experience, no current or recent effort to search for work. The jobless ghetto, in which work has disappeared, is a product of the growth in concentrated poverty, and especially the growth in the number of census tracts in which 40 percent or more of the population lives in poverty. The exodus of nonpoverty families, both white and black, from these areas has left them depopulated and bereft of the resources necessary for economic success.

One of the reasons work has disappeared from the inner-city ghettoes of Chicago, according to Wilson's meticulous urban research, is that more than 40 percent of the city's employers refuse to, or simply do not, advertise entry-level jobs in Chicago newspapers, preferring to recruit via employee referral or advertisements in ethnic neighborhoods or suburban newspapers outside ghetto areas (Wilson 1996). Wilson's jobless ghetto is a synthesis of several discrete arguments regarding changes in the nature of jobs, the location of jobs, and the attitudes of employers.

With regard to the changing nature of work, there is ubiquitous evidence that the returns to education have become more unequal, at least since the early 1980s (Kodrzycki 1996). This means that small differences in schooling now generate larger differences in earnings. The growing gap in returns to schooling is generally credited to trends in the supply and demand for highly educated workers. During the past fifteen years, the supply of college-educated workers expanded, but at a rate slower than demand. On the supply side, demography explains much of the slowdown: we have reached the end of the large baby boom cohorts entering the workforce. On the demand side, several possibilities are offered, though none has been demonstrated unequivocally to be true. They include shifts in the industrial mix toward more education-intensive industries; changing skill requirements within industries; technological change favoring workers with more education; and the role international trade has played in placing downward pressure on wages at the low end of the education distribution.

Linked to Ferguson's studies showing that differences in human capital explain most of the difference in black-white earnings, the finding of a growing wage gap related to schooling suggests that even as black education and test scores converge to those of whites, the racial earnings gap can still grow because of the increased return to differences in these factors. Hence, whatever progress we might be making toward equalizing school resources and therefore economic opportunity could be undermined by the growing importance of even small differences in school achievement.

One indication of the polarization in the U.S. job structure comes from the U.S. Bureau of Labor Statistics. An examination of employment growth between 1989 and 1995 finds that the proportion of jobs in the highest-earning occupation-industry groups grew, as did the proportion of jobs in the lowest-earning groups. The proportion of jobs in the middle declined (Ilg 1996). To the extent that this continues to be true, and to the extent that small differences in schooling now determine whether an individual makes it into a high- or low-wage job, even those small differences in human capital will have an amplified impact on earnings.

The Spatial Environment

There is a spatial dimension to the earnings distribution as well. Studies show that metropolitan areas experiencing slow employment growth—such as the older industrial cities of the Midwest—are the ones experiencing the sharpest declines in real wages and family incomes (Drennan, Tobier, and Lewis 1996). Since black workers are disproportionately concentrated in these cities, this helps explain the continued gap in black-white income ratios. In these areas, blacks are now disadvantaged by the loss of what were high-wage-premium industries—those like auto and steel, that pay well relative to the skills required. If whites live disproportionately in places like San Jose and San Diego and blacks are more concentrated in cities like Detroit, the racial gap will rise as a result of these larger wage and income trends in the economy.

Even for blacks living in high-growth metropolitan areas, Timothy Bartik of the Upjohn Institute has shown that the labor market benefits of such locations are different than for whites (Bartik 1992). For blacks, living in a high-growth city manifests itself mainly in greater employment—higher labor force participation and lower unemployment rates—rather than higher wages. For whites, the benefits are more evenly split between higher employment and higher pay (Bartik 1992). The benefits to living in a high-growth locale are especially robust for high school dropouts, youth, and blacks. According to Bartik, "These marginal groups are most dependent on a tight local economy to allow them to obtain better jobs or indeed any jobs at all" (Bartik 1992, p.59).

These findings are consistent with several other studies. Bound and Holzer found that during the 1970s, the decline in manufacturing employment accounted for one-third to one-half of the increased joblessness among young black male dropouts (Bound and Holzer 1993). Similarly, using a sample of individuals with no more than a high school diploma, Bluestone, Stevenson, and Tilly found that deindustrialization was responsible for nearly half the decline in young white men's annual earnings between the 1960s and the 1980s, and 40 percent of the even larger loss in young black men's annual earnings (Bluestone, Stevenson, and Tilly 1992).

There is also a possible spatial dimension to labor market success *within* metropolitan areas. In reviewing an enormous amount of research on the racial differences in labor market opportunity, Moss and Tilly paid particular attention to the spatial mismatch hypothesis, which suggests that blacks living in the central city—where most metropolitan-area black families are located—are at a disadvantage in terms of job opportunity because so much industry has moved from inner-city to suburban locations (Moss and Tilly 1991). Residential segregation is consequently a significant factor in the labor market. The theory is clear and reasonable enough. But empirical verification has been difficult to obtain. Given the high level of residential segregation in many cities, it is hard to tell whether an earnings gap is due to spatial mismatch, to outright discrimination, or even to differences in measured or unmeasured human capital.

Statistical Discrimination and "Cognitive" Maps

While "space" in its conventional geographic form may not provide a definitive explanation for the continuing racial earnings gap in many metropolitan areas, it is possible that residential location still plays a role through the "cognitive maps" that employers and employees use when it comes to job search. Employers may deliberately avoid inner-city neighborhoods when they search for new recruits. Inner-city workers may avoid seeking employment in suburban locations not because they cannot easily get to them, but because they believe that their attempts at seeking employment there will be fruitless.

Such behavior is more generally referred to as "statistical discrimination": a practice in which employers judge an individual not on his or her own credentials (which may be difficult, time-consuming, or expensive to ascertain), but on beliefs about the characteristics of the typical or average member of the demographic group to which the individual belongs. If employers experience better performance from a certain demographic group—or even if they just *perceive* better performance—then it is likely the employer will choose from this demographic group again and again when new employees are needed. Similarly, employers who have a bad experience with a number of members of a particular demographic group may tend to stay away from other members of this group in future hiring decisions. Interviews with Chicago-area employers by Joleen Kirschenman and Kathryn Neckerman (1991) in the late 1980s revealed that many employers there did practice statistical discrimination, judging individual job applicants according to what they believed to be true of the demographic group to which the individual belonged. Many employers surmised that a black applicant would not make as good an employee as, for example, a white immigrant. As such, many refrained from hiring blacks whenever other applicants were available.

Kirschenman and Neckerman found that some of those employers who were willing to hire black workers nevertheless practiced statistical discrimination along other dimensions. A black job applicant who lived in public housing or went to an inner-city public high school might be automatically placed at the end of the hiring queue, the employer taking a dim view of the applicant's likely success on the job. The result of statistical discrimination is that job applicants are, metaphorically, lined up in order of their desirability to the employer. Employers work their way down this job queue until they fill all their vacancies. If labor markets are not very tight, the vacancies are all filled before the employer reaches the end of the queue, and the remaining workers are left without jobs. In such a scenario, it would take extraordinarily low unemployment rates for the employer to reach the end of the queue (Thurow 1975).

Institutional Factors

The growth in earnings inequality and the deterioration of real earnings at the low end of the distribution has also been tied to institutional factors. The decline in the proportion of workers who are unionized, and the diminished effectiveness of unions in protecting their most vulnerable members, contribute to earnings inequality (Freeman 1990; Blackburn, Bloom, and Freeman 1990; Bluestone and Harrison 1987). Similarly, the decline in the real value of the federal minimum wage has meant that earnings at the low end are no longer shored up as they were in previous generations (Kodrzycki 1996; Moss and Tilly 1991).

Cultural Capital

In an effort to explain the prevalence of low wages in inner-city neighborhoods, a number of analysts have turned their attention from traditionally measured human capital to what Lawrence Mead has termed "cultural capital" (Mead 1986; 1992). Mead contends that high rates of joblessness and low earnings are due neither to structural constraints in the labor market nor to employer discrimination. Rather, poor economic outcomes reflect character deficiencies and deviant values of central-city residents. Edward Banfield (1970) suggested much the same thing nearly thirty years ago in his controversial book, *The Unheavenly City*. Instead of being constrained to unemployment or confined to low-wage jobs as a consequence of low skills, lack of jobs, or outright discrimination, "underclass" individuals choose not to work on a regular basis or choose to work in the casual or so-called underground economy. According to cultural capital theorists, inner-city culture has created negative attitudes toward work, along with other antisocial behavior. More generally, cultural capital refers to the impact of socioeconomic status, or the intergenerational transmission of social class: the role of family background variables such as parents' educational attainment, income, and occupation (Blau and Duncan 1967; Jencks 1972).

Harry Holzer (1994) attempts to reconcile the apparently conflicting viewpoints between Wilson and Mead by positing that the deterioration in labor market outcomes for young blacks may be the result of interactions between William Julius Wilson's demand-side forces and Mead's supply-side forces. He argues that while Wilson emphasizes the role of labor market demand shifts that disadvantage black workers, the result of those shifts has been a reduction in the wage rate. If Mead's arguments can be construed to mean that young black workers have a very elastic labor supply curve—that their willingness to work is highly sensitive to the going wage rate—then a reduction in labor demand, coupled with a highly elastic labor supply, would produce both low wages and large reductions in employment.

Social Capital

A relatively new approach to understanding labor market outcomes, under the rubric of social capital theory, focuses attention on how the social or institutional networks within which individuals are embedded constrain or expand labor market opportunities. James Coleman, one of the pioneers in this approach, notes at least three kinds of social capital (Coleman 1988).

The first involves obligations and expectations. If there is an expectation of reciprocity between two people, then actions by one individual on behalf of the other establish an expectation for the first and an obligation for the second. Essentially, individuals acquire "credit slips" that can be drawn upon, for example, when it comes to job search. In his best-selling novel *Bonfire of the Vanities*, Tom Wolfe refers to this as a "favor bank," with its own elaborate set of rules [Wolfe 1987].

The second form of social capital involves information channeling. Individuals embedded in "thick" social networks with high degrees of "connectivity" to good job prospects presumably can use the information supplied by those networks to good advantage (Montgomery 1991; Corcoran, Datcher, and Duncan 1980; Granovetter 1974, 1982). One aspect of this type of social capital is related to the concept of spatial mismatch studied by John Kasarda and William Julius Wilson (Kasarda

1988; 1990; Wilson 1987). A social network is potentially limited geographically. If individuals reside in one geographic area and job openings exist in another, it is possible that those individuals will not be part of a social network that informs about those job openings.

The third form of social capital identified by Coleman is similar to cultural capital. It involves the existence of norms and sanctions that can facilitate certain actions and constrain others.

Social capital exists within families, neighborhoods, and communities. In terms of the labor market, social capital takes a number of forms. An important one is worker job referrals. These can come from a sibling, a parent, or a friend. Social networks can also be important in terms of job promotion within a firm.

Networks, as a form of social capital, can take the form of either an asset or a liability. Certain networks lead to increased human capital investment; others to dropping out of school. Certain networks provide job leads that promote regular employment at decent wages; other networks socialize individuals to shun work in the regular labor market. In either case, social capital may play a significant role in explaining differences in individual employment and earnings outcomes. One may therefore think of social capital and cultural capital as providing an individual with a social structure of opportunity. In a study of female employment in metropolitan Los Angeles, researchers found that while cultural capital factors like growing up in a single-parent family, in a welfare-dependent family, and/or in public housing substantially reduced the likelihood that a black woman would be working, use of social networks among this group improved the odds of working (Stoloff et al. 1996).

The Determinants of Labor Market Success

With these various themes providing a foundation for our investigation of the Greater Boston labor market, we are now well situated to present empirical results based on our use of the GBSS data. In this chapter, we shall do this in the form of separate analyses for men and women who have limited education and are between the ages of twenty-one and sixty-five. We pay special attention to those who have not gone beyond high school, since it is the less well educated labor force that faces the greatest difficulties in the new information age economy. These two gender-based studies not only look at hourly wages, but also investigate the determinants of working time and annual earnings by analyzing labor force participation, unemployment, and weekly hours.

Here, we focus on racial and ethnic differences, trying to understand what factors explain lingering differences in labor market success as measured by labor force participation, unemployment, hours worked, hourly wages, and ultimately annual earnings. In the next chapter, we shall focus attention on who gets into what kinds of jobs and how human, social, and cultural capital affect such outcomes.

Study #1: How Are Noncollege Workers Faring in the Greater Boston Labor Market? The Case of Men

For more than two decades the average real wage rate of workers who have not attended college has dropped significantly. We know from various studies that the decline in wage rates—and the increase in overall earnings inequality—has many sources. Among the suspects are skill-biased technological change, increased global competition, accelerated capital mobility, deindustrialization, downsizing, the shift from manufacturing to services, industry deregulation, the decline in unionism, and an increase in low-skill labor supply as a result of immigration (Burtless 1990; Bluestone 1994). Controversy surrounds the question of how much each of these factors has contributed to this trend, but there is little dispute that workers with limited schooling have suffered.

Annual Earnings

We can begin our investigation of labor market earnings by examining "expected" annual earnings for black, Hispanic, and white men between the ages of twenty-one and sixty-five. Expected annual earnings for each group is calculated according to the following formula:

$$(8.1) \ Y = pr\,(LFP) \ \times \ (1 \ - \ pr\,(U)) \times H/Wk \times 52 \times W$$

> where: Y = expected annualized earnings
> $pr\,(LFP)$ = probability of participating in the labor force
> $(1 \ - \ pr(UR))$ = $(1 \ -$ probability of being unemployed)
> H/Wk = mean hours worked per week
> W = median hourly wage

Annual earnings are therefore a function of the group probabilities of being in the labor force and being employed, as well as each group's median weekly work hours and measured median hourly wages.[5]

Figure 8.1 compares the annual earnings of men with schooling beyond high school with those who have no more than the high school degree. Two things are immediately clear from inspection of this figure,

FIGURE 8.1   *"Expected" Annual Earnings, Men*

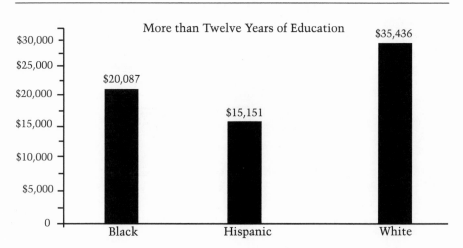

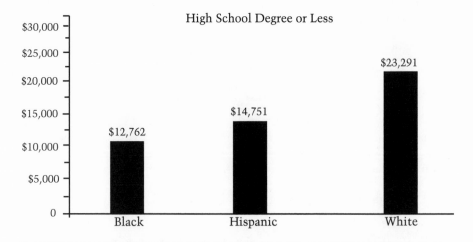

Source: Greater Boston Social Survey 1995.

which summarizes the impact of both schooling and race-ethnicity. Going beyond high school pays off handsomely, particularly for black and white men. At $20,087, the estimated "expected" annual earnings of black men with some college are 57 percent higher than those who have no more than a high school degree. For white men, additional education beyond high school provides expected annual earnings of a little more than $35,400, a premium worth over $12,000 a year, or 52 percent above the average for those with no more than a high school diploma.

Human capital clearly pays off in Boston, at least for blacks and whites. For Hispanics, schooling beyond high school also pays a premium, but it is quite small—only about 3 percent. This tiny college premium is something of a mystery, to which we shall return.

Figure 8.1 also demonstrates a large racial and ethnic gap in annual earnings, in line with the family income series presented earlier. For men with some college or more, blacks earn less than three-fifths (57 percent) of what whites earn; Hispanics only 43 percent as much. Some of this clearly reflects differences in the average level of education beyond high school attained by each of these groups. Three-fourths (75 percent) of the white men with more than high school educations have four or more years of college. The comparable figures for black and Hispanic men are only 47 percent and 11 percent, respectively.[6]

When we confine our examination to those with no more than a high school education, the racial and ethnic gaps in annual earnings are somewhat diminished, but by no means small. Blacks earn 55 percent of white men's earnings; Hispanics, 63 percent. Some of this difference is no doubt due to different high school completion rates. Less than 3 percent of white men in the GBSS did not finish high school. The comparable figures for black and Hispanic men are 20 percent and 58 percent, respectively. How much of the large earnings gaps can be explained by these different schooling levels will be examined later in this chapter.

Hourly Wage Rates

From the algorithm for expected annual earnings, it is obvious that the racial and ethnic gaps in annual earnings can be due to variation in labor force participation rates, unemployment rates, differences in weekly hours, and/or differences in wages. Figure 8.2 provides a preliminary look at hourly wage rates. Again, it is clear that there is an earnings gap due to education, as a comparison of the top and bottom panels of this chart suggests. Yet, as in the annual earnings chart, there are substantial differences in hourly wages even within the group with high school degree or less. Black men earn 83 percent as much as white men; Hispanic men have a median hourly wage rate just 71 percent as high as their white male counterparts.

A comparison of these hourly wage gaps with annual earnings ratios gives a clear indication of how working time plays a critical role in racially differentiated living standards. While the black/white male wage ratio for those with high school or less is 83 percent, the black/white annual earnings ratio is only 55 percent. On an annual basis, non-college white men earn almost double what black men make. The annual earnings gap for Hispanics is nearly as large (63 percent), but this reflects more a difference in hourly wages and less a difference in annual hours worked. Hispanic men with limited schooling earn more than

FIGURE 8.2   *Median Hourly Wage Rate, Men*

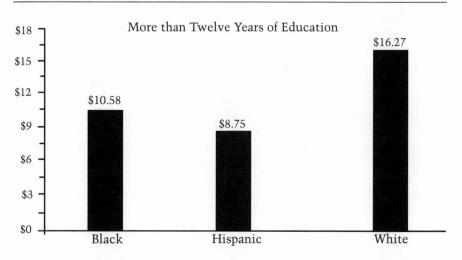

More than Twelve Years of Education

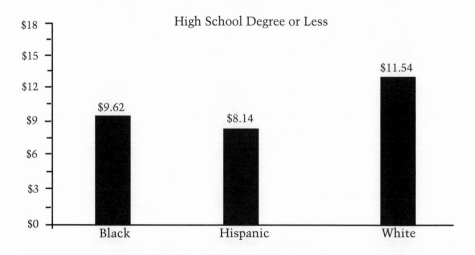

High School Degree or Less

Source: Greater Boston Social Survey 1995.

black men with more or less equivalent schooling not because they are better paid, but because they work more per year.

Annual Work Time

Differences in annual working time are depicted in figure 8.3.[7] For white men in the Greater Boston region, longer hours of work are correlated with more schooling, a finding consistent with national trends.[8] Over

FIGURE 8.3   *Expected Annual Work Hours, Men*

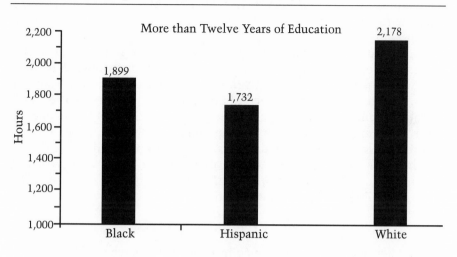

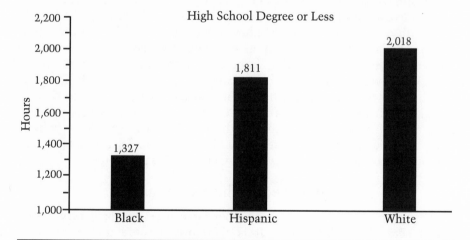

Source: Greater Boston Social Survey 1995.

the course of a full year, white men who have gone beyond high school work an average of 160 hours more than those who have never gone to college. The reverse seems to be true among Hispanic men, with those who are less educated working at least as many hours as those who have gone on to college.

By far, the largest education gap is found among black men. Those who have no more than a high school education can be expected to work nearly 575 fewer hours per year than those who have had some college—and only about *two-thirds* as much working time as less-educated white men. Hence, even if less-educated black men were at wage parity with white men, their annual earnings would trail by a huge amount.

This finding might appear to be consistent with the concept of the jobless ghetto. Black men in Greater Boston work, on average, a lot less than white men. Presumably, given our measure of "expected" annual hours, which is generated by combining labor force participation and unemployment rates with mean weekly hours, this could be due to lower workforce participation among inner-city blacks. If so, Boston would be following the same discouraging pattern found in other cities. But this does not turn out to be the case. Indeed, *black and Hispanic men in Greater Boston were just as likely to be in the labor force as white men*. This is clearly shown in figure 8.4.

Labor Force Participation

Among men with at least some college, about 90 percent of black, Hispanic, and white men reported being in the labor force at the time of the GBSS survey. Similarly, better than 85 percent of black and Hispanic men with no more than a high school education also reported that they were in the labor force. If anything, less well educated men of color were *more likely* to be in the labor force than comparably educated white men. When we further restrict our sample to black men with no more than a high school diploma who live in census blocks that are majority-black, the labor force participation rate remained high: above 82 percent. Even after restricting the sample to those living in census tracts where more than a quarter of the households live in poverty, nearly 70 percent of black men with limited education were in the labor force.

Employed in the Last Year

By definition, those who are in the labor force are either presently working or actively seeking work. It is therefore possible that each race-ethnic group could have the same proportion participating in the labor force as we have indeed found, but still have very different probabilities of actually working. This would mean that blacks, Hispanics, and whites could be equally present in the labor force, but blacks and/or Hispanics could have higher jobless rates. In this case, the image of the jobless ghetto would still survive.

To test this, we asked each respondent in the GBSS if they had worked anytime during the twelve months preceding the survey. As figure 8.5 amply demonstrates, education plays an important role in explaining whether an individual worked sometime during the previous

FIGURE 8.4   *Labor Force Participation Rate, Men*

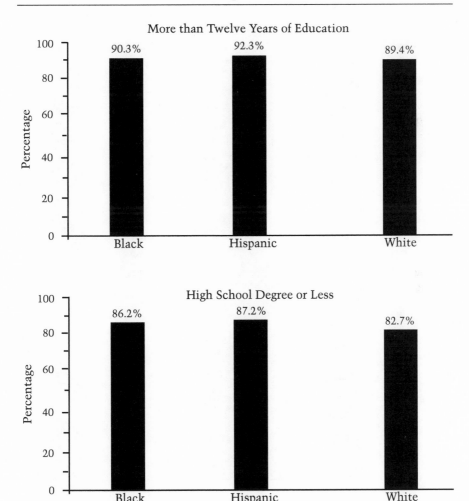

More than Twelve Years of Education

Source: Greater Boston Social Survey 1995.

year. Men with some college were more than 90 percent likely to have held a job. The percentage drops off sharply for those with no more than a high school degree, with only about 75 percent reporting having worked during the year.

But once again, the chart shows that there is no discernible difference in the probability of holding a job during the year across race and

FIGURE 8.5   *Employed in the Last Year, Men*

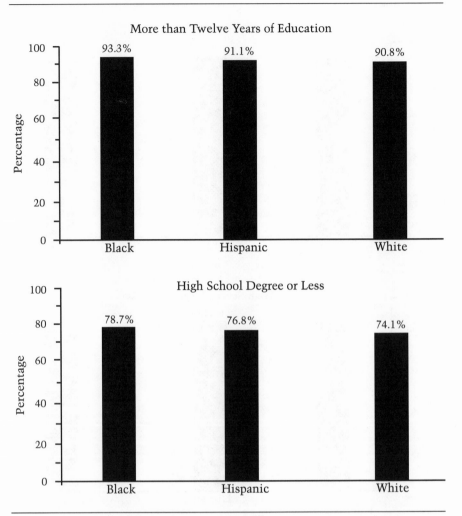

Source: Greater Boston Social Survey 1995.

ethnic groups. Black and Hispanic men in the Greater Boston region were just as likely to have worked sometime during the year as whites, once we control for education. Moreover, even for black men with no college, living in a "majority-minority" neighborhood, where more than a quarter of the families are in poverty, the likelihood of having worked at least sometime during the year was no less than 70 percent. This still leaves nearly a third of the potential black male labor force in the ghetto outside the world of work—but this is a far cry from all, or even most,

of them—and most black men in Boston, even those with little education, do not live in such heavily impoverished neighborhoods.[9]

That we find such high labor force participation and employment rates
for black men in Boston's booming economy has some precedent in earlier
work on the Boston labor market conducted by Richard Freeman in the late
1980s and related studies by Paul Osterman. Both found that as employment expanded rapidly and the labor market tightened during the
mid-1980s in Boston, the employment opportunities for disadvantaged
men improved significantly and the proportion of the inner-city poor who
found work increased accordingly (Freeman 1991; Osterman 1991).

But if there is no difference in labor force participation rates and no
difference in the probability of working sometime during the year, how
do we explain the large gap in annual working time among black, Hispanic, and white men? Part of the answer lies in the difference in education. In the Greater Boston region, over 68 percent of white men have
attended college, while only 53 percent of black men and 20 percent of
Hispanic men have. Given the lower labor force participation and employment rates for those with no college, the overall difference in working time by race and ethnicity could simply reflect differences in schooling. But recall that *within* schooling categories, black men still worked
many fewer hours per year than either Hispanics or whites. What is
responsible for this difference in working time?

Unemployment

Unemployment is one answer. Black men who have not attended college were twice as likely to be unemployed at the time of the GBSS
survey as either Hispanics or whites (see figure 8.6). This is unfortunately consistent with what has become a long-standing constant in
national labor force data: black unemployment rates have remained
stubbornly stuck at twice the prevailing aggregate unemployment rate,
year in and year out, throughout the entire post–World War II era.

One might find this result somewhat mystifying, given the finding
that black men are just as likely to have worked during the twelve
months prior to participating in the GBSS survey. How can the unemployment rate of black men be double the rate for Hispanic and white
men while the chances of working sometime during the year are nearly
identical? The answer reveals a great deal of what is going on in the
Greater Boston labor market for black men. While they are as likely to
work sometime during the year as Hispanic or white men, they are
much more likely to cycle in and out of jobs. As a result, at any single
point in time—for example, when they were interviewed for the
GBSS—they were more likely to be found unemployed. So black men
have more *spells* of unemployment over any discrete period of time, and

FIGURE 8.6   *Unemployment Rate, Men*

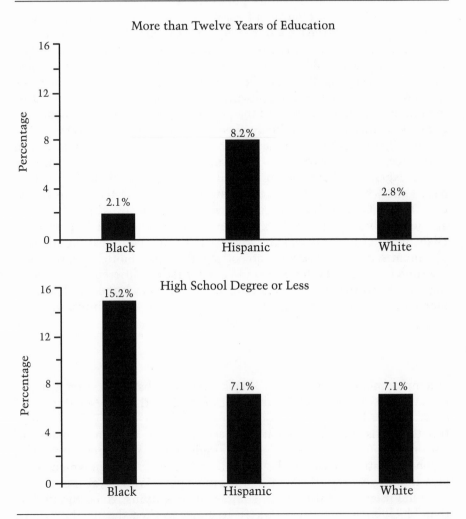

More than Twelve Years of Education

High School Degree or Less

Source: Greater Boston Social Survey 1995.

tend to hold a job for a shorter period of time. Hence, the problem in Greater Boston is not so much whether black men can find a job, but whether they can find one that provides them with steady employment. The booming Boston economy has provided work for those with even modest schooling, but for black men these jobs tend more often to be part-time, seasonal, and contingent.

This does not appear to be as serious a problem for Hispanics. To be sure, among Latino men with college, the unemployment rate appears to be exceptionally high compared with the estimates for black and white men. We do not have an explanation for this anomalous finding, with the exception that the sample size for this particular population is small. Recall that only 20 percent of all Hispanic men in our weighted sample have gone beyond high school. (The unweighted n for this subsample is only 38.) Therefore, it is possible that the 8.2 percent unemployment rate for this group reflects nothing more than a statistical fluke based on small sample size.

But what is extraordinary is the relatively low unemployment rate among Hispanic men with no more than a high school diploma. The rate is virtually the same as the white male rate and half the black rate. The surprise is compounded by the fact that even within this schooling category, Hispanics are much more likely never to have finished high school. Overall, nearly 60 percent of the Greater Boston weighted sample of Hispanic men did not complete high school, compared with 20 percent of black men and only 3 percent of white men. If schooling were the main determinant of joblessness, we would have expected Hispanic men to have the highest unemployment rate by far, cycling in and out of work at least as often as black men. That they do not suggests that other factors, including immigrant status, may explain this confounding finding.

Working Time-Weekly Hours

Part of the racial difference in annual hours is due to differences in the probability of being unemployed at least some time during the year. But there is another source every bit as important, particularly for black men. This is the difference in usual weekly hours, a reflection of part-time versus full-time work and the degree to which individuals engage in overtime. As figure 8.7 demonstrates, there are large differences in mean weekly hours by race and ethnicity, especially for men with no more than a high school degree. White men, regardless of education, appear to be workaholics, spending between 48.2 and 50.5 hours a week at work. Hispanics are more likely to work something closer to the standard 40-hour work week, those with less than college educations working a bit more than those who have been to college.

The group with the lowest average work time is noncollege black men. They average under 35 hours per week. Because of these large differences in working time, even if all men had the same wage rate and identical labor force participation and employment rates, white men would earn, on average, 45 percent more per year than black men and 17 percent more than Hispanic men. Working time is therefore a critical element in annual earnings differentials, especially for less-educated

FIGURE 8.7   *Mean Weekly Hours, Men*

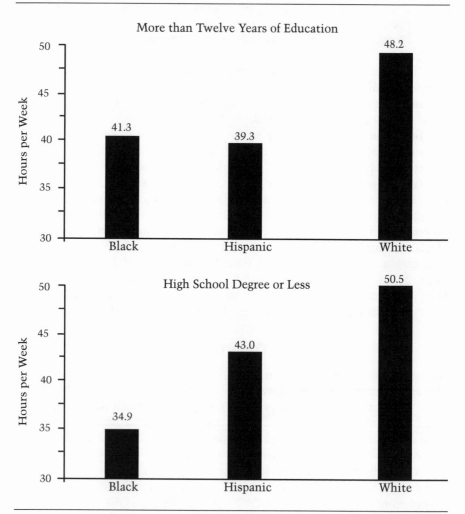

Source: Greater Boston Social Survey 1995.

black men. Given the large difference in working time, this single factor could be the most important component of the racial annual earnings gap. In the strong Boston economy, we seem to have not a jobless problem for black men, but one related to high job turnover and a high incidence of part-time employment.

Probing deeper into the GBSS data provides some insight into why minority men are working fewer weekly hours than whites. Nearly 25 percent of black men with a high school education or less reported working at part-time jobs averaging just 25 hours per week or less. Only 3 percent of Hispanic men and 5 percent of white men reported working this little. At the other end of the spectrum, blacks were much less likely to be working overtime. Only 5 percent of the noncollege black men worked more than 50 hours per week on a regular basis. Fully 30 percent of white men reported working this much, as did 11 percent of Hispanic men.

Moonlighting—working at two or more jobs in the same week—was also much more prevalent among white men. Those with a high school degree or less reported an average of 1.24 jobs each, while blacks and Hispanics both reported an average of 1.04. Over one-fifth of white men moonlight; less than one-twentieth of minority men do. An even stronger disparity occurs when it comes to self-employment. White men were much more likely to be self-employed—often working for themselves while they also held down a regular job. Nearly two out of five (38 percent) white men reported self-employment income, which means they were usually working extra hours. Only 4 percent of black men and 3 percent of Hispanic men worked for themselves.

These striking differences in the incidence of part-time work, in moonlighting, and in self-employment are crucial to understanding why black and Hispanic men remain far behind white men in the labor market. How much of this behavior is voluntary and how much is due to restrictions that minorities face in the labor market cannot be ascertained directly from the GBSS survey.

Nonetheless, at this point it is fair to suggest that only part of these large differences in working time can be attributed to blacks and Hispanics wanting more leisure time and whites desiring more cash income. Differences in location may affect the ability to moonlight in part-time jobs. Self-employment may require up-front investments that minorities have trouble financing, given their lack of financial assets. And blacks and Hispanics may be restricted to jobs and occupations that do not provide the same opportunities for overtime. While we cannot provide a definitive answer to any of these conjectures, in the next section of this chapter we will provide some circumstantial evidence.

Statistical Estimates of Labor Market Outcomes— Noncollege Men

Table 8.1 summarizes the empirical results we have presented so far. To probe more deeply into what is responsible for the labor market outcomes of men with no college experience living in the Greater Boston

225

TABLE 8.1   *Baseline Labor Market Components*

Men's Education: High School Diploma or Less (Age Twenty-One to Sixty-Five),
Greater Boston Labor Market, 1993 to 1994

	Black Men	Hispanic Men	White Men
Labor force participation rate	86.2%	87.2%	82.7%
Unemployment rate	15.2%	7.1%	7.1%
Average hours worked per week	34.9	43.0	50.5
Expected annual hours	1,327	1,811	2,018
Median hourly wage	$9.62	$8.14	$11.54
Expected annual earnings	$12,762	$14,751	$23,291
	Black/White	Hispanic/White	Black/Hispanic
Ratios			
Median hourly wage	83.4%	70.5%	118.2%
Expected annual earnings	54.8%	63.3%	86.5%

Source: Greater Boston Social Survey 1995.

region, we ran logit equations to estimate the determinants of labor force participation and unemployment rates, and ordinary least squares (OLS) regressions for weekly hours and hourly wages. This statistical treatment permits us, via the earnings algorithm, to ascertain the role of human capital, race, and residential location on expected annual income. The specific methodological protocol for the model is described in the appendix to this chapter.

Table 8.2 provides a complete list of the final variables and their definitions used in this model; table 8.3 provides the mean (or median) values for the dependent and independent variables in the final equations; and table 8.4 presents the entire set of final fitted equations. The sample for these equations included all men in the GBSS who were between the ages of twenty-one and sixty-five and who had formal education of twelve years or less. Sample sizes for each equation differ based on data availability. While we expected such variables as age, job experience, and being foreign-born to have an impact on labor force participation and unemployment, their coefficients did not prove statistically significant at the .10 level.[10] Therefore, in the final simulation equations, these variables were dropped.

One variable requires additional justification: STRAT (the dummy variable signifying whether an individual lives in a census block where a majority of residents are black or Hispanic). While generally identified here as reflecting the impact of neighborhood composition on labor market outcomes, this variable could be a proxy for any form of unmeasured

TABLE 8.2   *Variable List for Labor Market Simulation Model*

Variable Name	Variable Description
LFP	In labor force (dummy variable)
UR	Unemployed (dummy variable)
HRSWEEK	Usual hours worked per week
RLnHWAGE	Log of real hourly wage, including employment and self-employment earnings (adjusted for time elapsed since last job)[a]
BLACK	Non-Hispanic black (dummy variable)
HISPANIC	Hispanic (dummy variable)
STRAT	Live in black or Hispanic majority census block (dummy variable)
HSDEGREE	Completed twelve years of schooling (dummy variable)
ASSESSUQ	Interviewer's assessment of ability of respondent to understand questions on survey (1 = excellent to 5 = poor)
HEALTHDY	Health condition limits type or hours of work (dummy variable)
AGE	Age
AGESQ	Age squared
TOTJEXP	Years of experience in current or last occupation
ARMFORCE	Served in either active duty or military reserves (dummy variable)
FOREIGN BORN	Mother living outside United States when born
MARRIED	Ever married (dummy variable)
NUMJOB	Number of jobs held at time of survey
SELF-EMPLOYMENT	Self-employed on current or last main job (dummy variable)
SERVICE OCCUPATION	Current or last main job in service occupation (dummy variable)
SALES OCCUPATION	Current or last main job in sales occupation (dummy variable)
PUBSEC	Current or last main job in public-sector industry (dummy variable)
UNION MEMBER	Member of a craft, industrial, or trade union (dummy variable)
COMPUTER USE	Work with computer daily or weekly on job (dummy variable)
RECENTLY EMPLOYED	At work within past twelve months (dummy variable)

Source: Calculated from Council of Economic Advisers 1996, table B-43, 330.
[a]Inflation adjustment based on .2228 percent monthly increase in nominal average wages for production and nonsupervisory workers (1988 to 1995).

TABLE 8.3   *Mean-Median Values for Labor Market Simulation Model, Men (High School or Less, Age Twenty-One to Sixty-Five)*

Variable Name	Black	Hispanic	White
LFP	.862	.872	.827
UR	.152	.071	.071
HRSWEEK	34.9	43.0	50.5
HOURLYWAGE (Median)[a]	$9.62	$8.14	$11.54
STRAT	.782	.365	.006
HSDEGREE	.579	.282	.921
ASSESSUQ	2.475	2.902	1.589
HEALTHDY	.211	.238	.184
AGE	39	30	39
TOTJEXP (Median)	6	6	8
ARMFORCE	.162	.056	.304
FOREIGN BORN	.390	.656	.020
MARRIED	.540	.885	.734
NUMJOB	1.039	1.037	1.239
SELF-EMPLOYMENT	.041	.032	.381
SERVICE OCCUPATION	.114	.215	.041
SALES OCCUPATION	.054	.010	.204
UNION MEMBER	.277	.310	.122
COMPUTER USE	.103	.179	.321
RECENTLY EMPLOYED	.787	.768	.741

Source: Calculated from Council of Economic Advisers 1996, table B-43, 330.
[a]Inflation adjustment based on .2228 percent monthly increase in nominal average wages for production and nonsupervisory workers (1990 to 1995).

human capital that is shared by a large number of residents in minority neighborhoods and not prevalent in majority neighborhoods. Hence, we must exercise some caution in interpreting its meaning in this model.

Moreover, it is likely that a simultaneous relationship exists between labor market outcomes and STRAT. Those living in minority neighborhoods may find their chances for labor market success constrained by reason of where they live. Alternatively, limited labor market success may result in low incomes which, in turn, limit the types of neighborhoods these individuals can afford. As Keith Ihlanfeldt points out, one can deal with this problem by either estimating a system of equations that treats both employment and job access as endogenous variables or by restricting the sample to individuals for whom residential location is truly exogenous (for example, teenagers living with their parents) (Ihlanfelt 1992; see also Waddell 1992; 1993).

In our case, developing a full system of simultaneous equations, given the simulation methodology employed here, would have gener-

TABLE 8.4   *Logit and Regression Equation Results, Men, High School Degree or Less Schooling*

	LFP (logit)	UR (logit)	HRSWEEK (OLS)	RLnHWAGE (OLS)
Common Variables				
BLACK	1.5683	−.0127	−4.8153	−.2101
	(1.79)	(0.01)	(2.31)	(2.13)
HISPANIC	1.2878	−.4627	5.7463	.1834
	(1.21)	(0.45)	(2.00)	(1.59)
STRAT	−.6783	1.1985	.0151	−.1723
	(0.97)	(1.329)	(0.007)	(2.77)
Human Capital Variables				
HSDEGREE	.5257		2.0639	−.0007
	(0.80)		(1.27)	(0.01)
ASSESSUQ				−.1085
				(4.07)
HEALTHDY	−3.0707		−4.0835	
	(2.36)		(2.36)	
AGE			1.9332	.0514
			(4.22)	(3.29)
AGESQ			−.0221	−.0006
			(3.95)	(2.94)
TOTJEXP				.0083
				(1.68)
TOTJEXP × BLACK				.0197
				(3.19)
TOTJEXP × HISPANIC				.0062
				(0.73)
ARMFORCE				.0019
				(0.15)
ARMFORCE × BLACK				.1736
				(1.46)
Nativity-Family Status Variables				
FOREIGN BORN			−.7462	.2978
			(0.36)	(3.21)
FOREIGN BORN × BLACK				−.0634
				(0.54)
FOREIGN BORN × HISPANIC			−5.9200	−.5224
			(1.71)	(3.91)
MARRIED	.9801			
	(1.52)			
Job Characteristic Variables				
NUMJOB			10.4207	
			(4.27)	
SELF-EMPLOYMENT			6.3738	
			(2.02)	

229

TABLE 8.4   *Continued*

	LFP	UR1	HRSWEEK	RLnHWAGE
SERVICE OCCUPATION			−4.6126	
			(2.55)	
SALES OCCUPATION			10.2931	
			(2.35)	
UNION MEMBER				.2122
				(2.81)
COMPUTER USE				.1167
				(2.01)
Control Variable				
RECENTLY EMPLOYED				.1929
				(2.07)
Constant	1.5180	−2.6874	−7.7026	1.1537
N	318	252	279	245
F	1.36	1.27	4.68	14.35
Prob > F	.234	.287		
R-Squared			.256	.354
	(weighted)	(weighted)	(unweighted)	(unweighted)

Source: Greater Boston Social Survey 1995.
Note: T-statistics in parentheses.

ated a number of intractable problems. Since our sample excludes teen-agers, we could not follow the second method, either. The question, then, was whether to include STRAT at all. We chose to include this variable for two reasons. First, excluding this variable would have sub-jected the analysis to specification error as a result of a missing vari-able. By excluding STRAT from the analysis, it is likely that we would have obtained biased coefficients on such variables as race and eth-nicity. Moreover, as we noted in the last chapter, the distribution of rents paid by Boston-area minority families does not differ dramati-cally from that of whites. Hence, housing affordability per se does not appear to be a major factor constraining the decision to locate in a majority or a minority neighborhood. This suggests that while the rela-tionship between STRAT and labor market outcomes may still be si-multaneous, the causation appears to run primarily from residential location to labor success, not the other way around. Minority workers are constrained as to where they live as a result of factors other than income. As is, STRAT was not significant in three of the four equa-tions, suggesting that it plays only a modest role in labor market out-comes for this population.

With these methodological notes in mind, we can now look at the empirical results we derived from analyzing the GBSS data.

Labor Force Participation

A logit equation was used to examine the factors associated with whether an individual was either currently working or at least actively seeking employment at the time of the GBSS survey.[11] Recall that more than five out of six men in our study reported themselves to be in the labor force, with little variation by race or ethnicity. Hence, there is not much actual variation to explain. Only three variables of the six included in the equation proved statistically significant at the .10 level or better: BLACK, HEALTHDY, and MARRIED.

Of these variables, HEALTHDY and MARRIED have the expected signs. Those reporting a health condition that limits the type of work they can do, or their hours of work, were much less likely to be in the labor force. Based on a simulation of the labor force participation equation, black, Hispanic, and white men with no health limitations all had labor force participation rates (LFPR) of 90 to 92 percent. Those with health limitations have much lower estimated LFPRs: 40, 44, and 28 percent, respectively.

Marital status is not anywhere near as compelling a predictor of labor force participation, but it is nonetheless statistically significant. Using the equation to simulate LFPR's, we find a 10- to 16-percentage point difference between single and married men.[12] There is a positive association between being married and being in the labor force, but whether it means that married men are more motivated to work or that working men are more likely to be "marriageable" cannot be ascertained from our data.

The positive coefficient on BLACK was not originally expected, given the literature regarding labor market discrimination. But it is compatible with and reflective of the finding that the point estimates for the labor force participation rates of both black and Hispanic men with limited education are, if anything, slightly *higher* than the estimate for white men. Moreover, that the coefficient on STRAT—the variable that reflects whether an individual lives in a majority-minority neighborhood—was negative, as expected, but *not* statistically significant, suggests that after controlling for an individual's race, living in a racially segregated neighborhood does not appear to contribute much to reduced labor force participation, at least in Greater Boston. That is, race and ethnicity may play a major role in producing disadvantage in the labor market for people of color, but this is not manifested in labor force participation rates.

We tried other variables in the model—including foreign-born, age, high school completion, and veteran status—but none of these proved anywhere near statistically significant.[13] This was also true of variables created to proxy for transportation options, which might be related to an individual's ability to commute to a job. Overall, the logit equation itself has a low F-statistic, suggesting that the combination of variables used to explain labor force participation does a poor job of revealing the distinguishing characteristics of those who are in and out of the labor force. With the exception of race and marital and health status, labor force nonparticipation seems to be generally idiosyncratic for the less-educated men in the GBSS sample. More than 95 percent of healthy black men with limited schooling are in the labor force, as are 99 percent of the Hispanics and 93 percent of the white men.

Unemployment

Our attempt at explaining unemployment was somewhat problematic. An initial unemployment equation, conditioned on being in the labor force and based on unweighted data, proved highly unstable in simulation experiments. Moreover, it produced a rank order of jobless rates by race/ethnic group quite different from that found in table 8.1.[14] These results forced us to abandon this approach and turn to the weighted data, as we had in the case of the labor force participation equation. In the end, the weighted data provided for a suitably stable model that accorded with the relative rankings of unemployment rates.

Even then, none of the variables we used to ascertain the probability of being unemployed were statistically significant. The F-statistic for the equation was also quite low. The closest we came to a statistically significant variable was STRAT—suggesting that those who reside in minority neighborhoods may be disadvantaged when it comes to finding and retaining a job. Indeed, if we disregard the low t-statistic on this variable and insert its coefficient at face value in the unemployment rate module of the annual earnings simulation (to be discussed in the next section of this chapter), we find that moving black men from a minority neighborhood to a "white" neighborhood reduces their estimated unemployment rate from 15.2 percent to 6.7 percent—about the same as the white and Hispanic jobless rates. The same simulation reduces the Hispanic unemployment rate to just 4.4 percent, from 7.1 percent. The *spatial dimension* of the labor market therefore seems to be most pronounced when it comes to unemployment, not labor force participation—or hourly wage rates, as we shall demonstrate.

What was obvious from extensive experimentation with the unemployment equation is that many conventional variables do not seem to provide an explanation for differences in the probability of being unemployed. We expected that access to a car would help explain differences in unemployment, but this variable did not prove statistically significant. Similarly, we expected that those who searched for work using a network composed of family and friends would face lower unemployment. However, none of a series of network or social capital variables proved statistically significant, either. Perhaps in a much larger sample, they might have.

Weekly Hours

We had much greater success in explaining differences in weekly working time. While labor force participation and unemployment in the GBSS refer to current status, data on usual weekly hours and on hourly wages refer to current job *or* previous job within the past five years. This substantially eliminates the problem of selection bias, since we have hours and wage data for all those with any work experience over the past five years, even if they are not currently participating in the labor force or are currently unemployed. Hence, the equations for hours and wages are not conditioned on labor force status, obviating the need for implementing a procedure to correct for selection bias.[15]

A large number of GBSS variables enter the model with the expected signs and statistically significant coefficients. All together, our ordinary least squares (OLS) regression explains about a quarter of the variation ($R^2 = .256$). Other things being equal, race and ethnicity matter. Black men work an average of five hours *less* per week than whites; Hispanics work nearly six hours *more*. After controlling for race and ethnicity, we found no evidence of a ghetto effect or spatial mismatch on weekly hours. STRAT has the expected sign, but its coefficient was close to zero and insignificant.

Those with a health limitation not only are less likely to participate in the labor force, but when they are working they tend to work four hours less per week than others. Working time increases with age up to age forty-four and then slowly declines. Foreign-born men typically work about the same time as native-born.[16]

The most important set of factors determining working time has to do with the number and types of jobs that men with limited education obtain. As expected, those who work multiple jobs work longer hours—about ten hours more per week. This suggests that a not uncommon experience, at least for white men, is to work a regular job of forty hours plus a part-time job averaging about ten hours. The combination gives the mean 50.5 hour work week we found earlier for white men. Self-employment also contributes to longer work weeks. Those who are self-employed on a regular basis work six hours more per week than those who are not. Part of this differential may reflect moonlighting as well, with the self-employed working part of the week for someone else and part of the week for themselves.

Other things being equal, working in service occupations reduces reported working time by nearly five hours per week. In contrast and somewhat unexpectedly, working in sales occupations does the opposite—increasing weekly time by a whopping ten hours. For those who think of Kmart or a similar retail outlet as the locus for most sales jobs, this result might seem strange indeed. But sales occupations are found in a broad range of industries, not just retail trade. In financial services, insurance, banking, wholesale trade, and manufacturing, sales *representatives* make up a large share of total employment. These sales reps often work long hours out of offices or via telemarketing. The coefficient on SALES OCCUPATION is not counterintuitive once the distinction between "occupation" and "industry" is made.

The one variable that seems to play a minor role in working time is the high school degree. Those who have dropped out before completing high school suffer at most a two-hour deficit in hours worked. Altogether, then, we find that race, ethnicity, health status, age, moonlighting, self-employment, and occupation all affect working time—and therefore annual earnings.

How much of this important difference in weekly hours is voluntary? Do black men choose to work fewer hours, or is this an involuntary outcome? While this analysis cannot provide a definitive answer to these questions, there is strong reason to believe that racial differences in working time are not primarily a matter of individual choice. Much of this difference can be explained by the racial pattern of the occupational distribution in Greater Boston. Black men are only one-fourth as likely as white men to be in sales occupations—positions that generally offer significantly longer hours. On the other hand, black men are more than twice as likely to be in service occupations that generally offer shorter work weeks. To the extent that occupational choice is limited by various forms of racial discrimination, differences in working time is the result. Moreover, since 1983, black workers nationwide have increased their average weekly work time more than either white or Hispanic workers (Bluestone and Rose 1998). This suggests that motivation is probably not the key factor in the large hours gap we find in Greater Boston.

Hourly Wages

The final component in our labor market outcomes model is the hourly wage. The OLS regression for the natural log of real hourly earnings includes a large number of statistically significant variables related to human capital, family background, and job characteristics—as well as race and residence. Overall, the regression explains 35 percent of the total variance in wages.

Race is a highly significant variable, but it interacts in complex ways with occupational experience, veteran status, and nativity.[17] An evaluation of the regression results suggests that a native-born black who has only one year of occupational experience and has not served in the military will earn about 17 percent less than a comparable white. However, as his occupational experience increases, the racial wage gap declines. With six years of experience, the gap is down to 9 percent. By ten years, it disappears. An alternative to occupational experience is to have served in the armed forces. A black veteran who has just begun his career and has only one year of occupational experience will, according to the regression, earn about the same hourly wage as a comparably inexperienced white, regardless of the latter's veteran status.

Significant black disadvantage therefore exists in the Greater Boston region when it comes to hourly wages, but it declines with job experience. Additional years of experience in the same occupation permit black men in particular to move up the seniority wage ladder. Black men apparently enter occupations at the very bottom rung, but those who build up seniority benefit disproportionately. Such a wage pattern is consistent with a model of statistical discrimination. Hired in at low pay, black men who prove themselves to their employers move up the wage ladder more swiftly than either white or Hispanic men. Still, the problem is getting hired in the first place, and then continuing to be employed long enough in a given occupation to enjoy such benefits.

That statistical discrimination plays a large role in the labor market is also confirmed by the impact of veteran status. The variable ARMFORCE might be a proxy for either technical skills or social skills. But since the variable is important only for black men, the "signaling" role of veteran status is probably more pertinent. To the extent that black men need *better* credentials to compete for the same job opportunities as whites, veteran status is a highly valued credential.

In contrast to blacks, Spanish ethnicity per se does not appear to confer a disadvantage in terms of hourly earnings, even though Hispanic men have the lowest hourly wage of the three race-ethnic groups in our analysis. This suggests that other factors are responsible for the low hourly earnings of Hispanic men.

The variable STRAT enters the wage equation as statistically significant. According to its coefficient, employed men who live in minority-dominated neighborhoods suffer a 16 percent wage deficit. We generated terms for BLACK and STRAT and for HISPANIC and STRAT to check for interaction effects, but the coefficients on these terms proved both small and statistically insignificant. Therefore, it appears that race and ethnicity, on the one hand, and the neighborhood variable STRAT, on the other, have independent effects on hourly wages—although the race effect is conditioned on job experience and veteran status. If STRAT does measure spatial mismatch, then the spatial mismatch we find in Boston does not affect the probability of working per se, but may constrain the types of jobs inner-city residents can obtain and therefore the wages they can command.

A large number of human capital and demographic factors play a role in wage determination for noncollege men in the Greater Boston metropolitan region. While completing high school does not appear to have the expected "diploma" effect—its coefficient is small and insignificant—age and years of occupational experience are both significant. The normal age-earnings profile suggests that, on average, men reach their peak earning capacity at around age forty-three. This helps to explain why the Hispanics in our survey have lower wages than others; their median age is only thirty, compared with thirty-nine for both blacks and whites. If the age distribution of Latino men matched that of whites, a good portion of their hourly wage deficit would disappear.

The GBSS contains a number of questions regarding individual abilities and achievement. Among these are the results of a brief word-recognition test given each respondent (in English or Spanish, depending on what language was used in the interview) and interviewer assessments of the respondent's ability to understand English, to speak English clearly, and to answer the survey questions. Of these, one factor proved highly significant in the wage equation: ASSESSUQ, the interviewer's assessment of the ability of the respondent to understand the survey questionnaire.[18] While this measure is clearly subjective, the high t-statistic and the reasonable coefficient provide some confidence in this measure.[19] Given the attempt at race and ethnic matching between interviewer and respondent, there is reason to believe that the amount of systematic bias in these assessments based on the race or ethnicity of the interviewer is small.[20] Nevertheless, the mean scores vary significantly by race and ethnicity: 1.59 for white men; 2.48 for black men; 2.90 for Hispanics.[21] Hence, while the high school degree per se has no apparent role in wage determination for *this* group of men, differences in "ability"—as indicated by these assessments—seem to matter a good deal.[22]

That HSDEGREE was not significant in any of the component equations may seem surprising. What may explain this result is that in a regional economy with such a tight labor market, employers cannot afford the luxury of limiting their search to workers who are high school graduates. Indeed, a recent news story describes Boston-area employers' recruitment efforts inside homeless shelters in inner-city neighborhoods (Stein 1998). This is not to say that schooling never counts in such a labor market. In the next chapter, we shall present an analysis in which the data set was not truncated on years of education. In this case, schooling turns out to be a critically important factor in explaining differences in annual earnings.

Beyond the impact of human capital, the wage equation provides an interesting story about nativity. Evaluating the coefficient on FORBORN along with its two race-ethnic interaction terms suggests that foreign-born white workers—with limited education—are doing substantially better than native-born whites. Ceteris paribus, they earn about one-third more per hour (34 percent) than white men born in the United States. It may be true that those who come to the United States do so specifically for economic reasons—and working at a good job is one of them. Foreign-born blacks do better than their native-born counterparts, as well. Immigrants, primarily from the Caribbean and parts of Africa, are doing better than those who were born in the United States. The fact that nearly two out of five (39 percent) black men in the region with limited schooling are foreign-born makes this finding particularly salient. In the ordering of the labor market, whites dominate blacks and Hispanics, but foreign-born blacks dominate blacks who were born and raised here. The mean hourly wage of noncollege foreign-born blacks is $10.52 versus $9.56 for native-born.

According to the regression, the opposite pattern is true among Hispanics. Those who have recently come to the United States from abroad (or from Puerto Rico) would earn, if everything else were held constant, 25 percent less than Latino men who have lived here all their lives. This may reflect differences in language ability or growing familiarity with the local labor market. Given the data at hand, we were not able to distinguish between these two possible explanations.

As for the impact of job characteristics on the wage, two variables were statistically significant: UNION MEMBER and COMPJOB. Members of unions in the Greater Boston region receive a 24 percent wage premium. This is in line with national data demonstrating that the union-nonunion gap is generally of this magnitude (Mishel, Bernstein, and Schmitt 1999).[23] Black and Hispanic men particularly benefit from unions in Boston because approximately 30 percent of those with high school or less belong to them. Whites more often work in industries and occupations where unions are much less prevalent. The white unionization rate in our weighted sample is only 12 percent. According to our regression, if it were not for relatively high union density among black and Hispanic men, the racial and ethnic wage gaps would be significantly larger.

Those who work regularly with computers also receive a wage premium, on the order of 12 percent.[24] Unlike unionization, however, this wage premium favors white men. About a third (32 percent) of the non-college white men in our study reported working with computers on their jobs on a daily or at least weekly basis. Among Hispanics, only about half this proportion used computers, and among black men only one in ten. Clearly, access to jobs requiring computers is an important determinant of wages. Black men are least likely to have such an opportunity for labor market success.

The final variable in the hourly wage equation is a control variable, RECENTLY EMPLOYED, that indicates whether the sample individual actually had worked at any time during the previous twelve months. Because hourly wages in the GBSS are available not only for currently working men, but for those who have worked any time in the past five years, it is necessary to check for differences in wages that might be associated with current work status. The positive and significant coefficient on the control variable indicates that those who have worked sometime in the past year earn, ceteris paribus, 21 percent more than those who reported no work in the past year. This differential could be due to any number of factors, including differences in human capital that are not otherwise captured in the regression equation.

Simulating Labor Market Outcomes: Men

The final step in this labor market analysis is to bring all of the logit and regression results together into a single simulation model, so that we can evaluate how each of the factors we have addressed affects expected annual earnings. To accomplish this, we entered the four labor market component equations into a spreadsheet and then linked the equations by means of the labor market outcome formula reported as equation 8.1. By varying values of the "independent" variables in the model, we can simulate the impact on hourly wages and annual earnings. The complete baseline model is depicted in table 8.5.[25] The best way to summarize the simulation results is by way of a series of charts developed from the spreadsheet models.

Human Capital Factors

How much of the race-ethnic earnings gap could be closed if differences in education, age, health status, occupational experience, and veteran status were eliminated? Figure 8.8 provides the answer to this question. Inserting the white male human capital values into the simulation

TABLE 8.5   *Baseline Simulation: Factors Contributing to Male Annual Earnings Differences (High School or Less)*

Labor Force Participation					
	b	Black	Hispanic	White	All
BLACK	1.5683	1	0	0	0.071
HISPANIC	1.2878	0	1	0	0.091
HEALTHDY	−3.0707	0.211	0.238	0.184	0.187
MARRIED	0.9801	0.54	0.885	0.734	0.747
STRAT	−0.6783	0.782	0.365	0.006	0.097
HSDEGREE	0.5257	0.579	0.282	0.921	0.836
	Adj. Constant	Orig. Const			
Constant	0.9050	1.517983			

Simulation Predicted Values				
	Prob.	Mean	Adj. Prob	BM/WM	HM/WM
Black	0.894	0.862	0.862	104.14%	105.38%
Hispanic	0.903	0.872	0.872		
White	0.823	0.827	0.827		
All	0.842	0.842			

Unemployment					
	b	Black	Hispanic	White	All
BLACK	−0.0127	1	0	0	0.071
HISPANIC	−0.4627	0	1	0	0.091
STRAT	1.1985	0.782	0.365	0.006	0.097
	Adj. Const.	Actual Const.			
Constant	−2.6300	−2.6874			

Simulation Predicted Values				
	Prob.	Mean	Adj. Prob	BM/WM	HM/WM
Black	0.154	0.152	0.152	2.15	1.00
Hispanic	0.066	0.071	0.071		
White	0.068	0.071	0.071		
All	0.072	0.072			

TABLE 8.5   *Continued*

		Hours-Week			
	b	Black	Hispanic	White	All
BLACK	−4.815341	1	0	0	0.071
HISPANIC	5.746259	0	1	0	0.097
STRAT	0.0150958	0.782	0.365	0.006	0.097
HEALTHDY	−4.08354	0.211	0.238	0.184	0.187
NUMJOBS	10.42065	1.039	1.037	1.239	1.19
AGE	1.933214	39	30	39	38
AGESQ	−0.0220857	1521	900	1521	1444
SERVICE OCC	−4.612597	0.114	0.215	0.041	0.064
SALES OCC	10.29314	0.054	0.01	0.204	0.163
SELFEMP	6.373832	0.041	0.032	0.381	0.297
HSDEGREE	2.063944	0.579	0.282	0.921	0.836
FORBORN	−0.7461862	0.39	0.656	0.02	0.167
HISP FB	−5.919983	0	0.656	0	0.064

	Adj. Constant	Act. Const			
Constant	−7.702649	−4.84286			

		Simulation Predicted Values			
	Predicted	Mean	Adj. Pred	BM/WM	HM/WM
Black	40.46	34.90	34.90	0.691	0.852
Hispanic	41.53	43.00	43.00		
White	52.49	50.50	50.50		
All	50.22	50.22			

		LnHOURLY WAGE			
	b	Black	Hispanic	White	All
BLACK	−0.210096	1	0	0	0.071
HISPANIC	0.183387	0	1	0	0.097
STRAT	−0.172301	0.782	0.365	0.006	0.097
EMPREC	0.192868	0.787	0.768	0.741	0.76
AGE	0.051438	39	30	39	38
AGESQ	−0.000572	1521	900	1521	1444
COMPJOB	0.116709	0.103	0.179	0.321	0.323
ARMFORCE	0.001183	0.162	0.56	0.304	0.252
BLARMF	0.173601	0.162	0	0	0.012
TOTJEXPA	0.008258	6	6	8	8
UNION1/2	0.212160	0.277	0.31	0.122	0.144
HSDEGREE	−0.000740	0.579	0.282	0.921	0.836
BLEXP	0.019702	6	0	0	0.426
HISEXP	0.006216	0	6	0	0.582
FORBORN	0.297843	0.39	0.656	0.02	0.167

TABLE 8.5   *Continued*

LnHOURLY WAGE					
	b	Black	Hispanic	White	All
BLACKFB	−0.063432	0.39	0	0	0.028
HISPFB	−0.522463	0	0.656	0	0.064
ASSESSUQ	−0.108468	2.475	2.902	1.589	1.8365
	Adj. Constant	Act. Const.			
Constant	1.220600	1.153683			

Simulation Predicted Values

	LnHRWAGE	Median	Adj. LnHr	LnHR-WAGE BM/WM	HM/WM
Black	2.2536	2.2630	2.2630	92.5%	85.7%
Hispanic	2.2291	2.0970	2.0970		
White	1.4618	2.4460	2.4460		
All	2.4460	2.4460			

	exp(LnHR)	Median		exp(LnHR) BM/WM	HM/WM
Black	9.52	9.62	9.62	83.4%	70.6%
Hispanic	9.29	8.14	8.14		
White	11.73	11.54	11.54		

Annual Hours

Estimated from Equations

	Baseline	Simulated	BM/WM	HM/WM
Black	1,327	1,326	65.7%	89.7%
Hispanic	1,811	1,812		
White	2,018	2,019		

Annual Wage

Estimated from Equations

		BM/WM	HM/WM
Black	12762.15	54.8%	63.3%
Hispanic	14750.70		
White	23291.35		

Baseline

		BM/WM	HM/WM
Black	12762.15	54.8%	63.3%
Hispanic	14750.70		
White	23291.35		

Source: Greater Boston Social Survey 1994.

FIGURE 8.8   *Hourly Earning Ratios, Men*
              Impact of Human Capital Factors

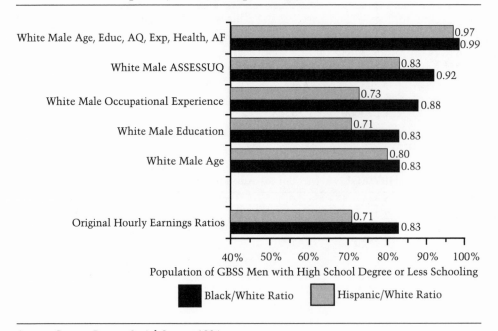

Source: Greater Boston Social Survey 1994.

model reduces the wage gap for both blacks and Hispanics—with slightly more improvement for Hispanic men. Since black men have the same median age as white men, there is no improvement in black hourly wages due to substituting the white median. But for Hispanics, the earnings ratio increases to .80 from .71—within just three percentage points of the black/white ratio. Because the coefficient on HSDEGREE is small (and insignificant), the impact of awarding blacks and Hispanics diplomas in the same proportion as whites has little impact on closing the wage gap. The same is true for health status, for while we found that adverse health conditions limit working time, they do not appear to have an independent impact on wages. Substituting the white male median for occupational experience does little for Hispanics, but raises the black ratio to .88. The combination of white male education and ASSESSUQ raised the ratios to .83 and .92 for Hispanics and blacks, respectively.

Finally, when we substitute white male age, education, ASSESSUQ, occupational experience, and veteran status, both the black/white and Hispanic/white ratios close nearly to unity (to .99 and .97, respectively).

As a result, after simulating equivalent human capital investments in all three groups of noncollege men, we find virtually no difference in hourly wages among white, black, and Hispanic workers. Any wage effect that might be deemed due to discrimination (as evidenced by the negative and statistically significant coefficient on the variable BLACK) is offset by advantages black men have in union membership and the apparently strong positive signals of occupational experience and veteran status. This particular finding of racial convergence in hourly wages after controlling for human capital is consistent with a growing literature on the black-white *hourly* wage gap referred to earlier (Ferguson 1993; O'Neill 1990).

But simulating the entire model for expected *annual* earnings yields a very different story, as figure 8.9 amply demonstrates. Recall that the original annual race/ethnic earnings ratios are .55 and .63 for blacks and Hispanics, respectively. As before, assigning the white median age to black men does nothing to close the earnings gap, because both racial groups have the same median age. But the generally younger Hispanic men gain substantially in this simulation, closing the Hispanic-white

FIGURE 8.9   *Annual Earnings Ratios, Men*
             Impact of Human Capital Factors

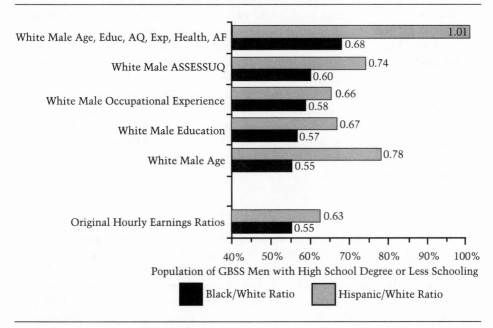

gap from .63 to .78. This occurs because, as young workers enter middle age *both* weekly hours *and* the hourly wage increase. As we artificially age Greater Boston's Hispanic population, two-fifths (40 percent) of the Hispanic-white male annual earnings gap of 37 percentage points disappears.

The completion of high school improves the black/white ratio slightly (from .55 to .57), and helps the generally more poorly educated Hispanic men somewhat more, closing the earnings gap by 4 percentage points. Equalizing occupational experience closes the gap a little bit as well. The combination of white male values for education and ASSESSUQ closes the gap to .63 for black males and to .79 for Hispanics. Yet, it is only when we simulate the model giving black and Hispanic men the entire set of white male human capital traits that the overall impact of human capital variables becomes dramatic. For black men the earnings gap closes by 13 percentage points (from .55 to .68), leaving black men still one-third (32 percent) behind the annual earnings of white men. *For Hispanics, however, closing the human capital gap eliminates the original annual earnings deficit altogether, as the Hispanic/white simulated earnings ratio closes to 1.01.* As Hispanic men become older, as they increase their education level and occupation experience, in the process likely increasing the skills measured by ASSESSUQ, they will come very close to gaining full earnings parity with white men. If their health and veteran status were to match that of white men, the annual earnings gap would disappear altogether.

Something well beyond education, years of occupational experience, and improved health is necessary to make further inroads into the large remaining earnings deficit experienced by black men who go no further than high school. Raising human capital levels to white averages improves black annual earnings by about $2,000. The same exercise raises Hispanic earnings by more than four times that amount—$8,800. After equalizing human capital, black men still dominate Hispanic men very slightly in hourly wages, but they fall well below them in what really counts: annual earnings.

Race and Residence

If improved human capital does not close the black-white earnings gap very much, what does? Clearly, one possibility might involve ending any racial discrimination and racial segregation—components of what we have called the opportunity nexus. As one test of the efficacy of such a strategy, we simulated the impact of treating both blacks and Hispanics as native-born whites and "moving" them into white neighborhoods. This is done by setting the variables BLACK, HISPANIC, and

STRAT to zero in the logit and regression equations. The results for hourly wages are found in figure 8.10.

Moving black men into white neighborhoods improves the black/white wage ratio to .95 from its original .83. Similarly, treating blacks as though they were white native-born (regardless of where they live) brings the ratio to .94. Doing both simultaneously actually reverses the hourly wage ratio, so that blacks dominate whites. This is because in the hourly wage regression, blacks have several factors in their favor, including higher unionization rates, a veteran's wage premium advantage, and the advantage of a higher proportion of foreign-born. Taking these into account, we estimate that blacks on average would earn 7 percent more than whites if they were "seen" as white and lived in white neighborhoods. Both race and neighborhood are therefore critical to understanding the existing wage deficit that black men with limited education face.

Hispanic men, on the other hand, improve their position relative to white men by 5 percentage points when they are "moved" into white neighborhoods, but are worse off when treated as white native-born.

FIGURE 8.10   *Hourly Earning Ratios, Men*
                Impact of Race and Residence

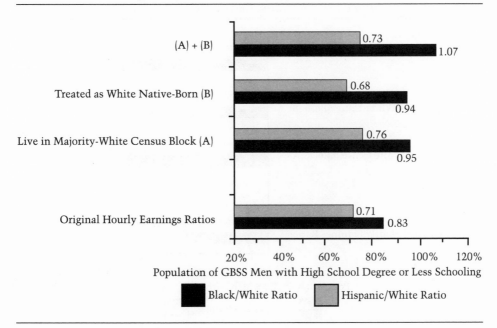

Source: Greater Boston Social Survey 1995.

Combining the two effects raises the Hispanic/white hourly wage ratio by only 2 percentage points, from .71 to .73. This corroborates our earlier conclusion that for Hispanics the major problem is a human capital deficit, not discrimination or residency per se. In this important aspect, these two minority groups face very different barriers to wage parity with whites.

Turning to expected annual earnings tells a related story, although the outcome for black men is not anywhere near as sanguine as it was in the case of hourly wages. Since black and Hispanic men with limited schooling have measured labor force participation rates that are higher than that of whites, "making" a black or Hispanic into a white actually reduces labor force participation and cuts overall hours. This naturally has a negative impact on expected annual earnings. On the other hand, moving blacks and Hispanics into white neighborhoods improves the earnings ratios considerably. Setting STRAT to 0 adds 7 percentage points to the black/white ratio and 8 points to the Hispanic/white ratio (see figure 8.11).

Even when we treat blacks as whites and have them live in white neighborhoods, they earn 26 percent less than whites on an annual

FIGURE 8.11   *Annual Earnings Ratios, Men*
Impact of Race and Residence

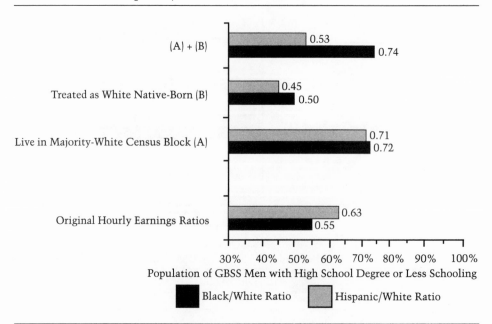

Source: Greater Boston Social Survey 1995.

basis. Ending "discrimination" in this way does more to close the earnings gap than improvements in human capital, but the gap remains large. For Hispanic men, the annual earnings gap actually increases when we run this simulation. Treating blacks as whites and placing them in white neighborhoods adds more than $4,000 to their annual earnings. Doing the same for Hispanics drops their annual pay by nearly $2,000. Again, discrimination matters for blacks; human capital deficits matter more for Hispanics.

What *could* close the black-white gap? To help answer this question, we ran an additional simulation in which all we changed were the job characteristics of black and Hispanic men. In this case, we gave the two minority groups the same average number of jobs as their white colleagues (NUMJOBS), the same number of years of occupational experience (TOTJEXPA), the same proportions in sales and service occupations (SALES; SERVICE), and the same percentage using computers regularly on the job. All these variables appear in the weekly hours regression.

The result of this simulation is found in figure 8.12. The black/white annual earnings ratio rises to .70 from .55, while the Hispanic/

FIGURE 8.12   *Annual Earnings Ratios, Men*
Human Capital, Residence, Job Types

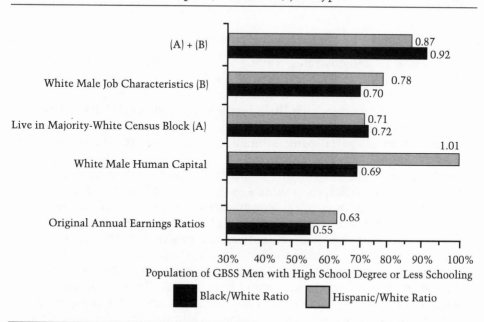

Source: Greater Boston Social Survey 1995.

white ratio rises to .78 from .63. In the same chart, we have added the simulation for human capital and for living in a white-majority neighborhood. Giving blacks the same job characteristics as whites does more for their annual earnings—by boosting their working time—than does equating human capital. Moreover, combining two simulations, giving blacks both the same job characteristics as whites and moving them into white neighborhoods ((A) + (B)), closes the annual earnings ratio to .92 from the original ratio of .55. This means that four-fifths (80 percent) of the annual earnings gap can be closed in this way (.37/.45), while equalizing human capital closes less than one-third (31 percent) of the original gap.

Study #2: How Are Noncollege Workers Faring in the Greater Boston Labor Market? The Case of Women

Have black women fared as poorly in the Greater Boston labor market as their male counterparts? How have Hispanic women done? What factors are responsible for any differences we find in hourly and annual earnings? We carried out a second study focusing on women interviewed in the GBSS to answer these questions.

Annual Earnings

As figure 8.13 demonstrates, among women in our study who have a high school education or less, blacks could expect to earn a little less than $7,200 a year. Hispanic women earn considerably more, nearly $10,400. White women do a little better still, at about $11,100. Hence, black women earn only about two-thirds (65 percent) as much as white women. Noncollege Hispanic women, on the other hand, have nearly reached parity with noncollege white women, earning 94 percent as much per year. For more highly educated women, the fate of black and Hispanic women relative to whites is reversed. College-educated black women, like their noncollege counterparts, earn about two-thirds (62 percent) of what white women earn. But the better-educated Hispanic women only earn half (50 percent) of the nearly $18,000 average expected annual salary of college-educated white women. Indeed, Hispanic women who have attended college appear to have *lower* annual earnings than those who never went beyond high school. These findings raise several questions. What accounts for the large *racial* difference in annual earnings among noncollege women while the annual ethnic (His-

FIGURE 8.13   *Expected Annual Earnings, Women*

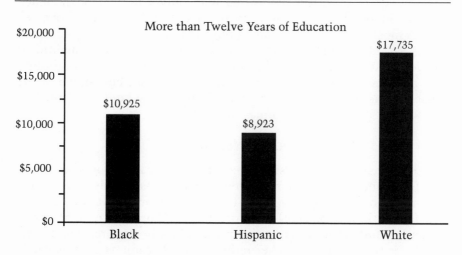

More than Twelve Years of Education

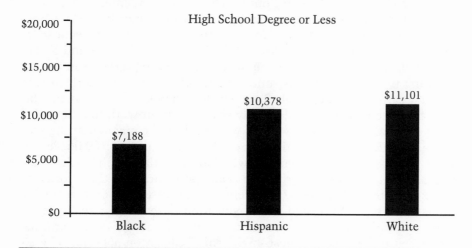

High School Degree or Less

Source: Greater Boston Social Survey 1995.

panic/white) earnings ratio is close to parity? Why do better-educated Hispanic women have such low annual earnings?

Part of the explanation for racial and ethnic differences among the college-educated group may be explained by the fact that white women are much more likely to be graduates of four-year colleges and universities, while black and Hispanic women are more likely to have completed only community college or left a four-year school before completing their degrees. In our study, 31 percent of the white women had at least four years of college, compared with only 9 percent of the black women and 10 percent of the Hispanic. Here the diploma or "degree" effect is most pronounced, a finding reflected in other studies (Bluestone 1993).[26] To solve the rest of the puzzle, it is necessary to pose additional questions. Given that annual earnings are the product of the hourly wage rate and the number of hours worked per year, how much of the explanation is tied to differences in the hourly wage rate? How much is explained by differences in annual work hours?

Hourly Wage Rates

An initial answer to the first of these questions can be found in figure 8.14. Black and Hispanic women are at a substantial disadvantage when it comes to hourly wages. Among noncollege women, blacks earn less than four-fifths (79 percent) of white median hourly wages. Hispanic women do somewhat better, with a median hourly wage ratio of 84 percent. As it turns out, the higher ratio for the Hispanic women is partly due to where they work. Three out of five (61 percent) employed noncollege Hispanic women work in the manufacturing sector in Greater Boston, which pays relatively well for workers who have limited education and weak English-language skills. Only 21 percent of white and 5 percent of black women work in this sector. The wage premium in manufacturing is so high that Hispanic women who choose to work in this industry earn, on average, only 2 percent less than Hispanic women who have attended college, who generally shy away from work in blue-collar fields. Noncollege Hispanic women who work in the manufacturing sector earn a 25 percent premium over those who do not: $9.06 versus $7.24 per hour. For black women with no more than a high school diploma, the black/white hourly ratio is almost identical to those for their better-educated colleagues (79 percent for hourly wages; 65 percent for annual earnings). While additional education raises wage rates for both black and white women, it does not appear to close the racial earnings gap. Because the payoff to post–high school education appears to be so low for Hispanic women, the ethnic earnings gap actually worsens with education: from .83 to .75. Again, the high proportion of noncollege Latina women working in manufacturing is responsible for this outcome.

Annual Work Time

The importance of working time is demonstrated in figure 8.15. In the top panel, white women with college clearly dominate in terms of expected annual work hours. At more than 1,500 hours per year, they work 26 percent more hours than black women and nearly 50 percent more than Hispanic women who have gone beyond high school. White

FIGURE 8.14   *Median Hourly Wage Rate, Women*

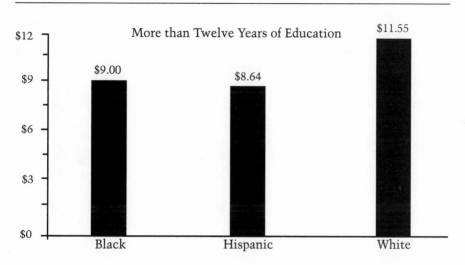

More than Twelve Years of Education

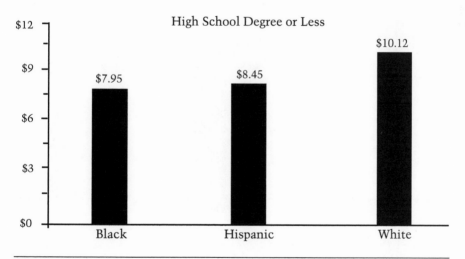

High School Degree or Less

Source: Greater Boston Social Survey 1995.

women's higher hourly wage *combined* with longer work hours is responsible for the nearly $18,000 average annual pay we reported earlier.
Since education level is a key variable that affects not only hourly wage
rates but also the probability of working full-time rather than part-time
(Blau, Ferber, and Winkler 1998), it is not surprising that black and
white women with more years of schooling work more hours per week

251

FIGURE 8.15   *Expected Annual Work Hours, Women*

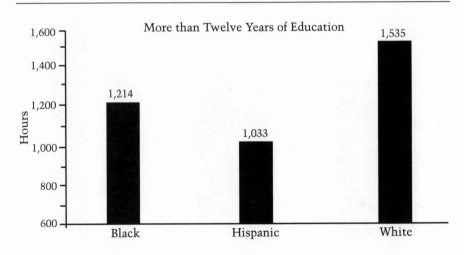

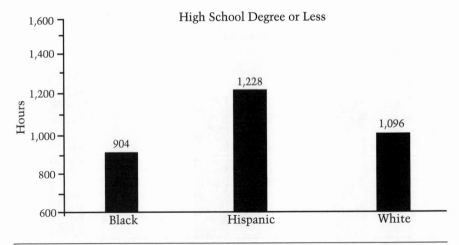

Source: Greater Boston Social Survey 1995.

than those with less, or that white women who spend the most years in school work the most when they enter the labor market.

That more-educated Hispanic women actually work *fewer* hours per year than their less-educated counterparts is one more piece of evidence suggesting the importance of manufacturing employment to explaining the labor market patterns of Latina women. Work in this industry permits Hispanics to work longer hours than either blacks or whites, regardless of education. Less-educated Hispanic women work 12 percent more hours than noncollege whites. This allows a 94 percent Hispanic/ white annual earning ratio, despite the fact that, on average, hourly pay is only 84 percent of what white women receive.

In investigating annual hours of work, we have peeled back another layer of the onion. But this raises still another question: Why do annual hours vary so much across race and ethnic groups? As in the case of men, this prompts us to examine several aspects of labor force attachment to understand the components of annual hours. What is the likelihood that a woman will be in the labor force, and what is the likelihood that she will have recent employment experience? What risk does she face of being unemployed? If she is working, how many hours per week does she work?

Labor Force Participation

Being part of the labor force is the norm for Greater Boston Area women, regardless of education level or race-ethnicity (see figure 8.16). Among women with a high school diploma or less, about two-thirds are in the workforce *regardless* of race or Hispanic ethnicity. What we found for men also applies to women: minorities in Greater Boston are just as likely to be in the labor force as whites.

The labor force participation rates (LFPRs) for better-educated black and Hispanic women are nearly identical to those of their less-educated sisters indicating that education does not play a significant role in this regard for minority women. This is not true, however, for whites, who benefit tremendously from additional schooling. White women with at least some college training are 25 percent more likely to be in the labor force than those who have not gone beyond high school. Indeed, at 86.1 percent, their LFPR is almost as high as that of white men (89.4 percent), reflecting, one would imagine, extraordinarily good labor market opportunities in Boston for well-educated women workers—particularly those who have completed at least four years of college.

Employed in the Last Year

Our alternative measure of labor market participation—employed sometime during the last twelve months—shows much the same pattern as for labor force participation. Even among women with limited education there is strong attachment to the labor force, and it does not vary substantially by race or ethnicity (see figure 8.17). Between 61 and 63 percent of black, Hispanic, and white noncollege women reported that they worked sometime in the year previous to the GBSS survey.

For black and white women, having additional years of schooling increases the likelihood of recent employment experience—to 76 percent for black women and to 86 pecent of white women with at least

FIGURE 8.16   *Labor Force Participation Rate, Women*

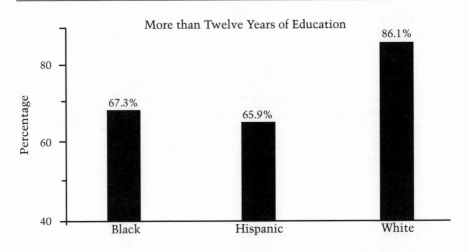

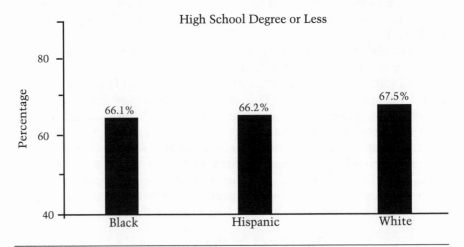

Source: Greater Boston Social Survey 1995.

some college. Surprisingly, this outcome does not hold true for Hispanic women with more years of schooling. Their rates of recent employment experience are almost the same as for less-educated Hispanic women. Since we have not controlled for family income or the presence of young children, it is possible that differences on these dimensions account for the unexpectedly low employment rate among better-educated Hispanic women. The opportunity for noncollege Hispanic women to work in manufacturing may play a role in this regard as well.

FIGURE 8.17   *Employed in the Last Year, Women*

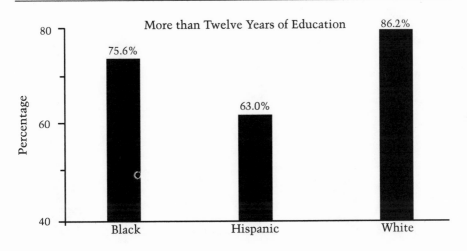

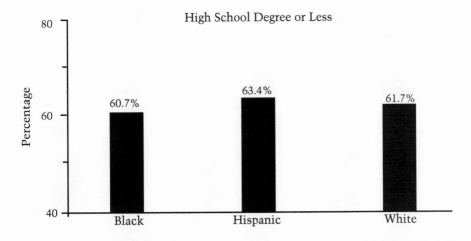

Source: Greater Boston Social Survey 1995.

Unemployment

The risk of being unemployed is much higher for black women than for white women, and the effect is compounded by having a limited amount of education (see figure 8.18). Black women with no more than a high school education had an unemployment rate of 20.6 percent, compared with a rate of 8.8 percent for white women and 6.7 percent for Hispanic women. This pattern is similar to the one we found for men,

FIGURE 8.18   *Unemployment Rate, Women*

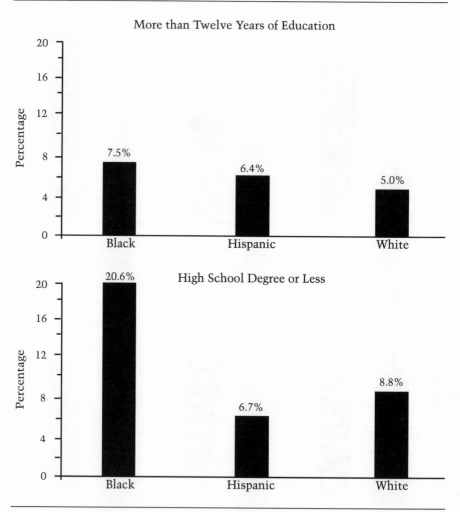

Source: Greater Boston Social Survey 1995.

indicating that high unemployment is a particular problem for less-educated blacks in Greater Boston, regardless of gender. Given racial parity in labor force participation and employment rates, it suggests that black women, like their male counterparts, are prone to cycle in and out of work more so than are other groups.

While college-educated black women also fared worse than the comparable group of white women, the racial unemployment ratio for this better-educated group was only 1.5, rather than the 2.3 ratio for the less educated. Schooling reduces the risk of unemployment for all groups, and this is especially true for black women in Greater Boston.

Among women with more than twelve years of education, the Hispanic unemployment rate was about midway between the high rate for blacks and the lower rate for whites. This, too, is a fairly commonplace finding. What is unusual in this case is that among less-educated workers, it was the Hispanic women who had the lowest unemployment rate. Again, we can conclude that this has something to do with the high concentration of Hispanic women in manufacturing. During a period when manufacturing might undergo a process of downsizing, it is possible that workers in this sector would have higher unemployment rates than others. But during the survey period, manufacturing in the Greater Boston region was relatively stable.

Working Time-Weekly Hours

Recall that for men, we found a sharp difference in weekly hours by education and by race and ethnicity. This is not the case for women. In general, as figure 8.19 demonstrates, there are only small differences in weekly working time on each of these dimensions. For white women, there is less than a two-hour difference between those who have gone to college and those who have not. For black women, the difference is about double this size: 37.5 hours versus 33.1 hours. The biggest difference is among Hispanics, and once again the longer hours are put in by those with less education.

The racial gap is small as well. Less-educated white women work only about one hour more per week than less-educated black women. Among college-educated women, the racial divergence is reversed, with the black work week about one and a half hours longer than the white. Consistent with all the other statistics reported, it is the better-educated Hispanic women who work the least.

To sum up, then, the racial and ethnic difference in annual earnings is due not only to differences in hourly wages, but also to differences in working time—in this case, most strongly related to the high unemployment rate experienced by less-educated black women. The one anomaly in the overall pattern is found among better-educated Hispanic women, who have relatively low expected annual incomes because of both unexpectedly low wages and low weekly hours. What accounts for these racial and ethnic differences?

To answer this question, we will do two things. First, we will see how blacks, Hispanics, and whites differ in terms of the variables that presumably influence annual earnings. This includes variables related to human capital, nativity and family status, and job characteristics. Then, we will statistically estimate how important each of these variables is

FIGURE 8.19   *Mean Weekly Hours, Women*

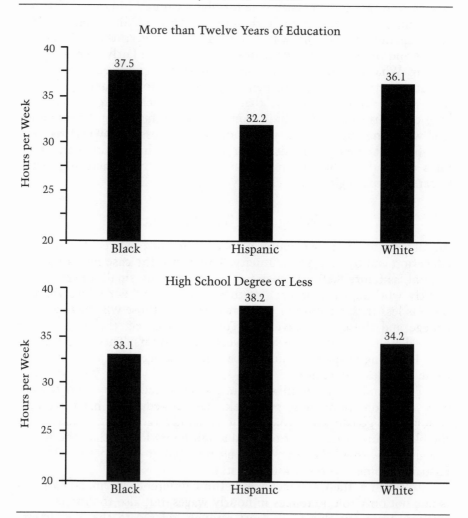

Source: Greater Boston Social Survey 1995.

to explaining differences in wages and the labor market components that contribute to annual hours.

Key Independent Variables: Differences by Race and Ethnicity

The demographic profiles for the black and Hispanic women in the GBSS differ substantially from that of the white women along many

TABLE 8.6   *Mean or Median Values for Labor Market Simulation Model, Women, High School Degree or Less, Age Twenty-One to Sixty-Five*

Variable Name	Black	Hispanic	White
LFP	.661	.662	.675
UR	.206	.067	.088
HRSWEEK	33.1	38.2	34.2
HOURLY WAGE (Median)[a]	$7.95	$8.45	$10.12
STRAT	.639	.358	.007
HSDEGREE	.598	.246	.766
HEALTHDY	.314	.139	.302
AGE	39	35	42
TOTJEXP (Median)	3	6.7	6
FOREIGN BORN	.294	.886	.083
MARRIED	.371	.675	.829
PRESKID (<7 YRS)	.371	.615	.299
NUMKIDS (< 19 YRS)	1.19	2.53	1.14
NUMJOB	1.048	1.012	1.219
LnFIRM SIZE	4.318	5.136	3.296
PUBLIC SECTOR	.155	.055	.160
SELF-EMPLOYMENT	.033	.040	.114
MANUFACTURING	.046	.606	.206
SERVICE OCCUPATION	.361	.170	.200
SALES OCCUPATION	.079	.053	.092
UNION MEMBER	.177	.231	.106
TELEPHONE USE ON JOB	.490	.131	.692
COMPUTER USE ON JOB	.237	.080	.529
RECENTLY EMPLOYED	.607	.634	.618

Source: Calculated from Council of Economic Advisers 1996, table B-43, 330.
[a]Inflation adjustment based on .2228 percent monthly increase in nominal average wages for production and nonsupervisory workers (1990 to 1995).

dimensions, as shown in table 8.6. For one, they live in different neighborhoods. About two-thirds of the black women and one-third of Hispanics with limited education live in minority neighborhoods (STRAT). While, by definition, these neighborhoods are less likely to contain whites, it is nevertheless striking that less than 1 percent of white women with limited education live in majority-minority neighborhoods.

There are also significant differences in terms of human capital variables. Only 25 percent of the Hispanic women had a high school diploma, compared with 60 percent of black women and 77 percent of white women. On the dimension of health limitations, the Hispanic women, who are, on average, much younger, are also much healthier. Only 14 percent say they have a health limitation affecting the type or amount of work they can do, compared with 30 percent of the white women (who are, on average, seven years older) and 31 percent of the black women (who are four years older). Despite the fact that the Hispanic women are younger, they are likely to have already spent more time in their current occupation. Their median years of occupational experience is 6.7, compared with 6 years for whites and only 3 years for blacks.

Black, Hispanic, and white women also differ substantially on a host of other factors. The Hispanic women, according to the GBSS, tend overwhelmingly to be newcomers to Greater Boston: 89 percent were born outside the U.S. mainland. Among black women, 29 percent are foreign-born; among white women, only 8 percent.

The family situations of women with limited education vary substantially by race and ethnicity. While 83 percent of the white women and 68 percent of the Hispanic women were married, only 37 percent of the black women were married at the time of the GBSS survey. Hispanic women have larger families—averaging two and a half children, compared with only a little more than one child for black and white women. Because they are younger, they are also more likely to have a child under age seven; 62 percent of the Hispanic women have a young child or children, compared with 37 percent of the black women and 30 percent of the white women.

Black, Hispanic, and white women with limited education occupy very different places within the workforce. Most strikingly, Hispanic women are heavily concentrated in manufacturing, as we have repeatedly mentioned. Fully three-fifths (61 percent) of them work in this one industrial sector, compared with 21 percent of white women and only 5 percent of black women. Hispanic women are less likely to work in the public sector—only 6 percent of Hispanic women are found there, compared with 16 percent for both white and black women. Differences in the rate of union membership are a reflection of these differences in the industrial distribution. Hispanic women have the highest unionization rate, at 23 percent, compared with 18 and 11 percent of black and white women, respectively. These differences in industrial distribution also account for differences in the nature of job tasks. White women are far more likely to use a computer on the job—53 percent, versus 24 percent for blacks and only 8 percent for Hispanics. White women are also far more likely to use a telephone on the job—69 percent, versus 49 percent for blacks and only 13 percent for Hispanics.

Thus, black, Hispanic, and white women have very different demographic and job profiles. Among women with limited education, Hispanic women are the least well educated but also the healthiest. The vast majority were born outside the U.S. mainland. They have more children and are more likely to have younger children. They are highly concentrated in the manufacturing sector, where rates of union membership are higher and where job tasks are less likely to include using a computer or speaking on the phone. Black women are most likely to live in segregated neighborhoods, and least likely to be married. White women are most likely to have completed high school, least likely to have been foreign-born, and most likely to be married. They are by far the most likely to work with computers, and also the most likely to use the telephone in their work.

Statistical Estimates of Labor Market Outcomes—Noncollege Women

The key question is, How does all this affect success in the labor market? Using a methodology similar to the one we employed to analyze men, we developed separate equations for individual labor force components and then combined them in a spreadsheet simulation. We used the same protocol as we did for the men for including and excluding independent variables in the overall model. Table 8.7 provides the entire set of final fitted equations for the women.

Labor Force Participation

We ran an unweighted logit equation for the probability that a woman with a limited education would be in the labor force. None of the common variables (BLACK, HISPANIC, or STRAT) significantly affected the likelihood of labor force participation. Human capital variables, however, have a highly significant impact. Finishing high school increases the likelihood of labor force participation (t = 5.12), while having health limitations reduces it (t = 9.25). The nativity/family status variables also play an important role. Married women are more likely to be in the workforce, while having a larger number of children and/or having a young child reduces the probability of labor force participation. With regard to nativity, being foreign-born increases the likelihood of labor force participation, but the interaction term for foreign-born Hispanics shows that these two attributes tend to offset each other.

Unemployment

A weighted logit equation was used to estimate the probability that a woman with limited education would be unemployed at the time of the survey interview. Among the common variables, HISPANIC had a nega-

TABLE 8.7   *Logit and Regression Equation Results, Women, High School*
Degree or Less

	LFP (logit)	UR (logit)	HRSWEEK (OLS)	RLnHWAGE (OLS)
Common variables				
BLACK	.2964	.1611	2.1720	.1237
	(0.97)	(0.15)	(1.29)	(1.42)
HISPANIC	.4301	−2.8918	.6965	.0342
	(0.99)	(2.15)	(0.44)	(0.42)
STRAT	−.3692	−.5620	1.7122	−.0153
	(1.29)	(0.60)	(1.08)	(0.21)
Human capital variables				
HSDEGREE	.9092	−2.4205	−2.4092	−.0294
	(5.12)	(3.18)	(2.19)	(0.56)
HEALTHDY	−2.1806			
	(9.25)			
TOTJEXP				.0133
				(3.87)
Nativity-family status variables				
FOREIGN BORN	1.0876			
	(2.24)			
FOREIGN BORN × HISPANIC	−1.5363			
	(2.44)			
MARRIED	.7491	−1.8157		
	(3.74)	(2.12)		
CHILD < AGE SEVEN	−.6934	3.0608		
	(3.02)	(3.26)		
NUMKIDS < AGE EIGHTEEN	−.2101			
	(2.51)			
Job characteristic variables				
NUMJOB			10.4982	
			(4.54)	
MFGDUMMY			5.3105	
			(4.75)	
SALES OCCUPATION				−.1750
				(2.11)
SALES × WHITE				−.3274
				(1.80)
PUBLIC SECTOR			2.7767	
			(1.88)	
UNION MEMBER				.2566
				(1.85)
LNFIRMSIZE				.0534
				(4.49)
UNION × LNFIRMSIZE				−.0351
				(1.54)

TABLE 8.7   *Continued*

	LFP	UR1	HRSWEEK	RLnWAGE
COMPUTER USE				.1036
				(1.77)
USE PHONE				.2011
				(3.40)
Control variable				
RECENTLY EMPLOYED				.1446
				(2.66)
RECENT EMPLOY				
× WHITE				.2343
				(1.97)
Constant	.6303	−.5450	22.7387	1.4347
N	677	307	416	381
F	12.87	7.94	8.18	12.99
R-Squared			.103	.284
	(unweighted)	(weighted)	(unweighted)	(unweighted)

Source: Greater Boston Social Survey 1995.
T-statistics in parentheses.

tive sign and was significant at better than the 5 percent level (t = 2.15): ceteris paribus, Hispanic women are less likely to be unemployed.

The significant coefficient on the one human capital variable—high school diploma—indicates that completing high school reduces the risk of unemployment. Among the nativity-family status variables, being married reduces the chance of unemployment; having a young child increases it.

Compared with white women, black women are more likely to have young children, less likely to be high school graduates, and far more likely to be single. According to this equation, these characteristics, rather than being black per se, account for their substantially higher unemployment rates.

Weekly Hours

An unweighted ordinary least squares (OLS) regression was used to ascertain the factors related to the number of hours worked per week by the women. None of the common variables was significant, and the best-fit equation produced one mystery. According to the regression, having a high school diploma actually *reduces* working time by nearly two and a half hours per week, after controlling for other factors. The coefficient is reasonably small, but statistically significant. If it were any larger, we would have pursued this issue further. As is, we do not have a good explanation for this unexpected finding.

What we did find, similar to the case for men, is that job characteristics play an important role in explaining the variance in working time. Among these variables, having more than one job increased work time by more than ten hours per week for each additional job—a result almost identical to the finding for men. Working in the public sector, where there tends to be a standard full-time work week, increases work time by almost three hours per week. Working in manufacturing, which also tends to have a long standard work week, increases work time by over five hours per week—a factor particularly important, as noted, for Hispanic women in the region. It is possible that the unexpected negative coefficient on HSDEGREE we found in this equation is due to the conflation of industry attachment and education. That Hispanic women work longer hours than either blacks or whites, despite the fact that they are much more likely not to have completed high school, may really be due to their disproportionate representation in manufacturing. However, tests with a series of interaction variables could not confirm this conjecture.

Hourly Wages

The final equation in the complete model provides an explanation for the variance in hourly earnings. As in the case for men, we ran an unweighted ordinary least squares regression equation for the natural logarithm of the hourly wage rate. None of the common variables were significant in this equation. Indeed, the variables BLACK and STRAT were not statistically significant in *any* of the labor market components for women. This is quite different from the fitted model for men, where we found a highly significant negative coefficient on STRAT in the hourly wage equation, in addition to a highly significant negative coefficient on the race variable BLACK. Moreover, the coefficient on BLACK in the male weekly hours equation was also negative and highly significant. This would seem to suggest that race and residence play a much larger role in labor market outcomes for black men than for black women. Being black and living in a minority community have an adverse impact on hourly wages and annual earnings for black men with limited schooling. The explanation for black women's poor labor market outcomes is more elusive.

Among the human capital variables, total years of experience in an occupation was significant, but the impact on the wage rate was relatively modest because the coefficient is so small. Having a high school diploma did not have a significant impact on the hourly wage rate at all, but several job characteristics did. Women working in sales occupations earned 19 percent less per hour. This is not surprising, for the sales occupations open to most noncollege women are in the low-wage retail trade sector. White women in sales occupations experienced an additional substantial wage penalty of 39 percent (t = 1.80), presumably because there is a better range of alternative employment available to white women, compared with black or Hispanic women.

Union members receive a 29 percent wage premium (t = 1.85), somewhat higher than that for men. Women working in larger firms receive a 0.5 percent wage premium for every 10 percent increase in the number of workers employed by the firm. However, the effect of these two variables is not strictly additive: the interaction term for the two together would reduce wages by 0.3 percent for every 10 percent increase in firm size (t = 1.54). So firm size appears to be more important in the nonunion sector than in unionized industries.

Job attributes that reflect certain tasks that are routinely required on the job also contribute to a higher hourly wage. Using a computer on the job raises the wage rate by about 11 percent (t = 1.77)—a somewhat smaller impact than for men. This might reflect the possibility that women are more likely to be using computers for data entry, while men are using computers in more highly valued assignments. Women who regularly use a telephone in their work are rewarded with a 22 percent wage premium—possibly reflecting higher-level clerical skills.

The control variable in this equation—recent employment experience—is particularly powerful for women. While recent employment experience has a positive impact on *all* women (a 16 percent wage premium), it has an additional (26 percent) positive impact on white women. Therefore, white women who have steady employment earn a large premium. White women are less likely than minority women to find themselves in jobs structured to accommodate unstable work habits, and therefore they experience an additional payoff to recent employment experience, beyond the payoff to minority women.

In sum, when it comes to the hourly wages of noncollege women, neither race nor ethnicity nor neighborhood seems to matter. Occupational experience matters, but the high school degree does not. Unionization is particularly important, as is working in desk occupations where the use of a computer and telephone are normal parts of the job. Steady employment is crucial as well, particularly for white women.

Simulating Labor Market Outcomes: Women

In our baseline equation for hourly wages, recall that black women earned 79 percent as much as white women; Hispanic women earned 84 percent as much. (See table 8.8 for a summary of the initial data.) On an

TABLE 8.8   *Baseline Labor Market Components*

Women, High School Diploma or Less (Age Twenty-One to Sixty-Five),
Greater Boston Labor Market, 1993 to 1994

	Black Women	Hispanic Women	White Women
Labor force participation rate	66.1%	66.2%	67.5%
Unemployment rate	20.6%	6.7%	8.8%
Average hours worked per week	33.1	38.2	34.2
Expected annual hours	904	1,228	1,096
Median hourly wage	$7.95	$8.45	$10.12
Expected annual earnings	$7,188	$10,378	$11,101
Ratios	Black/White	Hispanic/White	Black/Hispanic
Median hourly wage	78.6%	83.5%	94.1%
Expected annual earnings	64.8%	93.5%	69.3%

Source: Greater Boston Social Survey 1995.

annual basis, however, the two minority groups diverged significantly. The black/white ratio falls to 65 percent, while Hispanics nearly close the entire gap with whites, rising to 94 percent, based on long hours of work. We can now see how changes in human capital, in race and neighborhood residence, and in family structure affect the overall level of expected annual income and the earnings ratios among blacks, Hispanics, and whites.

Human Capital Factors

On an hourly wage basis, simulations that standardized for the human capital factors of education, occupational experience, and health turned up little impact on the wage ratios for either blacks or Hispanics (see figure 8.20). This is the case because the coefficients on the human capital variables in the hourly wage equation are either small or 0. Hence, differences in schooling (high school or less), health status, and occupational experience have a small impact on wages.

However, these factors have a larger effect on the components of expected annual hours, and therefore show up as more important in the annual earnings simulation. According to figure 8.21 the black/white annual earnings ratio rises to .77 from .65 when white means for HSDEGREE, HEALTHDY, and TOTJEXPA are inserted into the model. For Hispanics, the high school diploma makes the big difference, raising annual hours of work so much that if Hispanic women completed high school in the same proportion as white women, they would dominate

FIGURE 8.20   *Hourly Earning Ratios, Women*
              Impact of Human Capital Factors

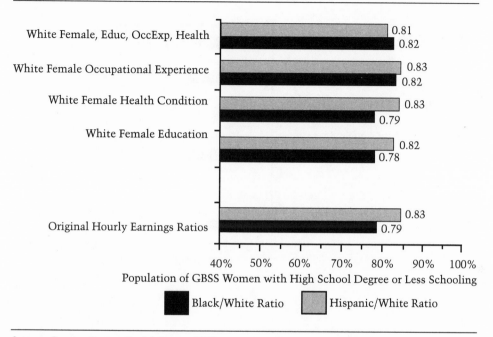

White Female, Educ, OccExp, Health — 0.81 / 0.82
White Female Occupational Experience — 0.83 / 0.82
White Female Health Condition — 0.83 / 0.79
White Female Education — 0.82 / 0.78
Original Hourly Earnings Ratios — 0.83 / 0.79

40% 50% 60% 70% 80% 90% 100%

Population of GBSS Women with High School Degree or Less Schooling

■ Black/White Ratio   ▨ Hispanic/White Ratio

Source: Greater Boston Social Survey 1995.

white women in annual earnings. So education is a key variable for Hispanic women, but not for black women—and it operates through higher labor force participation rates and lower unemployment rates, not through weekly hours or hourly pay.

Race and Residence

If improved human capital has only a modest effect on the earnings of black women, would treating them like whites and "moving" them to white neighborhoods make much of a difference in earnings? As far as hourly wages go, the answer appears to be no. As figure 8.22 demonstrates, there is no improvement in hourly pay for black women when we treat them as white, nor when we place them in white-majority census blocks. While Hispanic women benefit from being treated as white (the Hispanic/white hourly wage ratio rises from .84 to .91), they too receive no benefit from being placed in white-majority census blocks.

On an annual earnings basis, as figure 8.23 shows, the outcome for

267

FIGURE 8.21 *Annual Earnings Ratios, Women*
Impact of Human Capital Factors

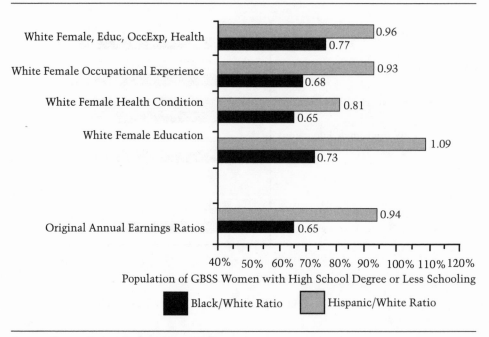

White Female, Educ, OccExp, Health — 0.96 / 0.77

White Female Occupational Experience — 0.93 / 0.68

White Female Health Condition — 0.81 / 0.65

White Female Education — 1.09 / 0.73

Original Annual Earnings Ratios — 0.94 / 0.65

40% 50% 60% 70% 80% 90% 100% 110% 120%

Population of GBSS Women with High School Degree or Less Schooling

■ Black/White Ratio   ▨ Hispanic/White Ratio

Source: Greater Boston Social Survey 1995.

black women actually gets worse. Since, other things being equal, our regression results indicate that black women would have higher labor force participation rates and longer weekly hours (the signs on these coefficients are positive, though insignificant), making them white is a disadvantage when it comes to expected annual hours of work. Given that they gain nothing on hourly wages, the overall outcome is negative. For Hispanics, we can close the annual earnings gap simply by treating Hispanic women as native-born, which raises their labor force participation rates. Indeed, if this is done, they wind up with expected annual earnings 11 percent greater than whites'. Then again, they did not have far to go to gain equality in annual earnings.

Family Structure

For black women, neither the race-residence-nativity variables nor the human capital variables produce dramatic improvements. So what does? Figure 8.24 provides a powerful clue. It shows annual earnings simulated for each of four family types. Regardless of race-ethnic group, annual earnings are by far the highest for women who are married but

FIGURE 8.22   *Hourly Earning Ratios, Women*
Impact of Race and Residence

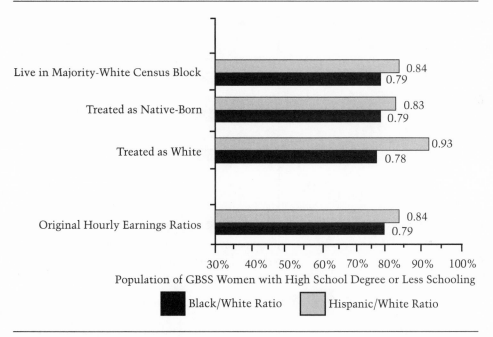

Population of GBSS Women with High School Degree or Less Schooling

■ Black/White Ratio   ▢ Hispanic/White Ratio

Source: Greater Boston Social Survey 1995.

have no children under age eighteen. Single women with no children under age eighteen have the second highest annual earnings—a bit higher than married women with children. But trailing way behind the rest of the pack are single women with children—*regardless* of race and ethnicity. When we simulate this group and "give" them two children, annual earnings drop dramatically for all three race-ethnic groups. Black women see their annual earnings fall to $1,383—only about 12 percent as much as black married women who have no young children. White single mothers also fare badly. Their earnings ($1,392) are about the same as that of black single mothers, and according to our simulation they make only about 10 percent as much as what married white women with no children under eighteen earn. Single Hispanic mothers are at less of a disadvantage. At $5,166, their expected annual earnings are higher than for similarly situated black and white single mothers— but only a third as high as their married colleagues who have no children under eighteen.

Family structure is therefore the single most important factor in explaining women's earnings, and it is where black women are at greatest disadvantage. Recall that only 37 percent of black women in our study

FIGURE 8.23   *Annual Earnings Ratios, Women*
             Impact of Race and Residence

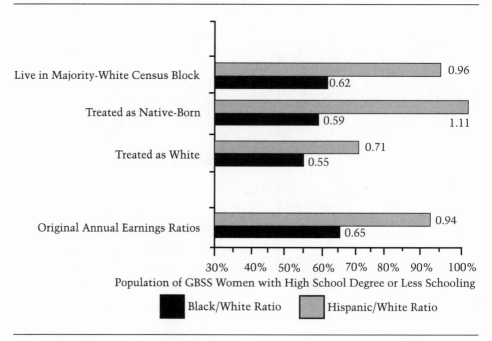

Population of GBSS Women with High School Degree or Less Schooling

■ Black/White Ratio   ▨ Hispanic/White Ratio

Source: Greater Boston Social Survey 1995.

were married, compared with 68 percent of Hispanic women and 83 percent of white women. Being single hits black women hard. This is particularly true when they are single parents. Among mothers with children under age eighteen, only 12 percent of white women and 30 percent of Hispanic women are unmarried, compared with 55 percent of black women.

Conclusion

This analysis of men and women with limited education suggests that the strong economy of the Greater Boston region has had beneficial effects on both labor force participation and the probability of having recent employment experience, particularly for blacks and Hispanics. Unlike the picture that might come from the inner cities of more economically distressed metropolitan areas, the strong Boston economy has provided the opportunity for most black and Hispanic men, as well as black and Hispanic women, to avoid the desolation of being completely disconnected from the labor market. The image of a jobless ghetto does not apply.

FIGURE 8.24   *Annual Earnings, Women*
              by Family Type

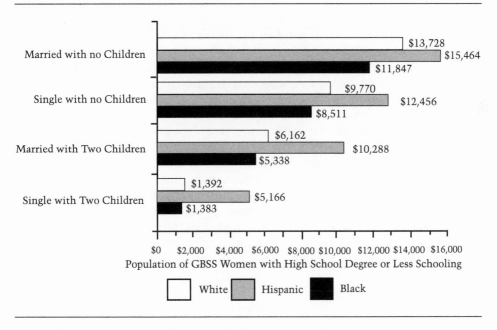

Population of GBSS Women with High School Degree or Less Schooling

White   Hispanic   Black

Still, there are serious problems that each of these demographic groups face relative to their white counterparts. The large gaps in both hourly wages and annual earnings facing Hispanic men are due almost exclusively to current human capital deficits. Accordingly, if there were convergence in human capital between Hispanic and white men, there would be convergence in earnings. This is not true for black men. Equalizing human capital equalizes hourly wages. But even after statistically providing black men with the same human capital as white men, a large annual earnings gap remains. This is due to higher unemployment and significantly lower weekly hours. For annual earnings convergence to occur, black men with limited education will have to be given the same opportunities as whites to find and retain full-time jobs, as well as the chance to supplement regular jobs with self-employment income—as is the case for many white men in the region.

The story for women is quite different. Hispanic women would actually have higher annual earnings than whites if they had the same education. This is true because, other things being equal, Hispanic women work more hours per week on average than their white counterparts and have a somewhat lower unemployment rate. Closing the annual earnings gap for black women proves much more difficult. Women in female-headed households with children tend to have the lowest annual earnings of all demographic types, regardless of race and ethnicity. But since black mothers are much more likely than whites or Hispanics to be single parents, black women on average have lower yearly pay.

The policy implications, which we shall take up in chapter 11, are driven by the observation that very different factors are responsible for the relative labor market success or failure of individual demographic groups in the Greater Boston region. But the circumstances faced by most groups in the metropolitan area are certainly not as adverse as those found in many communities where deindustrialization and joblessness are more widespread. The region's triple revolution has brought a new labor force to Greater Boston, but the strength of the economy has provided more labor market opportunity than is the case in many parts of the country. The opportunity nexus still plays favorites—with blacks at greatest disadvantage because of persistent racialist attitudes and housing segregation. But the region does not have a large jobless ghetto requiring massive investments in technical and social skills before any progress toward labor market equality can be made.

Appendix
Protocol for Estimating Annual Earnings Model

Because of the immense number of variables that theoretically could enter the model and the wide array of demographic information available in the GBSS, it was necessary to develop a protocol for entering variables into each equation. After much experimentation, the following rules were developed:

1. All variables included in the model had to represent factors highlighted by economic and sociological theory. These included variables related to human capital, nativity and family status, and job characteristics.

2. The data set was restricted to men age twenty-one to sixty-five who had no more than twelve years of formal schooling.

3. The original equations were run on *unweighted* data with four variables, which remain in the final equations regardless of their statistical significance. These account for race (BLACK), for ethnic group (HISPANIC), for neighborhood racial and ethnic composition (STRAT), and for high school completion (HSDEGREE). Our focus on race and

ethnicity, on neighborhood effects, and on human capital provides the rationale for entering these variables in each equation.

4. Additional variables were then tested in each model. These include a wide array of human capital and demographic factors, as well as variables related to the number and type of jobs held by working individuals. These were retained in the model if they met the 10 percent confidence level. Given the relatively small sample sizes for individual equations, this level of significance was deemed reasonable in order to reduce the possibility of Type II errors—rejecting valid hypotheses when they are true (Kennedy 1994).

5. The preference for using unweighted data in the estimated equations is based on a careful consideration of the tradeoff between inefficiency due to weighting versus bias due to not weighting (Graubard and Korn 1995). In a sample such as the GBSS, where some cases have very large weights relative to others, using weighted data for econometric analysis introduces enormous heteroskedasticity and therefore extremely inefficient parameters. On the other hand, the bias due to not weighting is a result of the stratification of the sample. Including stratification variables in each equation and attempting to specify each equation as carefully as possible in line with theoretical considerations should make the bias due to using unweighted data less detrimental than the inefficiency introduced by using weighted data.

6. Logit equations for labor force participation and unemployment rates were re-estimated with weighted data, because the unweighted specification produced coefficients that yielded highly unstable simulations.

While the original labor force participation and unemployment rate logit equations normally had the expected signs, counterfactual simulations based on the estimated coefficients yielded participation and unemployment rates that were overly sensitive to small changes in the simulated level of their explanatory variables. This turned out to be due to an interaction among three factors: the relatively small sample size, the use of a stratified, clustered sampling design for the survey, and the fact that the variables to be explained had mean values close to 1 (participation rate) and 0 (unemployment rate). (In related research on women where the participation rates were close to .6, this problem did not appear.) After a series of experiments with different forms of the equation, it was found that a model based on sample weighted data proved substantially more serviceable in the simulation model. In the unemployment equation, we also found that adding the HSDEGREE variable to the model generated instability. In this one case, the variable was dropped.

9

THE IMPACT OF HUMAN, SOCIAL, AND CULTURAL CAPITAL ON JOB SLOTS AND WAGES

IN THE last chapter we studied the determinants of hourly wages and annual earnings for black, Hispanic, and white workers with limited education. We devoted special attention to this group because those who are least advantaged in terms of schooling presumably are the ones who would be most adversely affected by Greater Boston's triple revolution.

In this chapter, we investigate the entire Greater Boston labor force, including those with more than a high school education. We search for the factors responsible for determining *where* people work: the industries, occupations, and firms in which people find employment. We develop separate models by race and ethnicity rather than by gender. This permits us to understand better how accumulation of human capital, social capital, and cultural capital affect the specific labor market prospects for each race-ethnic group—although at the cost of sacrificing some information about the impact of gender. Unfortunately, even with a data set with over 1,800 observations, subsampling by race, ethnicity, *and* gender leaves cell sizes too small for statistically reliable results.

We also delve into the factors responsible for differences in workers' education level, essentially asking how "investments" in social and cultural capital affect investments in human capital. A number of institutional factors are considered as well, in so far as they might affect how well workers fare on their jobs. Among these are the size of the firm where workers are employed and the racial and ethnic composition of the individual's workplace. Together with the previous chapter, the findings here round out our understanding of how the triple revolution and the opportunity nexus affect labor market outcomes throughout the region.

A Job Competition Model of the Urban Labor Market

We begin this deeper probing of the Boston labor market by elaborating a particular model of labor market behavior. Indeed, twenty-five years ago, Lester Thurow compared the study of labor markets to the game of chess:

> Imagine watching a chess game without knowing any of the rules of chess. Complicated moves are being made; players are being captured; games are being won. . . . Now imagine a more complicated game in which some of the moves are random events not determined by the explicit rules of the game. Accidents occur. The game is also being played by players who do not always act in accordance with the rules. They make mistakes. In such a game, constructing the rule book would be a monumental task. Yet it is just such a game that economists are trying to dissect. What are the rules of the economic game? How are the economic prizes distributed? What determines the actions of individual players?
>
> Ultimately the purpose of knowing the rules of any game is to be able to explain how the game works, to predict the outcome of the game, to play the game better, or perhaps, to design a better game. The starting point, however, is our knowledge of the outcome of the current economic game—a game played for life-and-death stakes. We can observe this game directly by looking at the distributions of earnings and wealth. These are the prizes that the economy has distributed. *Once we know the distribution of economic prizes, we can begin the task of working backward to understand the process whereby prizes are generated and distributed.* [Thurow 1975, vi–vii; emphasis added]

This passage, particularly the last line, provides an apt description of the approach we adopt here to understand the distribution of earnings in the Greater Boston labor market. We shall ask the question, Who gets which jobs in which industries and in which occupations, and how is he or she rewarded for getting there?

The model we employ here is based on "job competition" theory.[1] It focuses on the supply side of the labor market—on what workers bring to the firms that hire them. For present purposes, the demand side in this model is assumed to be exogenous. That is, the entire array of jobs, along with wage rates, is taken as given in the Boston labor market. Hence, we suspend the notion, found in the more common wage competition model, of smoothly functioning supply and demand functions setting wage and employment levels simultaneously.

In a job competition model, instead of competing against one another on the basis of the wages they are willing to accept, individuals compete against one another for job opportunities (or job slots) at more or less fixed wages. In jockeying for positions in the job queue, success for the individual worker rests on being able to signal to potential employers that he or she possesses a set of attributes (including credentials, behaviors, and attitudes) that firms find desirable (Thurow 1975). In Thurow's conception, "one set of factors determines an individual's *relative* position in the labor queue; another set of factors, not mutually exclusive of the first, determines the actual distribution of job opportunities in the economy. Wages are paid mainly on the basis of the characteristics of the job in question, and workers are distributed across job opportunities based on their relative position in the labor queue. The most preferred workers get the best jobs"[2] (Thurow 1975, 76).

Here we assume the labor market queue is given by the structure of industries and occupations in the region and by the preferences of employers. The principal task is to determine the factors responsible for how each worker (or groups of workers with similar characteristics) is allocated to a particular point in the queue: who gets the best jobs with the highest pay and who must settle for something less. We do not have firsthand evidence of the hiring process itself, nor information from employers on what characteristics go into establishing their labor demand queues. The data we have provide evidence of the hiring decision outcome: the ranking of employed workers in given industries, in given occupations, earning a given wage. From the analysis, we attempt to discern the key parameters of the hiring decision.

Employers do not know with certainty how well a new hire will perform on the job. Lacking direct information on the amount of training required to elevate a particular recruit to a level of acceptable job performance, employers rank workers on the basis of what they can learn of the workers' background characteristics. The objective of employers is to decipher what background characteristics best predict future work performance. In their search for a set of attributes with good predictive value, employers will likely consider such factors as formal education, previous work experience, and an individual's specific skills.

For jobs where the cost of making a hiring mistake is low—where the firm's investment in training costs and hiring costs is small relative to the total costs of employing the worker—employers will presumably search only *superficially*. To minimize search costs, employers will rely on easily identifiable worker traits such as formal education. Employers therefore use "statistical discrimination," choosing new employees who exhibit the most easily recognizable characteristics of successful employees they have hired in the past. This can obviously give rise to racial and ethnic discrimination or to gender and age discrimination (Reich 1981; Kirshenman and Neckerman 1991).

For jobs where the cost of a hiring mistake is high (one of the best examples being the hiring of a tenured full professor), employers will presumably search *intensively*, trying to learn as much as possible about a specific job candidate before committing themselves to what could be a multimillion dollar, long-term venture. Because different jobs require different skills, workers will appear at different places in the labor queue for different jobs.[3] One worker may be at the head of the queue for carpenters, given his or her training and skills, but way down in the queue for brain surgeons. Hence, in a complete job competition model, one needs to consider a segmented labor market in which noncompeting labor market queues coexist (Gordon, Edwards, and Reich 1982).

In this job competition model, identical individuals do not necessarily earn identical incomes, as they would according to the more typical wage competition model. Once in a job, individual workers will not normally receive the same on-the-job training or promotion opportunities. These are at least partially determined by the idiosyncratic practices of specific employers. In one firm, seniority alone might determine how high in the occupation one might rise; in another, racial, ethnic, or gender discrimination may foreclose promotion possibilities. As such, the job competition model is fully consistent with the observation of substantial variance in earnings among workers who have ostensibly identical human capital characteristics (such as education) and who provide equal work effort, but differ by race, ethnicity, gender, or any of a number of other characteristics not specifically related to job performance per se.

Clearly, research within a job competition framework must be seen as part of a "static" analysis. It entails a "snapshot" of a given labor market at a specific point and is used to explain how the characteristics of individual workers condition the positions they hold at that moment. In a "dynamic" analysis, one would want to examine how changes in workers' and employers' behavior contribute to altered outcomes (that is, a different matching pattern between workers and job slots). This is beyond the scope of the present research, but the static analysis provides important clues to what such a dynamic analysis might yield.

A Vector Description of a Labor Market

A diagram of the job slot-employee matching mechanism is provided in Figure 9.1. Each job slot in the labor market queue can be defined as a vector containing job requirements and job attributes established by the employer (or employers). To be considered for a particular job slot, prospective employees must demonstrate to the employer that they meet specific job requirements. These can include such factors as the amount

FIGURE 9.1   *Job Slot-Employee Matching*

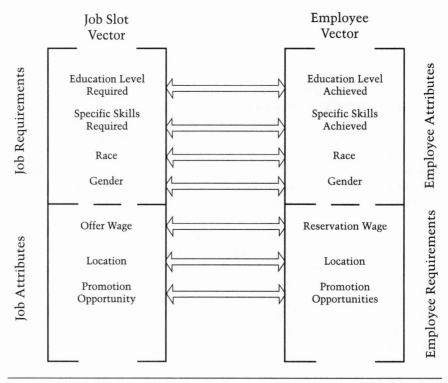

Source: Authors' compilation.

of schooling and specific skills the employer deems necessary to the job. Discrimination may also enter into the job "requirements" if employers have an implicit or explicit preference for a particular race or gender when considering potential workers for a specific job slot.

Each job slot also contains a set of job attributes. These include an offer wage, additional benefits conveyed in the compensation package, a spatial location, and the existence or absence of promotion opportunities. Presumably, in seeking to hire the best workers in the employee pool, employers compete by trying to offer an attractive compensation and benefits package. The job queue in any given labor market is simply a complete set of job vectors arrayed according to the quality of the job attributes embedded in each slot.

In analogous fashion, each potential worker in the labor market comes equipped with a set of employee attributes and a set of employee requirements. The attributes include education credentials and skill level. Each worker also has particular race, ethnic, and gender attributes—factors an employer might consider when making a hiring choice. On the employee requirements side, workers exhibit a reservation wage (a wage below which they will not accept employment), a reservation benefit package, a location requirement, suggesting a spatial limitation on which jobs will be acceptable from a commuting or amenities standpoint, and perhaps a set of requirements regarding potential promotion opportunities.

For a specific job-employee match to occur—that is, for a worker to be hired—there must be correspondence between a job's requirements and an employee's attributes. If an individual does not meet the minimum job requirements of the employer, the employee is rejected for the job. Likewise, there must be correspondence between what a worker requires in a job and a job's attributes for a successful match to occur. If, for example, the reservation wage of the applicant is above the offer wage of the job, the individual will reject the job. If the job's compensation package and promotion opportunities are satisfactory to the potential employee, but the job is located too distant from the applicant's residence (or in a neighborhood otherwise considered unacceptable by the job applicant), a match will not be consummated.[4]

In the static short-run analysis considered here, the set of job vectors and employee vectors are considered fixed.[5] The task before us is to identify the "successful" matches between worker characteristics and job slots, and from this exercise identify the specific employee attributes that contribute to high rankings in the job queues in the Greater Boston labor market. In this way, we can discern who gets what jobs and why.

Operationalization of the Job Competition Model

With the foregoing model as prologue, we can begin to consider a method for operationalizing the job competition model in order to, in Thurow's words, "begin the task of working backward to understand the process whereby prizes are generated and distributed." Our specific approach assumes a matching process in which individuals are first matched to (or screen themselves into) an industry-occupation cell. The "I/O cell" stipulates the broad industry and broad occupation category or job queue in which a worker competes for a position. Workers are then matched to a particular establishment or firm, and finally matched with a specific job slot within that establishment. That specific job slot is associated with a given wage, benefit package, and promotion ladder. Obviously, in the real world, the matching process involving I/O cells, firms, and job slots occurs simultaneously. At the moment someone takes a specific job, he or she hires into a specific occupation in a particular firm which is part of a given industry. In our operationalized model, we separate this process in order to gain an understanding of how the opportunity nexus surrounding a given individual affects what industries, occupations, and job slots he or she will be able to access.

Industry-Occupation Distribution

Every job in a local labor market can be identified as occupying one slot within a particular industry-occupation cell. For example, physicians working in the health industry are found in one I/O cell; painters employed in the construction industry are located in another; and salespersons within retail trade in a third. In Figure 9.2, each bar represents one I/O cell. The height of each bar represents the number of firms in a local labor market offering jobs that fall into this cell. In the hypothetical example here, there are ninety retail trade firms employing sales clerks, fifty construction firms employing painters, and forty health care providers employing physicians. The horizontal axis represents a particular observed characteristic of I/O cells—the average wage paid, for example,

FIGURE 9.2   *Distribution of Industry-Occupation Cells*

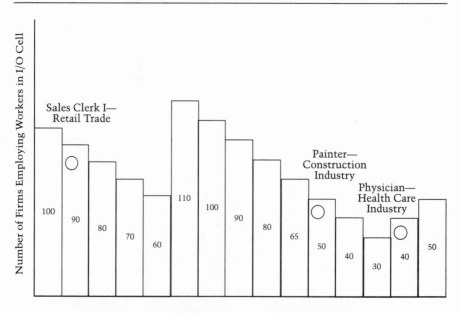

I/O Cells Arrayed by Cell Characteristics

Source: Greater Boston Social Survey 1995.

or the proportion of firms associated with the cell offering health insurance benefits to employees. In this example, retail trade jobs are generally in lower-wage I/O cells, while physicians are in an occupation within an industry that generally pays quite well.

Firm (or Establishment) Distribution

Within each I/O, there is then a distribution of firms (or establishments). Figure 9.3 presents a hypothetical distribution of *firms* within the construction industry. In this particular case, the distribution contains the set of fifty firms inside the figure 9.2 bar labeled "Painter—Construction Industry." The average wage (or another measure of remuneration offered workers in this establishment) is measured on the horizontal axis, and the number of firms within this I/O cell offering this pay package is measured on the vertical axis. Each firm in the figure 9.3 distribution is also associated with a set of characteristics that are potentially associated with its wage level.

In the diagram we depict two firms, one a small, nonunionized outfit and the other a large, unionized company. Presumably, workers who are fortunate to find jobs in the large unionized company enjoy better wages and benefits than those who end up in the other one. The amount of variance in the overall wage distribution within each I/O cell reflects the degree of market imperfection in the particular industry or occupa-

FIGURE 9.3   *Distribution of Firms (Employing I/O Cell Workers)*

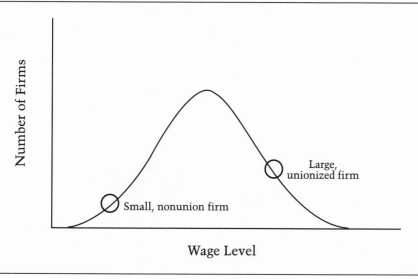

Source: Greater Boston Social Survey 1995.

tion depicted in the chart. Presumably, a market with few imperfections would be indicated by a more peaked distribution, with most firms offering similar wages and benefits; a highly imperfect market would appear as a flatter distribution, with much greater wage and benefit variance. The more imperfect the market, the more likely that nearly identical individuals will end up with different wages and benefits.

Job Slot Distribution

The final distribution in the model is found within a given firm or establishment (see figure 9.4). Within a firm, wages can vary across workers in the same occupation (as depicted in the diagram) because of a number of factors (for example, individual employee experience level, wages tied to piece-rate performance; or, for that matter, racial, ethnic, or gender discrimination within the firm). The actual compensation received by a specific worker is measured on the horizontal axis, and the number of workers within a firm receiving this wage is measured on the vertical axis.

Given this model of the labor market, we can see that the *wage paid to a specific worker* is the culmination of a wage determination process that operates at the level of the I/O cell (figure 9.2), the firm (figure 9.3), and finally the specific job within the firm (figure 9.4).

FIGURE 9.4   *Distribution of Jobs (Within I/O Cells Within Each Firm)*

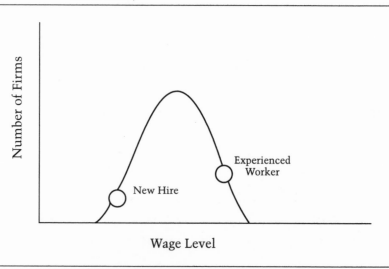

Source: Greater Boston Social Survey 1995.

This model does not assume anything about the active *or* passive behavior of the worker. Professionals are good examples of workers who play an active role in locating themselves in the I/O distribution. Individuals train to enter the health care industry as physicians or nurses, or train to become electrical engineers. For other workers, acquiring a location in the I/O distribution is passive or haphazard: a worker sees a Help Wanted ad and goes to the company to see what work it might have for him.

Model Specification

To operationalize this unique approach to wage determination for the purposes of empirical estimation, we developed the following specifications and a set of hypothesized relationships.

Industry-Occupation (I/O cell) Determination   Ideally, we would want to define each I/O cell on the basis of the general skill sets needed to perform the tasks within the cell. Because we do not have any readily available index to measure skill sets, we use the median hourly wage paid in 1990 to Massachusetts workers as a hedonic index of these characteristics. That is, while wages vary within a given I/O cell across individuals, based on the individual's particular skill level and other characteristics (including possibly race, ethnicity, and gender), we assume the median wage in a cell is a reasonable measure of the value of these skill sets in the overall labor market.[6] The I/O cell categorization we use includes fifteen industries and fourteen occupations, listed in the appendix to this chapter. Because of empty cells (there are no private household workers in the construction industry, for example), wage data exist for only 181 of the potential 210 I/O cells. The median wage figures were estimated for a sample that includes all men and women who reported wage or salary earnings.[7] Hence, we have combined full-time and part-time workers together, as well as self-employed workers, in making the median hourly wage calculations used in this study.

In the regressions to follow for individual race-ethnic groups, we hypothesize that the factors most influencing an individual's access to a particular I/O cell (or a range of I/O cells) are formal education, general training, and gender. The most powerful of these is expected to be education, as measured by years of schooling completed. On the assumption that formal credentialing is a requirement for many occupations, particularly those requiring more than a high school education, employers use education as a screening device when considering workers for skilled positions. A measure of general training is also included to take into account the types of credentials needed to enter a variety of technical and clerical occupations. Our measure refers to formal training received after high school, but excludes on-the-job training in order to limit simultaneity between training and occupational choice. Finally, we include gender in the I/O equation to account for possible industry or occupational segregation (Stevenson 1984; Treiman and Hartmann 1981; Kilbourne, England, and Bevon 1994).

Firm Determination   To identify the characteristics of an individual firm or establishment operating within an I/O cell, one might take its median wage, as we do for I/O cells. However, we do not have aggregate data on wages at the firm or establishment level and cannot use the limited GBSS sample to estimate such a measure. Instead we identify firms in this model by a number of characteristics likely to be correlated with wages. In particular, we expect the size of an establishment and the racial/ethnic composition of its workforce to be key indicators of a firm's position in the overall wage distribution. These two variables are available in the GBSS, and therefore we rely on them as proxies for the location of firms within each I/O cell. Large firms often pay higher wages than smaller ones, while firms that rely heavily on minority or women workers often pay lower wages than those employing mostly white men.[8]

A review of labor market studies suggests that the size of an individual worker's establishment is related to a number of factors. Workplaces in the public sector tend to be larger than the typical private-sector firm; workers who are self-employed tend to be associated with very small firms; and firms who hire new workers by relying on the "strong" networks (family and friends) of their current employees tend to be smaller as well. In addition, there may be a relationship between gender and firm size as well as age and education. We test for all of these in developing a model of firm size.

Whether a firm can be identified as having a large number of jobs "reserved" for minorities can be associated with the search behavior of the workers employed and the location of the firm in the I/O distribution. The more the firm relies on strong networks to hire workers, the more likely the firm hires large numbers of minorities. Firms hiring minority workers are also likely to be at the low end of the I/O distribution.

Job Slot Distribution   At the end of the overall matching process, workers find themselves in specific job slots within a given firm within an I/O cell. The observed hourly wage of the individual worker is used to identify this job slot—and thus the worker's position in the overall local labor market distribution. In accord with the standard practice used to estimate wages from microdata, we employ the natural logarithm of the hourly wage as the dependent variable in our empirical work.

Following the structure of the overall model as depicted in figures 9.2 through 9.4, an individual's hourly wage is a function of what I/O cell he or she enters and the two variables defining the individual's firm: the probability of working with minority coworkers and firm size. In addition, we employ a range of variables to further identify specific human capital attributes of the individual worker, all of which presumably rank the worker within the overall distribution of job slots within his or her firm. These include job experience in the particular occupation (as a measure of both skill and seniority effects), health status, and marital status (as a possible measure of worker "stability"). In addition, education and gender reenter the model to account for firm-specific effects beyond those associated with the impact of schooling and gender on I/O cell determination.

To make schooling endogenous in the model and thus account for one channel through which cultural capital and socioeconomic status can affect earnings, we model each individual's years of schooling as a function of the individual's background characteristics. These include age, gender, and several factors related to an individual's social and cultural capital accumulated before age sixteen.

The final wage simulation model for the Greater Boston labor market includes five equations of the following general form (a variable list is found in table 9.1).

(1) EDUCATION $= b_0 + b_1 AGE + b_2 SEX + b_3$ MOTHER'S EDUCATION $+ b_4$INTACT FAMILY

(2) IOCELL $= c_0 + c_1 EDUCATION$

(3) MINORITY FIRM $= e_0 + e_1 SEARCH + e_2 IOCELL$

(4) FIRM SIZE $= d_0 + d_1 SEARCH + d_2 SELF\ EMPLOYMENT + d_3 SEX + d_4 EDUCATION + d_5 PUBLIC\ SECTOR + d_6 AGE$

(5) HOURLY WAGE $= f_0 + f_1 IOCELL + f_2 FIRM\ SIZE + f_3 MINORITY\ FIRM + f_4 SEX + f_5\ OCCUPATION\ EXPERIENCE + f_6 AGE + f_7 AGE\ SQUARED + f_8 TEMPORARY/SEASONAL\ WORK + f_9 USE\ COMPUTER\ ON\ THE\ JOB + f_{10} EDUCATION\ +\ OTHER\ PERSONAL$ CHARACTERISTICS

TABLE 9.1   *Variable List for Labor Market Simulation Model*

Variable Name	Variable Description
IOCELL	Median wage for industry-occupation cell
MINORITYFM	Majority of employees at individual's establishment are black or Hispanic (dummy variable)
LnFIRMSZ	Natural log of the employment level in worker's establishment
RLnHWAGE	Natural log of real hourly wage, including employment and self-employment earnings (adjusted for time elapsed since last job[a]
EDUCATION	Years of schooling completed
EDUC (zero to eight)	Years of schooling completed (zero to eight) (categorical variable)
EDUC (nine to eleven)	Years of schooling completed (nine to eleven) (categorical variable)
EDUC (thirteen to fifteen)	Years of schooling completed (thirteen to fifteen) (categorical variable)
EDUC (over sixteen)	Years of schooling completed (over sixteen) (categorical variable)
SEX	Female = 0; Male = 1
MOTHERED	Years of schooling completed by mother of worker
INTACTFM	Worker lived with both parents most of the time until at least age sixteen (dummy variable)
GENTRAIN	Worker received training after high school *not* specific to the job (dummy variable)
SEARCH	Found job through family or friends (dummy variable)
PUBSEC	Employed in public-sector job (dummy variable)
SELFEMP	Worker's major job is self-employment (dummy variable)
TIMEUS	Percentage of life spent in mainland United States
AGE	Age
AGESQ	Age squared
OCCEXP	Years of total job experience in current occupation
CATHOLIC	Catholic (dummy variable)
JEWISH	Jewish (dummy variable)
TEENMARRY	Married before age eighteen (dummy variable)
EDOUTUS	Received at least some education outside mainland United States (dummy variable)
NUMORGS	Number of formal organizations individual belongs to (such as neighborhood, PTA, social club, sports teams, political organizations, church groups, ethnic and cultural organizations)
TEMPSEAS	Current work is in temporary or seasonal job (dummy variable)
COMPJOB	Work with computer daily or weekly on job (dummy variable)
MARRIED	Currently married (dummy variable)

TABLE 9.1   *Continued*

Variable Name	Variable Description
WORDTEST	Number of words correctly identified in wordtest (Max = 7)
HEALTHDY	Health or general condition limits amount or kind of work individual can perform (dummy variable)
ASSESSUQ	Interviewer's assessment of ability of respondent to understand questions on survey (1 = excellent to 5 = poor)
STRATUM	Live in black- or Hispanic-majority census block (dummy variable)
EMPREC	At work within past twelve months (dummy variable)
UNION	Member of a union (dummy variable)

Source: Calculated from Council of Economic Advisers 1996, table B-43, 330.
[a]Inflation adjustment based on .2228 percent monthly increase in nominal average wage for production and nonsupervisory workers (1988 to 1995).

In this set of equations, the hourly wage for the individual is a function of the I/O cell to which the individual worker's firm belongs, the characteristics of the firm that employs him plus the size of the firm, and a set of personal attributes that determine the worker's wage within the firm. These include such factors as age, sex, education, and occupational experience. A path diagram for this equation set is found in figure 9.5.

Testing Hypotheses with the Job Competition Model

For the purpose of demonstrating the power of this model, we attempt to test a number of general hypotheses about earnings determination in this chapter, including:

H_1: *Family background variables*—particularly those related to mother's education and the number of parents in the home when young—substantially affect the level of schooling received by individuals. Hence, socioeconomic status is a major constraint on the amount of schooling individuals receive and therefore on where they end up in the labor market.

H_2: The impact of *human capital variables* on industry-occupation access will be strongest for white men, as they suffer least from the various forms of labor market discrimination that tend to constrain I/O access for blacks, Hispanics, and women.

FIGURE 9.5   Path Diagram for Labor Market Simulation

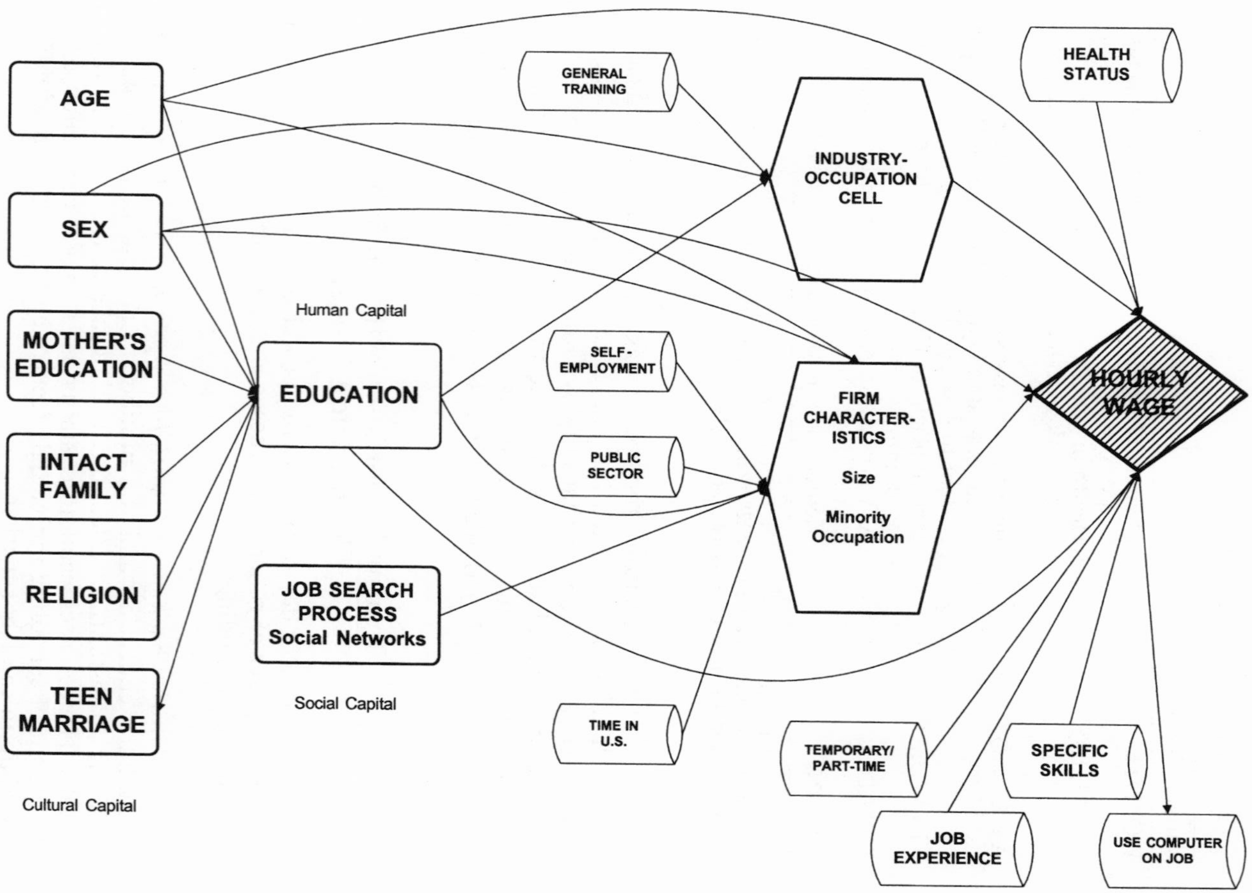

HEALTH STATUS

HOURLY WAGE

INDUSTRY-OCCUPATION CELL

FIRM CHARACTER-ISTICS
Size
Minority Occupation

SPECIFIC SKILLS

JOB EXPERIENCE

TEMPORARY/PART-TIME

USE COMPUTER ON JOB

GENERAL TRAINING

SELF-EMPLOYMENT

PUBLIC SECTOR

TIME IN U.S.

Human Capital

EDUCATION

JOB SEARCH PROCESS
Social Networks

Social Capital

AGE

SEX

MOTHER'S EDUCATION

INTACT FAMILY

RELIGION

TEEN MARRIAGE

Cultural Capital

Source: Authors' compilation.

H₃: The use of *strong network ties* (family and friends), particularly by blacks and Hispanics, to locate jobs in the Boston labor market will result in lower wages as a result of limiting job search to firms where coworkers are generally from minority groups. (This hypothesis has two parts: (a) that strong ties bind workers to minority jobs, and (b) that minority-concentrated jobs offer lower wages to their employees.)

H₄: The use of strong ties to find work will lead to employment in smaller firms.

H₅: Access to jobs that require the use of a computer will pay a premium wage.

Overall, the opportunity nexus for minorities and women is expected to be constrained at every stage of the wage determination process, from I/O cell location to the actual wage-setting patterns in individual firms. How much of the constraint stems from inadequate amounts of human capital and how much from social and cultural capital deficits is one of the key questions we investigate. The other is how much of any human capital deficit is itself a function of an individual's socioeconomic background. In the end, how well individuals do in the Greater Boston labor market, according to this model, depends on what industries, occupations, and firms they have access to—and this in turn depends in large measure on what life was like for them when they were growing up.

Explaining Wage Differences by Race, Ethnicity, and Gender

Baseline values for the "dependent" variables in the model are presented in table 9.2 for men and in table 9.3 for women. These statistics are for

TABLE 9.2   *Baseline Values, All Men*

	Black	Hispanic	White
Mean years of education	13.4	10.2	14.9
< ninth grade	5.1%	22.8%	1.3%
Nine to eleven years	13.7%	34.6%	0.1%
High school grad	25.8%	22.2%	26.1%
Some college	27.7%	18.4%	20.2%
BA +	27.7%	2.0%	52.2%
I/O cell median wage	$11.21	$9.34	$12.39
Minority occupation	26.4%	35.4%	1.1%
Firm size	593	287	410
Mean hourly wage	$11.24	$9.24	$17.04
Median hourly wage	$10.00	$8.14	$14.63

Source: Greater Boston Social Survey 1995.

TABLE 9.3   *Baseline Values, All Women*

	Black	Hispanic	White
Mean years of education	12.5	12.2	13.9
< ninth grade	7.3%	5.6%	0.7%
Nine to eleven years	14.5%	48.0%	6.6%
High school grad	32.2%	12.8%	32.4%
Some college	36.3%	21.3%	27.2%
BA +	9.6%	12.3%	33.0%
I/O cell median wage	$9.86	$9.78	$11.82
Minority occupation	26.8%	48.7%	2.5%
Firm size	571	291	446
Mean hourly wage	$9.58	$9.53	$13.87
Median hourly wage	$8.56	$8.49	$11.06

Source: Greater Boston Social Survey 1995.

individuals who reported they were working at the time of the GBSS survey, or who had worked sometime during the five-year period before the survey was undertaken. The mean values for all the remaining variables in the model are found in tables 9.4 and 9.5. All these statistics are weighted to account for the sampling design used in the survey.

Wages

In our chapter 8 study of workers with no more than high school educations, white men dominated black men in terms of hourly wages, and black men dominated Hispanic men. When we eliminate the truncation on education, the same rank ordering prevails. Non-Hispanic white men have the highest mean and median hourly earnings ($17.04 and $14.63, respectively), while Hispanic men have the lowest ($9.24 and $8.14)— indeed, even lower than Hispanic women. On average, Latino men earn only about 55 percent as much as white men, regardless of whether the mean or median is used for comparison. Black men do somewhat better than Hispanics, earning about two-thirds ($11.24 and $10.00) of the white male averages. These wage gaps are significantly larger than those we found when, in the last chapter, we compared men with no more than a high school degree. There we found Hispanic/white and black/white wage ratios of .71 and .83, respectively. Among women, the interracial and interethnic earnings gap is somewhat smaller. Black and Hispanic women have rough wage parity with each other, but earn just under 70 percent of the mean hourly wage of white women ($13.87) and 76 percent of the median ($11.06). Again, the wage gaps are larger than when we limit the analysis to just those with high school or less.

TABLE 9.4   *Descriptive Statistics for Employed GBSS Sample Respondents, Men, by Race, Ethnicity*

Characteristic	Black	Hispanic	White
AGE	35.8	34.1	39.1
Percentage CATHOLIC	19	60	52
Percentage who use Computer on job (COMPJOB)	32	19	63
Percentage educated outside of United States (EDOUTUS)	42	77	4
Years of schooling EDUCATION	13.4	10.2	14.9
Percentage receive general training (GENTRAIN)	18	12	17
Percentage w/ health limits (HEALTHDY)	8	16	14
Percentage raised in intact family (INTACTFM)	50	54	88
I/O cell median wage (IOCELL)	11.2	9.34	12.39
Percentage JEWISH	0	0	4
Est. employment Ln FIRM SIZE	3.82	3.61	3.79
Ln HOURLY WAGE	2.3	2.15	2.69
Percentage MARRIED	52	85	68
Percentage in minority-dominated job (MINORITYJB)	26	35	1
Mother's education (Years) (MOTHERED)	11.2	5.7	12.0
Percentage working in PUBLIC SECTOR (PUBSEC)	16	4	14
Percentage SELF-EMPLOYED	4	11	23
Percentage found job through family or friends (SEARCH)	43	79	35
Percentage Working TEMPORARY/ SEASONAL jobs	7	13	5
Occupational experience (in years) (OCCEXP)	8.4	6	11.7
Number of correct answers on WORDTEST (max. 7)	3.3	2.7	4.9
Percentage of lifetime in United States (TIMEUS)	76	50	98
Interviewer's assessment of respondent (ASSESSUQ)	2.04	2.73	1.40
Married as a teenager (TEENMARRY)	4.10	9.79	0.02
Membership in social organizations (NUMORGS)	1.36	1.4	1.0
Minority neighborhood (STRATUM)	73	40	1
Employed in last twelve months (EMPREC)	80.3	76.4	76.8

Source: Greater Boston Social Survey 1995 (weighted by PADJWGT).

TABLE 9.5   *Descriptive Statistics for Employed GBSS Sample Respondents, Women, by Race, Ethnicity*

Characteristic	Black	Hispanic	White
AGE	37.9	34.5	39.5
Percentage CATHOLIC	16	53	54
Percentage who use computer on job (COMPJOB)	39	28	66
Percentage educated outside of United States (EDOUTUS)	32	84	4
Years of schooling EDUCATION	12.5	12.3	13.9
Percentage receive general training (GENTRAIN)	23	21	31
PERCENT w/ HEALTH LIMITS (HEALTHDY)	23	7	13
PERCENT RAISED IN INTACT FAMILY (INTACTFM)	54	70	81
I/O CELL MEDIAN WAGE (IOCELL)	9.85	9.79	11.81
Percentage JEWISH	0	0	7
Est. Employment Ln FIRM SIZE	4.52	4.43	3.83
Ln HOURLY WAGE	2.15	2.16	2.4
Percentage MARRIED	36	68	69
Percentage in minority-dominated job (MINORITYJB)	27	49	3
Mother's education (Years) (MOTHERED)	10.4	6.6	12.3
Percentage Working in PUBLIC SECTOR (PUBSEC)	18	16	16
Percentage SELF-EMPLOYED	5	3	11
Percentage found job through family or friends (SEARCH)	44	58	25
Percentage working TEMPORARY/ SEASONAL jobs	16	9	3
Occupational experience (in years) (OCCEXP)	6.7	7.6	12.0
Number of correct answers on WORDTEST (max. 7)	3.4	3.2	4.7
Percentage of lifetime in United States (TIMEUS)	79	56	98
Interviewer's assessment of respondent (ASSESSUQ)	2.15	2.49	1.51
Married as a teenager (TEENMARRY)	12.4	35.7	12.5
Membership in social organizations (NUMORGS)	1.4	1.3	1.2
Minority neighborhood (STRATUM)	69	37	0
Employed in last twelve months (EMPREC)	60.8	60.3	63.3

Source: Greater Boston Social Survey 1995 (weighted by PADJWGT).

Education and Cultural Capital Variables

Some portion of these larger race-ethnic wage differentials are no doubt due to differences in the mean level of education. This would certainly follow from what we learned in the last chapter about the human capital roots of the Hispanic-white male earnings gap. Hence, analyzing education should prove even more fruitful when we eliminate the truncation on schooling.

In the GBSS sample, average African American schooling levels do not trail as far behind white levels as one might expect. Black men average 13.4 years of schooling, compared with 15.0 for white men. But, consistent with last chapter's findings, Hispanic men trail substantially behind, averaging only 10.2 years of education. Among blacks and whites, men average about one more year of schooling than women, but among Hispanics, women dominate men by about two years. How this plays out in the overall wage distribution will be the subject of analysis later in this chapter.

Distribution Across Industry-Occupation Cells

On average, Hispanic men work in industry-occupation cells with a median wage of $9.34. At the other end of the spectrum, white men work in industry-occupation cells with a median wage of $12.39. Each race-ethnic-gender group has a distinct distribution across occupation and industry categories, as illustrated in figures 9.6 through 9.9. Clearly, Boston's workforce is being sorted into different industries and I/O cells along the lines of race, ethnicity, and gender. Indeed, each group appears to occupy a different niche in the regional economy, as we have repeatedly observed in earlier chapters.

Black men, for example, have a bimodal occupation distribution, with 23 percent in professional work, mainly in large health, education, and social service institutions; and another 28 percent in service occupations, with 12 percent in protective service and 16 percent in other service occupations, including food service and cleaning and building services. Although 15 percent work in retail trade, only 7 percent are in sales occupations; the others work in inventory and warehouse operations with little face-to-face contact with customers.

Black women are concentrated overwhelmingly in service occupations (including food service and cleaning and building services), clerical occupations, and sales. Over two-thirds of all black women in the Boston region work in just these three occupations. Compared with black

(Text continues on p. 298.)

FIGURE 9.6   *Occupational Distributions, Men*

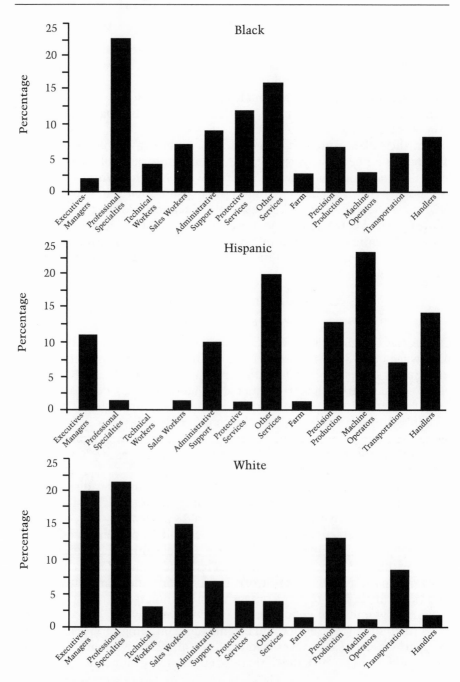

Source: Greater Boston Social Survey 1995.

FIGURE 9.7 *Industry Distributions, Men*

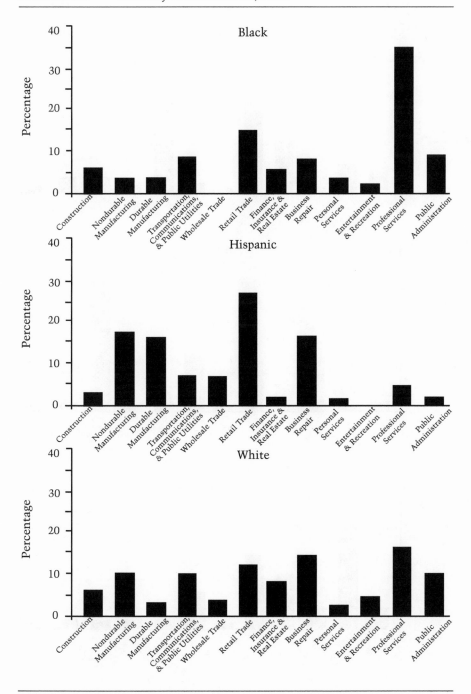

Source: Greater Boston Social Survey 1995.

FIGURE 9.8 Occupational Distributions, Women

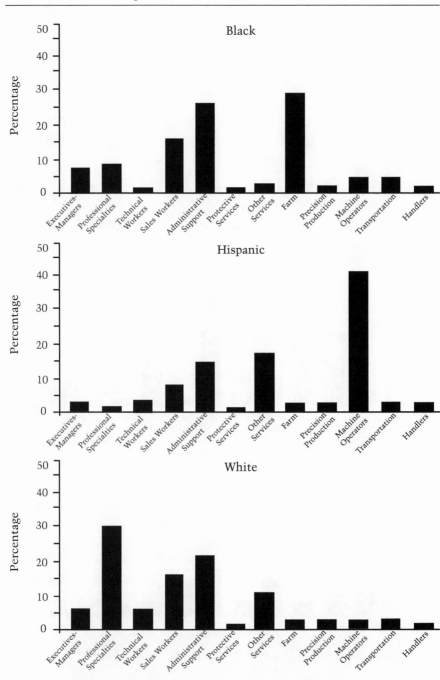

FIGURE 9.9 *Industry Distributions, Women*

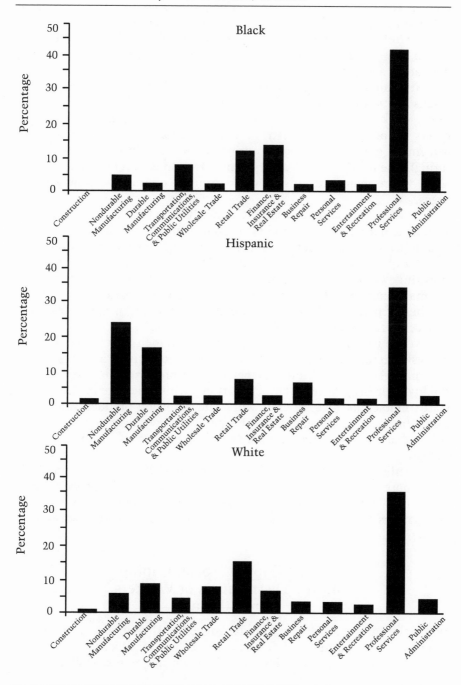

Source: Greater Boston Social Survey 1995.

men, a smaller proportion are in the professions, while a somewhat larger proportion are executives, administrators, and managers (8 percent), working primarily in professional service industries (such as health and social services), retail trade, and a small number in finance, insurance, and real estate.

Hispanic men have a dramatically different I/O distribution. Unlike blacks and whites, they are heavily concentrated in blue-collar occupations, working as factory operatives (23 percent) and handlers and laborers (14 percent). By industry, about a third are in manufacturing (17 percent in nondurable manufacturing, 16 percent in durable manufacturing). The other major industry concentration is in retail trade (27 percent), where many presumably work in local community shops and bodegas.

Very few Hispanic women in Greater Boston have gone beyond high school, and therefore the industry and occupational distributions we find here are almost identical to those we found in chapter 8. More than two out of five (41 percent) are employed as factory operatives in manufacturing (24 percent in nondurable manufacturing; 17 percent in durable manufacturing). Clerical, sales, and service occupations account for another 42 percent. Most of the remaining are found in the professional services sector, many in the health care industry.

At the top of the I/O cell structure, white men are clustered in the highest prestige occupations: 20 percent are executives, administrators, and managers; an additional 21 percent are professionals. Even within the lower-prestige blue-collar occupations, white men are in the higher-status blue-collar jobs, in craft work and precision production (13 percent). In contrast to blacks and Hispanics, they are more evenly distributed across industrial sectors, with less than one-fifth in any single industry.

Nearly a third of white women are in professional occupations, with another 22 percent doing clerical work and 15 percent working as salesclerks. On average, white women are much more likely to be in occupations where they are in face-to-face contact with their customers or clients.

Cultural Capital, Social Capital, and the Distribution of Workers Across Firms

While the information on particular niches in the labor market clearly shows a racial, ethnic, and gender pattern, not all blacks are found in service occupations, not all Hispanics are working in blue-collar factory jobs, and not all whites are executives and professionals. Cultural capital and social capital may influence which black, Hispanic, and white workers will end up in which labor market segments. Within the GBSS data set, we have a number of variables that can proxy for at least some cultural and social differences. One of these is religion. Given Boston's ethnic history, it is not surprising to find that a majority of both the whites and Hispanics, but less than one-fifth of the blacks, in our study are Catholic. Religious background could influence how much education an individual receives, on average, and this helps to explain what I/O cell he or she enters. Only about half of the black and Hispanic sample were raised in a two-parent family, compared with 80 percent of the whites. Having both a mother and father at home when one is young might influence the intergenerational transmission of education and therefore indirectly affect the job one gets and the wages one receives as an adult.

Job search behavior may also contribute to the types of firms where individuals find work. For blacks, 43 percent of the men and 44 percent of the women used "strong" ties (family or friends) to find their current (or last) job; among Hispanics, the corresponding proportions were extremely high: 79 percent and 58 percent among men and women, respectively. Here we have social capital investments at work. In contrast, only about a third of white men and a quarter of white women found jobs in this way; they were more likely to use formal channels to find work—consulting newspaper advertisements, private employment agencies, or the public employment service.

On-the-job experience varies significantly among these groups, too. White men and white women both averaged nearly twelve years of experience within their current occupations (although not necessarily with the same firm). Black men averaged only about eight; black women fewer than seven. Among Hispanics, women have more occupational experience: seven and a half years, compared to Hispanic men's six. Hence, the typical Hispanic male has only half the occupational experience of the typical white—a factor that might again prove powerful in explaining their current lagging position in the labor market.

Finally, computer use on the job varies enormously. Among whites, almost two-thirds report that they use a computer at work daily or at least weekly—about twice the rate we found for white men with limited schooling. Among blacks, computer usage is much lower: 39 percent for women and 32 percent for men. Hispanics report the lowest usage rates: 28 percent of the women and only 19 percent of the men. While substantially higher than we found in the last chapter, the racial and ethnic ranking of computer use is similar.

In the regression analysis to follow, we shall study how all these factors affect the jobs individuals end up in and how this ultimately affects their hourly wages.

The Regression Results

In estimating a recursive model such as the one just described, the explanatory (right-hand side) variables in each equation should be exogenous, or at least predetermined with respect to the dependent variable of the equation. In reality, almost nothing is exogenous—most variables affect most others, and so models rarely meet these requirements exactly. However, the labor market model presented here reasonably and approximately conforms to these requirements, except for the consideration of two variables, which we introduced in chapter 8.

One of these (EMPREC) indicates whether a person worked sometime during the last year (as opposed to sometime before a year ago). The other (STRAT) indicates whether the person lives in a minority stratum—a majority-minority neighborhood. Neither can confidently be classified as exogenous. According to labor theory, whether or not a person chooses to work depends in part on his or her expected market wage rate, so EMPREC is not purely exogenous in the model. Also, to the extent that earnings and incomes constrain where one can live, STRAT is also an endogenous variable. In a more complete modeling system, we would have additional equations with EMPREC and STRAT as dependent variables, and we would have estimated the system with a simultaneous equations estimator, but we leave this task for a future research project. Instead, we present two sets of equations for each dependent variable in the model. The basic equations exclude STRAT and EMPREC, and the augmented equations include them.

The Equation Set

For each race-ethnic group, we have calculated regression equations to explain education level (EDUCATION), an industry-occupation-cell "index" which, as noted, is the the median wage in an industry-occupation combination (IOCELL), the probability of working in an establishment in which the majority of immediate coworkers are African American or Hispanic (MINORITYFM),[9] the natural logarithm of firm size (LnFIRMSZ), and the natural logarithm of the individual's wage (RLnHWAGE) in 1994 dollars. For each set of equations, we compare the relative importance of selected variables, as well as the ability of the model to explain variation within each race-ethnic group.

Education Level In accord with standard models of cultural capital and social status attainment, we expect that an individual's own educational level is heavily influenced by the family environment in which he or she was raised. These attributes are largely outside the individual's control. Other things being equal, we expect that younger cohorts will have more schooling than older ones simply as a result of the increased emphasis placed on formal schooling in the post–World War II period (AGE). We also expect that men will have slightly more formal schooling than women, particularly due to higher college attendance rates (SEX). To proxy the effect of socioeconomic status (SES) and cultural variables, the baseline equations include mother's education (MOTHERED)[10] and a dummy variable for whether an individual was raised in a single-parent or intact family for most of the years before age sixteen (INTACTFM). The education regressions for blacks, Hispanics, and whites are found in table 9.6.

Generally, the standard hypotheses regarding these factors are supported in these regressions—but with some important differences between groups. For all three groups, MOTHERED is positive and highly significant. Using the ordered logit results in table 9.6, we can assess the impact of mother's education on an individual's schooling. For example, one additional year of mother's schooling beyond high school increases the probability of completing high school among whites by 1.6 percentage points, and of going to college by 5.7 points. In black families, these effects are in the same range: 1.7 and 4.1. For Hispanics, the percentage points gains are 3.3 and 4.5.

Growing up in an intact family increases the probability of finishing high school by 2.4 percentage points for whites and by 3.2 points for blacks. However, we did not find that family structure affects the education of Latino children. The coefficient is small and insignificant.

The expected negative sign on AGE was found for all groups, but was not significant for whites. Among Hispanics, a fifty-five-year-old is 22 percent less likely to have completed high school than is a twenty-five-year-old; among blacks, the estimated difference is 10 percent. Clearly, there has been a dramatic increase in education for these two groups, suggesting that the education gap between future-generation minority groups and whites can be expected to decline substantially, if this trend continues.

The impact of gender on education is small, but statistically significant. For whites, men are 2 percentage points more likely to finish high school than women. Among blacks, the opposite is true. Black men are about 2 percentage points less likely than black women to finish high school, but the difference is not statistically significant. Hispanic men are least likely of all to complete high school—and as much as 5 per-

TABLE 9.6   *Ordered Logit Equation Results*

| | Education | | | | | |
| | Black | | Hispanic | | White | |
	(1)	(2)	(1)	(2)	(1)	(2)
AGE	−.0296	−.0192	−.0395	−.0371	−.0026	.0028
	(3.53)	(2.21)	(4.63)	(4.26)	(0.42)	(0.42)
SEX	−.1390	−.0037	−.2655	−.9602	.4058	.6153
	(0.90)	(0.00)	(1.34)	(1.26)	(2.17)	(2.57)
MOTHER'S EDUCATION	.1673	.1703	.1843	.1778	.2668	.2464
	(5.61)	(5.65)	(8.12)	(7.81)	(7.86)	(7.17)
INTACT FAMILY	.2631	.3130	.0342	.0594	.3154	.3082
	(1.24)	(1.47)	(0.26)	(0.45)	(1.65)	(1.83)
CATHOLIC	.4163	.4883	−.1430	−.1935	−.3713	−.3824
	(1.44)	(1.65)	(0.77)	(1.03)	(1.92)	(1.95)
JEWISH	—	—	—	—	.7610	.7591
					(1.78)	(1.71)
TEEN MARRIAGE	−.0008	−.1509	−.3017	−.3398	−1.4153	−1.3156
	(0.00)	(0.43)	(1.38)	(1.54)	(4.19)	(3.80)
EDUCATED OUT OF U.S.	.6494	.4876	.1311	.0342	.2153	.0779
	(2.45)	(1.78)	(0.57)	(0.15)	(0.61)	(0.22)
STRATUM		−.0607		−.7588		−.5561
		(0.11)		(1.88)		(2.14)
STRATUM × SEX		−.2986		.5076		−.5382
		(0.33)		(0.65)		(1.41)
RECENT EMPLOYED		1.0953		.6894		.8150
		(4.77)		(3.58)		(3.90)
CONSTANT 1 (ED: zero to eight)	−2.1490	−1.2123	−1.5032	−2.0291	−.7111	−.5738
CONSTANT 2 (ED: nine to eleven)	−.8497	.1250	−.3903	−.8875	.8422	1.0282
CONSTANT 3 (ED: thirteen to fifteen)	.8203	1.8802	1.0100	.5479	2.7673	3.0633
CONSTANT 4 (ED: over sixteen)	2.5889	3.7280	2.6131	2.1910	3.8435	4.2047
N	323	323	440	440	442	442
Pseudo R-square	.070	.096	.089	.103	.110	.141
Log likelihood	−440.8	−428.7	−591.3	−582.3	−549.1	−530.4

Source: Greater Boston Social Survey 1995.
Z-statistics in parentheses.

centage points less likely than Hispanic women. This is fully in accord with the mean differences found in the sample. For Hispanics, whose overall educational attainment is substantially lower than for other groups, it is the women who are more likely to stay in school, the men who are more likely to enter the workforce before completing high school.

As expected, those who are currently working are likely to have had more education than those who are not currently working. For example, a white woman who is currently working is 5 percentage points more likely to have completed high school than one who is not working, and is 18 points more likely to have gone to college.

Living in a minority neighborhood (STRAT) is associated with lower educational attainment for whites, and marginally lower educational attainment for Hispanic women. For example, white men who live in minority neighborhoods are 4 percentage points less likely to have completed high school than white men who live in predominantly white communities.

Using these education regressions, we can simulate what the average educational attainment would be for each race-ethnic group by gender under a particular set of assumptions about mother's education and family structure. For evaluation purposes, the baseline person we use here is forty years old, his or her mother completed high school but did not go to college, and he or she grew up in an intact family. (The remaining variables in the regression are left at their mean values for each race-ethnic group and gender.)

As we see in table 9.7, even when we set mother's schooling and family structure constant across groups, educational attainment still differs dramatically by race and ethnicity, but there are strong improvements for Hispanics. Under this simulation, some 69 percent of His-

TABLE 9.7   *Probability (in Percentage) of Completing High School or Attending College*

	Men		Women	
	Completed High School	Went to College	Completed High School	Went to college
White	95	74	93	66
Black	85	52	87	57
Hispanic	69	35	74	42

Source: Greater Boston Social Survey 1995.
Note: Assuming age forty; mother completed high school but did not go to college; grew up in intact family

panic men would complete high school, compared with 95 percent of white men. But that simulated 69 percent compares with the actual figure of less than 43 percent high school completion or better among the GBSS sample of Hispanic men (recall table 9.2). College attendance rises from about 20 percent to 35 percent for this group. Hence, a not insignificant part of the Hispanic-white male education gap we see today is associated with the average low education achievement of these workers' parents. This is not the case among black or white workers. The same simulation raises the high school completion rate of black men by only 3 percentage points, to 85 percent, and the college attendance rate by nothing at all. The model estimates a higher educational attainment for white men than for white women, but higher educational attainment for minority women than minority men. This may suggest somewhat faster labor market improvements in the future for minority women.

Industry-Occupation Cell Median Wage (IOCELL)   The ordinary least squares regressions for I/O cell are contained in table 9.8. In accord with human capital theory, we hypothesize that education is the single most critical factor in arraying individuals across industry-occupation cells in a local labor market and, indeed, the education category variables performed as expected. High school completion is taken as the base group in this model. Note that the signs on EDUC (zero to eight) and EDUC (nine to eleven) are universally negative, indicating that those who have not completed high school are more likely to end up in lower-ranked I/O cells. Those who have attended some college end up, on average, in I/O cells that have median wages somewhere between 7 and 10 percent higher than the I/O cells of those who have only completed high school. Completing college really pays off in terms of getting into highly rated I/O cells. For blacks, those who have at least completed college find jobs in industry-occupation groups that have median wage rates more than one-third higher than the I/O cells for those who have merely finished high school. Indeed, when we control for education, the I/O cell wages are nearly identical for black and white men, indicating that education per se is not blocking black men from entering industries and occupations where higher wages are being paid.

The same is not true, apparently, for Hispanic men. With the same amount of education, they seem to be limited to much lower wage industries and occupations. Hispanics need a college degree to land a job in an industry and occupation that pays the same, on average, as one that whites or blacks need only a high school education to get (see table 9.9). Note that their restriction to such industries will likely affect their actual wages, but other factors operating at the firm level can

TABLE 9.8   OLS Regression Equation Results

| | Industry-Occupation Cell (Median Wage) | | | | | |
| | Black | | Hispanic | | White | |
	(1)	(2)	(1)	(2)	(1)	(2)
EDUC (zero to eight)	−.0461	−.0416	−.0699	−.0676	−.0522	−.0022
	(0.76)	(0.68)	(2.69)	(2.61)	(1.00)	(0.04)
EDUC (nine to eleven)	−.0884	−.0888	−.0703	−.0708	−.0619	−.0021
	(2.47)	(2.47)	(2.71)	(2.68)	(1.11)	(0.04)
EDUC (thirteen to fifteen)	.1019	.1007	.0710	.0699	.0999	.0951
	(2.67)	(2.64)	(1.96)	(1.94)	(2.35)	(2.25)
EDUC (over sixteen)	.3551	.3489	.2378	.2349	.2870	.2658
	(7.88)	(7.60)	(3.71)	(3.70)	(8.68)	(7.85)
SEX	.0563	.1147	.0429	.0669	.0215	−.0001
	(1.86)	(1.21)	(1.95)	(0.81)	(0.79)	(0.00)
GENERAL TRAINING	−.0485	−.0458	.0216	.0233	−.0204	−.0279
	(1.64)	(1.51)	(0.81)	(0.87)	(0.59)	(0.81)
STRATUM		.0137		−.0048		−.0750
		(0.23)		(0.08)		(1.89)
SEX × STRATUM		−.0666		−.0312		.0504
		(0.66)		(0.36)		(0.94)
RECENTLY EMPLOYED		.0201		.0230		.1362
		(0.53)		(1.15)		(3.85)
CONSTANT	2.2045	2.1768	2.1766	2.1668	2.2410	2.1606
	(76.14)	(31.68)	(102.27)	(33.66)	(73.63)	(50.54)
N	345	345	453	453	420	420
R-SQUARE	.253	.254	.119	.121	.200	.232

Source: Greater Boston Social Survey 1995.
T-statistics in parentheses.

TABLE 9.9   Estimated I/O Cell Median Wage Index by Education, Based on I/O Regression Model

| | High School (Twelve Years) | | College (Sixteen Years) | |
	Men	Women	Men	Women
White	10.09	9.78	12.02	11.66
Black	9.99	9.37	12.26	11.50
Hispanic	9.38	8.98	10.09	9.66

Source: Greater Boston Social Survey 1995.

offset this disadvantage. Similarly, blacks might be able with equal education to get into the same I/O's as whites, but still suffer a disadvantage at the level of the firm. Getting into a high-median-wage industry does not mean that one will necessarily get one of the better-paying jobs.

Men tend to get into better I/O cells than women, but the difference is not significant for whites. General training was not found to make much of a difference in determining what industry and occupation cell was attained, but it is possible that it is rewarded *within* each industry and occupation cell.

The relationship between the IOCELL median wage and whether one is currently employed (EMPREC) makes a significant difference only for whites, with whites currently employed working in industry-occupation groups whose median wage averages 14 percent higher than those whose last job was sometime in the prior five years. One would expect recently employed workers to be in occupations and industries that pay more, if only because they might generally have higher productivity and therefore greater employability. The fact that this is not the case for blacks and Hispanics suggests that the kinds of I/O cells they are more likely to have access to are those in which continuous employment is not particularly valued.

There does not appear to be any relationship between the industry and occupation cell of one's job and whether or not one lives in a minority stratum. Living in a minority neighborhood does not appear to restrict one's access to broad industry-occupation groupings. As we shall soon see, however, it will affect the actual wages *within* I/O cells for some race-ethnic groups.

Probability of Working in a Minority Position Within Firm (MINORITYFM) There is strong evidence from the literature that establishments that are "crowded" with minority workers pay lower wages (Bergmann 1974; Tomaskovic-Devey 1993; Bluestone 1974; Stevenson 1984). Therefore, we use a logit analysis to examine the factors that affect the likelihood that a given African American or Hispanic worker will work in a minority position within his or her firm. By *minority position*, we mean a job in which most of the respondent's immediate colleagues are black, Hispanic, Asian, or another minority. In order to estimate the effect of these factors reliably, we pooled the sample for blacks and Hispanics and then estimated a model with race-ethnicity interaction terms (see table 9.10). There are simply not enough whites in minority jobs to reliably assess the impact of this factor on them.

Using this regression we can ascertain the probability that individuals from specific race-ethnic groups will be working in minority-domi-

TABLE 9.10   *Logit Equation Results*

Minority Occupation Within Firm	BLACK-HISPANIC	
	(1)	(2)
SEARCH NETWORK	.4579	.4402
	(2.69)	(2.56)
EDUCATION	−.1051	−.0796
	(3.09)	(2.05)
TIME IN U.S.	−.3396	−.3423
	(0.82)	(0.82)
HISPANIC × EDUCATION	.0664	.0260
	(2.06)	(0.68)
HISPANIC × TIME U.S.	−.8692	−.9224
	(1.63)	(1.68)
STRATUM		−.1826
		(0.46)
SEX × STRATUM		.1280
		(0.69)
RECENTLY EMPLOYED		−.2222
		(0.78)
HISPANIC × REC. EMP		.9361
		(2.61)
CONSTANT	.6666	.6259
	(1.90)	(1.18)
N	658	658
F-Statistic	9.40	6.38

Source: Greater Boston Social Survey 1995.
T-statistics in parentheses.

nated occupations within the firms that have hired them. Blacks and Hispanics who are long-term U.S. residents and who are high school graduates, and who did not rely on a network of family and friends to find a job—"baseline" persons in table 9.11—are about equally likely to work in a minority occupation within their firm, the probability being approximately 28 percent for blacks and 27 percent for Hispanics. For both groups, the job search methods that are utilized are important. Using a network of family and friends to find a job increases the probability of working in a minority position by roughly 10 percentage points for blacks and Hispanics. Our results are similar to those found in a recent Atlanta study (Browne and Hewitt 1995). Such networks may improve the likelihood of finding work, but they tend to reduce the opportunity for working in positions where the majority of employees are white. Moreover, as we will see in the hourly wage equation, relying on family and friends to find a job has an adverse impact on black earnings.

TABLE 9.11   *Probability of Working in a Minority-Dominated Position Within a Firm*

	Black	Hispanic
Baseline: high school graduate, did not use a network of family and friends to find job, always resided in the United States	28.2%	26.8%
Baseline, except only an eighth-grade education	37.4	29.9
Baseline, except uses a network of family and friends	38.3	36.6
Baseline, except new to the United States	35.6	55.1

Source: Greater Boston Social Survey 1995.
T-statistics in parentheses.

The chance of ending up in a minority-dominated occupation declines with education. A black high school graduate is about one-fourth less likely to work mostly with other people of color than a black who has gone no further than the eighth grade.

Not unexpectedly, newer Hispanic immigrants to the United States are much more likely to find work in minority occupations than are lifelong residents of the United States (TIMEUS). For example, a Hispanic who is similar to the baseline person in table 9.11, but a recent immigrant, is estimated to be twice as likely to work in a minority occupation (55 percent versus 27 percent). The effect of recent immigration for blacks is smaller and statistically insignificant.

We did not find a significant correspondence between living in a minority stratum and working in a minority occupation. This does not mean that there is no relationship, but probably reflects the fact that our sample had too few minorities living outside minority strata to be able to measure the relationship with any reliability. One last finding is of particular interest. We might expect current or recently employed workers, who are likely to be more desirable to mainstream employers than those not currently working, to be less likely to be working in minority-dominated positions than those who last worked over a year ago. But that is not what we found. For blacks, there was no significant relationship, and for Hispanics, the opposite relationship was observed: those who were currently working or who worked sometime in the past year were *more* likely to be working in minority-dominated positions. This means that it is easier for Hispanics to find and retain a job if they seek work in a minority-dominated position than if they routinely look for work in "white" firms. Again, however, this is a two-edged sword: while it increases the probability of working, it also increases the probability of working in a lower-wage job.

Firm (Establishment) Size (LnFIRMSZ) There is evidence in the literature that while smaller firms are creating many new jobs, larger firms are still the employers that pay higher wages (Gordon 1979; Brown, Hamilton, and Medoff 1990; Harrison 1994). Therefore, in explaining differences in individual earnings, we would like to understand the factors that affect the size of the establishment in which workers are employed. Since those who are self-employed are likely to work in firms that are very small, we control for this factor (SELFEMP). As expected, there was a strong and significant negative correlation between firm size and self-employment (see table 9.12).

For all groups, workers with more education tended to work in larger firms, although the relationship is weak for Hispanics. For whites, education level and self-employment were the only variables that proved statistically significant. For blacks and Hispanics, however, several other factors were associated with access to larger firms. After con-

TABLE 9.12 *OLS Regression Equation Results*

	Ln Firm size					
	Black		Hispanic		White	
	(1)	(2)	(1)	(2)	(1)	(2)
SELF-EMPLOYMENT	−4.2005	−4.2477	−3.6993	−3.6760	−3.6572	−3.6879
	(13.49)	(12.11)	(16.84)	(15.56)	(16.87)	(16.34)
PUBLIC SECTOR	.3331	.3209	−.1235	−.1498	.2827	.2278
	(0.99)	(0.95)	(0.39)	(0.47)	(0.74)	(0.61)
SEARCH NETWORK	−.6325	−.6352	−.3522	−.3682	.0473	.0531
	(2.37)	(2.37)	(1.50)	(1.57)	(0.20)	(0.22)
SEX	−.6704	−1.7021	.1464	.1669	−.2174	−.0171
	(2.31)	(1.57)	(0.68)	(0.23)	(0.87)	(0.05)
EDUCATION	.1632	.1506	.0499	.0497	.1125	.0998
	(3.00)	(2.83)	(1.68)	(1.66)	(2.62)	(2.04)
AGE	.0094	.0081	.0256	.0258	−.0074	−.0071
	(0.60)	(0.53)	(2.29)	(2.30)	(0.67)	(0.64)
STRATUM		.1671		.1928		−.0173
		(0.30)		(0.45)		(0.04)
SEX × STRATUM		1.0414		−.0676		−.4953
		(0.94)		(0.09)		(0.99)
RECENTLY		.7562		.2180		−.0817
EMPLOYED		(2.54)		(1.06)		(0.24)
CONSTANT	2.4601	1.9720	2.6847	2.3946	2.7615	2.9930
	(2.87)	(2.04)	(4.81)	(3.36)	(4.42)	(4.09)
N	231	231	316	316	266	266
R-SQUARE	.217	.243	.196	.200	.268	.274

Source: Greater Boston Social Survey 1995.
T-statistics in parentheses.

trolling for other factors, black women tended to work in somewhat larger firms, reflecting the industries where many work. (Recall that more than two out of five of them work in "professional service" industries—primarily large hospitals.) For both blacks and Hispanics, using a family-and-friends network to find work led to employment in smaller firms, although the effect for Hispanics was statistically weak. Finally, among Hispanics, older workers tended to work in larger firms.

The addition of the stratum and EMPREC variables have little explanatory power, except for blacks. Those who worked in the past year tended to work in larger establishments than blacks who last worked more than a year earlier. Employment in larger firms tended to be more stable. As a result, the causation between recent employment and firm size probably ran in the opposite direction from that specified in the equation. Those who had been able to find work in larger firms were less likely to be unemployed and less likely to be cycling in and out of work. Given the high unemployment rates and incidence of part-time hours among black men found in the last chapter, this finding of firm size takes on greater significance.

Hourly Wage (LnHRWAGE) The ultimate objective of this inquiry, of course, is to ascertain how all these factors affect the hourly wages of black, Hispanic, and white workers. Hence our final equation in the model is for the natural log of the (real) hourly wage (see table 9.13). Our baseline regression equations include the I/O cell median wage, a series of education categories, plus a number of additional human capital variables, including age (and age squared), occupational experience,[11] and a dummy variable for health limitations. Other variables in the equation account for the individual's gender; whether an individual is married; whether a temporary or seasonal worker; whether he or she uses a computer on the job; whether the person is in an occupation within a firm where the majority of the workforce is minority; how the individual scored on a vocabulary test; and finally, how the individual respondent in the survey was assessed by the interviewer. These wage equations are reasonably robust, explaining between 27 and 46 percent of the variance depending on race-ethnic group.

The natural logarithm of the individual worker's industry-occupation cell wage (Ln IOCELL WAGE) is important and highly significant, but its effect varies across the three race-ethnic groups. It is most important for whites and least important for Hispanics. For whites, working in an industry-occupation that pays on average 1 percent more than another is associated with an individual's wage rate being .73 percent higher, everything else (education, age, and so on) held constant. In more technical terms, the elasticity for whites is .73. For blacks, the elasticity

TABLE 9.13   OLS Regression Equation Results

| | Ln Hourly Wage | | | | | |
| | Black | | Hispanic | | White | |
	(1)	(2)	(1)	(2)	(1)	(2)
Ln I/O CELL WAGE	.4790	.4750	.3169	.3098	.7158	.6928
	(5.15)	(5.20)	(2.53)	(2.48)	(6.16)	(5.92)
SEX	.0067	−.1576	.1339	.2782	.1256	.1773
	(0.15)	(1.01)	(2.53)	(2.95)	(1.98)	(2.18)
OCCUPATIONAL EXP.	.0126	.0122	.0143	.0129	.0159	.0148
	(4.03)	(4.20)	(3.00)	(2.67)	(4.06)	(3.82)
TEMP/SEASONAL WORK	−.1200	−.0819	−.0987	−.0804	−.2229	−.2209
	(2.00)	(1.26)	(1.27)	(1.02)	(2.24)	(2.18)
AGE	.0120	.0124	.0196	.0218	.0132	.0181
	(0.87)	(0.92)	(1.33)	(1.46)	(0.71)	(0.97)
AGE SQUARE	−.0001	−.0001	−.0002	−.0003	−.0002	−.0003
	(0.65)	(0.73)	(1.33)	(1.45)	(0.93)	(1.18)
USE COMPUTER	.0380	.0393	.2724	.2578	.1425	.1308
	(0.75)	(0.78)	(4.45)	(4.16)	(1.73)	(1.61)
Ln FIRM SIZE	.0317	.0290	.0443	.0421	.0022	.0024
	(3.04)	(2.75)	(4.16)	(3.90)	(0.15)	(0.17)
MINORITY OCCUPATION	−.0970	−.0863	−.0738	−.0711	−.1502	−.1162
	(2.12)	(1.97)	(1.54)	(1.46)	(1.04)	(0.79)
MARRIED	.0871	.0719	.0258	.0074	.0686	.0442
	(1.62)	(1.38)	(0.48)	(0.13)	(1.13)	(0.76)
EDUC (zero to eight)	.0481	.0555	.0968	.1017	.1101	.1607
	(0.58)	(0.72)	(1.37)	(1.44)	(0.58)	(0.89)
EDUC (nine to eleven)	−.0339	−.0267	.0507	.0433	−.0330	.0157
	(0.59)	(0.48)	(0.74)	(0.63)	(0.31)	(0.14)
EDUC (thirteen to fifteen)	−.0758	−.0943	.0075	.0034	−.0022	−.0109
	(1.27)	(1.58)	(0.10)	(0.04)	(0.03)	(0.13)
EDUC (over sixteen)	.1461	.1375	.2610	.2527	.0248	.0123
	(1.57)	(1.51)	(2.41)	(2.38)	(0.26)	(0.13)
WORD TEST SCORE	−.0074	−.0035	.0122	.0145	.0382	.0316
	(0.48)	(0.23)	(0.87)	(1.06)	(1.85)	(1.56)
HEALTHDY	−.1997	−.1602	−.0711	−.0491	−.2851	−.2369
	(3.22)	(2.71)	(1.39)	(0.93)	(2.87)	(2.26)
INTERVIEWER ASSESS	−.0350	−.0356	−.0237	−.0311	−.0468	−.0517
	(1.52)	(1.56)	(0.77)	(0.99)	(0.88)	(0.99)
STRATUM		−.1836		.0001		−.0192
		(2.58)		(0.00)		(0.23)
STRATUM × SEX		.1697		−.1690		−.1658
		(1.05)		(1.59)		(1.39)
RECENTLY EMPLOYED		.1802		.0894		.1438
		(3.00)		(1.57)		(1.66)
CONSTANT	.7365	.7682	.5967	.5408	.0942	−.0031
	(1.93)	(1.94)	(1.48)	(1.33)	(0.22)	(0.01)
N	297	297	389	389	358	358
R-Square	.439	.459	.263	.271	.361	.372

Source: Greater Boston Social Survey 1995.
T-statistics in parentheses.

is significantly lower, .55, and for Hispanics, it is only .35. Hence, as whites move up the industry-occupation ladder, their wage rates tend to rise along with their promotion. For blacks and especially for Hispanics, however, working in a higher-rated industry-occupation cell does not necessarily provide higher wages. As they rise up the industry-occupation ladder, they are more likely to find themselves constrained to the lower end of the I/O cell wage distribution. This is fully consistent with our earlier finding that, controlling for education, blacks are found in I/O cells with median wages similar to those of whites. Being in the same I/O cell ranking is no guarantee of ending up with the same wages (see table 9.14).

Black men, for example, are in industry-occupation cells that pay an average of 91 percent of the cell wages where white men work. Nonetheless, in the jobs in which they actually work, they earn only about two-thirds (66 to 68 percent) as much as white men. Hispanic men are in industries and occupations much lower in the I/O cell distribution than either white or black men. And within these cells they are constrained to the lowest-wage jobs. This phenomenon could be due to unmeasured human capital factors or to various forms of discrimination, an issue we will address in the labor market simulations to come. The ratios between I/O cell wage rates and actual wage rates are larger among women, reflecting somewhat smaller actual wage gaps between minority women and white women than for their male counterparts.

After the inclusion of IOCELL in these regressions (which, as we previously saw, is highly dependent on years of schooling), education below the college degree adds no additional information about the determinants of hourly wages. At the very top end of the education distribution, however, completion of college appears to help move blacks and Hispanics up the earnings ladder within individual I/O cells. Complet-

TABLE 9.14   *Median I/O Cell Wages Versus Hourly Wage Rates, Race-Ethnic Ratios*

	Black Males/ White Males	Hispanic Males/ White Males	Black Females/ White Females	Hispanic Females/ White Females
Median I/O cell wage	.91	.75	.83	.83
Median hourly wage	.68	.56	.77	.77
Mean hourly wage	.66	.54	.69	.69

Source: Greater Boston Social Survey 1995.

ing college, or going beyond to graduate or professional school, improves black hourly wages by about 15 percent. For the very few Hispanics in the region who have gotten this far in their schooling, the payoff is even greater—boosting hourly wages by more than 27 percent. This does not hold true for whites, suggesting that all the education effect for them is already conveyed at the level of the industry-occupation distribution.

Other human capital variables have a negligible impact on earnings after controlling for industry-occupation. Communication skills, as measured by a vocabulary test (WRDTESTH), are found to be statistically significant only for whites. Unlike the results in the last chapter for less-educated workers, interviewer assessments of the ability of respondents to understand the questionnaire did not appear as a significant variable for any group. However, it came closest to significance in the black equation.

Likewise, age is only marginally significant at best in these regressions. The effect of age is apparently accounted for by other variables included in the model, such as occupational experience and industry-occupation cell. Even so, in each case the quadratic specification for age takes the normal inverted-parabolic shape, indicating a positive effect on wage rates up to a given age and then a declining effect on wage rates. One suspects that the normal age-earnings profile would show up if we were investigating annual earnings, since the largest impact of age is normally on annual hours worked, not the hourly wage.

The two human capital variables that do make a difference are occupational experience and health status. Each year of experience is estimated to boost wages by 1.6 percent for whites, 1.2 percent for blacks, and 1.5 percent for Hispanics. These effects are statistically identical. Hence, as workers increase their seniority in an occupation, ceteris paribus, they move up the wage ladder. However, unlike the less-educated workforce we studied in the last chapter, black earnings do not, in general, rise faster than whites'—so seniority does not help close the racial gap in hourly wages for those who have gone beyond high school. Presumably, occupational experience is helpful as a signal of a black worker's ability for those with no more than a high school degree, while the associate's or bachelor's degree provides this signal for the more educated.

The presence of health limitations is quite powerful, reducing wages by 25 percent for whites, 18 percent for blacks, and 8 percent for Hispanics. Moreover, note that these are the estimated effects *on wages* for *workers*. Health limitations also lower annual earnings, as we saw in the previous chapter, by preventing some people from working at all—or restricting how many hours they can work.

Factors beside human capital have a substantial impact on wage rates, as well. For example, wages vary by gender (for whites and Hispanics, but not blacks), even after accounting for the indirect effects of gender differences through education, I/O cell, and firm size. Moreover, the size of the gender-based wage differential appears to vary according to where a worker lives. Evaluating the coefficients on the variables SEX, STRATUM, and the interaction term, STRATUM × SEX, suggests that white men earn 19 percent more than white women if they live in majority-white neighborhoods. However, this gender-based wage gap is essentially 0 among (the few) whites living in minority communities. Hispanic men dominate Hispanic women in terms of wages no matter where they live— although the wage gap is much higher for those living in white neighborhoods (32 percent) than those in minority communities (12 percent). This may suggest that upwardly mobile Hispanic men have been able to enter higher-paid occupations more easily as they leave the barrio, at least relative to Hispanic women. The gender wage gap for blacks is estimated to be only 4 percent and is not statistically significant.

The coefficient on MARRIED comes closest to statistical significance only for blacks. This may reflect still another instance of statistical discrimination and "signaling" phenomena: a married worker may signal to employers that the person is more stable and therefore less of a hiring risk.[12]

After controlling for all these human capital factors, we find that the type of job one obtains remains an independent and significant variable in wage determination. For example, being a seasonal or temporary worker is associated with lower hourly wages for all three groups, regardless of education and occupational experience. This is one of the factors that locates workers at different points in the wage distributions within individual I/O cells. The wage differential is steep for whites and blacks: 19 percent for whites and 15 percent for blacks. For Hispanics, seasonal or temporary workers make 10 percent less than otherwise. Given that both blacks and Hispanics are more likely to be temporary or seasonal workers (see tables 9.4 and 9.5), this factor helps explain the lower wages of minority groups. Black women are five times more likely to be in such jobs than white women (16 percent versus 3 percent); Hispanic men are nearly three times as likely as white men to be in such part-year or temporary jobs (13 percent versus 5 percent). In the last chapter we saw how part-time work and cycling in and out of work affected adversely the *annual* earnings of black men. Here we find that seasonal and temporary work affect the *hourly* wage as well.

The wage differentials associated with being in jobs that regularly require use of a computer also vary substantially by race and ethnic group, but not exactly as we expected. For Hispanics, workers who regularly use a computer earn a wage premium estimated to be 28 percent over those Hispanic workers who do not. For whites, the premium is estimated to be 15 percent, and only marginally statistically significant. For blacks, the premium is estimated to be only 5 percent, and not statistically significant. These differences likely reflect the way computers are used in the occupations where these workers are employed. Hispanics are least likely to be using computers on the job, as tables 9.4 and 9.5 demonstrated. Yet, in the manufacturing jobs in which many of them are employed, the use of computers may set them aside in better-paid jobs. For whites and blacks, many more who use computers may employ them in simple tasks (such as data entry) and therefore earn only a small wage premium at best. This is particularly true among women, as we saw in the last chapter.

Firm size is statistically significant for minorities, with an elasticity of .032 for blacks and .042 for Hispanics. This means, for example, that a doubling of establishment size is associated with a 2 to 3 percent higher wage rate for blacks and Hispanics.

Working in a minority-dominated position within a firm is associated with lower wage rates for all groups, although for whites the small number of such workers makes the estimate unreliable. Blacks who work in a minority job within an establishment are estimated to suffer a 9 percent lower wage rate, and Hispanics, a 7 percent penalty.

Overall, then, minorities are at a disadvantage in the Greater Boston labor market because they are more likely to be in temporary or seasonal work, less likely to be working with computers, more likely to be in smaller firms, and more likely to be "crowded" into jobs with other minorities.

The augmented regressions using the STRATUM and RECENTLY EMPLOYED terms suggest additional differences among workers. Workers who are currently working or who worked in the last year make significantly more than those who worked only sometime in the prior five years. The estimated difference is 19 percent for whites, 23 percent for blacks, and 14 percent for Hispanics. This could reflect either unmeasured differences in worker human capital and productivity affecting their employment experience or various forms of discrimination. In either case, this result suggests that the high incidence of cycling in and out of jobs we associate with blacks has a powerful influence on their wages.

Place of residence is associated with variation in wage rates, but not universally by race or by gender. For both white and Hispanic men, but not women, living in a minority neighborhood is associated with lower wage rates: 17 percent less for whites, and 16 percent less for Hispanics. For black men, the measured difference is only about 1 percent, and far from significant due to the small number of blacks in the sample who live in nonminority neighborhoods. However, black women who live in minority neighborhoods are estimated to make 17 percent less than black women who live outside minority neighborhoods, a result that is significant at the 5 percent level. These results are consistent with the presence of statistical discrimination, in which employers use an applicant's address as one criterion in making hiring decisions.

Simulation Results

The overall results from such a complex model of wage determination are not at all easy to summarize. To make them more manageable we resort to simulations, as we did in the last chapter, which allow us to explore two interesting questions:

1. How much of the differences in the wage rates between whites, blacks, and Hispanics, and men and women, are accounted for by differences in observable human capital characteristics? In other words, if these groups had the same education, age, occupational experience, and so on, how much closer would their wage rates be, and how large would the remaining differences be?

2. What are the relative contributions of human, cultural, and social capital to earnings for each of the race-ethnic and gender groups?

In each simulation, input variables are changed and their results are traced through the model. For example, we can stipulate a change in the average mother's education of a particular race-ethnic-sex group and then see how it affects each element in the model and finally the estimate of hourly wage. Given the estimated parameters in the education equation, an increase in mother's schooling will increase the average education level of a group we are studying. In turn, this will boost the group's I/O cell wage index, reduce the probability that members of the group will be in minority occupations within an establishment, and increase the average firm size of the group. Inserting all these new values into the hourly wage equation will then provide an estimate of how the group's hourly wage varies as a result of all the direct and indirect changes that follow from the single change in mother's education. Similar simulations can be estimated for various human capital, cultural capital, and social capital variables, or sets of variables. Depending on what values are changed, it is possible to compare across or within race-ethnic gender groups.

Human Capital Simulations

The first set of simulations compares wages across race-ethnic groups as we vary human capital attributes. Note first the distribution of human capital variables across the four equations in the simulation model:

	Education	Age	Health	Occupational Experience	General Training	Word Test Score
I/O cell	X	X			X	
Minority occupation	X					
Firm size	X	X				
Hourly wage	X	X	X	X		X

Education enters into each of the equations, while age enters into all but minority occupation. In addition, the health limitations variable, the years of occupational experience variable, and the word test score enter into the hourly wage equation alone.

In preparing the simulations, we estimate each dependent variable based on substituting white male values for the black and Hispanic values in the black and Hispanic equations. By chaining the equations together, we ultimately obtain estimates of the black/white and black/Hispanic hourly wage ratios under varying human capital conditions.

For example, in estimating the impact of educational differences on the male race and ethnicity wage ratios (BM/WM hourly wage ratio; HM/WM hourly wage ratio), we first substitute the white male education category values (for example, Educ [zero to eight], Educ [nine to eleven]) into the black and Hispanic I/O cell median wage equations. In this case, this raises the black male I/O cell value from its original $11.21 to $12.31. The Hispanic male value rises from $10.15 to $10.96. These new I/O cell values are, in turn, substituted into the black and Hispanic hourly wage equations to yield new simulated wage rates, assuming blacks and Hispanics had the same (higher) education level of white men. The end result of this simulation is that the black/white male hourly wage ratio rises from its original value of .68 to .77 simply by raising the average education of black men to the white male level. Similarly, the black/Hispanic ratio increases from .56 to .67 (see figure 9.10). Hence, a little more than one-quarter of the original black-white male wage gap (9 of 32 percentage points) and exactly one-quarter of the original black-Hispanic male wage gap (44 percentage points) disappear by equalizing formal schooling at the white male level.

Figure 9.10 demonstrates that equalizing health conditions across race and ethnicity does virtually nothing to close the race-ethnic wage gaps. The same is basically true of age, despite the somewhat lower mean age of Hispanic men. Occupational experience, however, does improve the wage ratios, especially for Hispanics. Education is quite powerful, as we demonstrated in our example. Finally, when we simulate the model with white male values for all the human capital variables, we find that we improve the black/white male and Hispanic/white male wage ratios to .81 and .79, respectively. That means that *differences in*

FIGURE 9.10   *Hourly Earnings Ratios, Men*
              Impact of Human Capital Factors

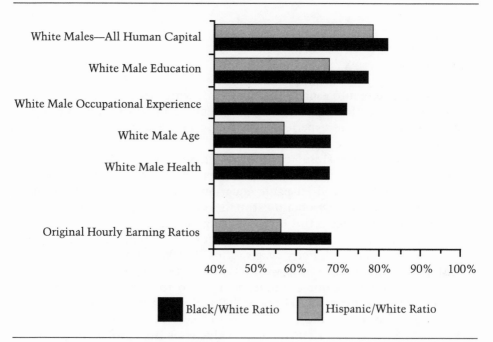

Source: Greater Boston Social Survey 1995.

human capital explain about two-fifths (41 percent) of the original black-white male wage differential and over half (52 percent) of the original Hispanic-white male wage difference.

These results can be compared with those we found in the last chapter. There we found that among those with no more than a high school education, differences in human capital explained virtually all the racial and ethnic wage gap. Here we find that across all education groups, the impact of closing the human capital gap is not anywhere near as salutary. This suggests that for black and Hispanic workers with *more than a high school degree*, there are large wage gaps not closed by equalizing human capital. As we move up the occupational hierarchy, it appears the racial and ethnic wage gaps are larger, not smaller. The tight labor market in the Greater Boston metropolitan region has leveled human capital and equalized wages at the low end of the labor market, but not at the high end, where white professionals and technicians appear to get the best-paying jobs of all.

FIGURE 9.11   *Hourly Earnings Ratios, Women*
                Impact of Human Capital Factors

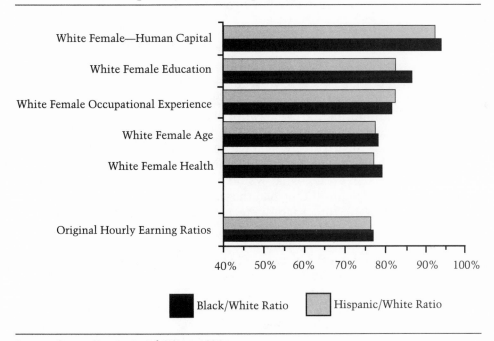

Source: Greater Boston Social Survey 1995.

The analysis for women is found in figure 9.11. Again, we find little improvement if we equalize health condition or age. Occupational experience helps a little more, and education still further. When we add in the white female values for all human capital variables, the amount of the original wage gaps eliminated is relatively large: nearly three-quarters of the original black-white female wage gap (.17 of .23) and two-thirds of the black-Hispanic female wage gap (.15 of .23). Hence, *we have closed most of the female race and female ethnic wage gaps by equalizing human capital.*

Again, this result stands in contrast to the findings we presented in the last chapter. There, more of the female hourly wage gap remained unexplained after equalizing human capital. This suggests that unlike men, better-educated black and Hispanic women have been able to compete with better-educated white women for higher-paying professional and technical jobs. Black and Hispanic women with college educations have been able to find nearly comparable employment to white women in nursing, teaching, social work, and apparently other professions as well. College-educated black and Hispanic men have not been as fortunate with regard to their white male counterparts.

Determinants of Educational Level

Human capital cannot close the hourly wage gaps across race-ethnicity groups entirely, but as we have seen, it surely matters. That finding leads naturally to inquiring about why human capital levels are different by group. The information we have in the GBSS, as extensive as it is, cannot provide anywhere near a complete answer to this question. However, we can use the first regression we ran to simulate group differences in education level, the single most important of the human capital factors. We do this by asking what would be the expected education level of blacks and Hispanics if they had the same "cultural" capital variables (mother's education, intact family, teen marriage rates, and religion) as white men.

Recall from table 9.4 that white men's mothers on average have completed high school (12.0 years). This is nearly a year more schooling than what black men receive (11.2 years) and more than double the education received by the mothers of the Hispanic men in the GBSS sample (5.7 years). Nearly 90 percent of white men were raised in intact families. Only about half of black and Hispanic men were fortunate enough to have both parents present. In addition, virtually none of the white men were married as teenagers, while 4 percent of the black men and nearly 10 percent of the Hispanic men were. The "cultural" capital backgrounds of black and Hispanic women were similar, with the exception that they were much more likely to be married as teenagers (recall table 9.5). Indeed, nearly 12 percent of the black women and over a third (36 percent) of the Hispanic women were married before they reached the age of twenty.

These cultural factors have their impact on education level, as figure 9.12 demonstrates. If black men had the socioeconomic advantage of white men, they would, on average, complete community college (14.0 years of education). Hispanic men, instead of falling shy of high school graduation by nearly two years, would be high school graduates. Black women would be well along toward completing two years of college, while Hispanic women would leap from being high school graduates to being community college grads. In brief, family background matters. Hence, we have additional information linking education to labor market success and socioeconomic and cultural variables to education. The web of causation is coming together.

FIGURE 9.12   *Education Level Simulation*
Education If White Male Cultural Capital

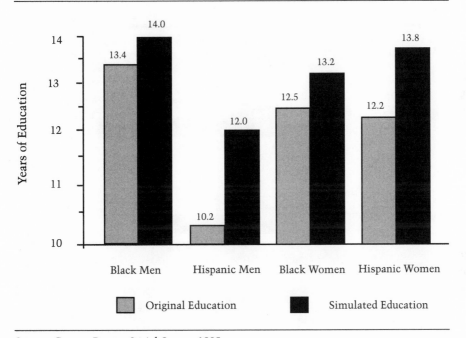

Source: Greater Boston Social Survey 1995.

Attributes Versus Wage-Generating Functions

An alternative way to demonstrate our findings is to compare simulations where black and Hispanic values for *all* variables are substituted into the white male equation with simulations in which white male characteristics for *all* variables are inserted into the black and Hispanic equations. The first simulation (White Male Equation Simulation) asks the question: What would black and Hispanic men earn if they had their own characteristics but were treated as white men in the labor market? The second asks the opposite question: What would black and Hispanic men earn if they were treated as blacks and Hispanics, but had all the characteristics of white men (for example, their education, marital status, and occupational experience). The results for men are shown in figure 9.13.

Substituting the entire set of white male characteristics into the set

FIGURE 9.13   *Hourly Earnings Ratios, Men*
White Male Characteristics versus White Male Equation

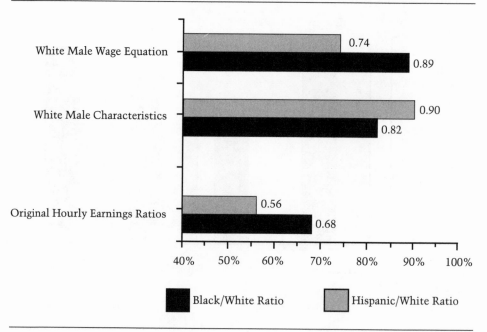

Source: Greater Boston Social Survey 1995.

of black male equations improves black/white hourly earnings ratio from 68 to 82 percent. The same substitution makes an enormous difference for Hispanic men—eliminating more than three-quarters (77 percent) of the original wage gap. These results reinforce the findings we reported in the last chapter. When Hispanic men have the same set of characteristics as white men, save their Hispanic ethnicity, they end up in the labor market in positions close to where white men end up.

However, when black men are given the same characteristics as white men, save their racial identity, they still fall short of white male success in the Greater Boston labor market by nearly 20 percent—almost double the Hispanic deficit. This again suggests the primacy of race as a continuing economic burden on black men in the Boston region.

Reversing the simulation and inserting black and Hispanic male characteristics into the white male wage-setting equations reveals the same pattern. Because of their disadvantages in human and cultural capital, Hispanic men trail white men in hourly earnings by a simulated 25 percentage points. Black men who are more like white men in their human and cultural capital attributes trail white men by only about 10 percentage points. Hence, black men's major failing is not so much their lack of "good" human and cultural capital as the fact that they are still treated as "black" when it comes to employment opportunities in the Greater Boston labor market. Given the findings in the last chapter, we are forced to conclude that this form of discrimination is most acute not for black men with the largest human capital deficits, but for those who have the smallest. Apparently, in today's Boston labor market, well-educated white men have a substantial advantage in making it into the best occupations and highest-paying industries over their black male counterparts who are equally well educated. More human capital closes the hourly wage gap for less-educated black workers, but not for those who have made it into college or beyond.

Figure 9.14 provides a similar analysis for women, with quite different results. Substituting white female characteristics into the black and

FIGURE 9.14   *Hourly Earnings Ratios, Women*
            White Female Characteristics Versus White Female
            Equation

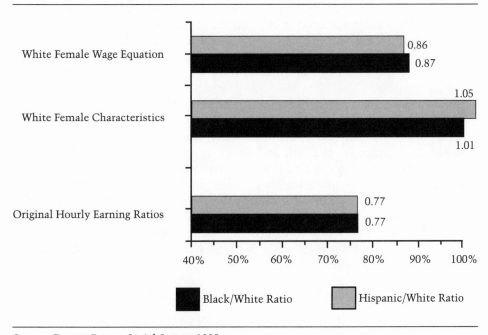

Source: Greater Boston Social Survey 1995.

Hispanic wage-generating equation set totally eliminates any racial or ethnic gap in earnings. This means that if black and Hispanic women had the same human capital and cultural capital as white women, they would end up in similar positions in the wage distribution. Racial discrimination per se in the Greater Boston region seems to be aimed mostly at black men, not black women.[13] Much of the remaining racial and ethnic gap in women's wages is due largely to the human capital and cultural capital deficits black and Hispanic women have relative to their white counterparts. Both black and Hispanic women earn only about 87 percent of white women when we provide them with the same wage-generating equation (that is, the same labor market opportunities) as white women.

Human Capital Versus Cultural Capital Versus Social Capital

One last set of simulations permits us to weigh the relative contributions of human capital, cultural capital, and social capital to the hourly earnings of each of our race-ethnic-gender groups.

For each of these simulations, each group is assigned the same (mean population) attributes. The factor of interest is then varied from a "low" value to a "high" value, and the outcomes on wage rates are observed. The "low" and "high" values of human, cultural, and social capital are chosen to be the 10th and 90th percentiles of each of their component variables for the GBSS sample population at large. In the case of dichotomous variables, such as marital status, we estimate the model based on whether the attribute in question is present. Standardizing on certain percentiles allows one to compare the relative magnitudes of the wage rate effects of the different capital concepts. The 10th and 90th percentiles were chosen in order to obtain a significant range of change for each concept.

For many of the simulations, the proportional changes for men and women, but not the levels, are essentially the same. This characteristic of the simulation is artificial, and arises from the way we specified the models. Where gender enters the basic equations, it enters simply as a dummy variable. A more realistic, more richly specified model would have entailed interactions of gender with other independent variables, or separately estimated equations for each race-ethnic and gender group. We did not do this because our primary focus was on race-ethnic differences, but the methodology could easily be extended to do this. An analysis of the simulations follow.

Human Capital Simulation

The human capital simulation varies several characteristics according to table 9.15. The results for men and women are presented in figures 9.15 and 9.16.

TABLE 9.15   *Human Capital Simulation*

Attribute	Low (10th Percentile)	High (90th Percentile)
Education	7 years	16 years
Experience in occupation	4 years	17 years
Vocabulary test score	1	5
General training	no	yes

Source: Greater Boston Social Survey 1995.

Two highlights emerge from this simulation. First, human capital is important, far more important than we shall find for cultural capital or social capital, in augmenting wage rates. For both white and Hispanic men, the difference between the 10th and 90th percentiles in human capital is associated with an 88 percent difference in mean hourly wage

FIGURE 9.15   *Human Capital Simulation, Men*
"Low" Versus "High" Human Capital

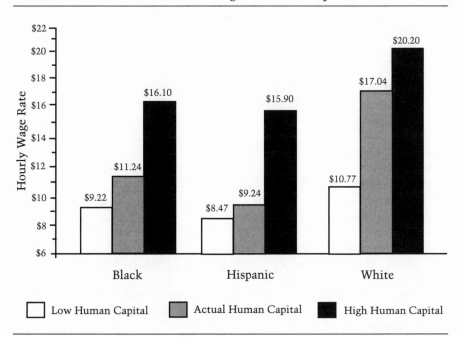

Low Human Capital   Actual Human Capital   High Human Capital

Source: Greater Boston Social Survey 1995.

FIGURE 9.16   *Human Capital Simulation, Women,*
                    "Low" Versus "High" Human Capital

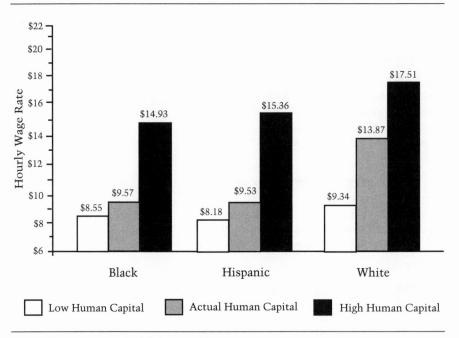

Source: Greater Boston Social Survey 1995.

rates. That means the white male well endowed with human capital will earn over $20.00 per hour compared with about $11.00 for his poorly educated, inexperienced counterpart. For Hispanic men, the difference is nearly $16.00 versus only $8.50. For blacks, the difference in wage rates amounts to 77 percent ($9.22 versus $16.10). Noneducational aspects of human capital, such as experience and vocabulary (perhaps a proxy for communication skills), are more important for whites and Hispanics than for blacks, according to the original regression results. What is also interesting—but not surprising, given the results in the last chapter—is that at low levels of human capital, there is very little disparity between the groups. Disparities increase as the level of human capital rises, with whites earning the highest rates of return to human capital investments.

Given the limited nature of the regression model (that is, gender enters as a single variable in each equation), the results for women are nearly identical to those of men.

Cultural Capital Simulation

The cultural capital simulation varies the following characteristics listed in table 9.16.

The results for men and women are presented in figures 9.17 and 9.18. Cultural capital is important for whites and for blacks, but not as important as human capital is. The main transmission mechanism for whites and blacks for cultural capital is through education, and the single most important factor is mother's education. For both whites and blacks, differences between the 10th and 90th percentiles in cultural capital are associated with differences of 25 to 27 percent in wage rates. These impacts are significant, but much less than those of human capital. The transmission line from, say, mother's education to son's wage is much weaker than from son's own education to his wage.

For Hispanics, cultural capital makes little difference. An increase from the 10th to 90th percentile gains Hispanics only 4 percent in wage rates. The story again is education. For example, at the 10th percentile of cultural capital, less than 1 percent of all groups have a four-year college education. At the 80th percentile of cultural capital, only 2 percent of Hispanic males do. In contrast, at the 80th percentile, 82 percent of white men have a four-year college education and 35 percent of black men do.

Social Capital Simulation

Social capital, as measured in our model, has only a tiny impact on wage rates (see figures 9.19 and 9.20). After much experimentation with sev-

TABLE 9.16   *Cultural Capital Simulation*

Attribute	Low (10th Percentile)	High (90th Percentile)
Mother's education	none	14 years
Raised in an intact family	no	yes
Religion	not Catholic or Jewish if black; Catholic if not black	Catholic if black; Jewish if not black
Married as a teenager	yes	no
Currently married	no	yes
Percentage of time resided in the United States	19%	100%

Source: Greater Boston Social Survey 1995.

FIGURE 9.17   *Cultural Capital Simulation, Men*
              "Low" Versus "High" Cultural Capital

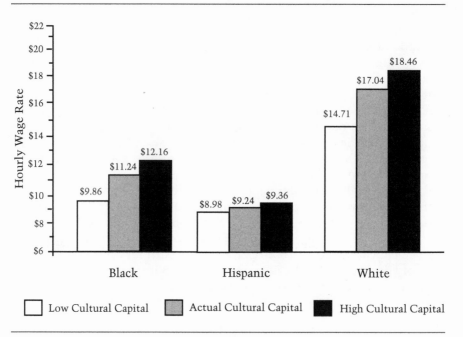

Source: Greater Boston Social Survey 1995.

eral variables and specifications, only one social capital variable remained in the model. That was whether or not a person used family or
friends to search for a job. For whites, the variable had essentially no
effect. For blacks and Hispanics, it increased the probability of working
in a minority establishment and led to employment in a smaller-sized
establishment. Both of these have a negative impact on wage rates, but
the direct and indirect effects are so small as to make little difference in
wage rates. For blacks, using family or friends to find a job resulted in
finding a job that paid 3 percent less than otherwise; for Hispanics, 2
percent less.

Combined with the findings from the last chapter, we can conclude
that searching for jobs through family and friends appears to increase
the chances of finding a job but, at least for blacks and Hispanics, the
types of jobs found are likely to be in lower-wage industries and occupations. The good news of "more work" is offset by the bad news of "less
pay."

FIGURE 9.18   *Cultural Capital Simulation, Women*
              "Low" Versus "High" Cultural Capital

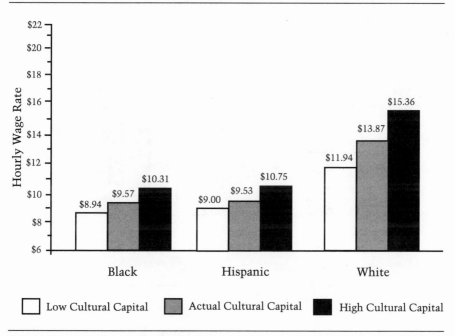

Source: Greater Boston Social Survey 1995.

Conclusion

This brings us to the end of our journey into the realm of Greater Boston workers—at least in terms of wage determination. While there is much detail about the wage-generating process that has been learned, there are several conclusions that stand out as particularly important:

- Differences in human capital matter a great deal, regardless of race, ethnicity, or gender. In Boston's new mind-based economy, very large wage differentials are associated with differences in such factors as education and occupational experience. As a result, closing the existing human capital gaps between blacks and Hispanics, on the one hand, and whites, on the other, will help close a good part of the existing racial and ethnic wage gap. This is particularly true for Hispanics—a finding that mirrors the results we found in chapter 8.

- There is a strong intergenerational transmission line when it comes to education. Cultural capital in the form of mother's education, being raised in an intact family, religious background, and early mar-

FIGURE 9.19   *Social Capital Simulation, Men*
"Low" Versus "High" Social Capital

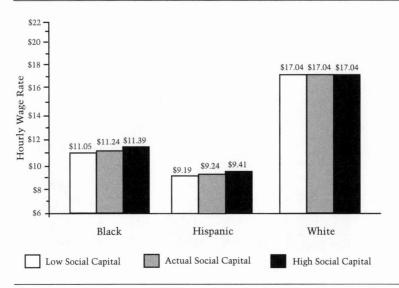

Source: Greater Boston Social Survey 1995.

riage all influence an individual's education level. Because of large differences in these cultural variables by race and ethnicity, there is ultimately a substantial racial and ethnic wage differential related to these factors.

- For black men, however, closing the human capital gap is insufficient to bring wage equality with whites. While they are found in industry-occupation cells that have a median wage 90 percent as high as white men, their median hourly wage rate is only 68 percent as high as whites. When we raise their human capital values to white levels, the black/white male wage ratio remains at 82 percent. This suggests that a good deal of racial discrimination still exists in the Greater Boston labor market—and its greatest impact is on hourly wages of those at the high end of the education distribution, not the low end, given our chapter 8 findings.

- The elasticities of hourly wage rates with respect to I/O cell median wage rates are relatively low for blacks and Hispanics, suggesting that even as these workers move up into higher-rated industries and occupations, they still tend to be confined more often to jobs at the lower end of the wage distribution. Despite the presumed higher costs of making a hiring mistake at the high end of the jobs distribution, the evidence here suggests that there is still a substantial amount of sta-

FIGURE 9.20   *Social Capital Simulation, Women*
              "Low" Versus "High" Social Capital

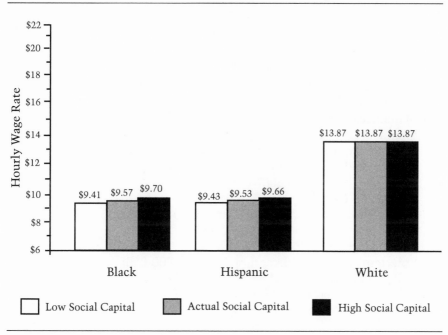

Source: Greater Boston Social Survey 1995.

tistical discrimination employed in the selection of candidates for high-end jobs.

- Blacks and Hispanics tend more often to use family and friend networks when searching for work. While this may improve their chances of finding jobs, these jobs tend to be in smaller firms and in minority-dominated occupations. As a result, the wages earned by such job seekers tend to be a little lower than those earned by workers who use more formal channels to locate employment.

- Residential location has an impact on earnings. In general, living in a minority neighborhood has an adverse impact on hourly wages.

In sum, the model employed here suggests that a good deal of progress could be made through policies aimed at equalizing human capital. But this will not be a sufficient remedy for the remaining wage gap, especially between black and white men. To close this gap will require policies and practices aimed at reversing the adverse impact of discrimination in the hiring hall and on the job. Where one works matters a great deal.

Appendix
List of Industries and Occupations in
I/O Cell Matrix
(with Census Codes)

Industries:

Agriculture, forestry, fishing, and mining (010-050)
Construction (060)
Manufacturing (Nondurable) (100-222)
Manufacturing (Durable) (230-392)
Transportation, Communications, and Public Utilities (400-472)
Wholesale (Durable) (500-532)
Wholesale (Nondurable) (540-571)
Retail (580-691)
Finance, Insurance, and Real Estate (700-712)
Business and Repair Services (721-760)
Personal Services (761-791)
Entertainment and Recreation Services (800-810)
Professional and Related Services (812-893)
Public Administration (900-932)
Active Duty Military (940-960)

Occupations:

Executive, Administrative, and Managerial
Professional Specialty
Technicians and Related Support
Sales
Administrative Support
Private Household
Protective Occupations
Service, except Protective and Household
Farming, Forestry, and Fishing
Precision Production, Craft, and Repair
Machine Operators, Assemblers, and Inspectors
Transportation and Material Moving
Handlers, Equipment Cleaners, Helpers, and Laborers
Military

10

WHAT DO BOSTON AREA EMPLOYERS SEEK IN THEIR WORKERS?

IN THE two preceding chapters, we examined how labor markets operate from the vantage point of the individual worker. We asked a series of questions, including: What factors affect the likelihood that an individual will be in the labor force? Be unemployed? Occupy a particular job slot? Work a certain number of hours per week? Earn a specified hourly wage? We focused on the supply side of the labor market—the attributes of workers who offer their services to employers. But just as the market for apples is influenced not only by those who want to *sell* apples but by those who want to *buy* them, so too is the labor market influenced not only by those who want to sell their labor (the supply side of the labor market: the workers) but also by those who want to buy labor (the demand side of the labor market: the employers).

What are employers looking for when they hire workers? What decision rules do they follow in selecting those applicants they think will turn out to be good workers, and rejecting those applicants they deem to be unacceptable risks? As part of the Ford and Russell Sage Foundation–funded Multi-City Study of Urban Inequality, of which the Greater Boston Social Survey (GBSS) was one part, two surveys of employers were mounted in Boston as well (as in Atlanta, Detroit, and Los Angeles). Both surveys have generated important insights into how employer actions and attitudes affect the job opportunities of Greater Boston's minority residents. In both, we inquired primarily about jobs that require no more than a high school diploma, and the results we examine here are limited to those low-qualification jobs. Thus, the subset of jobs we look at is restricted in a manner that is analogous to the restrictions placed on the subset of workers we examined in chapter 8.

The first of these surveys was a quantitative survey done by telephone, polling about 900 employers in the Greater Boston area. The survey asked a variety of questions about the characteristics of the jobs the employers offered, including the tasks performed on the job, the credentials needed by applicants, the recruiting and screening methods used, the demographic characteristics of the person who was most recently hired, and the demographic characteristics of the firm's other employees, and well as of its customers. The second survey was conducted face to face with forty-five employers and probed more deeply into skill demand, recruiting and hiring strategies, and attitudes about different workers and city-versus-suburban locations through structured but open-ended interviews.

Using these surveys, we are able to focus on four factors that potentially constrain the job opportunities of minority workers living in Boston and other central cities within the metropolitan area:

1. The skills demanded by firms and changes in the skills sought;
2. Employers' relocation away from population concentrations of urban minority workers;
3. The effects of recruiting and screening methods on minority workers; and
4. Employers' attitudes regarding workers of color.

We find that all four of these factors appear to constitute important barriers to full employment opportunity for black and Hispanic workers, given Greater Boston's triple revolution. Most jobs in the Boston area require multiple skilled tasks and multiple credentials, and demands for both "hard" (technical) and "soft" (social) skills are rising. Skill and credential requirements tend to reduce the chances that a black or Hispanic applicant will be hired, and particularly cut against black and Hispanic men. People of color, particularly blacks, remain residentially concentrated in Boston proper, but the "effective unemployment" rate (measuring vacancies against job-seekers) is much higher in the hub than in the suburbs. Moreover, given the region's spatial revolution, businesses are far more likely to relocate from Boston to the suburbs than the other way around, and many employers expressed concerns about crime and workforce quality in inner-city areas. In terms of screening, when formal tests are used, fewer blacks and Hispanics are hired, presumably because of these groups' disadvantage in average education and skill levels. But use of a pre-employment interview has the same effect, and we suggest that the subjectivity inherent in interviews increases the impact of employer stereotypes of minorities. Indeed, a substantial minority of employers report that other employers, coworkers, or customers hold negative attitudes toward people of color, perhaps exacerbated by the demographic revolution. Negative employer perceptions are of particular concern because, as we find in our in-depth inter-views, these influence employers' assessments of the skills of potential workforces and of the relative safety of neighborhoods.

All these factors help elaborate the opportunity nexus of racial atti-tudes, residential segregation, and labor market outcomes, and all help to explain the racial and ethnic disparities in hourly wages and annual earnings we described, particularly among workers with limited educa-tion.

Job Tasks, Skills, and Credentials

We can begin by asking what tasks Boston-area employers require entry-level workers to perform. The quantitative survey asked employers the frequency that certain tasks—such as talking face to face or on the tele-phone to customers, reading instructions at least a paragraph long, writ-ing paragraphs or memos, doing arithmetic, or working with com-puters—are done on a given job.[1] The results are presented in table 10.1. All the tasks, except for writing, are performed daily on at least half the jobs reported. Clearly there appears to be a strong need for cognitive and personal skills to handle the daily tasks in entry-level noncollege jobs.

Given these tasks associated with entry-level jobs, what credentials do Greater Boston employers want of their new entry-level employees? The second panel of the table shows the type of credentials employers report they require. The most frequently cited is references, but even prior vocational or other training is needed to obtain 30 to 40 percent of available jobs. The results also indicate that a higher fraction of em-ployers in the city of Boston proper require each of the hiring creden-tials, except for vocational training. The lowest is found in the region's central cities outside Boston, including Brockton, Cambridge, Fra-mingham, Gloucester, Haverhill, Lawrence, Lowell, Lynn, Salem, and Waltham—where a higher proportion of jobs are in manufacturing.

Taken together, the two panels of table 10.1 tell a sobering story. The hurdle to qualify for entry-level jobs, especially in Boston itself, appears to be high. This suggests that less-educated minority workers face a potential skills mismatch in their local labor markets.

Given this set of demands, how many Boston-area jobs are actually available to workers with little experience or skill accumulation? Harry Holzer has calculated the fraction of all jobs in the central cities, the suburbs, and other places in the four metropolitan areas that involve few or no skilled job tasks, such as those we saw in table 10.1, and few or no hiring credentials (see Holzer 1996b, 62–66 and table 3.9; see also Holzer and Danziger, forthcoming). We replicate those calculations in table 10.2.

TABLE 10.1   *Frequency of Task Performance and Hiring Requirements, Boston Area*

	Daily	Weekly	Monthly	Almost Never
Frequency of task performance				
Talk face to face with customers	56.6%	5.1%	2.1%	36.1%
Talk on the phone with customers	52.6	6.4	3.1	38.0
Read instructions	53.1	21.3	7.4	17.8
Write paragraphs	31.5	16.8	8.7	42.8
Do arithmetic	64.4	13.6	2.9	19.1
Use computers	50.8	5.9	2.8	40.3

	Boston	Suburbs	Other Central Cities in Boston CMSA
Hiring requirements by city and suburb			
High school diploma	80.3%	75.0%	61.4%
General experience	77.5	71.0	72.0
Specific experience	68.9	57.9	61.4
References	81.3	80.7	80.2
Vocational or other training	43.4	43.6	29.3

Source: Multi-City Telephone Employer Survey.
Note: Sample size for tasks performed was 799–800; sample size for hiring requirements was 798–800. (There is a range of sample sizes because there are missing values in some categories.)

Very few of the jobs available now require none of the job tasks or none of the credentials—and there are actually fewer yet in the Boston area than in the other metropolitan areas studied. This obviously reflects the shift to the mind-based economy discussed in earlier chapters of this book. If the pool of jobs obtainable by entry-level workers is expanded to include those that only require talking to customers, the situation improves somewhat but remains fairly bleak. Overall, only one in seven entry jobs would be available to workers who had trouble reading instructions, writing paragraphs, doing arithmetic, or using computers. Only one in twenty jobs requires no high school diploma, training, experience, or references. Importantly, the fraction of low-requirement, low-credential jobs is actually lower in the city of Boston, where less-educated and less-experienced workers are more likely to live.

Jobs that entail no or few specific tasks or credentials also pay wages significantly lower than the average for all entry jobs in the em-

TABLE 10.2   *Task and Credential Requirements for Boston Area Jobs*

	Boston	Suburbs	Other Central Cities	Total
Proportion of Jobs				
Perform none of major tasks daily	2.2%	6.4%	16.0%	7.4%
Perform none of major tasks, except talking to customers	12.3	12.7	21.6	14.3
Requires no high school diploma, training, experience, or references	3.6	5.9	4.8	5.3
Requires only high school diploma	4.8	7.6	5.5	6.7
Requires only high school diploma and general experience	7.1	9.7	6.2	8.6
Wage levels				
All jobs	$9.71	$9.18	$8.97	$9.23
Perform none of major tasks daily	a	$7.44	$8.21	$7.66
Perform none of major tasks, except talking to customers	$7.27	$7.32	$7.89	$7.50
Requires no high school diploma, training, experience, or references	a	$7.08	$7.04	$6.87
Requires only high school diploma	$6.75	$6.99	$7.06	$6.97
Requires only high school diploma and general experience	$7.08	$7.55	$7.16	$7.16

Source: Multi-City Telephone Employer Survey.
[a]Very small number of observations.
Note: Sample size for proportion of jobs was 800; sample size for wage levels was 560.

ployer survey. Compared to all noncollege jobs in Greater Boston reported in the employer survey, jobs that entail no specific tasks pay 17 percent less. A typical such job pays $15,320 for full-year, full-time work, compared with $18,460 for the average of all noncollege jobs in the central cities of the region. Jobs located in the city of Boston that do not require a high school degree, training, experience, or references pay even less: $13,740.

To the degree that the trend of skill demands is rising, this mismatch is likely to worsen. The results in table 10.3 suggest that we should indeed expect a growing mismatch, at least for the near term.[2]

TABLE 10.3   *Proportion of Boston-Area Employers Reporting Change in Skills Sought for the Sample Job*

	All Jobs	Clerical	Customer Service	Blue-Collar	Other
Report a change in skills	39.0%	50.8%	31.2%	34.9%	42.5%
Of those reporting a change					
Skills risen	98.7	98.4	98.2	98.6	99.1
Skills declined	1.3	1.6	1.8	1.4	0.9
Of those reporting a rise in skills					
What kind of skills					
Basic reading, writing, numeric	31.8	32.2	27.7	30.0	34.9
Social and verbal	20.7	11.3	37.4	17.9	19.5
Both	22.4	29.0	11.1	24.4	23.1
Other	19.6	26.0	23.9	20.5	13.1
Reasons for the rise					
New technology	81.6	96.8	64.6	72.2	88.1
Computers	71.0	98.4	62.1	38.8	81.7
New products	46.9	32.2	47.8	56.7	48.3
Higher product quality	63.4	60.0	45.0	64.1	74.6
New services provided	64.1	51.5	74.5	57.1	70.9
More customer contact	51.6	49.9	74.4	30.9	54.9
Organizational change	76.7	77.3	72.2	75.3	79.6
Sample size	800	127	210	239	221

Source: Multi-City Telephone Employer Survey.

Boston-area employers were asked to report if the skills needed to perform the sample job were changing and, if so, whether they were rising or declining, and why. Less than half (40 percent) of all hub employers reported a change in the level of skills required on the entry-level jobs. But, among those that did report a change, essentially all reported an increase in skill requirements. Basic reading, writing, and verbal skills—so-called hard skills—are most frequently cited as the kind of skills that will increasingly be needed to compete for even the simplest entry jobs. Close behind are the social and verbal skills—soft skills—or a combination of both hard and soft skills.

The greater need for basic skills appears to derive from the introduction of new technology or the use of computers. The heightened demand for social and verbal skills, on the other hand, seems to originate from more need for customer contact and, as our qualitative data also suggest, from organizational change, which frequently involves more use of teams and, for most employees, increased personal interaction across the organization.

The pattern of skill upgrading is similar across occupations, but with some notable differences. A larger fraction of employers report skill increases for clerical occupations, and this appears to be driven by the widespread introduction of computers into clerical work. As might be expected, blue-collar occupations are relatively more likely to require more basic skills, and customer service jobs are relatively more likely to demand greater social and verbal skills.

In addition to the quantitative information gleaned from the telephone surveys, we gathered qualitative data from face-to-face interviews with employers. These interviews tell us that there is often more to skill upgrading than meets the eye. For example, consistent with the telephone survey data, employers most commonly reported no change in skill requirements. But in some cases, employers stated that there had been no changes and then later in the interview described upgrading. Consider this interchange with the owner of a contract cleaning company:

Interviewer: So, have there been changes in the skills and qualities you look for over time?

Respondent: No, the same. . . . We've been looking for the same kind of people for twenty years.

. . .

Respondent: But you know, there is one thing that has happened is . . . that recycling is a big issue now. So, the cleaners have had to be a little more aware and do a little more thinking than in the old days when they just had to dump the trash because now you've got a trash barrel, you've got a recycling barrel, and now there's starting to be multiple recycling barrels for different kinds of trash, and so, you know, they have to be a little more aware of that. Certainly, there's a lot more high-tech office equipment now than there was twenty years ago . . . so in the old days you could just clean your phone until you were content, nothing would happen. Now, the phones are computers, so you have to be very careful. They're learning that the office equipment is more sensitive, so they do have to be a little more on the ball, I think.

On the other hand, while numerous respondents described the computerization of various jobs, a substantial minority reported no resulting increase in the skills sought. A Boston construction supply wholesaler had just spent $250,000 on a new computer system, but was not looking for anything different among clerical hires, because "if it's not broke, don't fix it." In a warehouse that has adopted computerized materials-handling and -tracking equipment, skills required for the entry-level warehouse worker job have remained unchanged, because: "It's still a manual [job], lifting the cases and lifting and staging and picking, that's really what it comes down to." Others commented that it has been easy to train people to use computers and other new automated equipment. In fact, the human resource director at a bank commented that she does not look for prior computer knowledge in new hires "because our computers are different. I mean all systems are different. They have to learn our system and that's what they're trained in." Similarly, some managers observed that general workforce skills had changed in step with the business's technical requirements, or even ahead of them. At a prison where "computers are everywhere now," this has not affected who they are looking for as prison employees because "the pool already had the skills before we even went out and looked for them."

Moreover, in some cases computerization has a tremendous impact on the workforce that has nothing to do with skill. In a fascinating second-hand story, gleaned from the Los Angeles employer survey, a local mortgage company executive recounted a story about a Boston-area financial institution:

> Two to three years ago, their mortgage company decided that they were going to equip all of their salespeople with laptop computers. And they were going to be required, rather than fill out the loan application long-hand and deliver it to the processor for closing, to enter the information [into the machine]. They had a 95 percent turnover in their sales force. They just quit. . . . It's because of the different attitudes about using the computer at that time. Typing is women's work, and the male loan officers considered it beneath them. Demeaning.

(He went on to add that male attitudes had changed, and that now his sales force is "begging for us to buy them computers.")

Despite all these caveats, a growing need for computer skills was the most common skill change reported. We also heard repeatedly about three other kinds of increased technical or hard skill requirements. First, some businesses have placed new emphasis on such basic skills as literacy, often in response to new equipment, new worker involvement in statistical process control, or new standards for customer or worker safety, all of which may require reading written instructions or keeping written records. Second, employers told of a need for workers to handle a broader range of tasks, or to possess a more analytical overview of how their tasks fit into broader processes. Officials at a public agency, for example, told us they seek clerical workers who are "able to do two or three, four different things." Third, a variety of industry-specific changes call for added skill: home care aides, for example, need added technical knowledge because managed care is inducing hospitals to discharge sicker patients, according to the director of one Boston agency.

More frequent than any of the hard skill shifts except for computer literacy, however, were heightened demands for soft skills. Managers of retail, service, and clerical workers spoke of greater needs for the interaction skills involved in customer service—in some cases linked to a declining need for hard skills: "It's becoming more and more important that people have good communication skills and be people-oriented, along with having your basic typing and word processing skills. There's not that many secretarial jobs anymore where you just sit in front of a computer and type all day."

As Moss and Tilly (1996a) reported in earlier research, employers related these new needs back to competitive pressure and to a competitive strategy designed to win over customers, "really trying much more hard to meet the needs of the customer," as one government agency manager put it. Less commonly, managers expressed a need for stronger interaction skills stemming from the adoption of team forms of organization.

Skill Requirements Disadvantage Particular Groups

Table 10.4 shows the association between the need for certain job tasks or the use of particular hiring credentials and the proportion of new hires in each of six race-ethnicity-gender groups (white, black, Hispanic, by male and female).[3] The results are striking. Looking at daily task use, white women are substantially more likely to be hired if *any* of the tasks are required daily, compared to the case when the tasks are not required. This is particularly so for the use of computers and talking on the phone, which, as Holzer notes, may result from the concentration of white women in clerical and sales jobs (see Holzer 1996b, 81). This gender effect also holds for Hispanic women, but not for blacks.

Black and Hispanic men are hit hard when any of these tasks must be performed daily. Talking face to face or on the phone particularly disadvantages Hispanic men, and one can speculate that this is due in part to poorer English-language skills. There is also a large effect on Hispanic males when computers are used. Both black and Hispanic

TABLE 10.4   *Gender and Race of New Hires by Daily Task Use and Hiring Requirements (Ratio of Percentage in Cell to Percentage in All Jobs)*

	White Males	Black Males	Hispanic Males	White Females	Black Females	Hispanic Females
All jobs	32.5%	6.6%	6.2%	46.7%	3.5%	4.3%
Daily tasks						
Talk face to face with customers						
No	1.06	1.03	1.65	0.86	1.03	1.09
Yes	0.96	0.98	0.53	1.10	0.97	0.93
Talk on the phone with customers						
No	1.24	1.48	2.02	0.55	1.31	1.65
Yes	0.79	0.61	0.18	1.39	0.71	1.00
Read instructions						
No	0.92	1.32	1.44	0.94	1.37	0.91
Yes	1.07	0.70	0.69	1.05	0.69	1.12
Write paragraphs						
No	1.07	1.11	1.39	0.86	1.20	1.14
Yes	0.86	0.80	0.26	1.30	0.54	0.70
Do math						
No	0.81	2.05	1.82	0.77	1.80	1.51
Yes	1.11	0.39	0.56	1.13	0.51	0.70
Use computers						
No	1.33	1.45	1.87	0.63	0.51	1.05
Yes	0.67	0.56	0.02	1.37	1.49	0.95
Requirements for hiring						
High school diploma						
No	1.08	1.92	2.66	0.51	1.37	1.67
Yes	0.97	0.68	0.45	1.17	0.86	0.77
General experience						
No	0.95	1.61	1.87	0.80	1.31	1.12
Yes	1.02	0.77	0.69	1.08	0.86	0.98
Specific experience						
No	0.96	1.14	1.82	0.87	1.14	1.21
Yes	1.02	0.92	0.50	1.09	0.89	0.88
References						
No	1.11	1.76	1.18	0.73	1.80	1.07
Yes	0.98	0.83	1.00	1.06	0.80	1.00
Vocational or other training						
No	0.94	0.98	1.34	0.96	1.29	1.26
Yes	1.09	1.05	0.60	1.05	0.60	0.67

Source: Multi-City Telephone Employer Survey.
Note: Sample size was 688–92. Except for the first row (which shows the percentage in all jobs), the table shows the ratio of the percentage of hires in a race-gender group in that cell to the percentage in that race-gender group across all jobs.

men's numbers plunge when writing or arithmetic is required. White men's proportion of the workforce tumbles noticeably when customer service and computer tasks are needed, but increases if reading or math is required.

A similar but not identical pattern of associations is evident for hiring credentials. White females are hired in greater numbers when any of the hiring requirements are utilized, compared to when the credential is not necessary. In contrast, black and Hispanic males get clobbered when any of the hiring credentials are applied. Black females are less in evidence, as well, when such credentials are necessary in order to be hired. As with job tasks, white females receive a higher proportion of jobs than their male counterparts when any of the hiring credentials are applied. This gender pattern is not apparent for Hispanic men and women.

Table 10.4 completes a discouraging jobscape for less-educated workers, particularly those of color. The overwhelming majority of jobs involve skilled tasks, educational or skill credentials, or both. Businesses are seeking higher levels of qualifications and abilities in their workers. Workers with limited education, and black and Hispanic men in particular, are disproportionately selected out of the jobs that have such skill requirements. Furthermore, the small number of jobs offered with few requirements pay poorly.

This is confirmed by the findings of the Greater Boston Social Survey of households reported in chapter 8. The annual earnings of black and Hispanic men who have no more than a high school diploma are substantially lower than those of comparably educated white men. This is due in part to the kinds of jobs that these groups are able to secure. Over 20 percent of the white men in the GBSS study worked in sales occupations, which normally require high levels of interaction with customers. Only 5 percent of black men and only 1 percent of Hispanic men were found in these occupations. This is important not so much because of the hourly wages these jobs pay, but because of the opportunity for longer weekly hours available in these occupations. As we noted in chapter 8, on average, men working in sales positions work ten more hours per week than other workers. This translates into significantly higher annual earnings. Moreover, about a third of white men are working in jobs that use computers. Less than one-fifth of Hispanic men and only one-tenth of black men are in such jobs. *Being locked out of sales jobs and computer-based occupations takes a large toll on black and Hispanic men's earnings and contributes to the large gap in annual earnings between minority men and whites.* Our employer interviews suggest this phenomenon could get worse, if the schooling and skill acquisition of minorities, especially Hispanics, do not keep pace.

The qualitative findings reflect and contribute added detail to this discouraging picture. As the quantitative data indicate, higher hard-skill requirements may exclude people of color, who disproportionately lack such skills. Rising soft-skill requirements are also likely to reduce access for workers of color, as we have argued at length elsewhere (Moss and Tilly 1996a). Here issues of objective skill levels are mingled with employer stereotypes about the interaction and motivation skills of particular groups, as well as customer and coworker racial and ethnic preferences. As we will discuss, employer, customer, and coworker biases are widespread, so augmented soft-skill requirements inevitably leave a substantial opening for heightened discrimination.

Location of Jobs

Another potential impediment to employment for many workers of color is physical distance from the jobs for which they are qualified. As noted earlier in this book, the notion of a spatial mismatch between black communities and metropolitan area jobs is an old one (Kain 1968). Recent research (Kasarda 1993) shows continuing shifts of employment from the central city to the suburbs, and provides growing evidence that distance and commuting-cost barriers contribute significantly to black labor market disadvantage in many cities. This is particularly true for younger workers and shows up in the most recent data (Jencks and Mayer 1990; Holzer 1991; Ihlanfeldt 1997; Moss and Tilly 1991).

Where are the entry-level jobs in the Boston area? Table 10.5 shows the distribution of firms in the survey across Boston, its suburbs, and other central cities in the region. Entry-level noncollege jobs are concentrated in the suburbs. These findings raise the concern that the geography of jobs could be a barrier to central-city minority workers, especially if the red-hot Boston economy were suddenly to cool.

TABLE 10.5   *Proportion of Boston-Area Jobs and Vacancies by Boston, Suburbs, and Other Central Cities*

	Boston	Suburbs	Other Central Cities
Proportion of firms located in each area	18.3%	63.2%	18.5%
Proportion of firms reporting a vacancy in each area	56.6%	39.7%	44.7%
Mean number of vacancies among firms reporting a vacancy	22.2	9.4	5.5

Source: Multi-City Telephone Employer Survey.
Note: Sample size was 799–800.

344

Nevertheless, while more jobs are located in the suburbs, suburban firms are less likely to report a current vacancy than either Boston firms or those located in other local central cities. In fact, a considerably higher fraction of firms in Boston, and a somewhat higher fraction in other central cities such as Brockton and Cambridge, report a current vacancy. Furthermore, the mean number of vacancies in the firms that report having one is quite a bit lower among firms in the suburbs than in what are generally larger central-city firms and institutions like hospitals, universities, and large insurance and financial companies.

This should be good news for central-city residents, especially minority workers. But the good news is tempered by the fact that suburban commuters take a significant number of the available jobs in the hub city, leaving a higher unemployment rate among central-city residents. Thus, as Holzer has shown, the *effective* level of unemployment, accounting for the size of the labor force and commuting patterns of suburban and city residents, is higher in primary central cities such as Boston (see Holzer 1996, 32–37 and table 2.4). We replicate his results in table 10.6. In this table, we present the ratio of filled jobs, vacant jobs, and unemployed workers, respectively, to the resident labor force in Boston versus the suburbs (in this case, including central cities in other areas). The effective unemployment level, and the gap between effective unemployment and the number of vacancies, are shown as well, scaled by the size of the labor force in the area. Effective unemployment is calculated by first assuming that unemployed residents will have the same commute patterns as employed residents, and then apportioning the unemployed residents in each area to the central city or outside the central city using the commute pattern of the employed residents. The

TABLE 10.6   *Ratios of Filled Jobs, Vacancies, and Unemployed Workers in the Boston Area*

	Boston	Suburbs + Other Central Cities
Filled jobs/Labor force	1.472	0.816
Vacancies/Labor force	0.037	0.021
Unemployed, as percent of labor force	6.8%	6.5%
Effective unemployment, as percent of labor force	10.8%	5.8%
Effective unemployment − vacancies, as percent of labor force	7.1%	3.7%
Effective unemployed people per vacancy	2.919	2.762

Source: Holzer 1996, tables 2 to 4 (33).

final line in the table gives the ratio of effective unemployment to job vacancies.

The results in table 10.6 show more labor market distress in Boston than in the suburbs and other local central cities. Effective unemployment is roughly twice as high in the hub than elsewhere in the metropolitan area, as is the gap between effective unemployment and job vacancies. So, despite the higher vacancy rate in the city, the likelihood of unemployment is higher as well.[4]

Table 10.7 shows descriptive information from the quantitative survey on firms' current and past locations, and whether they plan to move in the near future. Firms throughout the Greater Boston area have a fairly high average tenure. Because the distribution is skewed upward by a relatively small number of values near 100 years, we also present the median number of years a firm has been at its present site. By either measure, suburban firms have more recently moved to or opened in their current location. Despite substantial average tenures, the proportion of businesses that have relocated in the past ten years is also strikingly high: 55 percent across all businesses, and 59 percent for suburban firms in particular. Firms in the region's other central cities—

TABLE 10.7   *Location Characteristics of Boston-Area Firms by Boston, Suburbs, and Other Central Cities*

	Boston	Suburbs	Other Central Cities	All Firms
How long at the present location				
Mean number of years	25.8	20.3	29.8	22.9
Median number of years	15.0	14.0	20.0	
Moved in the last ten years	52.5%	58.5%	43.6%	54.8%
Is a move planned?	9.0%	7.7%	11.1%	8.6%
Plan not to keep firm open indefinitely	1.5%	1.3%	2.2%	1.5%

	Moved but Stayed in Category	Moved to Boston	Moved to Suburb	Moved to Other Central City	Total
Started in					
Boston	14.0%	—	23.0%	8.0%	100.0%
Rest of metro area	8.0%	0.3%	—	—	100.0%

Source: Multi-City Telephone Employer Survey.
Note: Sample size was 727–56.

many of which are aging industrial centers—are even older and less likely to have recently shifted location. About 10 percent of all Boston-area firms are planning a move, and among those, there is not much difference across Boston, suburb, and other central cities. Almost no firms in this survey report that they are likely to close in the foreseeable future.

The last panel of this table addresses the question: For firms that *started out* in a given part of the metropolitan area, how many moved elsewhere in the metro area, and to where? (Because this is based on a retrospective question of firms currently located in the metro area, it excludes businesses that moved out of the area altogether.) Of firms in the sample that started out in Boston proper, nearly a third (31 percent) had moved to the suburbs or other central cities at the time of the survey. This is far more common than the reverse move, undertaken by less than 1 percent of businesses that started out elsewhere in the metropolitan area. Even taking into account that Boston represents only one-fifth of business sites in the metro area (so that even businesses relocating at random would be more likely to move out than in), there is a strong net flow of relocating business away from the hub. Such is the nature and impact of the region's spatial revolution.

Why Are Employers on the Move?

Employers are shifting to suburban areas, at greater distances from inner-city communities of color. But what can we learn about *why* they are doing so, and *how* they view such inner-city communities both as potential business locations and as potential sources of labor?

The qualitative data reveal that racial composition figures prominently in employers' cognitive maps of space. This information about race combines with other perceptions of an area to form signals about its desirability as a business location, and the quality of its workforce. Most Boston-area employers do not view concentrated minority and/or low-income areas—particularly black neighborhoods—as desirable locations. While for many suburban managers, the inner city and its workforce were so remote from their experience as to be of little concern, managers located within or close to central cities often openly stated negative views. The reasons for these views include crime, congestion, and lack of access to desired labor supply, as well as in some cases outright racial antipathy. Concerns with safety and its potential effect on recruiting employees, for instance, were voiced by several service agencies. The comments were moderated, however, with statements that the view of the inner city from the outside was exaggerated and the problem was not one that seriously compromised their ability to do their work.

The comment of the director of a medical facility in a largely black area of Boston's inner city was illustrative:

> I'm not unaware that this is considered to be a dangerous area. Its reputation far exceeds the reality, but it's certainly been a long-standing concern in terms of patients and employees. There are people who have a problem coming into this area. People will respond to an ad, and when they drive through the area or come into the area, they won't work. They won't want to. They're afraid.

Spatial lines defined in black and white still exist within Boston, of course. Interestingly, the strongest explicitly *racialized* statement of concern for safety was voiced in the context of blacks traveling to work in South Boston, an overwhelmingly white area with a long history of animosity toward blacks. Three city employers raised this concern. Stated one:

> I find parts of Boston are difficult. And, I'm not talking about Roxbury and Dorchester, where you hear about all the drive-by shootings. The big thorn in my side, and I've been trying to work it for years, is South Boston. Now, keep in mind that most of our workforce are men and women of color. They, for appropriate reasons, I feel, refuse to go to South Boston.

In addition to safety concerns, most hub employers have a negative assessment of the workforce available in concentrated minority and/or low-income areas—again, particularly predominantly black areas. A hotel manager in a suburb close to Boston explained that no inner-city Boston residents are employed at the desk, because:

> You have to have people in that area that show some interest. You can't have somebody standing behind the front desk with a long face on who doesn't want to be there and looking at their watch every five minutes. It doesn't look good to [guests] when they're paying $159 a night . . . to stay here.

Race, class, and location all contribute to most employers' assessment of workforce skills, typically with substantial overlap among the three. In this regard, the Boston public schools came in for special criticism from local-area employers. Comments by one administrator for a contract cleaning firm responsible for servicing a major Cambridge employer captured this relatively widespread sentiment:

> The difference in the education, I can see very clearly. . . . You can have a high school degree from Boston and you can have a high school degree from, let's say, Medford, Somerville, or somewhere else, and the abilities of

the people to comprehend and write and read are far greater for the people in the outlying areas.

Similarly, a public-sector human resource director declared,

> I think we have a real problem. I think the problem is centered in the Boston public school system. In my opinion, the school system in this city is not producing young people with the educational skills to get into the workforce, and in many cases, perform.

This manager went on to link differences in education to disparities in skill by race:

> In most cases, the white . . . has gone either to private school or gone almost overwhelmingly to the Catholic parochial school system in the city through high school, which is very expensive, up to five, six thousand dollars a kid. . . . [Compare that with] minority kids who either went to school in the deep South, where the per capita expenditure for education is as low as you can imagine, or they graduated from the Boston public school system. In either case, we've had, historically, a much larger failure rate among minority . . . than white. . . . That's been a very significant problem.

As we noted in chapter 2, the Boston public schools have been a flash point for race relations in the city of Boston for many years, even before the confrontation over busing in the 1970s. The schools have become predominantly minority, as white residents have left them for private schools or fled to the suburbs. Given the demography of the schools and the history of controversy, it is difficult to pull apart the conundrum of educational preparation in the public schools from the issues of race, class, and space that the Boston public schools have come to symbolize. At times, complaints about the Boston schools surely mean exactly no more than what is said; at other times, they represent a coded way of expressing an aversion for inner-city workers.

In contrast, several blue-collar businesses located in or near the satellite cities Lawrence and Lowell show a very different set of attitudes about the inner city as a place to do business, and the available workforce in inner-city areas. These firms base their economic strategy on the availability of the immigrant inner-city workforce in these cities. They complained about the problems of an inner-city location—in particular, crime, drugs, safety—but, for the time, these concerns appear to be counterbalanced by the availability of a inner-city workforce well suited to their economic needs. Two examples illustrate this situation. A manager of a Lawrence manufacturing facility whose production workforce is over 70 percent Hispanic from the Lawrence inner city described the location of his firm as "an issue . . . for us. It's all crack houses and prostitutes out here. . . . And it's tough for us right now to bring in customers." But when asked about problems with getting qualified workers in the area, he responded, "that hasn't been too, too difficult."

The owner of a small metal-coating firm told a very similar story about locating business in Haverhill, an old mill city just to the northeast of Lawrence. He described Haverhill in starkly negative terms: "Well . . . you have to be aware that there's pretty good drug traffic two or three blocks from here. . . . [Haverhill] has an inner city. It has homeless people . . . and drug traffic." But shortly afterward he added, "But . . . I view the workforce as an asset and not really as a problem. They really aren't a problem."

The workforce attracted by the firm significantly distorted this (Anglo) business owner's perception of Haverhill, as evidenced by his comment that: "I don't know much about it because I have only been here a couple of years, but I just know that it's . . . Hispanic, almost majority now, I would say. A lot of Spanish stores, a lot of Spanish people." In fact, the Hispanic population of Haverhill stood at only 5 percent in 1990, up from 2 percent in 1980. In any case, this active pursuit of a minority workforce remains the exception; businesses are more likely to hold negative views of such a workforce.

As employers pursue location decisions, recruiting, and screening, they act on this set of perceived *signals* about cities and their local populations. Given the highly segregated settlement patterns in Boston, particularly in the case of blacks, most people of color are in fact spatially concentrated. In practice, businesses' reservations about concentrated minority neighborhoods lead them to locate farther and farther away from most people of color. Of course, a wide range of other reasons exist why businesses might choose to move to suburban locations, including less traffic congestion and proximity to the residential locations of their managers. Nonetheless, these location decisions impose *barriers* of distance to jobs for those who live in the central city—particularly if they do not have their own cars. One Waltham manufacturer explained that no blacks apply for jobs because: "You can't get there from here, Waltham. You have to take three or four buses. I remember one of the guys . . .we opened up at 8:00 in the morning and he had to leave at 6:00 in the morning to get here on three or four different buses."

The *signal and barrier effects* both contribute to the disadvantages suffered by black men in the Boston labor market, as the 17 percent hourly wage deficit (*after* controlling for human capital differences) revealed in chapter 8 attests. The story is about more than just distance, as suggested by some employers' comments about the inner-city work-force. Moreover, some firms in the inner suburbs who could hire more Boston inner-city residents recruit immigrants from elsewhere. And, in a number of cases, we found that immigrants who work at suburban firms and even farther from Boston manage to overcome the friction of space through carpools and vanpools. Blacks in Boston might more readily use this transportation mode, as well, if they were the workers of choice, and/or these were the jobs they wanted.

Recruiting and Screening Methods

A key variable in recruiting and hiring procedures is their degree of for-mality. Formality in hiring may affect the probability of employment of minorities in several ways. Formal hiring procedures may be more ob-jective, reducing the opportunity for biases, stereotypes, or social net-works to drive recruitment and selection processes. Businesses may use formal procedures when they require higher levels of skill, or seek to reduce variation in skill levels of new hires. In some cases, however, the use of greater formality in screening may actually be a reaction to the increased number of black or Hispanic applicants, given many em-ployers' negative perceptions of black and Hispanic skill levels. Alter-natively, and somewhat more benignly, highly formal screening pro-cesses may be adopted by highly visible, well-paying employers, who must select from very large applicant pools. Such employers may also attract disproportionate numbers of black applicants. Higher levels of public scrutiny and political pressure, or higher levels of intrinsic com-mitment to diversity, are likely to result in reliance on more formal procedures.

A long literature documents that the quintessential informal screening device, the pre-employment interview, incorporates the racial predilections of the interviewer (Dipboye 1982; Word, Zanna, and Coo-per 1974). In an earlier study, we found a strong negative statistical link between the importance of the interview as a screening device and the level of black male employment in a given firm (Moss and Tilly 1995a). Our qualitative findings reinforce this connection (Moss and Tilly 1996b). Neckerman and Kirschenman (1991) reported that use of imper-sonal tests in place of face-to-face interviews was positively associated with increased black employment. If followed and enforced, affirmative action policies work precisely by introducing greater formality and pre-sumed objectivity into recruiting and screening.

As we will show, the type of recruiting and screening methods used by employers result in different racial and ethnic hiring patterns. Some part of the explanation may be discrimination; some part may be a confounding of cultural differences and stereotypes with perceptions of differences in certain types of skills (notably, personal interaction and motivation skills); and some may be the effect of lower skills and less access to effective job networks on the part of workers of color. The quantitative results reported here directly observe outcomes but cannot easily disentangle the sources of these outcomes. The qualitative evidence is more suggestive about how employer subjectivity can confound skills assessment with stereotyping of different groups.

Table 10.8 shows the recruiting method that generated the last hire, as well as screening methods employed in hub-area firms. While there is some variation across Boston, suburb, and other local central cities in the use of these methods, the patterns are fairly similar. More formal methods include the use of newspaper ads or referrals from employment agencies, community agencies, schools, or unions. Together, these for-

TABLE 10.8   *Recruiting and Screening Methods Used by Boston-Area Employers, by Boston, Suburb, and Other Central Cities*

	Boston	Suburb	Other Central Cities	Total
Recruiting method for the last employee hired				
Newspaper ad	22.2%	31.2%	28.7%	29.1%
Help Wanted signs	1.8	5.0	2.9	4.0
Walk-in	10.2	12.3	10.9	11.7
Referrals from				
Current employees	28.1	27.6	31.5	28.5
State employment service	0.2	3.6	3.6	3.0
Private employment service	18.0	4.1	3.3	6.4
Community agency	2.2	0.2	0.7	0.7
Schools	2.5	4.4	1.4	3.5
Union	0.8	0.2	1.4	1.4
Other (acquaintances, etc.)	14.3	11.3	12.4	12.4
Used affirmative action in recruiting	59.6	48.9	46.8	46.8
Screening methods used				
Written application	79.7	77.9	79.1	78.4
Interview	89.9	86.5	81.1	86.1
Physical and/or drug test	16.0	4.4	5.6	6.8
Tests and/or other	39.3	31.3	35.9	33.7
Verify education	36.1	23.8	22.5	25.9
Check criminal record	30.5	22.1	28.0	24.8
Used affirmative action in hiring	47.8	32.4	27.8	34.3

Source: Multi-City Telephone Employer Survey.
Note: Sample size was 709–99.

TABLE 10.9   Race and Gender of Last Employee Hired in Boston area Firms,
by Recruiting Method and by Use of Hiring Screens
(Ratio of Percentage in Cell to Percentage in all Jobs)

	White Males	Black Males	Hispanic Males	White Females	Black Females	Hispanic Females
All Jobs	31.5%	6.9%	6.3%	47.6%	3.5%	4.2%
Recruiting method						
Newspaper ad	1.01	1.13	0.52	1.12	0.37	0.52
Help Wanted signs	1.56	0.67	0.83	0.77	1.29	0.00
Walk-in	0.91	0.41	1.49	0.87	1.23	3.21
Referrals from						
Current employees	0.89	0.87	1.67	0.96	1.83	0.86
State employment service	1.17	1.64	1.63	0.65	1.49	1.26
Private employment service	0.68	0.33	0.03	1.45	0.66	1.10
Community agency[a]	1.30	3.84	4.08	0.00	1.80	0.10
Schools	1.21	0.74	0.00	1.08	1.54	0.00
Union[a]	0.00	3.70	0.00	1.57	0.00	0.00
Other (acquaintances, etc.)	1.30	1.59	0.75	0.80	0.40	0.98
Used affirmative action in recruiting						
Yes	0.92	0.77	1.06	1.04	1.63	0.90
No	1.17	1.13	0.92	0.91	0.40	1.21
Hiring screens						
Written application						
Yes	0.95	1.06	1.14	0.99	1.03	1.14
No	1.31	0.64	0.46	0.95	0.83	0.64
Interview						
Yes	1.03	0.81	0.86	1.04	0.74	1.12
No	1.09	1.87	1.97	0.64	2.20	0.50
Physical and/or drug test						
Yes	0.65	0.90	0.63	1.30	1.17	0.95
No	1.59	1.12	1.63	0.75	0.84	1.06
Tests and/or other						
Yes	1.07	0.55	0.78	1.01	1.71	0.81
No	1.17	0.97	1.29	0.85	0.71	1.29
Verify education						
Yes	1.03	0.71	0.83	1.06	1.17	0.79
No	1.18	0.87	1.22	0.87	0.60	1.26
Check criminal record						
Yes	1.08	0.75	0.95	0.88	2.43	1.10
No	1.13	0.81	1.17	0.93	0.63	1.17
Used affirmative action in hiring						
Yes	0.82	0.88	1.19	1.13	1.00	0.79
No	1.14	0.94	0.92	0.91	0.94	1.19

Source: Multi-City Telephone Employer Survey.
[a]Very few observations in this row.
Note: Sample size was 615–91. Except for the first row (which shows the percentage in all jobs), the table shows the ratio of the percentage of hires in a race-gender group in that cell to the percentage in that race-gender group across all jobs.

mal methods generated roughly 44 percent of the hires, with newspaper ads accounting for almost two-thirds of that total. The other 56 percent were generated by more informal recruiting procedures, with employee referrals yielding nearly half this group. For screening, most businesses use a written application and an interview, and close to half use some form of testing.

How do the different recruiting and screening methods affect who gets hired by Boston area businesses? In table 10.9 the race-ethnicity and gender of the latest hire of surveyed employers is arrayed by the recruiting and screening methods used. Compared to their rate of representation in all jobs, black and Hispanic men are substantially more likely to be the hire when employers have taken a referral from a state employment agency or community agency. Black women enjoy a smaller employment boost from these referral sources. These two recruiting methods are used fairly rarely, however, as table 10.8 indicates. Again, compared to their representation in all jobs, use of employee referral improves the representation of Hispanic males. Somewhat surprisingly, employee referrals hurt white males, have only a very small negative effect on black males and white females, and have a positive effect on black females. Use of affirmative action in recruiting cuts against white men, as expected, but also, to a much smaller extent, black men and Hispanic women. As it turns out, black women seem to be the greatest beneficiaries of affirmative action recruiting.

Use of interviews and physical tests is associated with lower rates of hiring of black and Hispanic men. Interviewing is also associated with lower rates of hiring black women, while testing raises their rate of hire. Use of a written application is associated with higher employment of blacks and Hispanics of both genders. Use of background checks on education is linked to greater probability of hiring black and white women. Where Boston-area employers use affirmative action in making the hiring decision, white men lose by about the amount white women gain.

Based on these results, the relationship between procedural formality and the racial composition of Greater Boston workplaces is not simple. Consider black men, for example. Certain formal methods (written application, newspaper advertising) increase the chances that a black man will be hired; certain less formal or more subjective procedures (pre-employment interview) dampen those chances. But the use of other formal procedures, such as testing and verifying education is associated with *lower* black male employment. In another paper (Moss and Tilly 1996b), we examine the data with multiple regression, and find the same complex pattern:

- Interviews reduce black male employment because they offer an opening for biases, whereas written applications provide more objective information.

- Skill tests are more common in higher-skill jobs. Since relatively fewer blacks are likely to qualify, given their somewhat lower average education level, the use of this screening method is associated with lower black employment.

But correlations in the quantitative data cannot establish causality. For this, we must turn to qualitative data that can offer important additional insights about why and how formality matters for the racial composition of hiring.[5]

Heretofore, we have emphasized *why* formal hiring is associated with particular racial mixes of employment. *How* formality plays out can vary greatly. Formality in hiring procedures varies widely in terms of content, implementation, context, and hence implications. A highly formal procedure such as a test can—by design or otherwise—strongly favor one group over another. Our qualitative data provide illustrations of both why *and* how formality is associated with racial representation.

For one, informal recruiting, particularly recruiting driven by current employee referrals, privileges employer and incumbent employee networks. For example, a supervisor at a Boston-area manufacturer explained the high number of Asian workers in the plant as follows: "I think a lot of internal references . . . so that may have a lot to do with it. I see amongst that group, a lot of people trying to help members of their family and friends. Get them a job, get them in the company."

Such informal recruiting does not always cut against black employment. For instance, a Boston home care provider serving low-income, largely minority neighborhoods recruits via referrals from clients who suggest neighbors or friends to provide care to them. Consequently, this firm has a workforce that heavily represents black women. In this particular case, rising skill and certification demands have shifted recruiting toward training programs—and this more formal recruiting is yielding *fewer* black employees.

Changing the racial composition of a firm's workforce may require supplementing formal channels with more informal ones. For example, in a public agency using uniformed personnel, the leader of a black employees' group noted how his agency gave time off to employees to do recruitment and reassigned workers to take on the role of recruiter.

Much of the hiring literature argues that reliance on interviews disadvantages black applicants because of the subjectivity involved. Our own data amply document the subjectivity of pre-employment interviews. As the manager at one Boston-area home health agency stated, "Everything else aside, even if someone has all the pieces in place, but I just don't have a good feeling about her, we don't want her." In fact, at a public agency grappling with issues of affirmative action, a manager told us:

> We don't place a great deal of emphasis on interviews. . . . We do not have an interview board or panel because the consent decree requires that we have very detailed reasons for rejecting a candidate, so we have to be on sound footing, and the results of an interview really aren't that in my opinion. You know, it's too subjective.

In a related example, in a Boston-area public-sector agency, even though the interview is the key screen, it is carefully structured. When asked what part of the process is the most important in making decisions, the respondent said: "It's certainly the interview process. That has to be handled with care and it has to be completed thoroughly and fairly. Everybody should be asked the same questions. Everybody should be treated the same. And you don't spend two minutes with one applicant and an hour and a half with another."

As with recruiting, formality in screening does not altogether eliminate subjectivity. Even in civil service environments constrained by consent decrees, there are loopholes to be found if personnel directors are looking for them. A black employees' leader in a uniformed public service agenda claimed that despite the organization's efforts at recruiting minorities, there's still a lot of nepotism. And a white human resource official in a different uniformed public service agency revealed that the agency's cadet program has become an alternate access route to jobs—a route that "becomes subverted as a way around affirmative action, to be quite honest. . . . It is a way to have politically connected people get appointed a cadet and bypass the veteran, nonveteran, and affirmative action standards."

Moreover, formal selection methods can be adopted to screen blacks and other people of color in, but also to screen them out. A large suburban manufacturing facility, which had never tested applicants for blue-collar jobs, began aptitude testing when the surrounding area's population tilted toward people of color. Other changes surely contributed to this shift—the company faced a labor surplus and was upgrading skill requirements—but the timing of the change is suggestive, especially in combination with managers' disparaging remarks about inner-city workers.

Affirmative action typically contributes to formality in recruiting and screening, and is most highly developed in large firms and in the public sector. At one Boston-area federal agency, for example, the division chief remarked, in comments that also touched on the strong diversity objectives of many government agencies: "We have to be very conscious and cognizant as a federal employer that we have guidelines and mandates that we have to follow, and therefore I have a full-time EEO officer and she has two or three people who work for her."

Employer attitudes toward affirmative action vary widely. Some employers we interviewed openly opposed affirmative action, at least in its present form. Such respondents were typically white males, and the complaint, as might be expected, was reverse discrimination. For instance, the white male CEO of a Boston-area health care facility declared: "I'm anti–affirmative action, I have to tell you that. . . . I don't know of a better way, having said that. But I think basically I'm against it." When asked why, he said, "Because it's reverse discrimination."

Similar opinions were voiced in both the private and the public sector, particularly in public sector agencies under consent decrees. Moreover, a number of firms indicated that while they try to abide by their affirmative action goals, affirmative action has a chilling effect on the willingness to hire minorities because firing them is so difficult.

Other managers, however, spoke in support of affirmative action. While such statements sometimes appeared pro forma, in other cases they seemed to reflect sincere conviction. According to one African American human resources director for a Boston-area home care provider:

> If we look at reversing affirmative action, then [minorities will] never catch up. . . . There will be, in the year 2000, more women and minorities in the work force or eligible to be in the workforce. Yet people who run or who are in charge of major corporations and things are white males, OK? So [in the absence of affirmative action] nothing will change.

Employer Attitudes

In Greater Boston, as across the country, employer perceptions of and attitudes toward racial and ethnic groups ineluctably infiltrate hiring decisions. In earlier work done by our colleague Joleen Kirschenman, based on in-depth face-to-face interviews with employers in Chicago (Kirschenman 1991; Kirschenman and Neckerman 1991; Neckerman and Kirschenman 1991), and by us based on comparable interviews in Detroit and Los Angeles (Moss and Tilly 1995b, 1996b), researchers found that many employers rate black workers worse than others in terms of soft and hard skills; few, if any, rate them better; and some employers voice negative, stereotypical views of blacks. Waldinger

(1993) reported similar results from a Los Angeles study. While some of these negative perceptions surely stem from actual average-skill differences, bias clearly plays a part as well. Audit studies that sent out job applicants with identical qualifications found that employers chose white applicants more often than black and Hispanic ones (Bendick, Jackson, and Reynoso 1994; Fix and Struyk 1994). The employer surveys provide added leverage for understanding employers' views of various racial and ethnic groups in the Boston area.

Employers might reduce their hiring of minority workers if they themselves are biased against such groups. But they might also resist minority hiring if they think customers or their existing employees hold these negative views (Becker 1957). The quantitative survey asked employers about each of these three sources of potential bias by asking whether customers, employees, or other employers in the industry prefer to deal with people of their own race or ethnicity. Employers were also asked directly whether they felt that inner-city residents made poorer job applicants or employees than residents of other areas. The results are reported in table 10.10. Overall, about 30 percent of employers reported racial or ethnocentric preferences by customers, employees, or other employers. Thirteen percent held a negative view of inner-city residents. Although Boston bears a stigma of racism stemming from the conflicts over school busing in the 1970s, these results are quite similar to those reported in the Atlanta, Detroit, and Los Angeles metropolitan areas (Moss and Tilly, forthcoming). Somewhat surprisingly, city of Boston employers were more likely to report racial or ethnocentric bias on the part of customers, employees, or employers than their counterparts in the suburbs.

Another, less direct indicator of employer attitudes is the ratio of new hires to applicants by racial, ethnic, and gender group. The employer survey demonstrates that businesses hire a greater proportion of Hispanic and white applicants than black male and female applicants. Some of these differences no doubt result from differing qualifications in the applicant pools. In addition, if Hispanics disproportionately obtain jobs through personal contacts, they will represent a smaller proportion of the formal applicant pool, driving up their ratio of hires to applicants. Nonetheless, this result is consistent with some degree of employer underestimation of black qualifications, or even antipathy toward black applicants. Such evidence helps to explain why we found in chapter 8 that once we held human capital constant among blacks and Hispanics with no more than a high school degree, the Hispanic-white annual earnings gap disappeared, but not the black-white gap.

In-depth interviews add additional substance and context to this picture of employer attitudes, confirming and extending previous litera-

TABLE 10.10   *Proportion of Boston-Area Employers Reporting Ethnocentrism by Customers, Employees, and Other Employers*

	All Employers	Boston	Suburbs	Other Central Cities
Employers Reporting				
Customers prefer to deal with employees of their own race or ethnic group	17.7%	21.3%	17.8%	13.7%
Employees prefer other employees of their own race or ethnic group	19.1	27.0	18.0	15.6
Other employers in your business prefer employees of their own race or ethnic group	19.8	23.8	19.6	16.9
Any of the types of ethnocentrism	29.6	38.4	27.7	27.4
Inner-city residents are weaker job applicants or employees	13.1	11.9	14.1	11.2

Source: Multi-City Telephone Employer Survey.
Note: Sample size was 686–743.

ture based on such interviews. Interviewers asked managers whether they saw differences in skill or worker quality among whites, blacks, Hispanics, and Asians. The questioning focused on differences between black and white workers.

Many employers described such differences, although the majority answered "I don't know" (sometimes citing the fact that their workforce is too segregated to assess different groups) or "I don't see any differences." In fact, Boston-area employers were less likely to identify racial or ethnic differences in worker quality than their counterparts in Atlanta, Detroit, or Los Angeles. Based on context, some of their answers appear to be sincere, whereas others were no doubt offered as the socially acceptable answer. As one public-sector respondent wryly remarked, "We have to be so politically correct these days." A few managers referred to equal employment opportunity laws in ways that seemed to indicate discomfort at drawing racial distinctions. "That's a loaded question," said another public-sector manager. "You know, the direction of your question was towards, for lack of a better term, 'protected populations' and I cannot articulate any particular reason why those populations and/or employees would have any more of a hurdle with regard to their work that I know of." Moreover, a number of respondents gave mixed responses, at some points delineating racial differences and at other points denying them.

When hub-area employers did note black-Hispanic-white differences, they sometimes pointed to a black or Hispanic disadvantage in hard skills—reading, writing, math, and so on. For example, the manager of clerical workers at a hospital stated,

> I think [minorities'] education is maybe on a lesser level. . . . This is not a racial remark . . . but I can still say that I think that the white secretaries that I have are much more professional. I'm not sure it's fair to say more intelligent but they certainly present themselves that way. . . . They are higher caliber.

A bank manager commented, "Well, I have to say the Hispanics, as you know, most of them don't pass the [math] test," and a number of others pointed to language problems with Hispanic, Asian, and Haitian immigrants. (Of course, in a number of businesses serving immigrant communities, bilingualism, or even speaking the immigrant language, is instead a plus.)

Many respondents who noted racial skill differences attributed them—especially those between blacks and whites—to educational attainment or school quality. Overall, however, relatively few employers *explicitly* acknowledged racial hard-skill differences, but as noted, many complained about the quality of the "inner-city" workforce, and attributed these problems to the degeneration of the public schools in Boston and other central cities.

Soft skills came up more frequently. We heard about personal interaction issues: for instance, "with the black workforce . . . for some reason, I've had people say that they weren't being treated fairly," that American women of color "occasionally will have what I call 'the attitude,'" and that "Hispanic males are very proud . . . ego, or macho." We also heard about motivation problems: blacks who lack self-esteem because of the welfare system, African Americans who are "not as dependable" as the predominantly immigrant workforce at a food service facility because "their job is not as . . . important to them," and Hispanics who "are more slow-paced because of their background and the countries they came from . . . [that] don't have the hustle and bustle of the United States."

In fact, employers' criticisms of blacks' hard skills sometimes shaded over into discussions of soft skills. When the hospital manager quoted earlier elaborated on what it meant to be "professional," she focused on dress and articulateness. Similarly, others said that many inner-city African Americans and Hispanics don't know how to apply for a job, in terms of dress, grooming, and style of speech. One manufacturer located in Lawrence offered a litany of complaints and stereotypes about his inner-city, Hispanic workforce:

> A big problem I have is attendance. . . . And that is an inner-city problem, right? Every day I have people out for . . . court appearances. I have guys calling me from jail. . . . The Hispanic people tend to get sick more. . . . You know, somebody said to me one time when we were talking about the education level . . . and so forth. It's, unfortunately for these guys . . . related to race. They're probably from a dysfunctional family. They probably never ate good healthy meals like a lot of us were fortunate enough to eat growing up. And that just carries over into adulthood. So your education is down . . . your life's guidance was down a little bit, and your nutrition goes down.

On the other hand, some managers described racial and ethnic differences as cultural differences that simply had to be managed correctly. Some employers viewed black workers' assertiveness as understandable or even positive:

> Those people who have been the underdogs are stronger fighters than the people who have had an easy road of it. And perhaps this is where antagonism is created . . . but it's understandable. If you are an underdog, you're going to fight to do better. And if you're on the other end of the stick where it's been very easy for you to progress and to achieve and to become successful, you can feel very threatened.

In addition, criticisms of a particular racial or ethnic group did not always translate into serious dissatisfaction with that group, let alone reluctance to hire members of the group. Furthermore, negative comments about Hispanics were somewhat counterbalanced by paeans to the immigrant work ethic—in the Boston area, primarily applying to Hispanics, Asians, and Afro-Caribbean migrants. In Atlanta, where African Americans occupy some of the same positions in the job ladder as immigrants in Boston, a few employers lauded the African American work ethic in similar terms; such comments were rare in the Boston area. On the other hand, with respect to Hispanics, the following sentiment was not uncommon: "Spanish people are more willing to work. They are willing to work longer hours. . . . I think the ones that I've known are . . . very dedicated to their jobs."

Greater Boston employers particularly heaped praise on Asian immigrants, sometimes connecting the strong work ethic to their newness in the country: "Your Asian workforce, because it's the newest immigrant in the country, has a completely different work ethic. You need them for seventy-two hours a day, they'll be there for seventy-two hours a day." In one instance, a factory supervisor rated Asians well above Hispanics: "[Hispanics] take a lot of pride in what they do but they also can get very insulted. . . . As a spectrum I see the Asians on the high end of work ethic and working hard and privately and quietly. You know, and I probably see Hispanics on the other end because of that pride in their culture."

Some employers compared immigrants favorably to native whites. The remarks of two Boston-area managers are striking in this regard.

Manager No. 1

Respondent: [The Hispanics] work pretty well. . . . They're trying to support . . . their family, or families, or whatever they have. . . .

Interviewer: Would say you have more problems in getting the white people to work?

Respondent: Absolutely. Not that we won't hire them, but . . . we will look twice before we hire just a regular white guy for a floor job.

Manager No. 2

Respondent: The Cape Verdean guys back there [in the kitchen] are my hardest workers. These guys are absolutely fantastic workers. . . . When I was younger . . . in all restaurants, you always had young, white, American boys washing dishes. Now, you know, I almost try to stay away from them in a way because they're so lazy at times. . . . I get Cape Verdean kids in here and they bust their butt. You know, I get these white kids in here, they're young, sixteen, seventeen, eighteen years old, and they think they're just going to hang out and just be lazy all day.

In other cases whites are not applying for the jobs in question, so employers compared immigrants favorably to blacks alone.

Boston-area employer views about the dependability of black workers varied by employee gender. Joleen Kirschenman (1991) and Ivy Kennelly (1995) have pointed out that managers have a schizophrenic perception of black women: on the one hand, they see black women as motivated workers because they tend to be single mothers supporting a family; on the other hand, they see single mothers as unreliable because of family demands—"the kids issues that come up and the disturbances about their work," as a hospital manager put it. In our Boston-area sample, we were not able to get many employers to speak about gender differences within race, but to the extent that we did, we heard some views from each side of this division.

Conclusion

In summary, then, Greater Boston employers frequently describe negative views of minorities held by themselves or others. A substantial minority of respondents described racial or ethnocentric preferences by customers, employees, or fellow employers. In addition, a non-negligible minority of employers voiced negative views of blacks as workers; their views of Hispanics appear to be more ambivalent, and their views of Asians on the whole relatively positive. Some of the expressed views clearly fall into the category of stereotypes. This suggests that we should view the data on skill and minority employment, discussed earlier in the chapter, with some caution. Though skill shortfalls in African American and Hispanic populations represent a real, serious problem, differential access to jobs requiring skills appears likely to be in part due to slanted employer perceptions of the hard and soft skills of different racial and ethnic groups. As we have argued elsewhere (Moss and Tilly 1996), it is particularly difficult to distinguish between legitimate, skill-based screening and discrimination when soft or social skills are involved.

Several key unifying points emerge from the analysis of labor demand in the Boston area.

- *Skill requirements, location, and discrimination all pose significant barriers to minority workers, particularly blacks.*

Job tasks such as using computers, writing paragraphs, and interacting with customers reduce the likelihood that black and Hispanic job seekers will land the job. The situation is worst for black and Hispanic males. Hiring requirements such as high school diploma, experience, or references have the same effect. Employers in general express negative views of inner-city workers and of the inner city itself as a place to do business, and businesses are considerably more likely to move out of cities than to move in. A number of managers explicitly state negative judgments of black and Hispanic workers' skills, and stereotypes often enter these judgments. Employers also report ethnocentrism among customers and workers—attitudes likely to further curtail minority access to jobs.

- *Jobs with few requirements are extremely rare in number and offer low wages in the new Boston economy.*

The fraction of noncollege jobs without major requirements is around 5 percent throughout the Boston metropolitan area and lowest in the city of Boston itself. Relaxing some of the job tasks required expands the pool of jobs, but not by much. Wages for jobs with few or no requirements pay around $7.00 or less an hour (in nominal terms of 1992 to 1994, when those data were collected), not enough to support a family and hardly enough to support an individual living alone.

- *Many employers pointed to the Boston public schools as a problem area.*

Even assuming that for some employers, criticisms of the public schools are a coded way of talking about race, the misgivings about the Boston schools were expressed so widely and across such a varied cross-section of employers that they must be taken seriously. The Boston public schools were contrasted unfavorably with suburban schools, as well as private and parochial schools. Though there have been some signs of progress since the in-depth interviews were completed in 1996, these criticisms are relatively fresh.

- *Skill requirements and location are confounded with race.*

No matter how hard we try, we cannot cleanly separate the effects of skill requirements, location, and race, and, therefore, policy aimed at one will be hindered by the connections among the problems. To be sure, greater policy effort is needed to invest in the skills of inner-city minority workers. Efforts need to be made to enhance soft skills as well as hard skills. Increased access by inner-city workers to the growth of jobs in the suburbs, as well as economic development efforts within the city, will pay dividends. To the degree that employers act on stereotypes they hold, or practice statistical discrimination, the combination of more skills and better ability to communicate one's skills will be particularly effective. However, what our research and that of the other authors in the Multi-City Study of Urban Inequality series bring to light is that race not only continues to matter a lot, but that it influences employers' perceptions of skills and of the desirability of different locations as business sites and areas from which to recruit. The success of policies to develop the skills and mobility of minority workers will be compromised if they are not combined with an innovative antidiscrimination strategy.

Appendix

The Employer Surveys

The telephone survey of employers was administered by Professor Harry Holzer of Michigan State University, with an extension carried out by Joleen Kirschenman and the authors. Eight hundred to 1,000 employers in each of the four cities were interviewed between May 1992 and May 1995, including 891 in Boston. The survey questions addressed the characteristics of the establishment of the last person hired into the firm, and of the job the person filled. Respondents were asked about frequency of performance of certain tasks, recruiting and screening procedures, other hiring requirements, the demographics of the worker hired, the demographics of the persons applying for the job, and the demographics of the firm's employees and customers. About 250 of the firms' interviews in Greater Boston were generated by respondents in the Greater Boston Social Survey (GBSS), who reported the name and address of their employers. The rest of the firms were drawn from lists of firms from Survey Sampling, Inc., which, in turn, were generated from phone directories. The response rate for the telephone survey (including only firms that passed the screener) was about two-thirds. Holzer (1996) has already reported many of the major findings from these data; our discussion covers some of the same ground but presents new results as well. Results reported here differ from those reported by Holzer because they include responses from ninety additional telephone interviews in the Boston area.

The sample for the in-depth employer survey was drawn from firms that had been identified by household respondents holding jobs requiring no more than a high school education, and that had successfully completed a telephone survey. Interviews were conducted at forty-six firms in Boston, with similar numbers in the other three metropolitan areas. The survey design targeted up to three interviews per business (a top executive, a human resource official, and a direct manager of the job selected for special attention). In Boston, a total of 103 interviews were completed, for an average of 2.3 per business. Firms were surveyed between the summer of 1994 and the summer of 1996. The response rate for the in-depth survey was about two-thirds.

The in-depth survey involves a series of structured questions and follow-up probes. Questions gather the details of the recruiting, screening, and hiring procedures used in filling the sample job, and what each procedure is designed to do. All questions were open-ended, and interviewers were trained to encourage respondents to elaborate, telling the story of their business's relationship to the labor market.

Findings from telephone and face-to-face surveys often have different focuses and may sometimes appear to be inconsistent. The purpose of this chapter is not to iron out or adjudicate any such differences, but to present results from both surveys, and to point to potential conflicts or ambiguities as triggers for further research.

All the quantitative tabulations and qualitative evidence reported in this chapter refer only to jobs that require no more than a high school degree.[6] Given this limitation, the sampling and weighting schemes are designed to approximate an employment-weighted sample of the universe of businesses employing people who have no more than this amount of formal schooling. The employment-weighting means that a business's probability of appearing in the sample is roughly proportional to the number of people it employs; larger employers are more strongly represented.

11

SHARING THE FRUITS OF GREATER BOSTON'S RENAISSANCE

To succeed over the long run, every metropolitan area must periodically reinvent itself, as the leading industries of one generation become the sunset industries of the next. Some areas seem better able to do this than others. The phenomenal resuscitation of Greater Boston, from economic basket case of the 1950s, 1960s, and 1970s to exemplar of urban and metropolitan rejuvenation at the end of the twentieth century, has been a central theme of this book.

Another has been the transition from what used to be one of the most lily-white regions of the country to one that is rapidly becoming multiracial and multicultural. While the region's population is still overwhelmingly white (nearly 90 percent in 1990), the increase in the black, Hispanic, and Asian populations in just the past quarter-century has been prodigious. Of the 154 towns and cities in the Greater Boston area, only one—the city of Boston itself—had a minority presence as high as 5 percent in 1950. Even by 1970, there were only eight other towns that reached this level. Twenty years later, however, one third of the region's cities and towns were at least 5 percent minority, and fifteen of them had reached the 10 percent level. In four of the largest cities in the region—Boston, Cambridge, Lawrence, and Lowell—the minority population ranged from nearly a quarter to half the total population. In Boston itself, more than 40 percent of the population was black, Hispanic, or Asian. Demographic projections suggest the hub of the region could be majority-minority by the time the results of the 2000 census are in.

Moreover, unlike Detroit and Atlanta, where diversity is limited largely to native-born blacks and whites, Greater Boston is attracting ever larger numbers of Hispanic and Asian immigrants, as well as blacks from the Caribbean and Africa. Greater Boston cannot yet be considered a true multicultural center, like Los Angeles or Miami, but it is surely moving in this direction. By 1990, of the 234,000 minority residents in

Boston proper, nearly two out of five were Latino, Asian, American Indian, or of mixed parentage. Lawrence's dominant group is Hispanic; Lowell, Quincy, and Brookline's most numerous minority group is Asian.

The social, economic, and political geography of the region is also changing rapidly. Not long ago, the city of Boston dominated the region in almost every regard. Today, its population comprises less than 15 percent of the regionwide total, and business and industry continue to shift to the suburbs and beyond. Unlike other cities, however, this has not meant that the region's largest central city is becoming a deindustrialized, deteriorating relic. Just the opposite is true. Boston has become an even more vibrant economic and social center, with downtown office vacancy rates close to the lowest in the nation. Its financial district is buzzing with activity, as are its hotels, restaurants, and other tourist attractions. Its universities continue to expand, along with its premier health care sector and its high-tech industries. East Cambridge, just across the river from downtown Boston, has been the center of the most explosive growth in high-tech industry anywhere in the nation. When you walk down the streets of even the most dilapidated neighborhoods in Boston, you do not get the impression of utter devastation and hopelessness, too often the case in cities like Detroit, Newark, or Chicago. The region's triple revolution of demographic, industrial, and spatial change has transformed this New England metropolitan area in ways that would have been unimaginable to its typical resident in 1950—and well beyond the expectations of researchers studying the region even two decades ago. Greater Boston is truly a renaissance region.

The Impact of the Triple Revolution

The triple revolution has been the product of a wide array of institutional factors (decisions made by judges, legislators, and administrators in federal, state, and local government and by corporate leaders in the private sector) as well as market forces (those impersonal changes in prices and profits that cause resources to flow out of one area and into another). The region has certainly benefited from being in the right industries at the right time. As higher education, health care, and high-tech boomed in the late twentieth century, Boston was exquisitely placed to take advantage of the computer and information revolutions. But it also benefited from the huge outlays for defense goods and defense R&D that the U.S. Congress lavished on the region during the Reagan era.

One consequence of the triple revolution is that the opportunity nexus—the interplay of racial and ethnic attitudes, housing market segregation, and labor market outcomes—has been shaped by the transformation of Greater Boston, and provides a set of advantages and disadvantages that are unique to the area. In this book, we have been especially interested in mapping the dimensions of urban inequality in the region. Our findings suggest that, in general, Boston does not fit the mold of other cities and regions around the country. We believe that the specific ways in which demographic, industrial, and spatial change occurred in Boston over the past century explain why.

The current demographic revolution had its precursors in the nineteenth century, when immigrants from Ireland, French Canada, and then Eastern and Southern Europe were absorbed amid hostilities based on cultural and religious differences. At one time, ethnic background divided the region: the English against the Irish, in particular. Later, as the Irish gained a foothold in the economic and political landscape of the region, social class became the main axis of conflict. The working-class Irish of South Boston found themselves at odds with the lace-curtain Irish who were moving to more affluent suburban neighborhoods. With the growth in black, Hispanic, and Asian immigration to the region, the depopulation of the area's older cities ended and social conflict shifted to the dual axis of race and class.

Greater Boston experienced its period of industrial restructuring much earlier than the rest of the country. It was the home of the original Industrial Revolution in the United States, with its textile and shoe production, but it was already experiencing its industrial decline when other parts of the country were going through their initial period of rapid industrialization. In the 1920s, when Detroit's auto industry was just gaining momentum, the majority of New England's textile producers had already moved South, leaving hundreds of factories shuttered and tens of thousands of workers without jobs. For the next half-century, Boston trailed much of the rest of the country in job creation and population growth.

Today, the economy of Greater Boston has been the "advance scout" for the postindustrial age based on high technology and professional services. The rise of government-university-corporate collaborations was one of the institutional factors that originated in this area and shaped the new economy.

While some of the institutional factors—such as the advent of FHA-insured mortgages—and market forces—like the increase in real incomes that caused decentralization in most U.S. cities after World War II—affected Boston as well, the story played out somewhat differently there. The Boston area began its decentralization much earlier than the rest of the nation, in the pre-automobile era. Therefore, many of Boston's suburbs, especially the older ones, are well served by public transportation. While other cities were still annexing adjacent areas as economic activity spilled over the city's boundaries, the process of annexation came to a halt earlier in Boston. Finally, since the production centers of the nineteenth century were from the age of water power, eastern Massachusetts contained several major industrial cities north, south, and east of Boston itself. As the Boston suburbs expanded, they grew in the interstices between these industrial cities. This spatial pattern, with its more extensive public transportation networks and its stock of working-class housing in the old industrial centers, has probably reduced the degree of spatial mismatch between where people work and where they live, compared with other metropolitan areas.

The New Racial and Ethnic Divisions in Greater Boston

Utilizing the Greater Boston Social Survey (GBSS) conducted in 1993 to 1994, as well as existing census data, we have been able to ascertain how this triple revolution affected the well-being of the racial and ethnic groups that now comprise the region. Not surprisingly, white households have the highest average incomes, and they are well above the national average. While black families had rapid income gains during the 1980s, their mean income still trails behind whites by a good 38 percent. Hispanic families, the newest to arrive in the region, trail whites by even more: 45 percent.

Moreover, whites are the only ones with any appreciable net financial assets. The average black family has almost none, while Hispanics are deeply in debt. White families are also most likely to own their own homes, and much more likely than minorities to own them free and clear. Whites benefit, on average, from being somewhat better educated than blacks and substantially better educated than Hispanics, who often come to Boston with relatively few years of schooling. Whites have been able to parlay their education—and, in some cases, their skin color—into the most prestigious and best-paying occupations in the area.

We have also relied on the GBSS to explore a set of detailed questions about each aspect of the opportunity nexus: racial and ethnic attitudes, residential segregation, and labor market outcomes. This exploration has provided us with insights into why the hierarchy of race and ethnicity continues to be so prevalent.

Greater Boston has a legacy of prejudice, going back to the days of NINA—"No Irish Need Apply"—in the mid-nineteenth century. Today, there is considerable evidence indicating the persistence of negative stereotypes, now based on race and ethnicity more than religion or country of origin. In response to one of the GBSS questions, almost half the

whites surveyed rated whites as more intelligent than blacks or Hispanics. They were also more likely to rate minorities as "harder to get
along with." On the other hand, half of white respondents admit that
whites tend to discriminate against minorities, and a majority of whites
favor special job training and education programs for minorities, although relatively few favor giving preferences to minorities through affirmative action hiring.

White perceptions of their group's discriminatory behavior is borne
out by the experience of substantial numbers of blacks and Hispanics.
Thirty-eight percent of Hispanics and 44 percent of blacks say they have
experienced workplace discrimination. Nearly half of blacks and nearly
two-thirds of Hispanics believe that whites are more likely to discriminate than are members of their own group.

These racial and ethnic attitudes affect the choices each group
makes about where to live. While low income might reduce a family's
housing options, income alone cannot explain the extent of residential
segregation in Greater Boston. The variation in housing expenditures
among blacks, whites, and Hispanics is surprisingly small, indicating
that affordability cannot explain the patterns of residential segregation
we find in the region. Nor does a lack of knowledge about housing availability constrain minority families, for in answering pertinent GBSS
questions, it is clear that they have a reasonably accurate perception of
the housing market in various communities beyond their own.

Skin color turns out to be the single most compelling factor associated with housing segregation, with blacks living in the most segregated
neighborhoods. Hispanics, many of whom are white, appear to face less
discrimination than blacks in the housing market. Black respondents
are far more likely to believe that they miss out on good housing because white owners will not rent or sell to them; because real estate
agents will not show them homes in white neighborhoods; and because
banks and lenders will not lend money to them to purchase a home in
many communities. Whites as a group, in our GBSS sample, tell us that
their "ideal community" is 62 percent white, 15 percent black, 10 percent Hispanic, and 13 percent Asian. It is not surprising that many
blacks would be uncomfortable moving into such an area. Blacks and
Hispanics say their ideal community would be composed of about 40
percent their own group, about 25 percent white, about 16 percent
Asian, and about 20 percent the other minority group. Based on these
sentiments, one can see that black, white, and Hispanic preference maps
are mutually exclusive. Even beyond institutional discrimination in the
housing market, these preferences provide a potent force for the persistence of residential segregation.

The Greater Boston Labor Market

As two elements of the opportunity nexus, housing markets and labor markets are interconnected. In some instances, residential location can have a profound impact on a household's employment options. Similarly, the high-tech revolution has upgraded skill requirements, while the spatial revolution has shifted the location of many businesses to the suburbs and beyond. Given these dramatic industrial and spatial changes in the region, one would expect that workers with limited education would do very poorly.

Just as the housing market is segregated by race, the labor market tends to be segregated by race, ethnicity, and gender. White men dominate executive and professional positions in the region, black men are heavily concentrated in services, and Hispanic men prevail in manufacturing. White women are found disproportionately in professional services, black women in personal services and clerical positions, and Hispanic women in the factories.

Among men with limited education, we found that labor force participation is as high for blacks and Hispanics as for whites. The booming Boston economy has provided so many jobs that even those at the end of the labor market queue have been able to find work. There is a catch, however. Even though black men are as likely as white or Hispanic men to have worked, they are less likely to have found steady work, and suffer a much higher unemployment rate. They also work far fewer hours per week, compared with whites and Hispanics, because they are more likely to hold part-time jobs, less likely to work overtime, and less likely to moonlight or be self-employed. As a result, even though Boston does not have a jobless ghetto, as in the case of many other cities, black men end up with much lower annual earnings than white men—and even lower than Hispanics. This is despite the fact that the median hourly wage paid to black men in Boston exceeds the median wage of Hispanic men by nearly 20 percent.

Using econometric analysis, we were able to simulate various scenarios of the labor market. For example, what if black or Hispanic men had the same amount of human capital (for example, age, education, training, health status) as whites? What if they lived in the same kinds of neighborhoods? These simulations show that from an initial Hispanic-white annual earnings ratio of 63 percent, providing Hispanic men the same human capital as whites would bring their annual earnings up to par with whites. For black men, however, improving human capital would have a much more modest impact, raising the black-white ratio from 55 to only 68 percent. Hence, solving the low-income problem for Hispanics means focusing on education and training, much more than anything else. The same will not work for black men. For them, we need to deal with a variety of labor market barriers and outright discrimination.

In a simulation for black men, "placing" them into jobs with the characteristics of white men's jobs (for example, a higher proportion in sales occupations, a lower proportion in service occupations, a higher proportion using computers at work, and more years of experience in the occupation) and "moving" them into neighborhoods with white majorities brought the earnings ratio up to 92 percent.

A similar analysis for women with limited education showed that here, too, labor force participation is high across all three race-ethnic groups, as is the proportion with recent work experience. However, black women have a very high unemployment rate, more than double the rate for whites. In the women's simulations, giving Hispanics the same human capital as whites would close the annual earnings gap, as it did for Hispanic men. In the women's case, however, the original annual Hispanic/white earnings ratio was already 93 percent—because Hispanic women work at full-time jobs in manufacturing, a sector of the economy that offers relatively good wages for poorly educated workers. While still earning lower hourly wages than white women, they work more hours per year, offsetting most of the hourly wage disadvantage.

For less-educated black women, giving them white women's human capital improves the annual earnings ratio from 65 to 77 percent. The major impediment to further improvement is family structure rather than market discrimination, as in the case of black men. The high proportion of black women who are single parents brings the average annual wage well below that of either Hispanic or white women.

Although we are especially concerned with the impact of the triple revolution on workers with limited education, the GBSS also provides a rich source of data for examining wage differences throughout the labor force, including workers with higher levels of schooling. Using a job competition queuing model to understand how workers are matched up with jobs, we found that equalizing human capital would play an important role in equalizing wage rates, especially for Hispanics. But again, this would not be enough to reduce the wage gap for black men. Our simulations indicate that black men face more job discrimination than any of the other groups, almost regardless of their education level.

Cultural capital, we found, plays a large role in explaining why educational attainment differs across race-ethnic groups. Differences in mother's education, religion, and whether a worker was brought up in an intact family all have an effect on how much schooling that worker completes. Therefore, there is significant social transmission of economic status. Breaking this transmission line is particularly important for young Hispanics, who will need to acquire substantially more years of schooling than their parents did.

As for social capital, blacks and Hispanics are more likely than whites to use social networks to find employment. In the labor market, this turns out to be a double-edged sword. Minority workers who use family and friends to find jobs are more likely to be employed at any given time, but their wages tend to be lower. Using social networks is more likely to land a minority worker in a firm with minority coworkers, and these firms tend to be smaller and to pay lower wages for comparable jobs.

The complementary surveys we fielded with employers provided some first-hand knowledge of why discrimination continues to be a serious problem, especially for black job seekers. A telephone survey and follow-up personal interviews with company managers revealed that changes in skill requirements, relocation of workplaces to outside the central city, the recruitment and screening methods used by personnel departments, and employer attitudes toward minority workers all serve to constrain job opportunities for blacks and, in some cases, Hispanics. According to these surveys, less than 6 percent of the job vacancies in Greater Boston do not require a high school diploma or some training or experience; only 6.7 percent require nothing more than a high school diploma. Wage rates for these jobs are very low, about $7 per hour (in 1995 to 1996 dollars). Although it is difficult to pin down with certainty, some of the location decisions made by companies and some screening procedures used by managers seem to be derived from the negative stereotypes of minorities expressed in some interviews.

The racial attitudes we uncovered in the household surveys, along with the patterns of residential preferences, help explain where blacks, Hispanics, and whites live in the new demographically and spatially diverse Greater Boston metropolitan region—and how the attitudes of company managers are formed. The end result is a booming region where employment opportunities exist, but where prosperity is still unequally shared.

A SWOT Analysis of the Greater Boston Region

We have combined historical information describing the triple revolution with the evidence provided by the GBSS on racial and ethnic attitudes, residential segregation, and labor market outcomes and further evidence from employer surveys to better understand how well individual racial and ethnic groups fared in Boston at the end of the twentieth century. To explore what all this might mean for the future, we turn to a

SWOT analysis to learn something of the Strengths, Weaknesses, Opportunities, and potential Threats to future progress in this renaissance region.

Strengths

Greater Boston's greatest strength lies in its enormously successful economy. Being in the right place at the right time has always conferred advantage to one region over another. In the nineteenth century, the newly invented power loom required a source of energy other than the hands and feet of its human operator. Lawrence and Lowell became the center of the nation's Industrial Revolution because the Concord and Merrimack rivers could be harnessed to turn the water wheels that powered the industry. The rivers had existed for thousands of years, but only when invention, entrepreneurship, and capital came together could this natural resource finally be used to create tens of thousands of jobs.

In a sense, the same thing was true of Boston at the end of the twentieth century. For at least a hundred years, the region had been home to the highest concentration of higher-educational institutions in the country. For nearly as long, its hospitals, including Mass General (MGH) and the other teaching hospitals connected to the Harvard, Boston University, and Tufts medical schools, have constituted one of the nation's premier centers for advanced medical care. The mutual fund industry was invented in Boston in the mid-1920s. However, it was only in the postindustrial era well after World War II that the services offered by universities, hospitals, and financial institutions became the driving force of the global economy.

The universities not only provided the brainpower for high-technology industry in the region, but with the growing demand for postsecondary education, Boston's universities became a major "export" industry—bringing in hundreds of thousands of students from other states and abroad. Billions of dollars a year flow into the region from tuition and from the grants, contracts, and gifts awarded to Greater Boston's forty-two universities and colleges. In addition, the students who come here from outside the region spend at least as much on everything from rent and food to haircuts and entertainment. Today, universities are a booming industry, and they helped make Boston a renaissance region.

The same is true of Boston's hospitals and clinics. Patients from throughout the country and from other nations come here for the state-of-the-art medical care available from MGH and a host of other teaching hospitals. As medical care has become a larger and larger sector of the economy—doubling to 14 percent of the nation's Gross Domestic Product in the past fifty years—Boston was ideally placed to take advantage of this shift in consumer dollars. In the process tens of thousands of jobs have been created, not only for the most highly skilled surgeons, but for medical technicians, nurses, orderlies, and janitors.

Likewise, the mutual fund industry has blossomed in Boston. Not until the late post–World War II era would private pension funds be large enough, and would families have enough savings, to make these financial institutions a big industry. Today, it is a $5-trillion-dollar-a-year industry, centered in downtown Boston.

These are but three of the six pillars undergirding the renaissance of the Boston economy. In addition, there is high-tech industry itself. The minicomputers designed and built in the region by the Digital Corporation, Data General, Prime, and Wang no longer lead the information processing industry, but these companies helped spawn a software industry in the region, which employs tens of thousands. As military weapons grew ever more sophisticated, Boston became a major supplier because of its universities and high-tech companies. In Lexington, Raytheon provides Patriot missiles to the armed forces, while General Electric in Lynn and Everett, just north of the hub, is one of the three leading suppliers of military jet engines in the world. The entire region was able to take advantage of the explosion in defense spending fostered by the Reagan administration and the Congress in the 1980s.

And, finally, tying all this together has been the boom in construction in both the private and public sectors. New office towers are going up all through the region, in response to an extremely low vacancy rate. Moreover, as Boston bids to become a large convention city, new hotels are going up in record numbers. New housing construction and extensive housing renovation is keeping smaller contractors fully employed. In the public sector, the city has just completed the Ted Williams tunnel connecting South Boston to Logan Airport and the massive Deer Island water treatment plant. It is in the midst of depressing a major elevated highway, the central artery, that runs through the heart of the city.

Greater Boston is at the very top of its economic game with this diverse set of booming industries. Unemployment in the region is consequently extremely low and, barring a national recession, should stay that way. This means that the tight labor market that has provided job opportunity even for workers with limited schooling has a good chance of being sustained.

Economists fear, however, that too much economic growth can place enormous strain on labor markets, leading to such rapidly rising wages that old firms in the region consider moving out and newer firms eschew moving in. But here is where the demographic revolution confers an added advantage on Greater Boston. It has brought in many newcomers who are quite attractive to employers. At the higher end of the education spectrum, many immigrants continue to come here specifically for the area's higher education offerings, both at the baccalaureate and postbaccalaureate level. They are joined by others who received their professional training elsewhere, but found job opportunities here. Innumerable doctors, nurses, engineers, and computer scientists in the area are first-generation Americans, and the region has benefited from their high levels of skill and expertise. Without them, there would have been severe labor shortages in these skilled professions.

At the lower end of the education spectrum, immigrants have come in to take the less remunerative of the blue-collar jobs—the ones that many native-born workers spurn. Foreign-born workers are the factory operatives and hospital aides, the security guards and taxi drivers. In their absence, severe labor shortages would have occurred in these fields as well.

The spatial revolution has also treated Greater Boston kindly. In other metropolitan areas, the decentralization of residences and businesses has often left a hollowed-out core where the central city used to be. Boston's population is smaller now than in 1950, but it stopped declining nearly twenty years ago. Unlike similar areas in other cities, the low-income neighborhoods of Boston can still support retail trade, whether in the form of traditional commercial main streets or the more recently arrived central-city shopping malls. As Michael Porter points out, although incomes may be lower in the inner city, households live at much higher density than in the suburbs, so purchasing power per acre may be similar (Porter 1995).

While it is true that median incomes in Greater Boston are higher in the suburban ring than in the central city, the contrast is not as stark here as it is elsewhere. There is a historical reason for this. Greater Boston's unique story of spatial change—residential decentralization filling in the spaces between nineteenth-century industrial cities—means that tony suburbs like Weston bordered gritty cities like Waltham. Some suburban employment opportunities may be inaccessible to inner-city minorities, but the nature of spatial change here makes spatial mismatch less severe than in other metropolitan areas. Regional planners in Massachusetts worry about suburban sprawl and its attendant ecological and traffic problems, but here again, the history of high-density settlement has made the problem less severe in Boston than in many of the lower-population-density metropolitan areas of the Sunbelt states.

The triple revolution has consequently brought great strength to the region, strength that could keep employment at high levels, unemployment low, family incomes rising, and abundant economic opportunities even for those whose education and skills would place them at great risk in a less buoyant market.

Weaknesses

The triple revolution also leaves the region with some important weaknesses. The fruits of the economic boom are distributed unevenly, and the boom itself has created some critical problems for the region.

Residential Segregation and Turf Battles   While the region has rapidly become multicultural and multiracial, its neighborhoods remain highly segregated. This is particularly true for blacks. Some of this segregation is accounted for in the personal preferences of both blacks and whites, but banking and real estate institutions have not been blameless in perpetuating this pattern of separate communities identified by race. As the companion employer survey to the GBSS demonstrated, many employers appear to have "cognitive maps" regarding where they believe they can find appropriately skilled and "socialized" potential employees. These maps tend to exclude areas with high concentrations of minorities, particularly blacks. This could continue to disadvantage blacks in the labor market, while segregation itself can undermine cooperation between the races on a whole range of social and political issues. A lack of cooperation constrains urban planning, as turf battles are fought along racial lines.

Persistent Poverty   Despite the booming economy, poverty remains extremely high—especially for Hispanics and Asians. While the poverty rate for black households is now relatively low in Boston compared with other central cities, it is relatively high for Hispanic and Asian families. Of the top 77 central cities in the nation, Boston had the 11th highest poverty rate for Hispanics and 18th highest for Asians. In the rest of the Greater Boston region, the poverty ranking for Hispanics and Asians was even higher. Clearly these new immigrant groups are not sharing in the region's bounteous economy as much as they might—at least so far.

Part of the problem is related to the continued erosion in the manufacturing base of the region. Hispanics, in particular, and to some extent Asians, have gained a foothold in the economy through employment in the remaining textile and other blue-collar industries that still operate throughout Greater Boston. But these manufacturing facilities are in a precarious position, facing growing competition from Third World countries. For manufacturers, it is often much cheaper to use Third World workers who still reside in developing countries than to keep employing Third World workers who have come to live in Greater Boston.

If the slide in manufacturing employment continues, or if a recession were to adversely affect this sector, both Hispanics and Asians could see their already high poverty rates increase still further. This would be unfortunate for these new immigrants, but its impact would extend to everyone else in the region. The combination of extremely high incomes, particularly for well-educated whites, and extremely low incomes for less-educated, mostly foreign-born immigrants creates a great social class divide that strains relations throughout the region.

The Housing Market   Boston's superb economy also has a downside when it comes to the housing market. Metropolitan areas like Dallas or Phoenix have ample room to build new housing on the undeveloped outskirts of town, but Boston has no such possibility. With the economic boom the demand for housing is growing faster than supply, and prices are consequently rising sharply. In 1990, the city ranked fourth in median household rent and third in rent as a percent of monthly median household income. Moreover, Boston's homeownership rate is very low, given the extremely high prices that homes are bringing. During the 1980s, the economic boom in Boston was so strong that the city of Boston ranked number one in increased home prices, while the entire region ranked No. 2 in the runup in housing costs. While this increase in home values was welcome news for many existing homeowners, it poses insurmountable financial barriers for younger families and families with limited income and assets. Unless measures are taken to increase the housing stock, affordability will continue to be a problem. If nothing is done to reverse the soaring cost of shelter in the region, it will be difficult to attract new businesses and new workers.

Recent newspaper articles have underlined this potential weakness in Greater Boston. According to one account, young and well-educated workers who aspire to homeownership have a strong incentive to move to other parts of the country, thus exacerbating labor shortages among skilled workers. It is hard to blame them. While Massachusetts ranks fourth in per capita income among the states, its rank falls to twenty-first once income is adjusted for housing costs (Blanton 1998). The other problem is that in some neighborhoods that have historically had the lowest housing values in Boston, prices and rents are rising proportionately faster than anywhere else. This has fed fears that soon no neighborhood in the entire city will offer affordable housing (Flint 1999). While it is preferable to deal with the problems of economic success, rather than the problems of economic decline, these issues relating to housing affordability are nonetheless serious, and difficult to solve in an era when both the federal and state governments have reduced their commitments to increasing the stock of affordable housing.

Unequal Public Services   Finally, we might note a weakness in public services in some neighborhoods. While all racial and ethnic groups view city services and property upkeep with near equally high satisfaction, the same does not hold true for the quality of police protection and public schools. Blacks rank these services much lower than Hispanics or whites. The continuing feeling on the part of blacks that they are on the short end of the stick when it comes to the provision of fair and equal policing and good schools adds to the level of political frustration and sometimes outrage in the region.

Opportunities

Despite a lot of good news about the region, all these weaknesses need attention. Fortunately, if the economy remains strong, the resources needed to redress these problems should be available. The combination of the strengths and weaknesses highlighted here suggest that there are opportunities for the region that are still to be realized. We can mention a few here.

Reducing Underemployment With unemployment rates below 5 percent, employers often need to search the region thoroughly for qualified employees. What the GBSS indicates is that unlike some other cities, there is a large pool of workers with strong labor force attachment but who nonetheless are presently underutilized. This is particularly true of black workers. Unlike the image of the jobless ghetto, the overwhelming majority of blacks in Boston are willing and able to work. In fact, they are working and have recent job experience. They are "underemployed," not "unemployable." Hence, there is a natural symbiosis between the needs of employers and the needs of many inner-city residents. Here is a golden opportunity to fill at least some of the employment needs of companies while simultaneously improving the annual earnings of currently disadvantaged black workers.

That underemployment, and not a total absence of skills and employment experience, is at the root of black disadvantage in the Greater Boston labor market needs to be publicized. Employers need to be made aware that a group with recent work experience is available for jobs, especially jobs offering steady work. If employers do not substantially alter their perceptions of the black workforce and the overly grim picture they have of the inner-city neighborhoods where many live, it is hard to imagine that the black-white annual earnings gap can be closed. Fortunately, given the strong employment growth in the region, there is a persistent problem of labor supply shortages in some fields, which could provide more employment opportunity for the presently underemployed.

Many of the region's machinists, for example, are nearing retirement age, and new training programs have been necessary to replenish the supply (Ackerman 1997). Extending these to inner-city residents and immigrant newcomers will increase economic opportunity in minority-dominated neighborhoods and simultaneously help solve the labor shortage crisis. Training more of the region's labor force in computer skills should help a good deal, given the high return to computer usage we found in our labor market studies. In the case of black men, however, we need to figure out how to overcome job discrimination, which still hinders this particular segment of the workforce more than any other. In the case of black women, many of whom are single parents, there is a need for better provision of child care to reduce this barrier to full participation in the workforce.

Similarly, expanding education and training programs for new immigrants to the region could pay off handsomely for both workers and employers. As the region continues to develop its mind-based industries requiring highly educated workers, those with limited education will see their opportunities shrink. Even in manufacturing, skill requirements are likely to increase as technology transforms production. This is a concern for all workers, but especially for minority workers, whose educational attainment tends to be lower than whites'.

Hispanic workers tend to have the least education and the highest school dropout rates in the region. Recently, the Hispanic-American Chamber of Commerce initiated programs aimed at reducing the school dropout rate among Massachusetts Hispanic students (McCabe 1999). GBSS data on attitudes indicate that while opposing affirmative action hiring programs, a majority of even the white population nevertheless acknowledges the existence of racial and ethnic discrimination and would support programs to improve education and training for disadvantaged minorities. In a region where labor markets are close to full employment, significant expansion in high-quality human capital enhancement programs represents a positive-sum policy game, improving job opportunities for minorities without substantially reducing them for anyone else.

Residential Segregation   In an era of exclusionary zoning and gated communities, suburbs have tended to develop as places segregated both by race and by income. Efforts that require communities to provide affordable housing have often been disappointing, whether it be judicial decisions, as in the Mount Laurel case (New Jersey), or legislative action, as in the case of Massachusetts. Although a 1969 law set a goal for every city and town in Massachusetts to put aside 10 percent of its housing stock as affordable, only 21 out of 351 Massachusetts cities and towns are in compliance thirty years later (MacQuarrie 1999).

Nevertheless, examples of stable, integrated communities do exist—places where an increase in the black population has not caused white flight. Recent research by Ingrid Gould Ellen argues that it is not racism per se that causes whites to leave, but the fear that the advent of blacks will leave the community with less economic and political power to preserve the level of public services and the quality of life for residents (Ellen 1997). Hence, "affirmative marketing" efforts, such as those used in Shaker Heights and Cleveland Heights, two Ohio communities, included strategies to preserve the quality of housing and public services, especially the quality of local public schools (Galster 1990). Other examples of communities with stable racial integration resulting from explicit design include Sherman Park in Milwaukee, Vollintine-Evergreen in Memphis, Park Hill in Denver, and West Mount Airy in Philadelphia (U.S. Department of Housing and Urban Development 1998).

While segregation by income and segregation by race are two different dimensions of exclusion, the resistance of many suburban communities in Massachusetts to the former (even when it means something as innocuous as building affordable housing for the elderly) does not bode well for the latter. Those communities that are willing to accept a diverse population should receive state government assistance for carrying out community enhancement programs and implementing "affirmative marketing" strategies to help reduce white flight and attract new white families as well as minority households to integrated neighborhoods.

Encouraging Community Economic Development   If low-income minority households could improve their earnings, and if programs to reduce residential segregation were more effective, there would be fewer neighborhoods with concentrated poverty in Greater Boston. It is unlikely, however, that low-income neighborhoods would simply disappear, and therefore it is necessary to ensure that they are made livable, safe, and secure. To that end, we point to the Dudley Street Neighborhood Initiative (DSNI) as a model for community economic development.

The Dudley Street neighborhood in Roxbury-North Dorchester (what is now the DSNI core area) saw arson, disinvestment, racial change, and depopulation in the period from 1950 to 1980, when its total population dropped by more than half and the neighborhood shifted from 95 percent white to 84 percent minority. By 1984, when the Riley Foundation agreed to help support community efforts to rebuild the area, 30 percent of the land, excluding streets, was vacant. The area is one of the poorest in the commonwealth, with low per capita income, high unemployment, and a high percentage of female-headed households. It is estimated that in 1990, the population of the DSNI core area was about 7 percent non-Hispanic white, 29 percent Hispanic, 25 percent Cape Verdean, and 37 percent African Americans who were neither Hispanic nor Cape Verdean. The story of how DSNI came to be a truly representative multiracial, multicultural organization of local residents, rather than a top-down organization of planners and agency representatives, is told in detail in *Streets of Hope*, co-authored by DSNI's first executive director (Medoff and Sklar 1994). The resident-controlled board of DSNI chose as its first project cleaning up and fencing off the vacant lots and closing the illegal trash transfer stations that had been operating in the area. The 1986 "Don't Dump on Us" campaign was successful not only in attaining its stated goal, but also in involving growing numbers of residents in the process of rebuilding the community.

Although there was a large amount of vacant land within the DSNI area, it would not have been easy to redevelop it, because ownership of the vacant lots was scattered among numerous private individuals, and even those lots owned by the city of Boston tended to be small and not contiguous. To solve the overwhelming problem of site assembly, DSNI needed the power of eminent domain, the very power that had been used against many residents of the area who moved there after having been displaced by urban renewal projects elsewhere in the city. It was unprecedented for a grassroots community organization to be granted such power, but DSNI was given the right of eminent domain by the BRA in 1988. To ensure that housing built on the land acquired by eminent domain (as well as the land given by the city) remains affordable, DSNI created a community land trust, Dudley Neighbors, Inc., which owns the land in perpetuity (Medoff and Sklar 1994). Thus, the story of redevelopment in the Dudley Street area is the antithesis of Boston's early post–World War II urban renewal projects in the New York Streets and West End neighborhoods within the central city (see chapter 4). The power of eminent domain in urban redevelopment is no longer synonymous with the power to displace poor people and disrupt their communities. Expanding the Dudley Street model to other parts of the city and the region is well worth exploring.

Supporting Regional Cooperation   According to 1990 census data, the Boston CMSA was the seventh largest in the nation, while the city of Boston itself was only the twentieth largest city (Cisneros 1993). The city of Boston contains an unusually small share of the metropolitan-area population, and many of the area's problems are beyond the capability of any single municipality to solve. Issues of open space, water supply, and transportation planning are regional in scope and need regional solutions, as does the issue of reducing residential segregation.

Although the Greater Boston region has experienced a substantial amount of spatial decentralization in terms of housing and business location, the region still maintains a high level of population density. The city of Boston ranks fourth out of 77 cities in population density, and the suburban ring ranks tenth. This high density makes expanded public transit a viable option for the region.

The growing presence of minorities within many of the cities and towns in the region should make it increasingly possible to foster regional cooperation among the various political jurisdictions, despite the high degree of local neighborhood residential segregation. The opportunity is greater here for this type of activity than in metropolitan areas where the demographic distribution is polarized between what has been described as "chocolate city" and "vanilla suburbs."

Building on Global Trade In addition to its geographic advantage for international trade, given its seaport status, Greater Boston's multicultural community has the potential for providing abundant opportunities for continued success in the global economy. Trade with Spanish- and Portuguese-speaking Latin America, trade with Asia, and future trade with nations of the former Soviet Union could all be enhanced, as large numbers of immigrants have come from these regions, speak the native languages, and understand the customs by which business is conducted. In the new global economy, Boston is therefore positioned for success not only because of its leading industries, but precisely because of the immigrants it has attracted.

Threats

The opportunities for expanding on the recent success of the Greater Boston region are legion. But success is never guaranteed, as the history of Boston amply demonstrates. The region's nineteenth-century shipping industry lost out to other ports on the East Coast and to other forms of transportation. The textile mills that promised employment to waves of immigrants closed their doors and moved south or out of the country altogether. The boom in minicomputers fizzled when personal computers—designed and built elsewhere—became so powerful that they displaced the computers built in Boston. In the new, highly competitive global economy, Boston faces numerous threats that must be avoided if its renaissance is to be sustained. There are a number of internal threats that the region can try to handle on its own. There are also a number of external threats against which the corporate leaders and public officials in Greater Boston could use their influence to help chart the course of national policy.

Public Schools   One of the most important goals to be accomplished within the region is to improve the public schools, especially within the central cities of the metropolitan area. While there is reason to believe that the public schools in general are reasonably good in Greater Boston, almost no one denies the relatively poor quality of the schools in cities like Lawrence and Boston itself. More resources are needed in those schools where the most disadvantaged students are housed. The "best-practice" techniques of successful inner-city schools need to be emulated. What we know from the labor market research is that no group will be better served by such improvements than Hispanics, whose major disadvantage in the labor market seems to be uniquely tied to human capital deficits. While better schools alone would not entirely close the earnings gap between blacks and whites, improved schools would increase black earnings substantially.

Affordable High-Quality Higher Education   While most of the emphasis on school quality has been focused on the K–12 public school system, it is just as crucial to improve access to high-quality postsecondary education and to improve Boston's public institutions of higher education. In the immediate post–World War II era, private institutions of higher education like Boston College (BC) and Northeastern University (NU) had large cadres of commuter students from working-class families in the region. The University of Massachusetts at Boston did not exist, and the University of Massachusetts at Lowell was still in its previous incarnation as a technical school. As BC and NU grew in size and scope, they became national universities, and the local working-class commuters were increasingly replaced by more affluent students coming from other states and other countries. First-generation college students are now more likely to be found in the area's public institutions, where they are subject to the vagaries of the commonwealth's budget.

While the education one receives at UMass Boston and UMass Lowell is provided by top-notch scholars committed to providing excellent teaching to their students, the reputations of these schools lag far behind many of the private universities and colleges in the area. This disjuncture can be a disadvantage for graduates entering the job market.

In contrast, the reputation of the public universities often surpasses that of the privates in a number of Midwestern and Western states. UCLA in Los Angeles is one example; Wayne State in Detroit is another. Clearly, there is an opportunity to improve the standing of UMass, Boston, and UMass, Lowell, both by increasing state resources devoted to them and by improving their physical infrastructure and the quality of their academic programs. According to one study, the rate of return to the state treasury of investing in UMass, Boston, is on the order of 8.9 percent per year. That is, the increased incomes earned by its graduates—the overwhelming majority of whom remain in the region after graduation—is so high that they pay enough in additional income and sales taxes to more than pay back the state subsidies to the school (Bluestone 1993).

Improvements in the area's community colleges are also needed. While these schools have tried to compensate for the lack of academic preparation of many of the region's inner-city high school graduates, the students who graduate from Roxbury Community College, Bunker Hill Community College, and Middlesex Community College often need remedial work if they go on to four-year colleges or universities. Again, here is an opportunity to help sustain the region's economy by investing in its future labor force.

Affordable Housing We have already noted the region's potential Achilles' heel in its soaring housing costs. Rent control was abandoned in 1996, when a state referendum outlawed such housing regulation. In the aftermath of its demise, rents have skyrocketed in Cambridge, Boston, and Brookline, the last three cities where rent control was still in effect.

The alternative to keeping rents down directly by regulation is to produce enough additional housing that the resulting stock is sufficient to meet the demand. Accomplishing this in an already crowded region will first require assembling parcels of land that are underutilized or that can be converted into residential use. Here the city planning agencies can play a role in setting aside as much land as possible for new housing developments. Proponents of the new urbanism have demonstrated ways to design attractive high-density housing, avoiding the high-rise sterility of mid-century housing projects. Boston has made considerable progress in building attractive low-rise garden-style public housing. Expanding the supply of such housing, whether through public ownership, limited equity cooperatives, or incentives to the private market, will help alleviate the region's housing shortage.

Unionization One of the factors that has most benefited minority workers in the Greater Boston labor market has been their relatively high rate of unionization. Indeed, our labor market simulations suggest that black and Hispanic earnings would trail white earnings even more if it were not for the higher union-density rates among minorities. But unions are generally in decline. If this continues, there will be a disproportionately negative impact on these already disadvantaged groups. Moreover, the rates are declining not so much because unions are losing members in the manufacturing sector as because employment is growing most rapidly in those sectors where unionization is practically nonexistent. Unfortunately, these are the sectors where Boston-area minorities are increasingly likely to work (such as services, retail trade, and wholesale trade). If these trends continue, we will again see the earnings and income gaps growing sharply between whites and everyone else.

As Ralph Whitehead, Jr., Barbara Dafoe Whitehead, and Robert J. Lacey have recently shown, two important factors contributing to higher family incomes among those who did not attend college are a union card and a marriage license. The average income in the United States of "double union" families—married couples with at least one spouse holding a union card—has increased from $50,600 in 1973 to $57,793 in 1997 (in real dollars). "Single union" families—households that include either a married couple or a labor union member, but not both—had lower incomes and saw less improvement in income over time. In 1973, they averaged $40,988 per year; by 1997, their income had increased by only a thousand dollars. "No union" households—those that include neither a married couple nor anyone with a union card—trail the rest of the pack by a large margin and have actually seen their real income decline. In 1973, they averaged only $21,689; by 1997, their average income had slipped to $21,080 (Whitehead, Whitehead, and Lacey 1999).

Given the findings in our labor market analysis, this research applies most directly to black women. Less than 18 percent of black women with a high school degree or less are union members, and 55 percent of black women with children are unmarried. The combination is deadly, giving black women the very lowest annual earnings of any group we studied.

While there is not much that local public officials can do to encourage more unionization, they can defend statewide legislation requiring payment of prevailing wages and they can lobby Congress for labor-law reform to help level the playing field between organized labor and the corporate world. Regional unions can also redouble their efforts at organizing firms that employ large numbers of minority workers and increase the number of minorities in union-controlled or joint union-management training and apprenticeship programs.

In each of these areas—public schools, higher education, affordable housing, and unionization—the region can go a long way toward meeting a series of potential threats to its sustained prosperity. But there are threats that emanate from outside the region that must be considered as well.

National Recession   The success of the Greater Boston region in terms of growing family income, high levels of labor force attachment, and substantial economic progress for black, Hispanic, and Southeast Asian households has been predicated on rapid, sustained economic growth throughout much of the 1980s and 1990s. Any major slowdown in economic growth, as a result of national macroeconomic policy or any exogenous decline in demand for the region's traded goods, could seriously jeopardize continued progress in these areas. Periodic increases in interest rates by the Federal Reserve Board could undermine growth, as it did at the beginning of the 1980s when the Fed deliberately engineered a national recession to bring inflation under control. An overzealous attempt at building up federal budget surpluses could do the same if federal spending cuts are maintained even in the face of slowing growth rates and increased unemployment. While the region can do little to avoid this threat, its political and private industry leadership needs to weigh in on these matters in Washington (see Bluestone and Harrison 2000).

Persistent Inequality   Despite the growth in employment and incomes, Greater Boston, like most parts of the country, has a high degree of income inequality. In 1990, it had the 36th highest degree of income inequality in the top seventy-seven metropolitan areas. If income inequality continues to grow, it could undermine the progress that has been made by creating sharper political and social divisions within and between communities. Nothing so exacerbates income inequality as a slow-growing economy, which intensifies job competition among whites, blacks, Hispanics, and Asians (Bluestone and Harrison 2000). Obviously, a slowdown in economic growth would also impede any potential progress toward reducing the high poverty rates in many minority neighborhoods.

This requires leadership again on the growth issue, this time on equity grounds. When the Fed deliberately tries to slow the economy down as a hedge against inflation, it normally uses higher short-term interest rates to do so. This normally drives up unemployment rates, not as some mere unintended consequence but as an intended policy. With more people out of work, spending is supposed to slow, cooling down the economy and prices. What is unintended, perhaps, is that the main victims of this strategy are less-educated blacks, Hispanics, and Asians. It is strange that for the "good" of the overall economy, we punish the most disadvantaged to benefit everyone else.

Declining Public Investment   The current theory in vogue in Washington is that if cutting the federal deficit helped bring about a surge in the economy, building up the largest federal surplus is necessary to sustain the economy's return to health. But this thinking fails to recognize the critical role the public sector plays in economic growth through investments in public infrastructure, R&D, and human capital that help foster new technology and train technically proficient workers in its use. We know this from past experience. If the government had not invested enormous resources into radar and sonar during World War II, we might have delayed improvements in communications and television by another decade or so. If we had not built thousands of miles of interstate highways beginning in the 1950s, the blossoming of the post–World War II auto industry would have been stunted. The former, designed in MIT laboratories during the war, played an invaluable role in making Boston a center of high technology research, development, and production in the entire postwar period—just as the latter provided the roads that fueled Detroit's boom economy from the 1950s through the late 1970s.

More recently, it was the need for massive computing power to run modern defense systems that helped fund the design and construction of powerful mainframe computers. The requirement of miniaturized guidance systems for ICBMs and NASA rockets led the government to underwrite a good portion of the development costs of microprocessors and the software for programming them. It was the federal government's investment in the ARPANET that led to the modern-day Internet and the World Wide Web. Without these investments, today's ubiquitous e-commerce would never have come about—or would have been delayed, perhaps by decades.

No wonder, then, that the United States is doing so well today in computers and information technology relative to our most advanced trading partners, and why the Greater Boston region is doing so well relative to everyone else. The massive investments the federal government made in these technologies has put American high-tech firms, including ones like Greater Boston's own $4 billion EMC Storage Devices Corporation, well ahead of the global pack. Similarly, medical research emanating from government-funded laboratories has provided the region with a leg-up in biotechnology. We need to maintain a vital private-public partnership to assure that all the ingredients for sustained technological innovation and economic growth are present.

Unfortunately, the federal government has been destroying vital elements of this partnership since the late 1970s. One of the chief victims of the deficit-cutting and budget-balancing mania has been public spending on infrastructure and research and development. Since 1979, the share of federal investment in public nondefense infrastructure, education, and research has fallen steadily. In the 1970s, when we were putting in place the investments in information technologies, infrastructure, and education that would eventually pay off in the 1990s, federal investment in these activities averaged better than 2.5 percent of GDP. The percentage shrank dramatically during the 1980s under the Reagan and Bush administrations and has continued to decline under President Clinton and the Republican-dominated Congress. By 1998, it was down to only 1.5 percent of GDP. To get back to the spending level of the 1970s would cost more than $80 billion.

Under current projections, however, the entire investment role of the federal government will continue to shrink. Total discretionary federal funding (excluding Social Security, Medicare, Medicaid, and interest on the federal debt) was 13.6 percent of GDP in 1968. Even as late as 1986, it amounted to 10 percent. Twelve years later, it was down to 6.6 percent and is scheduled to fall to only 5.5 percent by 2004 (Bluestone 1999).

The private sector can hardly compensate for these losses, even if we used the surplus to cut taxes or lower interest rates. The financial exigencies of the stock market force firms to put more of their resources into practical development work rather than basic research. Transportation infrastructure and large-scale water treatment plants will not be constructed by private enterprise. Industry may invest in specific job training for its own needs, but it will hesitate to invest the resources necessary to boost the general skills of the workforce. All these investments require large-scale government participation and a substantial amount of government funds.

The critical point here is that no region of the country will suffer more from these cutbacks in the federal commitment to research and development in science and medicine than Greater Boston. The universities centered around Boston rely on federal grants and contracts to underwrite basic research. Federal aid to higher education helps pay for tuition and room and board. Federal funds from the National Institutes of Health pay for much of the leading-edge medical research done in the area's teaching and research hospitals. And federal highway funds are critical for completing the depression of the central artery and related projects. Hence, the new obsession in Washington over budget surpluses poses a real threat to the Boston economy. In the end, it may be the nation's infatuation with limiting the economic role of the federal government that most undermines Greater Boston's renaissance.

Closing Thoughts

Whether the Greater Boston region can take advantage of its strengths and opportunities and deal with its weaknesses and threats cannot be known with certainty. But one thing seems to be clear after studying this renaissance region for many years: for Greater Boston to maintain its growth and distribute the fruits of it equitably, everyone in the region must be willing to take another look at how we perceive and treat one another. That means a recommitment on the part of business to utilize a minority labor force ready and willing to work and ready and willing to seek out more education and more training. That means a commitment on the part of public officials to meet the needs of its poor neighborhoods every bit as much as the desires of those who live in its wealthiest communities. That means a commitment of leaders in the 154 towns and cities in the region to find more and better ways to work together to solve common problems. And, finally, it means that every racial and ethnic group in the region must begin to deal more effectively with the attitudes and actions that divide them.

All in all, we believe there are ways to maximize opportunities in the Greater Boston region and deal with the potential threats. While some of the mechanisms are beyond our local jurisdiction (such as federal fiscal and monetary policy), the region does have the ability to deal with intergroup perceptions and work toward equalizing economic and social opportunity in the workplace and in our neighborhoods. The future for the Greater Boston region is an extremely sanguine one if we can build on our strengths and continue to pay attention to correcting our weaknesses. In a renaissance region with so much potential, it would be a shame not to deal with the racial, ethnic, and social class divisions that keep many of its residents from enjoying the economic and cultural amenities this wonderful area has to offer.

Notes

Chapter 1

1. Our original research plan included special attention not only to blacks and Hispanics, but also to the rapidly growing Asian population in the region. Because of funding limits, however, it was not possible to "oversample" Asians in our survey. As a result, while we have new data that allow us to explore in some depth issues facing blacks and Hispanics, we do not have comparable data to do the same with Asians. One would hope that this shortcoming will be remedied in future research.

Chapter 3

1. Between 1980 and 1985, for instance, the real dollar value of prime defense contracts won by Massachusetts firms incresed by almost 60 percent; at the peak of the boom years, the Commonwealth ranked fourth among all states in contract awards (Dukakis and Kanter 1988, 39).

2. Ironically, former CEO Arnold Hiatt told President-elect Clinton's economic conference of Stride Rite's commitment to the Roxbury community just *four days* prior to his former firm's announcement.

Chapter 4

1. Upper-class suburbs in the late nineteenth century were not as economically segregated as their homogeneous equivalents are today. Tax lists for Newton's Chestnut Hill section between 1850 and 1890 show that up to a third of the residents were laborers, operatives, gardeners, servants, and others—primarily serving the upper-tier businessmen who commuted into Boston (Jackson 1985).

2. In 1907, for instance, the civic leader Edward Ginn constructed a "model tenement," Charlesbank, in hopes of inspiring redevelopment efforts; the public housing advocate Nathan Straus recom-

mended clearing the entire West End in the late 1930s in favor of public housing units (O'Connor 1992)

Chapter 5

1. In generating the sample frame, we used computer-drawn maps obtained from the University of Massachusetts Office of Computing Services, which utilized U.S. census TIGER files. These maps were checked and features were elaborated by reference to local street atlases. Segments were visited from November 1992 to January 1993 by trained listers who checked the maps, then made complete listings of all addresses of residences on selected blocks. Sampling of addresses was done in the central office. The overall sample, consisting of the five major strata, was subdivided using equiprobability sampling methods into five approximately equal-sized groups or replicates. Each group, or random subsample, is therefore similar to the overall sample in its relative overrepresentation of minority and low-income groups.

2. The structure of families in the Greater Boston region differs somewhat from the national distribution—particularly among Hispanic and white households. Nationwide, in 1990, 45 percent of black families had two (or more) adults; in Greater Boston the proportion was 47 percent. Hispanics in Boston tend to live in single adult units more often than they do elsewhere in the nation (76 percent versus 65 percent). Part of this may be due to the recent immigrant status of many Latinos in this region. Whites in Boston are also more likely than whites nationwide to live in single-adult households. Nationwide, 80 percent of all whites live in multi-adult families. According to the GBSS, only 71 percent do in Boston. The large student population may be responsible for this difference.

3. The mean values in Greater Boston are amazingly close to national medians. The national median family income in 1996 was $47,100, compared with the 1993 to 1994 mean in the Boston region of $48,600. The national-regional comparison for Hispanics was $26,200 versus $26,700. The largest discrepancy was among black families. Nationally, the 1996 median was $26,500; in Boston, it was $31,210. This is consistent with the data we reported in chapter 1 showing that blacks in Boston do well relative to blacks in other cities when it comes to family income.

4. Limiting our sample to families in which there are no elderly (age > sixty-five) persons does not significantly change the levels or the size of the race-ethnic income gaps. Nonelderly black family incomes average $32,182; Hispanics, $26,994; whites, $51,981. In this case, the black/white and Hispanic/white ratios are .62 and .52, respectively.

5. For the purposes at hand, we report "mean" rather than the more conventional "median" family income. Normally, the median is used as a measure of central tendency in income reporting in order to minimize the impact of extreme values in the income distribution. However, we found that in our sample the difference between the mean and median was not great, so that the two measures provide similar results. Using the broad income categories in the GBSS to calculate a median tends to obscure the underlying variation in family income. This is particularly true for subsamples by gender and family structure where the number of cases is limited.

6. The extremely high percentage of Hispanics who report living in public housing may reflect a misunderstanding of immigrant populations regarding this term. Those living in large apartment complexes or receiving housing subsidies may have inadvertently reported that they lived in public housing. The GBSS did not contain an independent means for verifying their responses.

7. Those born in Puerto Rico are U.S. citizens and not usually counted as immigrants. For our purposes, we have included those born on the island as foreign-born.

8. The incentive payment was increased to $20.00 per interview on June 1, 1994, to expedite attainment of the survey goals.

9. The following table provides a breakdown of the number of GBSS interviewers by race and ethnicity and the number of interviews conducted.

Number of Interviews Completed by Race of Interviewer

Number of Completed Interviews	Number of Interviewers	Race of Interviewer			
		Asian	White	Black	Hispanic
159	1				1
76 to 92	4		3		1
52 to 68	6		4	1	1
32 to 46	6		5		1
20 to 28	14		8	4	2
13 to 19	10		6	3	1
10 to 12	6		4	2	
5 to 9	16	1	5	6	4
4	7		2	4	1
3	4		3	1	
2	6		1	5	
1	12		4	7	1
	92	1	45	33	13

Source: Greater Boston Social Survey 1995.

10. These estimated rates *assume* that all noninterviews from each stratum (that is, blocks grouped according to census estimates of racial composition) follow the same race-ethnicity distribution as the interviews from that stratum.

11. The interview staff was persistent in attempting to solicit answers to all relevant questions. However, complete data on all cases was not achieved. On such variables as age, sex, and nativity, data on all 1,820 respondents was obtained. But on education, for example, there are 9 missing cases; on labor force participation, 27 missing cases. Among currently employed workers, we have valid wage data on 839 out of 899 cases—a question response rate of 93 percent. In order to obtain as much wage data as possible and to avoid selection bias, we asked earnings data on the current or last job. As a result, we have valid hourly wage data on 1,217 cases, even though only 1,003 respondents were working at the time of the survey. The use of retrospective questions—particularly regarding hours of work and wages noticeably improves the availability of data.

Chapter 6

1. See, for example, Bobo and Kluegel 1997; Feagin and Vera 1995; Hochschild 1995; Jaynes and Williams 1989; Kluegel and Smith 1986; Sigelman and Welsh 1991; Sniderman and Hagen 1985; in support for policies to reduce economic inequality, see Bobo and Kluegel 1993, 1997; Bobo and Smith 1994; Jacobsen 1985; Kluegel 1990; Sniderman and Piazza 1993; Tuch and Hughes 1996.

Chapter 8

1. See U.S. Department of the Treasury, Internal Revenue Service, *Statistics of Income—1992, Individual Income Tax Returns*, table 1.3. Taking into account government transfers does not alter the fact that work is by far the primary source of family income. In 1989, the median family in the United States realized 76.4 percent of its income from wages, salaries, and self-employment; 9.9 percent from government transfers; 7.4 percent from rent, interest, and realized capital gains; and 6.4 percent from other sources (Mishel and Bernstein 1994, table 1.13, 45).

2. Among the top 1 percent of all families by income, wages, and salaries plus self-employment income averaged $288,000 in 1989. This was just half (51 percent) total family income of $560,000 (Mishel and Bernstein 1994, table 1.18, 54). Over 46 percent came from capital sources and less than 1 percent from government transfers (Mishel and Bernstein 1994, table 1.13, 45).

3. In related research, the California State University at Hayward economist Nan Maxwell comes to similar conclusions using the NLSY (Maxwell 1994). She finds that the main source of the remaining black-white wage differential is the racial difference in the quality rather than the quantity of schooling, where quality is measured in terms of AFQT test scores. These differences in quality, Maxwell argues, are tied to the residential segregation and social isolation in the inner city, which leaves blacks with inferior schooling and a lack of positive peer and adult influences.

4. It is interesting to note that the one region where Ferguson found that increased racial disparity in earnings could not be explained by test score differences was the North Central region. In the Midwest states, the price of skill as measured by test scores could not account for the increased black-white wage disparity for young men with high school education or less after 1985. John Bound and Richard Freeman conclude that the large earnings losses for these young men are due to a combination of declining unionism, a large loss in manufacturing jobs, and the growth in the relative supply of young black males (Bound and Freeman 1992). To the extent that black men in the Midwest benefited disproportionately in the 1950s, 1960s, and 1970s from jobs in the auto, steel, and related industries and from union membership, the loss of these jobs in the 1980s was particularly devastating for them.

5. In generating expected annual earnings for each demographic group we study, we chose *median* values for hourly wages instead of the more conventional *mean*. This was done in order to minimize the impact of outlying values in the reported GBSS data. Given the relatively small sample sizes for various subgroups and the weighting procedure used in the GBSS stratified, clustered survey frame, it is possible that a few cases with outlying values *and* particularly high weights can have a distorting effect on mean values. By using medians for hourly wages, we reduce this potential distortion.

6. In our population weighted GBSS sample, two-thirds (68 percent) of white men have some schooling beyond high school. A little over half of black men (53 percent) have at least some college. In contrast, only about one in nine (11 percent) Hispanic men have gone beyond the high school degree. Hence, the education differences are quite substantial.

7. Following the annual earnings algorithm, "expected" annual hours for each group is equal to $[\text{pr (LFP)} \times (1 - \text{pr (U)}) \times \text{H/Wk} \times 52]$. As such, hours worked here do not refer to the working time of employed workers, as would be true of conventional measures, but to the expected hours of work, including those who report zero hours because they are out of the labor force or currently unemployed.

8. Among all workers age sixteen and over, an analysis of *Current Population Survey* data suggests that those with a college degree or more worked an average of 41.6 hours per week in 1995. This compares with a 39-hour work week for those who are high school graduates and only about 35 hours per week for high school dropouts (Bluestone and Rose 1998).

9. In our population weighted GBSS sample, over 80 percent of black men with no more than a high school education lived in neighborhoods where a majority of the households were black or Hispanic. Only 34 percent lived in neighborhoods where at least 25 percent of the households were officially poor. Only 8 percent were living where the poverty rate equaled or exceeded 40 percent.

10. In addition to these variables, many others were created from the GBSS survey and introduced into the equation set. These included such factors as years living in Boston, religion, prison record, firm size, percent minority in establishment, public-sector employment, and on-the-job training. While we might have expected these to prove statistically significant based on existing literature and economic theory, they did not. Hence, they too were excluded from the final equations used in the simulation.

11. As noted in this chapter's appendix, we were forced to rely on weighted data to estimate the equations for labor force participation and the unemployment rate. This was necessitated by the poor simulation model behavior of unweighted equations for these two expected annual earnings components. When we tried to use unweighted equation coefficients in the simulation model, we found that the model became severely unstable. For example, turning a black worker into a "white" worker could send the simulated labor force participation rate plummeting toward zero.

12. The simulated mean labor force participation rates for single and married men are as follows:

LFP Rates	Single	Married
Black men	.80	.90
Hispanic men	.77	.88
White men	.70	.86

13. We expected that education and age would be statistically significant in this equation. Neither was. Further analysis provided some insight into why this was true. If we restrict the sample to those who are healthy (HEALTHDY = 0), both AGE and AGESQ have the expected signs and are statistically significant. Health condition so dominates age, however, that it remains the significant variable in equations in which HEALTHDY is not restricted. On the other hand, education was never statistically significant in any

of our runs, even when the sample was not truncated on this variable and when alternative measures of education were specified. Education is a critical variable in other labor market components, but not labor force participation.

14. Given that the population weighted mean unemployment rate for less-educated black men is more than double the rates for Hispanics and whites, we naturally expected the coefficient on the race variable to be positive, large, and statistically significant. While nominally positive, it and its t-statistic were close to zero. What could have caused this peculiar finding? It turns out the pattern of coefficients in this equation can be explained by comparing weighted and unweighted data. Recall that the weighted unemployment rates for blacks, Hispanics, and whites are 15.2, 7.1, and 7.1 percent, respectively. However, given the GBSS oversample in poorer minority neighborhoods, the sample (unweighted) unemployment rates were quite different. The highest unweighted rate was among Hispanics at 20 percent followed by blacks and whites at 12.7 and 11.6 percent, respectively.

15. For the weekly hours equation, there are valid data on the dependent variable for 245 out of 252 current labor force participants. Of these, 212 were currently employed and 33 currently unemployed. In addition, there are valid data on weekly hours in thirty-four cases where the respondent worked at some time within the past five years of the GBSS, but was not at work when interviewed. Similarly, for the hourly wage equation, we have valid data on the dependent variable for 228 of the 252 current labor force participants. Of these, 197 were currently employed, while 31 were unemployed. In addition, we have valid data on hourly wages in twenty-three cases where the respondent worked at some time in the previous five years, but was either out of the labor force or unemployed at the time of the survey. Among those currently in the labor force, we have valid weekly hours data for 245, but valid wage data for only 228 because 17 respondents did not provide data from which an hourly wage could be calculated.

16. An exception is found, however, for the largest group of immigrants: foreign-born Hispanics. They average about seven hours *less* work per week than native-born Hispanics (FORBORN: $(-.746)$ + FORBORN $\times$ HISPANIC: (-5.92)).

17. The percentage difference in the hourly wage rate is calculated according to the following algorithm: percent difference in hourly wage = $(e^{(b \times 1)} - 1) \times 100$, where b is the regression coefficient.

18. The assessment of English-speaking ability did not prove statistically significant in any of the equations. This could be due to the fact that within this sample, restricted to those with a high school degree or less, many may be working in ethnic enclaves or in occu-

pations that do not require great facility with the English language. The overall ability to understand the questionnaire, on the other hand, may reflect a broader indication of competence.

19. Overall, the difference between white and black men on this variable is .89 units. This translates, according to the hourly wage regression, into a wage differential of about .01 log points.

20. In fact, analysis of the interviewer assessment of respondent understanding of the questionnaire (ASSESSUQ) indicates that white interviewers of black respondents tended to rate the ability of these respondents somewhat *higher* than the average rating given black respondents by black interviewers. On the ASSESSUQ scale of 1 = excellent to 5 = poor, the average score for black men with no more than a high school degree was 2.35 in the cases of white interviewers; 2.65 in the cases of black interviewers. Hence, the point difference is small and there does not appear to be any tendency for white interviewers to downgrade the assessment of blacks. White interviewers tended to score Hispanic respondents a little bit lower in ability than Hispanic interviewers did, but again the differences were not large. The average ASSESSUQ across all Hispanic male respondents with no more than high school was 2.90; the average score for respondents interviewed by whites was 3.17.

21. We found a substantial difference between whites and the two minority groups when it came to their test scores on the survey's word-recognition test. Whites scored an average of 3.84 correct answers out of a possible 7. Blacks and Hispanics scored 2.28 and 2.30, respectively. Difficulty with English was not a factor in this test, since it was given with a set of Spanish words for those Latinos who wished to conduct the entire interview in that language. Unlike the interviewer assessments, the word test is not subject to interviewer bias. That the results of the word test are correlated with the interviewer assessment rankings, we find additional reason for having confidence in the survey's assessment questions.

22. Moreover, to test for the possibility of interaction effects masking the impact of high school completion, we generated interaction terms for HSDEGREE and AGE, and HSDEGREE and a dummy variable for employed in manufacturing. However, neither of these interaction terms proved statistically significant, nor did they materially raise the t-statistic on the education variable. We are forced to conclude that in this truncated sample, the high school degree per se is not a key variable in the determination of labor market success in this particular labor market.

23. According to an analysis of pay data, Lawrence Mishel, Jared Bernstein, and John Schmitt (1999) found that the union hourly pay

premium in 1997 was 23.2 percent for all workers. It was especially large among blue-collar workers (50 percent).

24. This finding of a positive relationship is consistent with national studies. Using 1989 national data and a wage equation not unlike ours, the Princeton economist Alan Krueger (1993) found that the use of a computer at work is associated with an 18.8 percent wage differential. In a more recent paper, John E. DiNardo and Jörn-Steffen Pischke (1996) have challenged the conventional wisdom regarding the importance of computers in terms of wage and productivity premia. Using German data, they have shown that computer use is indeed associated with higher wages. But so is the use of pencils, calculators, and telephones! What they argue is that it is not the computer use per se that contributes to higher productivity and pay, but the jobs that require any kind of higher-level technical and social skills.

25. Several adjustments were needed in the model in order to align our estimates with the population weighted means for each labor market outcome component. After much experimentation, we chose the following adjustments as most appropriate:

(1) After entering all logit or regression coefficients for each component in the baseline spreadsheet and calculating mean outcomes for black, Hispanic, white, and all men, the constant in the fitted equation for each component was adjusted in order to bring the fitted mean value for *all men* into alignment with the actual mean value.

(2) After this was completed, any difference between the fitted mean value and the actual mean value for *each race-ethnic group* in the baseline spreadsheet was adjusted to zero by adding or subtracting to the fitted value until it was aligned with the mean value.

This process permits us to begin the simulation with race-ethnic group "fitted" means equal to the actual sample weighted means for each race-ethnic group. Moreover, this adjustment process permits the values estimated in the various simulations to reflect differences from the actual weighted baseline means, rather than differences from the means estimated on unweighted data.

26. In a study of the expected rates of return to students at the University of Massachusetts, Boston, Bluestone (1993) used *Current Population Survey* (CPS) data for the six New England states to estimate the present discounted value of achieving various levels of schooling. Among women, he found that one to three years of college provided a return of $128,000 above the return to the high school

degree. However, completing just one more year of college (and presumably earning a bachelor's degree) added an additional $194,000 to the present discounted stream of a woman's lifetime earnings. This suggests a substantial "diploma" effect.

Chapter 9

1. An alternative theoretical backdrop for labor market analysis is given by efficiency wage theory. The theory was developed in the 1970s and 1980s to provide a neoclassical explanation for involuntary unemployment, the existence of high- versus low-wage sectors, differing wage rates and unemployment rates between demographic groups, and statistical discrimination. Job competition theory and efficiency wage theory share several central ideas. One could argue that the only major difference is the style and language in which these ideas were presented to their respective audiences: one style, job competition, for institutionalists; and another style, efficiency wages, for neoclassicists.

   Efficiency wage theory explains these labor market observations by a combination of sectoral technological differences, imperfect information, and institutional characteristics. The theory gets its name from a central result that, at market-clearing wages in which the demand and supply for labor are equal, firms may not be maximizing profits. Firms may find it optimal to set wages above the market-clearing level, resulting in involuntary unemployment or underemployment. (We will refer to both simply as *unemployment* in this section.) There is no single efficiency wage theory, but several variations that stress different mechanisms. By the mid-1980s, there were three main branches, which may be labeled "adverse selection," "shirking," and "turnover" (Janet Yellen 1984).

   In the adverse selection branch of the field, the information on the quality of workers is imperfect in one sector, A, and is perfect in the other sector, B. These sectors correspond roughly to the primary and secondary sectors of dual labor market theory. There is also an institutional imperfection: wages in the sector A are identical for all workers in the same job category, even if their true quality differences are later learned by the employer. Employers in sector A cannot trust job applicants to divulge their true productivity, and cannot learn these from sector B employers. Andrew Weiss (1980) gives a clear presentation of adverse selection. He calls a person's innate productivity his or her "labor endowment," measured in efficiency units. Workers can always find employment in sector B, where they get paid according to their actual labor endowment; but they also seek employment in sector A, where employers cannot observe their actual endowment. Instead, sector A employers know that workers' acceptance wages and labor endowments are positively related by some known function. They also know the distribution of acceptance wages. From this information, they choose an optimal wage rate and employment level that minimizes labor cost per expected efficiency unit. If this wage level exceeds the market-clearing rate in sector B, there is involuntary unemployment. An unemployed worker cannot successfully bid for a job in sector A by offering a lower wage than the optimum set by sector A employers, because such a wage bid would signal the probability that the worker has a low labor endowment, and his or her labor cost per efficiency unit would be too high. Different unemployment rates by demographic group can arise if employers determine that they have different acceptance wage-endowment functions; and two workers of equal endowments would receive different wage rates if they worked in different sectors.

In the shirking branch of efficiency wage theory, information on the effort of workers is imperfect in sector A—being too costly to determine—and is perfect in sector B (Shapiro and Stiglitz 1984; Bulow and Summers 1985; Eswaran and Kotwal 1985). The information imperfection is related to the technology of production in sector A. For example, in an economic consulting firm, an associate is staring out the window. Is that employee daydreaming, or generating hypotheses? In contrast, a manufacturing establishment that pays piece-rate in sector B has a virtually costless system in measuring work effort. In order to discourage loafing and boost productivity, sector A employers find it optimal to pay a wage premium, giving workers in sector A an incentive not to shirk: if they *are* caught shirking, they pay the penalty of being banished to the lower-paid sector B. No such premium is necessary in sector B, since productivity is costlessly observed. Workers who shirk there are always caught and disciplined or fired. All workers are paid their marginal revenue product, but the higher marginal revenue product in sector A "pays" for the wage differential between the two sectors by restricting employment, so there is involuntary unemployment. Different unemployment rates between demographic groups can arise if these groups have different quit rates. For example, suppose women have higher quit rates than men. Sector A employers thus know that women's employment horizon is shorter than men's. Therefore, women must receive a greater inducement if they are not to shirk (with a shorter employment horizon, they are less likely to be "caught" then men). But if wages for men and women are required to be equal for the same job, then equilibrium requires that women have a smaller probability than men of moving from sector B to sector A—in other words, higher unemployment (underemployment).

In the turnover branch of efficiency wage theory (Salop 1973, 1979), workers have imperfect information about the working conditions of firms. These working conditions differ from firm to firm, and workers have (nonidentical) preferences for them. These firm attributes are learned on the job. Workers job-hop to learn about working conditions of alternative employers. Involuntary unemployment results when there are hiring costs or training costs for new employees in sector A, and institutional or capital market imperfections inhibit the payment of these employment costs by workers. Employers who have training costs thus must bear "turnover costs" when an employee quits and a replacement must be hired and trained. In this case, employers may find it optimal to pay a wage premium to lower the quit rate, thus saving on turnover costs. The wage premium again results in involuntary unemployment, as sector B does not incur training costs and therefore has no need to pay a wage premium. Demographic differences in employment and involuntary unemployment (underemployment) would result if different groups had different quit-rate functions, even if they simply involved different constants independent of wage rates. Since sector A employers are required to pay equal wages for the same job, they would find it profitable to order new hires by the groups' quit-rate functions. Groups with lower quit-rate functions would be more than proportionately represented in sector A.

Thus, efficiency wage theory provides various neoclassical explanations for intersectoral wage differences; the existence of involuntary unemployment and underemployment; and for differences in wages, sectoral employment, and unemployment-underemployment by demographic group. Furthermore, several key phenomena that account for the theory's conclusions, such as imperfect information on worker's productivities, training costs, and statistical discrimination, are shared by the job competition model.

2. Thurow's model conceptualizes jobs as "training slots." Workers with general skills compete for jobs that provide on-the-job training opportunities. Employers search for workers who can most readily attain an adequate level of performance at lowest employer training cost.

3. At 5'6" tall and with no jumping ability to speak of, it is unlikely that at least one of authors of this book will be ranked high in the labor market queue of the National Basketball Association. It is equally true (and blessedly fortunate!) that most NBA stars will not rank very high in the queue for labor economists.

4. Beside its usefulness in modeling the nature of job matching in the job competition model, this particular formulation of the labor market can be used for distinguishing among types of unemployment. *Frictional* unemployment exists when there are sufficient job slot vectors to accommodate the demand for jobs on the part of employees and the requirements and attributes of the jobs match the attributes and requirements of those seeking work. Any unemployment in this case is frictional in the sense that it is simply a temporary condition cured as soon as employees find jobs for which they

are qualified and which meet their reservation requirements. *Structural* unemployment can be said to exist when the number of job vectors equals or exceeds the number of employees seeking work, but there is a mismatch between job slots and employees. In this case, unemployment exists because the characteristics of potential workers do not meet the job requirements set by employers. *Deficient demand* unemployment exists whenever employers as a whole are satisfied with the attributes of potential employees, but their demand for such employees falls short of supply.

5. In a dynamic model, of course, the elements in both sets of vectors will change, depending on shifts in aggregate demand conditions and changes in technology. Slower growth in the local economy might result in employers raising the requirements for specific jobs if employers believe there is a sufficient number of more highly qualified candidates who would take the jobs, given existing offer wages and other job attributes. Faster growth in the local economy might force employers to lower job requirements or improve job attributes in order to find a sufficient number of workers to meet their needs. Changes in the local economy also affect workers' reservation wages.

6. These medians were generated for the BUIRG project by the Massachusetts Institute for Social and Economic Research (MISER) at the University of Massachusetts, Amherst, and are based on the 1990 PUMS 5 percent census sample for the entire state.

7. The median, rather than the mean, was selected as the best measure of central tendency in order to neutralize the impact of extreme outliers in the wage distribution. These outliers enter the data as a result of errors in reported usual weeks worked or usual weekly hours and because of the existence of negative hourly wages in a few cases of self-employed workers.

8. There is a rich literature on racial and gender "crowding" in terms of occupations and industries (see, for example, Bergmann 1974; Stevenson 1984). Here we extend this concept of crowding to the level of the firm.

9. We did not attempt to estimate this equation for non-Hispanic whites, since only 1.2 percent of our sample of employed whites worked in such minority establishments.

10. Mother's education was used to proxy parent's education rather than father's education for two reasons. First, because of assortative mating, there is a high correlation between mother's and father's formal schooling levels, and therefore one of these variables is sufficient. Moreover, in our sample, there is less missing data on mother's education, thus providing larger sample sizes for the regression.

11. We use a variable for total job experience—total years of experience within the occupation—which our survey data allow us to calculate directly, rather than having to adopt the widely used practice of calculating an imputed value based on age and years in school. This variable is only partially correlated with age and schooling, and particularly improves on analyses of women.

12. It is also possible that the effect of marital status on hourly wage differs by gender, although we did not test for this effect. Being married may signal "stability" for men, while it may introduce a greater likelihood of intermittent labor force participation for women of childbearing age. (See Blau, Ferber, and Winkler 1998.)

13. Note that we have focused on racial and ethnic differences in this chapter, rather than gender differences per se. Hence, we have not attempted to estimate the degree to which minority women (or, for that matter, white women) might face statistical discrimination on the basis of gender.

Chapter 10

1. As Harry Holzer notes, the use of computers can be quite varied and potentially ambiguous in interpretation. The range might include the very simple tasks of operating a grocery store checkout scanner or meal-ordering machine in a fast food restaurant, to word processing, to more technical computer use (see Holzer 1996b, 46, n 4).

2. As demand for and, most likely, return to skill increases, we are likely to see a supply response. To the degree they can, both white and nonwhite young people will invest in getting more skill, as they have done increasingly in the last two decades. Demand shifts tend to occur more rapidly than supply shifts, so that the labor market difficulties we attribute to increasing skill demand may continue to worsen for some time. (We thank Harry Holzer for this point.)

3. In this section and later sections, we analyze the race, ethnicity, and gender of the most recent hire in the firm. Many of the issues we raise about skill, attitudes, and screening procedures pertain as well to employer decisions *after the point of hire*. For example, decisions to train, to promote, or to fire may be affected by skills, perceptions, and procedures as well. Our data limit us to hiring outcomes.

4. See Tilly, Moss, Kirschenman, and Kennelly, forthcoming, for a socioeconomic analysis of the city-suburb distinction in each of the cities, and Holzer and Danziger, forthcoming, for a fuller treatment of potential mismatches between available jobs and workers.

5. This section draws heavily on, and excerpts material directly, from Moss and Tilly 1996b.

6. The qualitative survey considered only jobs that did not require more than a high school degree. The quantitative survey was intended to do so as well, but about 9 percent of the observations gathered information on jobs that require some college. Holzer (1996, 38) excluded these observations from the majority of his reported results, except in a few instances when he wanted to compare jobs that require some college with those that do not. Following Holzer, we restrict our analysis to jobs that do not require college.

References

Ackerman, Jerry. 1997. "Machinists Wanted." *Boston Globe*, December 17, 1997.

Action for Boston Community Development and United Community Services of Metropolitan Boston. 1972. "Five Ethnic Groups in Boston: Blacks, Irish, Italians, Greeks and Puerto Ricans." Boston (June 1972).

Adamic, Louis. 1938. *My America*. New York: Harper & Brothers.

Adams, Russell B. Jr. 1977. *The Boston Money Tree: How the Proper Men of Boston Made, Invested, and Preserved Their Wealth from Colonial Days to the Space Age*. New York: Crowell.

Albelda, Randy, and Chris Tilly. 1997. *Glass Ceilings and Bottomless Pits: Women's Work, Women's Poverty*. Boston: South End Press.

Altshuler, Alan, and David Luberoff. 1996. "Mega-Project: A Political History of Boston's Multi-billion Dollar Artery/Tunnel Project." John F. Kennedy School of Government, A. Alfred Taubman Center for State and Local Government, Harvard University. Rev. ed., April.

Amory, Cleveland. 1947. *The Proper Bostonians*. New York: Dutton.

Atkinson, Robert D., Randolph H. Court, and Joseph M. Ward. 1999. "The State New Economy Index: Benchmarking Economic Transformation in the States." Technology and New Economy Project, Progressive Policy Institute (July).

Aucoin, Don. 1993. "The 23rd Ward: Can a New Mayor Lure the Middle Class Back to Boston?" *Boston Globe Magazine* (September 12).

———. 1995. "Weld Takes a Hard Line on Welfare." *Boston Globe*, January 12, pp. 1, 20.

Babson, Jennifer. "Rents Go Up, While Diversity Declines." 1998. *Boston Globe*, January 31, 1998.

Bakanic, Von. 1995. "I'm Not Prejudiced, But . . . : A Deeper Look at Racial Attitudes." *Sociological Inquiry* 65(1): 67–86.

Banfield, Edward. 1970. *The Unheavenly City*. Boston: Little, Brown.

Barnes, Linda. 1995. *Hardware*. New York: Delacorte Press.

Bartik, Timothy J. 1992. "Economic Development and Black Economic Success." Draft final report. Kalamazoo, Mich.: W. E. Upjohn Institute for Employment Research. (October).

Becker, Gary S. 1957. *The Economics of Discrimination*. Chicago: University of Chicago Press.

——. 1985. "Human Capital, Effort, and the Sexual Division of Labor." *Journal of Labor Economics* 3(January, suppl.).

Bendick, Marc Jr., Charles W. Jackson, and Victor A. Reinoso. 1994. "Measuring Employment Discrimination Through Controlled Experiments." *Review of Black Political Economy* (Summer): 25–48.

Bergmann, Barbara R. 1974. "Occupational Segregation, Wages, and Profits When Employers Discriminate by Race or Sex." *Eastern Economics Journal* 1(April/May).

Biddle, Frederic M. 1993. "Kentucky Wins Stride Rite Shopping Center." *Boston Globe*, January 8, 1993.

Biddle, Frederic M., and Josh Hyatt. 1992. "City, State at Odds over Stride Rite Plan." *Boston Globe*, December 19, 1992.

Blackburn, McKinley L., David E. Bloom, and Richard B. Freeman. 1990. "The Declining Economic Position of Less Skilled American Men." In *A Future of Lousy Jobs?*, edited by Gary Burtless. Washington, D.C.: Brookings Institution.

Blalock, Hubert M. Jr. 1967. *Toward a Theory of Minority-Group Relations*. New York: Capricorn Books.

Blanton, Kimberly. 1998. "Workers Flee Mass. High Costs." *Boston Globe*, December 6, 1998.

Blau, Francine D., Marianne A. Ferber, and Anne E. Winkler. 1998. *The Economics of Women, Men, and Work*, 3rd ed. Upper Saddle River, N.J.: Prentice-Hall.

Blau, Peter, and Otis Dudley Duncan. 1967. *The American Occupational Structure*. New York: Wiley.

Bledsoe, Timothy, Susan Welch, Lee Sigelman, and Michael Combs. 1995. "Residential Context and Racial Solidarity Among African Americans." *American Journal of Political Science* 39(2): 434–38.

Blewett, Peter F. 1976. "The New People: An Introduction to the Ethnic History of Lowell." In *Cotton Was King: A History of Lowell, Massachusetts*, edited by Arthur L. Eno Jr. Lowell, Mass.: Lowell Historical Society.

Blouin, Francis X. 1978. *The Boston Region 1810–1850: A Study of Urbanization*. Ann Arbor, Mich.: UMI Research Press.

Bluestone, Barry. 1974. "The Personal Earnings Distribution: Individual and Institutional Determinants." Ph.D. diss., University of Michigan.

——. 1990. "The Great U-Turn Revisited: Economic Restructuring, Jobs, and the Redistribution of Earnings." In *Jobs, Earnings, and Employment Growth Policies in the United States*, edited by John D. Kasarda. Boston: Kluwer.

——. 1993. "UMass/Boston: An Economic Impact Analysis." University of Massachusetts at Boston: John W. McCormack Institute of Public Affairs (January).

——. 1994. "The Inequality Express." *The American Prospect* (November).

Bluestone, Barry, and Bennett Harrison. 1987. "The Growth of Low-Wage Employment, 1963–1986." *American Economic Review Papers and Proceedings* 78(May).

———. 2000. *Growing Prosperity: The Battle for Growth with Equity in the 21st Century*. Boston: Houghton Mifflin.

Bluestone, Barry, and Stephen Rose. 1997. "Overworked and Underemployed: Unraveling an Economic Enigma." *The American Prospect* (April).

———. 1998. "The Growth in Working Time and the Implications for Macro Policy." Public Policy Brief. Annandale-on-Hudson, N.Y.: Jerome Levy Institute of Bard College.

Bluestone, Barry, Mary Huff Stevenson, and Chris Tilly. 1992. "An Assessment of the Impact of Deindustrialization and Spatial Mismatch on the Labor Market Outcomes of Young White, Black, and Latino Men and Women Who Have Limited Schooling." Boston: John W. McCormack Institute of Public Affairs.

Bobo, Lawrence, James H. Johnson, Jr., and Melvin L. Oliver. 1992. "Stereotyping and the Multicity Survey: Notes on Measurement, Determinants and Effects." Occasional Working Paper Series 1991–1992, vol. 2, no. 8. Los Angeles: UCLA Center for the Study of Urban Poverty.

Bobo, Lawrence, and James R. Kluegel. 1991. "Whites' Stereotypes, Social Distance and Perceived Discrimination Toward Blacks, Hispanics, and Asians: Toward a Multiethnic Framework." Paper presented at the 86th Annual Meeting of the American Sociological Association. Cincinnati, Ohio (August 23–27, 1991).

———. 1993. "Opposition to Race-Targeting: Self-Interest, Stratification Ideology or Racial Attitudes?" *American Sociological Review* 58(4): 443–64.

———. 1997. "Status, Ideology and Dimensions of Whites' Racial Beliefs and Attitudes: Progress and Stagnation." In *Racial Attitudes in the 1990s: Continuity and Change*, edited by Jack Martin and Steven Tuch. Westport, Conn.: Praeger.

Bobo, Lawrence, and Ryan A. Smith. 1994. "Antipoverty Policy, Affirmative Action, and Racial Attitudes. In *Confronting Poverty: Prescriptions for Change*, edited by Sheldon H. Danziger, Gary D. Sandefur, and Daniel H. Weinberg. New York/Cambridge, Mass.: Russell Sage Foundation/Harvard University Press.

Bobo, Lawrence, Camille L. Zubrinsky, James H. Johnson, and Melvin L. Oliver. 1995. "Work Orientation, Job Discrimination, and Ethnicity: A Focus Group Perspective." *Research in the Sociology of Work* 5: 45–85.

Bolster, W. Jeffrey. 1997. *Black Jacks: African American Seamen in the Age of Sail*. Cambridge, Mass.: Harvard University Press.

Borges-Mendez, Ramon. 1994. "Urban and Regional Restructuring and Barrio Formation in Massachusetts: The Cases of Lowell, Lawrence, and Holyoke." Ph.D. diss., Massachusetts Institute of Technology, Department of Urban Studies and Planning (October).

Borjas, George. 1994. "The Economics of Immigration." *Journal of Economic Literature* 32(4): 1667–1717.

——. 1996. *Labor Economics*. New York: McGraw-Hill.

Boston Globe. 1990. "Walking Boston's Racial Hate Beat, Where No Crime Is Minor." Metro/Region, September 1, 1990, p. 26.

——. 1992. "1992 Rental Picture Improves." December 30, 1992, p. 59.

——. 1993a. "A community of contradictions." Metro/Region, February 22, 1993. p. 13.

——. 1993b. "South Boston High Erupts; 200 Youths Clash in Racial Brawl After Week of Tensions." Metro/Region, May 7, 1993. p. 1.

——. 1994a. "S. Boston Parents Say State Fueling Racial Tension," April 17, 1994, p. 29.

——. 1994b. "Housing Project Residents Cite Race in South Boston Incidents," June 13, 1994. p. 15.

——. 1994c. "2 Asian Men Beaten in S. Boston Attack," June 21, 1994. p. 16.

——. 1994d. "2 White Teenagers Hurt in South Boston Attack," July 18, 1994. p. 13.

——. 1995. "High Court Says Veterans Can Bar Gays from Parade; Speech Rights at Issue in St. Patrick's event." Metro/Region, June 20, 1995, p. 1.

——. 1996. "2 Hispanics Charged in S. Boston Attack," April 5, 1996. p. 25.

Boston Herald. 1994. "Law Must Work Equally for All, Unless You're in Massachusetts," January 2, 1994, p. 6.

Boston Redevelopment Authority, Economic Development and Industrial Corporation. n.d. "A Brief History of Boston's Planning, Economic, and Industrial Development Agency."

Boston Redevelopment Authority, Policy Development and Research Department. 1993. "Digital and Stride Rite Cause Roxbury Job Loss." Insight: A Briefing Report on a Topic of Current Interest (January 15).

Bound, John, and Laura Dresser. 1999. "The Erosion of the Relative Earnings of Young African American Women During the 1980s." In *Latinas and African American Women at Work: Race, Gender, and Economic Inequality*, edited by Irene Browne. New York: Russell Sage Foundation.

Bound, John, and Richard Freeman. 1992. "What Went Wrong? The Erosion of the Relative Earnings and Employment of Young Black Men in the 1980s." *Quarterly Journal of Economics* 107(1): 201–32.

Bound, John, and Harry J. Holzer. 1993. "Industrial Shifts, Skills Levels, and the Labor Market for White and Black Males." *Review of Economics and Statistics* 75(3): 387–96.

Bound, John, and George Johnson. 1992. "Changes in the Structure of Wages in the 1980s: An Evaluation of Alternative Explanations." *American Economic Review* 82(3): 371–92.

Boyer, Richard O., and Herbert M. Morais. 1972. *Labor's Untold Story,*

3rd ed. New York: United Electrical, Radio and Machine Workers of America.

Bradbury, Katherine L., Anthony Downs, and Kenneth A. Small. 1982. *Urban Decline and the Future of American Cities.* Washington, D.C.: Brookings Institution.

Braddock, JoMills H., and James M. McPartland. 1987. "How Minorities Continue to Be Excluded from Equal Employment Opportunities: Research on Labor Market and Institutional Barriers." *Journal of Social Issues* 43: 5–39.

Brooks, Thomas R. 1971. *Toil and Trouble: A History of American Labor,* 2nd ed. New York: Dell.

Brown, Charles, James Hamilton, and James Medoff. 1990. *Employers Large and Small.* Cambridge, Mass.: Harvard University Press.

Brown, Jeffrey. 1982. "Profile of Boston 1929–1980: Economic and Demographic Characteristics." Boston Redevelopment Authority Research Department (October).

Browne, Irene, and Cynthia Hewitt. 1995. "Networks, Discrimination or Location? Explaining Job Segregation Among African Americans." Paper prepared for Russell Sage Foundation Conference on the Multi-City Study of Urban Inequality (September).

Browne, Lynn. "High Technology and Business Services." 1988. In *The Massachusetts Miracle: High Technology and Economic Revitalization,* edited by David Lampe. Cambridge, Mass.: MIT Press.

Browne, Lynn, and Geoffrey M. B. Tootel. 1995. "Race and Mortgage Lending: Dissecting the Controversy." Regional Review, Federal Reserve Bank of Boston. (Fall): 19–24.

Bulow, Jeremy L., and Lawrence Summers. 1985. "A Theory of Dual Labor Markets with Application to Industrial Policy, Discrimination, and Keynesian Unemployment." Working paper 1666. Cambridge, Mass., National Bureau of Economic Research, July.

Burtless, Gary. 1990. *A Future of Lousy Jobs?* Washington, D.C.: Brookings Institutions.

———. 1996. "Trends in the Level and Distribution of U.S. Living Standards, 1973–1993." Working paper. Washington, D.C.: Brookings Institution.

Burtt, Everett J. 1961. "Changing Labor Supply Characteristics Along Route 128." Research report to Federal Reserve Bank of Boston #17.

Bushnell, Davis. 1999. "Lowell Gains Momentum." *Boston Sunday Globe,* May 23, 1999.

Cahn, William. 1980. *Lawrence 1912: The Bread & Roses Strike.* New York: Pilgrim Press.

Campbell, Robert. 1994. "The New Urban Ring Would Give the Hub an Economic Rim." *Boston Globe,* October 30, 1994.

Campen, Jim. 1995. "Changing Patterns: Mortgage Lending in Boston, 1990–1993." Paper. Massachusetts Community and Banking Council (July).

———. 1996. "Changing Patterns III: Mortgage Lending to Traditionally Underserved Borrowers and Neighborhoods in Boston, 1990–1995." Massachusetts Community and Banking Council (December).

Canellos, Peter S. 1989a. "After 20 Years, Anti-snob Zoning Found Ineffective." *Boston Globe*, January 1, 1989.

———. 1989b. "Many Try to Slam Door on Subsidized Housing." *Boston Globe*, January 2, 1989.

———. 1989c. "Changes in Rules, Attitudes Prescribed on Housing Logjam." *Boston Globe*, January 3, 1989.

Cappelli, Peter. 1993. "Are Skill Requirements Rising? Evidence from Production and Clerical Jobs." Industrial and Labor Relations Review 46(3): 515–30.

Carlaw, Christopher. 1976. "Boston and the Flight to the Sunbelt." Boston Redevelopment Authority, Research Report.

Carnoy, Martin. 1994. *Faded Dreams: The Politics and Economics of Race in America*. New York: Cambridge University Press.

Carrington, William J., and Kenneth R. Troske. 1995. "Gender Segregation in Small Firms." *Journal of Human Resources* 30(3): 503–33.

Carroll, Walter F. 1989. *Brockton: From Rural Parish to Urban Center, An Illustrated History*. Northridge, Calif.: Windsor Publications.

Chacon, Richard. 1996a. "Minority Families File Suit Against BHA." *Boston Globe*, December 18, 1996.

———. 1996b. "Plan Released for Land Above Artery." Boston Globe, March 7, 1996.

Chiu, Alexis. 1997a. "Blacks Answering Suburbia's Call." *Boston Globe*, July 24, 1997.

———. 1997b. "Chelsea at Bottom in Reading Test Score." *Boston Globe*, August 15, 1997.

Chu, Doris C. J. 1987. "Chinese in Massachusetts: Their Experiences and Contributions. Boston: Chinese Cultural Institution.

Chung, Tom L. 1995. "Asian Americans in Enclaves—They Are Not One Community: New Modes of Asian American Settlement." *Asian American Policy Review* 5: 78–94.

Cisneros, Henry G., ed. 1993. *Interwoven Destinies: Cities and the Nation*. New York: W.W. Norton.

Citizens Commission on Civil Rights. 1986. "The Federal Government and Equal Housing Opportunity: A Continuing Failure." In *Critical Perspectives on Housing: Philadelphia*, edited by Rachel Bratt, Ann Myerson, and Chester Hartman. Philadelphia: Temple University Press.

City of Boston. 1995. "Boston's Economy: Excerpt from the Official Statement of the City of Boston, Massachusetts. $75,000,000 General Obligation Bonds." (September.)

Clark, W.A.V. 1986. "Residential Segregation in American Cities." *Population Research and Policy Review* 5: 95–127.

———. 1988. "Understanding Residential Segregation in American

Cities: Interpreting the Evidence: Reply to Galster." *Population Research and Policy Review* 7: 193–97.

———. 1991. "Residential Preferences and Neighborhood Racial Segregation: A Test of the Schilling Segregation Model." *Demography* 28(1): 1–19.

———. 1992. "Residential Preferences and Residential Choices in a Multiethnic Context." *Demography* 29(3): 451–66.

Coate, Stephen, and Glenn C. Loury. 1993. "Will Affirmative-Action Policies Eliminate Negative Stereotypes?" *American Economic Review* 83(5): 1220–40.

Cole, Caroline Louise. 1997. "School Board Cool to Lawrence Plea." *Boston Globe*, August 15, 1997.

Coleman, James. 1988. "Social Capital in the Creation of Human Capital." *American Journal of Sociology* 94, suppl. P.S. 96.

Colman, William G. 1975. *Cities, Suburbs and States: Governing and Financing Urban America*. New York: Free Press.

Commonwealth of Massachusetts. Division of Employment and Training. 1999a. "Employment and Wages in Boston." ES-202 Series.

———. 1999b. "Labor Force and Unemployment Rate Data."

Conzen, Michael P., and George K. Lewis. 1976. *Boston: A Geographical Portrait*. Cambridge, Mass.: Ballinger.

Cook, Clifford. 1997. *City of Cambridge, Massachusetts: Demographic and Socio-Economic Statistics*. Planning Data Manager, Cambridge Community Development Department, September 8, 1997.

Corcoran, Mary, Linda Datcher, and Greg Duncan. 1980. "Information and Influence Networks in Labor Markets." In *Five Thousand American Families: Patterns of Economic Progress*, edited by Greg Duncan and James Morgan. Ann Arbor, Mich.: Institute for Social Research.

Corcoran, Mary, Colleen M. Heflin, and Belinda I. Reyes. 1999. "Latina Women in the U.S.: The Economic Progress of Mexican and Puerto Rican Women." In *Latinas and African American Women at Work: Race, Gender, and Economic Inequality*, edited by Irene Browne. New York: Russell Sage Foundation.

Corcoran Mary, and Sharon Parrott. 1998. "Black Women's Economic Progress." In *Latinas and African American Women at Work: Race, Gender, and Economic Inequality*, edited by Irene Browne. New York: Russell Sage Foundation.

Council of Economic Advisers. 1997. *The Economic Report of the President*. Washington: U.S. Government Printing Office.

Cromwell, Adelaide M. 1994. *The Other Brahmins: Boston's Black Upper Class, 1750–1950*. Fayetteville: University of Arkansas Press.

Curran, Karen. 1997. "Affordable Housing Posts a Victory in Dover." *Boston Globe*, May 10, 1997.

Damico, R., and N. L. Maxwell. 1995. "The Continuing Significance of Race in Minority Male Joblessness." *Social Forces* 73: 969–91.

Dauphinais, Paul R. 1996. "Être a l'ouvrage ou être maîtresse de maison:

French-Canadian Women and Work in Late Nineteenth-Century Massachusetts." In *Women of the Commonwealth: Work, Family, and Social Change in Nineteenth-Century Massachusetts*, edited by Susan L. Porter. Amherst: University of Massachusetts Press.

Davis, Mike, Steven Hiatt, Marie Kennedy, Susan Ruddick, and Michael Sprinker, eds. 1990. *Fire in the Hearth: The Radical Politics of Place in America*. London: Verso.

DiNardo, John E., and Jörn-Steffen-Pischke. 1996. "The Returns to Computer Use Revisited: Have Pencils Changed the Wage Structure Too?" Working paper. MIT Department of Economics (April).

Dipboye, Robert L. 1982. "Self-fulfilling Prophecies in the Selection-Recruitment Interview." *Academy of Management Review* 7: 579–86.

Dorfman, Nancy. 1988. "Route 128: The Development of a Regional High Technology Economy." In *The Massachusetts Miracle: High Technology and Economic Revitalization*, edited by David Lampe. Cambridge, Mass.: MIT Press.

Dreier, Peter. 1995. "Boston's West End 35 Years After the Bulldozer." *Planning* (August): 14–17.

Drennan, Matthew, Emanuel Tobier, and Jonathan Lewis. 1996. "The Interruption of Income Convergence and Income Growth in Large Cities in the 1980s." *Urban Studies* 33(1): 63.

Dublin, Thomas. 1994. *Transforming Women's Work: New England Lives in the Industrial Revolution*. Ithaca, N.Y.: Cornell University Press.

Dukakis, Michael, and Rosabeth Moss Kanter. 1988. *Creating the Future*. Cambridge, Mass.: MIT Press.

Early, Frances H. 1991. "The French-Canadian Family Economy and Standard-of-Living in Lowell, Massachusetts, 1870." In *The Continuing Revolution: A History of Lowell, Massachusetts*, edited by Robert Weible. Lowell, Mass.: Lowell Historical Society.

Edel, Matthew, Elliott Sclar, and Daniel Luria. 1984. *Shaky Palaces: Homeownership and Social Mobility in Boston's Suburbanization*. New York: Columbia University Press.

Ehrlich, Bruce D. 1987. "The Politics of Economic Development Planning: Boston in the 1980s." Masters thesis, Massachusetts Institute of Technology, Department of Urban Studies and Planning.

Eisenmenger, Robert. 1967. *The Dynamics of Growth in New England's Economy, 1870–1964*. Middletown, Conn.: Wesleyan University Press.

———. 1968. "The New England Region: Problems of a Mature Economy." Papers and proceedings of a conference held at the University of Connecticut (November 18, 1967). General Series #2 (March).

Ellen, Ingrid G. 1997. "Welcome Neighbors? New Evidence on the Possibility of Stable Racial Integration." *The Brookings Review* 15(1): 18–21.

Ellison, C. G., and M. A. Musick. 1993. "Southern Intolerance—A Fundamentalist Effect." *Social Forces* 72(December): 379–98.

Ellison, C. G., and D. A. Powers. 1994. "The Contact Hypothesis and Racial Attitudes Among Black Americans." *Social Science Quarterly* 75: 385–400.

England, Paula, George Farkas, Barbara Kilbourne, and Thomas Dou. 1988. "Explaining Occupational Sex Segregation and Wages: Findings from a Model with Fixed Effects." *American Sociological Review* 53 (4): 544–58.

Estle, Edwin. 1968. "A Summary of the New England Economy: Past, Present and Future." Federal Reserve Bank of Boston (April).

Eswaren, Mukesh, and Ashok Kotwal. 1985. "A Theory of Two-Tier Labor Markets in Agrarian Economies," *American Economic Review* 75(1): 162–177.

Falbel, Stephen, and Sonia Hamel. 1989. "The Demographics of Commuting in Greater Boston." Central Transportation Planning Staff.

Farley, Reynolds. 1996. *The New American Reality: Who We Are, How We Got Here, Where We Are Going.* New York: Russell Sage Foundation.

Farley, Reynolds, and Walter R. Allen. 1987. *The Color Line and the Quality of Life in America.* New York: Russell Sage Foundation.

Farley, Reynolds, Sheldon Danziger, and Harry J. Holzer. 2000. *Detroit Divided.* New York: Russell Sage Foundation.

Farley, Reynolds, and William H. Frey. 1994. "Changes in the Segregation of Whites from Blacks: Small Steps Toward a More Integrated Society." *American Sociological Review* 59(1): 23–45.

Farley, Reynolds, Howard Schuman, Suzanne Bianchi, Diane Colasanto, and Shirley Hatchett. 1978. "Chocolate City, Vanilla Suburbs: Will the Trend Toward Racially Separate Communities Continue?" *Social Science Research* 7(December): 319–44.

Farley, Reynolds, Charlotte Steeh, Tara Jackson, Maria Krysan, and Keith Reeves. 1993. "Continued Racial Residential Segregation in Detroit: 'Chocolate City, Vanilla Suburbs' Revisited." *Journal of Housing Research* 4: 1–39.

Farley, Reynolds, Charlotte Steeh, Maria Krysan, Tara Jackson, and Keith Reeves. 1994. "Stereotypes and Segregation: Neighborhoods in the Detroit Area." *American Journal of Sociology* 100(3): 750–80.

Feagin, Joe R. 1991. "The Continuing Significance of Race: Anti-Black Discrimination in Public Places." *American Sociological Review* 56(1): 101–16.

Feagin, Joe R., and Douglas Lee Eckberg. 1980. "Discrimination: Motivation, Action, Effects, and Context." *Annual Review of Sociology* 6: 1–20.

Feagin, Joe R., and Melvin P. Sikes. 1994. *Living with Racism: The Black Middle Class Experience.* Boston: Beacon.

Feagin, Joe R., and Hernan Vera. 1995. *White Racism.* New York: Routledge.

Featherman, David L., and Robert M. Hauser. 1978. *Opportunity and Change.* New York: Academic Press.

Federal Writers Project of the Works Progress Administration for the

State of Massachusetts. 1937. *Massachusetts: A Guide to Its Places and People.* Boston: Houghton Mifflin.

Ferguson, Ronald. 1991. "Paying for Public Education: New Evidence on How and Why Money Matters." *Harvard Journal of Legislation* 28.

———. 1993. "New Evidence on the Growing Value of Skill and Consequences for Racial Disparity and Returns to Schooling." Paper R93-34 (September). Cambridge, Mass.: John F. Kennedy School of Government.

———. 1995. "Shifting Challenges: Fifty Years of Economic Change Toward Black-White Earnings Equality." *Daedalus* 124 (1) Winter.

———. 1996. "Shifting Challenges: Fifty Years of Economic Change Toward Black-White Earnings Equality." In *An American Dilemma Revisited: Race Relations in a Changing World*, edited by Obie Clayton, Jr. New York: Russell Sage Foundation.

———. 1996. "Additional Evidence on How and Why Money Matters: A Production Function Analysis of Alabama Schools." In *Holding Schools Accountable: Performance-Based Reform in Education*, edited by Helen F. Ladd. Washington, D.C.: Brookings Institution.

———. 1997. "Evidence that Schools Can Narrow The Black-White Test Score Gap." In *The Black-White Test Score Gap*, edited by Christopher Jencks and Meredith Phillips. Washington, D.C.: Brookings.

———. 1998. "Evidence That Schools Can Narrow the Black-White Test Score Gap." In *The Black-White Test Score Gap*, edited by Christopher Jencks and Meredith Phillips. Washington, D.C.: Brookings Institution.

Firebaugh, Glenn, and Kenneth E. Davis. 1988. "Trends in Anti-Black Prejudice, 1972–1984: Region and Cohort Effects." *American Journal of Sociology* 94(2): 251–72.

Fix, Michael, and Raymond Struyk. 1994. *Clear and Convincing Evidence.* Washington, D.C.: Urban Institute Press.

Follett, Robert S., Michael P. Ward, and Finis Welch. 1993. "Problems in Assessing Employment Discrimination." *American Economic Review* 83(2): 73–78.

Formisano, Ronald P. 1991. *Boston Against Busing: Race, Class, and Ethnicity in the 1960s and 1970s.* Chapel Hill: University of North Carolina Press.

Freeman, Richard B. 1990. "How Much Has De-Unionization Contributed to the Rise in Male Earnings Inequality?" In *Uneven Tides: Rising Inequality in America*, edited by Sheldon Danziger and Peter Gottschalk. New York: Russell Sage Foundation.

Freeman, Richard B., and James Medoff. 1984. *What Do Unions Do?* New York: Basic Books.

Galster, George C. 1990. "Neighborhood Racial Change, Segregationist Sentiments, and Affirmative Marketing Policies." *Journal of Urban Economics* 27(3): 344–61.

Gamm, Gerald H. 1995. "In Search of Suburbs: Boston's Jewish Districts, 1843–1994." In *The Jews of Boston: Essays on the Occasion of the Centenary (1895–1995) of the Combined Jewish Philanthropies of Greater Boston*, edited by Jonathan D. Sarna and Ellen Smith. Boston: Combined Jewish Philanthropies of Greater Boston.

Gans, Herbert. 1962. *The Urban Villagers: Group and Class in the Life of Italian-Americans*. New York: Free Press.

Garreau, Joel. 1992. *Edge City: Life on the New Frontier*. New York: Doubleday.

Glaab, Charles N., and A. Theodore Brown. 1967. *A History of Urban America*. New York: Macmillan.

Glaessel-Brown, Eleanor E. 1991. "A Time of Transition: Colombian Textile Workers in Lowell in the 1970s." In *The Continuing Revolution: A History of Lowell, Massachusetts*, edited by Robert Weible. Lowell, Mass.: Lowell Historical Society.

Glickman, Norman J., Michael L. Lahr, and Elvin K. Wyly. 1996. "The State of the Nation's Cities: America's Changing Urban Life." Working paper. Center for Urban Policy Research, Rutgers University, New Brunswick, N.J. (April).

Goetz, Rolf, and Mark Johnson. 1993. *1990 Census of Population and Housing—Page Profiles for Boston's 16 Planning Districts*. Boston Redevelopment Authority (March).

Gordon, David M. 1979. *The Working Poor: Towards a State Agenda*. Washington, D.C.: Council of State Planning Agencies.

Gordon, David, Richard Edwards, and Michael Reich. 1982. *Segmented Work, Divided Workers*. Cambridge, U.K.: Cambridge University Press.

Gosselin, Peter G. 1997. "Market Up; Bonuses, Too: Profits Promote Living Large." *Boston Globe*. December 21, 1997.

Granovetter, Mark. 1974. *Getting a Job: A Study of Contracts and Careers*. Cambridge, Mass.: Harvard University Press.

———. 1982. "The Strength of Weak Ties: A Network Theory Revisited." In *Social Structure and Network Analysis*, edited by Peter V. Marsden and Nancy Lin. Beverly Hills, Calif.: Sage Publications.

Halter, Marilyn. 1995. *New Migrants in the Marketplace: Boston's Ethnic Entrepreneurs*. Amherst: University of Massachusetts Press.

Handlin, Oscar. 1959. *Boston's Immigrants, A Study in Acculturation*, rev. ed. Cambridge, Mass.: Harvard University Press.

Harrison, Bennett. 1984. "Regional Restructuring and 'Good Business Climates': The Economic Transformation of New England Since World War II." In *Sunbelt/Frostbelt: Urban Development and Regional Restructuring*, edited by William K. Tabb. New York: Oxford University Press.

———. 1994. *Lean and Mean: Why Large Corporations Will Continue to Dominate the Global Economy*. New York: Basic Books.

Harrison, Bennett, and Barry Bluestone. 1988. *The Great U-Turn: Corporate Restructuring and the Polarizing of America*. New York: Basic Books.

Harrison, Bennett, and Lucy Gorham. 1992. "Growing Inequality in Black Wages in the 1980's and the Emergence of an African-American

Middle Class." *Journal of Policy Analysis and Management* 11(2): 235–53.

Hart, Jordana. 1992. "Blacks Tell AG of Trouble with Brockton Police." *Boston Globe*, May 30, 1992.

Heilbrun, James. 1987. *Urban Economics and Public Policy*, 3rd ed. New York: St. Martin's Press.

Herbers, John. 1974. "Suburban Resistance to Subsidized Housing." In *Suburbia in Transition*, edited by Louis H. Masotti and Jeffrey K. Hadden. New York: New Viewpoints.

Herrnstein, Richard. 1971. "I.Q." *The Atlantic Monthly* (September).

Herrnstein, Richard, and Charles Murray. 1994. *The Bell Curve: Intelligence and Class Structure in American Life*. New York: Free Press.

Hicks, J. R. 1932. *The Theory of Wages*. London: Macmillan.

Hill, Catherine. 1996. Ph.D. Candidate, Rutgers University. Interview, August 22, 1996.

Hochschild, Jennifer L. 1984. *The New American Dilemma: Liberal Democracy and School Desegregation*. New Haven, Conn.: Yale University Press.

———. 1995. *Facing Up to the American Dream*. Princeton, N.J.: Princeton University Press.

Holmes, Steven A. 1997. "New Survey Shows Americans Pessimistic on Race Relations." *New York Times*, June 11, 1997, p. A16.

Holzer, Harry J. 1991. "The Spatial Mismatch Hypothesis: What Has the Evidence Shown?" Urban Studies 28(1): 105–22.

———. 1994. "Black Employment Problems: New Evidence, Old Questions." *Journal of Policy Analysis and Management* 13(4).

———. 1996a. "Employer Hiring Decisions and Antidiscrimination Policy." In *Demand-Side Strategies for Low-Wage Labor Markets*, edited by R. Freeman and P. Gottschalk. New York: Russell Sage Foundation.

———. 1996b. *What Employers Want: Job Prospects for Less Educated Workers*. New York: Russell Sage Foundation.

———. 1996c. "Why Do Small Firms Hire Fewer Blacks Than Large Ones?" Discussion Paper, Institute for Research on Poverty, University of Wisconsin at Madison.

Holzer, Harry J., and Sheldon Danziger. Forthcoming. "Are Jobs Available for Disadvantaged Groups in Urban Areas?" In *Urban Inequality: Evidence from Four Cities*, edited by Lawrence Bobo, Alice O'Connor, and Chris Tilly. New York: Russell Sage Foundation.

Holzer, Harry J., and David Neumark. 1996. "Are Affirmative Action Hires Less Qualified? Evidence from Employer-Employee Data on New Hires." Mimeo. Department of Economics, Michigan State University.

Howe, Peter J. 1995. "Tough Welfare Rules Set for Weld Signature Today." *Boston Globe*, February 10, 1995, p. 1.

Howell, David, and Edward Wolff. 1991. "Trends in the Growth and Distribution of Skill in the U.S. Workplace, 1960–1985." *Industrial and Labor Relations Review* 44(3): 481–501.

Hoy, John C. 1988. "Higher Skills and the New England Economy." In *The Massachusetts Miracle: High Technology and Economic Revitalization*, edited by David Lampe. Cambridge, Mass.: MIT Press.

Huff, Mary. 1966. "Alleviation of Blight and Slums: The Problem, the Alternatives, a Case Study." Senior honors thesis, Economics Department, Brandeis University.

Hughes, Bruce. 1997. "Overall Economic Development Strategy Plan." Old Colony Planning Council (March 20).

Ihlanfeldt, Keith. 1997. "The Geography of Economic and Social Opportunity Within Metropolitan Areas." Prepared for the Committee on Improving the Future of U.S. Cities Through Improved Metropolitan Area Governance, National Research Council/National Academy of Science (February).

———. 1992. "The Spatial Distribution of Black Employment between the Central City and the Suburbs." *Economic Inquiry*: 693–707.

Ilg, Randy E. 1996. "The Nature of Employment Growth, 1989–1995." *Monthly Labor Review* 119(6): 29–36.

Jackman, Mary R., and M. Crane. 1986. "'Some of My Best Friends Are Black . . .' Interracial Friendship and Whites' Racial Attitudes." *Public Opinion Quarterly* 50(4): 459–86.

Jackson, B., E. R. Gerber, and B. E. Cain. 1994. "Coalitional Prospects in a Multi-Racial Society—African-American Attitudes Toward Other Minority Groups." *Political Research Quarterly* 47(2): 277–94.

Jackson, Kenneth. 1985. *Crabgrass Frontier: The Suburbanization of the United States*. New York: Oxford University Press.

Jacobs, Jane. 1961. *The Death and Life of Great American Cities*. New York: Vintage.

Jacobsen, Cardell K. 1985. "Resistance to Affirmative Action: Self-Interest or Racism?" *Journal of Conflict Resolution* 29: 306–29.

Jaynes, Gerald David, and Robin M. Williams, Jr. 1989. *A Common Destiny: Blacks and American Society*. Washington, D.C.: National Academy Press.

Jencks, Christopher. 1972. *Inequality: A Reassessment of the Effect of Family and Schooling in America*. New York: Basic Books.

Jencks, Christopher, and Susan Mayer. 1990. "Residential Segregation, Job Proximity, and Black Job Opportunities." In *Inner City Poverty in the United States*, edited by Laurence E. Lind and Michael McGeary. Washington, D.C.: National Academy Press.

Jencks, Christopher, and Meredith Phillips. 1996. "Does Learning Pay Off in the Job Market?" Paper prepared for the Meritocracy and Equality Seminar at the Kennedy School of Government. Cambridge (April 18, 1996).

Johnson, George, and Kenwood Youmans. 1971. "Union Relative Wage Effects by Age and Education." *Industrial and Labor Relations Review* 24(January).

Johnson, James H., Melvin L. Oliver, and Lawrence Bobo. 1994. "Understanding the Contours of Deepening Urban Inequality: Theoretical

Underpinnings and Research Design of a Multi-city Study." *Urban Geography* 15(1): 78–90.

Johnson, Violet. 1995. "Culture, Economic Stability, and Entrepreneurship: The Case of British West Indians in Boston." In *New Migrants in the Marketplace: Boston's Ethnic Entrepreneurs*, edited by Marilyn Halter. Amherst: University of Massachusetts Press.

Jones, Henrik. n.d. "The Conflict of Regional Planning and Private Initiative in the Development of Route 128." Unpublished paper.

Juravich, Tom, William F. Hartford, and James R. Green. 1996. *Commonwealth of Toil: Chapters in the History of Massachusetts' Workers and Their Unions.* Amherst: University of Massachusetts Press.

Kahn, E. J. 1986. *The Problem Solvers: A History of Arthur D. Little.* Boston: Little, Brown.

Kain, John F. 1968. "Housing Segregation, Negro Employment, and Metropolitan Decentralization." *Quarterly Journal of Economics* 82(May): 175–97.

Kasarda, John. 1988. "Jobs, Migration, and Emerging Urban Mismatches." In *Urban Change and Poverty*, edited by Michael G. McGeary and Laurence E. Lynn. Washington, D.C.: National Academy Press.

———. 1990. "City Jobs and Residents on a Collision Course: The Urban Underclass Dilemma." *Economic Development Quarterly* (December).

———. 1993. "Inner-city Concentrated Poverty and Neighborhood Distress: 1970 to 1990." *Housing Policy Debate* 4(3): 253–302.

Kennedy, Lawrence W. 1992. *Planning the City Upon a Hill: Boston Since 1630.* Amherst: University of Massachusetts Press.

Kennedy, Marie, Mauricio Gaston, and Chris Tilly. 1990. "Roxbury: Capitalist Investment or Community Development?" In *Fire in the Hearth: The Radical Politics of Place in America*, edited by Mike Davis, Steven Hiatt, Marie Kennedy, Susan Ruddick, and Michael Sprinker. London: Verso.

Kennedy, Peter. 1994. *A Guide to Econometrics.* Cambridge, Mass.: MIT Press.

Kennelly, Ivy. 1995. "'That Could Come from Lack of Nurturing': Employers' Images of African-American Women." Master's Thesis, Department of Sociology, University of Georgia.

Kenney, Charles. 1987. "The Aftershock of a Radical Notion." *Boston Globe Magazine.* April 12, 1987.

Kiang, Peter N. 1993. "Education and Community Development Among Nineteenth-Century Irish and Contemporary Cambodians in Lowell, Massachusetts." *New England Journal of Public Policy* 9(1): 51–64.

Kilbourne, Barbara, Paula England, and Kurt Bevon. 1994. "Effects of Individual, Occupational, and Industrial Characteristics on Earnings: Intersections of Race and Gender." *Social Forces* 72(4): 1149–76.

Kinder, Donald R., and Tali Mendelberg. 1995. "Cracks in American Apartheid—The Political Impact of Prejudice Among Desegregated Whites." *Journal of Politics* 57(2): 402–24.

King, Mel. 1981. *Chain of Change: Struggles for Black Community Development*. Boston: South End Press.

Kirschenman, Joleen. 1991. "Gender Within Race in the Labor Market." Presented at the Urban Poverty and Family Life Conference. Chicago (October 10–12, 1991).

Kirschenman, Joleen, and Katherine Neckerman. 1991. "'We'd Love to Hire Them, But . . . ': The Meaning of Race for Employers." In *The Urban Underclass*, edited by Christopher Jencks and Paul E. Peterson. Washington, D.C.: Brookings Institution.

Kleinpenning, G., and L. Hagendoorn. 1993. "Forms of Racism and the Cumulative Dimension of Ethnic Attitudes." *Social Psychology Quarterly* 56: 21–36.

Kluegel, James R. 1990. "Trends in Whites' Explanations of the Black-White Gap in Socioeconomic Status, 1977–1989." *American Sociological Review* 55: 512–25.

Kluegel, James R., and Eliot R. Smith. 1982. "Whites' Beliefs About Blacks' Opportunity." *American Sociological Review* 47: 518–32.

———. 1986. *Beliefs About Inequality: American Views of What Is and What Ought to Be*. Hawthorne, N.Y.: Aldine de Gruyter.

Kodrzycki, Yolanda. 1996. "Labor Markets and Earnings Inequality: A Status Report." *New England Economic Review* (May/June).

Kravitz, D. A., and J. Platania. 1993. "Attitudes and Beliefs About Affirmative Action—Effects of Target and of Respondent Sex and Ethnicity." *Journal of Applied Psychology* 78: 928–38.

Krueger, Alan. 1993. "How Computers Have Changed the Wage Structure: Evidence from Microdata, 1984–1989." *Quarterly Journal of Economics* 108 (February): 33–60.

Krushnic, Richard. 1974. "Postwar Industrial Development on the Periphery of Metropolitan Boston." Working paper 13. Boston Studies in Urban Political Economy, Brandeis University.

Krysan, Maria, Howard Schuman, LesLi Jo Scott, and Paul Beatty. 1994. "Response Rates and Response Content in Mail Versus Face-to-Face Surveys." *Public Opinion Quarterly* 58: 381–99.

Kuhn, Sarah. 1982. "Computer Manufacturing in New England: Structure, Location and Labor in a Growing Industry." Cambridge, Mass.: Joint Center for Urban Studies of MIT and Harvard University.

Lakshmanan, Indira A. R. 1993. "Planners Envision Linking the Hub's Spokes with a Ring." *Boston Globe*, September 20, 1993.

Lambert, A. J. 1995. "Stereotypes and Social Judgment: The Consequences of Group Variability." *Journal of Personality and Social Psychology* 68: 388–403.

Lampe, David, ed. 1988. *The Massachusetts Miracle: High Technology and Economic Revitalization*. Cambridge, Mass.: MIT Press.

La Plaza. 1991. "Who's Cleaning Boston?" WGBH television documentary.

Lehigh, Scot. 1997. "Area's Russian Jews Bridge Two Worlds." *Boston Globe*, April 9, 1997.

Lehr, Dick. 1997. "Classroom Buzz." *Boston Globe*, February 11, 1997.

Leonard, Jonathan. 1990. "The Impact of Affirmative Action Regulation and Equal Opportunity Law on Black Employment." *Journal of Economic Perspectives* 4(Fall): 47–63.

Levine, Hillel, and Lawrence Harmon. 1992. *The Death of an American Jewish Community: A Tragedy of Good Intentions.* New York: Free Press.

Levy, Frank, and Richard Murnane. 1992. "U.S. Earnings Levels and Earnings Inequality: A Review of Recent Trends and Proposed Explanations." *Journal of Economic Literature* 30(September): 1333–81.

Lewis, Diane E., and Tatiana W. Ribadineira. 1997. "Shift from Farm Work Yields Few Gains for Many." *Boston Globe*, May 29, 1997.

Lieberson, Stanley. 1980. *A Piece of the Pie: Blacks and White Immigrants Since 1880.* Berkeley: University of California Press.

Lieberson, Stanley, and Glen Fuguitt. 1967. "Negro-White Occupational Differences in the Absence of Discrimination." *American Journal of Sociology* 73(2): 188–200.

Little, Arthur D., Inc. 1970. *Fostering Industrial Growth in Massachusetts.* Vol. 1. *Cutbacks in Defense Spending and the Economy of Massachusetts, 1968–1972.* Prepared for Governor Francis P. Sargent, Commissioner Carroll P. Sheehan, Department of Commerce and Development, Commonwealth of Massachusetts. (October).

Logan, John R., and Richard D. Alba. 1993. "Locational Returns to Human Capital—Minority Access to Suburban Community Resources." *Demography* 30(2): 243–68.

Lukas, J. Anthony. 1985. *Common Ground: A Turbulent Decade in the Lives of Three American Families.* New York: Knopf.

Lupo, Alan. 1995a. "A Theory Looking for Clout." *Boston Globe*, October 29, 1995.

———. 1995b. "Some Commuters Ready Now for a Circumferential System: Making a Case for the Ring." *Boston Globe*, December 24, 1995, City Weekly, p. 1.

Lupo, Alan, Frank Colcord, and Edmund P. Fowler. 1971. *Rites of Way: The Politics of Transportation in Boston and the U.S. City.* Boston: Little, Brown.

Maassen, G. H., and M. P. M. Degoede. 1993. "Stereotype Measurement and Comparison Between Categories of People." *International Journal of Public Opinion Research* 5: 278–84.

MacQuarrie, Brian. 1999. "Lawrence Seeks Neighborly Solutions." *Boston Globe*, February 28, 1999.

Maio, Gregory R., Victoria M. Esses, and David W. Bell. 1994. "The Formation of Attitudes Toward New Immigrant Groups." *Journal of Applied Social Psychology* 24(19): 1762–76.

Marquand, John P. 1936. *The Late George Apley: A Novel in the Form of a Memoir.* Boston: Little, Brown.

Massachusetts Commission Against Discrimination/Massachusetts Advisory Committee, U.S. Commission on Civil Rights. 1974. "Route 128: The Road to Segregation."

424

Massachusetts Department of Commerce and Development. 1973. "The Golden Semi-circle." (Pamphlet.)

Massachusetts Institute of Technology. 1958. "Economic Impact of Massachusetts Route 128."

Massagli, Michael P. 1993. "Interim Progress Report to the Ford and Russell Sage Foundations. Boston: Center for Survey Research. November 18, 1993.

Massey, Douglas S., and Nancy A. Denton. 1987. "Trends in the Residential Segregation of Blacks, Hispanics, and Asians." *American Sociological Review* 52: 802–25.

———. 1988. "The Dimensions of Residential Segregation." *Social Forces* 67(2): 281–315.

———. 1993. *American Apartheid: Segregation and the Making of the Underclass*. Cambridge, Mass.: Harvard University Press.

Massey, Douglas S., and Zoltan L. Hajnal. 1995. "The Changing Geographic Structure of Black-White Segregation in the United States." *Social Science Quarterly* 76(3): 527–42.

McCabe, Kathy. 1997. "Change and Dollars: Lynn Fosters Minority Firms in Hopes of Renewing Downtown." *Boston Globe*, June 18, 1997.

———. 1999. "From the Bodegas to the High-Tech Job Markets of Today." *Boston Globe*, August 11, 1999.

McKim, Jenifer B. 1997. "A Burial Ground Rich in History: Irish Advocates, Native Americans Want Respective Histories Honored." *Boston Sunday Globe*, June 1, 1997.

Mead, Lawrence. 1986. *Beyond Entitlement: The Social Obligations of Citizenship*. New York: Basic Books.

———. 1992. *The New Politics of Poverty: The Nonworking Poor in America*. New York: Basic Books.

Medoff, Peter, and Holly Sklar. 1994. *Streets of Hope: The Fall and Rise of an Urban Neighborhood*. Boston: South End Press.

Meléndez, Edwin. 1993a. "Latino Poverty and Economic Development in Massachusetts." In *Latino Poverty and Economic Development in Massachusetts*, edited by Edwin Meléndez and Miren Uriarte. Boston: Mauricio Gaston Institute for Latino Community Development and Public Policy, University of Massachusetts at Boston.

———. 1993b. "Understanding Latino Poverty." *Sage Race Relations Abstracts* 18(2): 3–43.

Metropolitan Area Planning Council. 1994. "MetroPlan 2000: The Regional Development Plan for Metropolitan Boston" (April).

———. 1999. "Comprehensive Economic Development Strategy."

Miller, Marc S. 1988. *The Irony of Victory: World War II and Lowell, Massachusetts*. Urbana: University of Illinois Press.

Miller, Steven E. 1974. *The Boston Irish Political Machines, 1830–1973*. Working paper 15. Heller School, Brandeis University (March).

Mincer, Jacob. 1970. "The Distribution of Labor Incomes: A Survey." *Journal of Economic Literature* 8(March): 1–26.

Mishel, Lawrence, and Jared Bernstein. 1994. *The State of Working America*. Armonk, N.Y.: M. E. Sharpe.

Mishel, Lawrence, Jared Bernstein, and John Schmitt. 1999. *The State of Working America*. Ithaca, N.Y.: Cornell University Press.

Montgomery, James D. 1991. "Social Networks and Labor Market Outcomes: Toward an Economic Analysis." *American Economic Review* 81(5): 1408–18.

Moss, Philip, and Chris Tilly. 1991. "Why Black Men Are Doing Worse in the Labor Market: A Review of Supply-Side and Demand-Side Explanations." Working paper. Social Science Research Council, New York (August 1991).

———. 1993. "A Turn for the Worse: Why Black Men's Labor Market Fortunes Have Declined in the United States." *Sage Race Relations Abstracts* 18(1).

———. 1995a. "Raised Hurdles for Black Men: Evidence from Employer Interviews." Working paper 81. Russell Sage Foundation, New York.

———. 1995b. "Skills and Race in Hiring: Quantitative Findings from Face-to-Face Interviews." *Eastern Economic Journal* 21(3).

———. 1996a. "Informal Hiring Practices, Racial Exclusion, and Public Policy." Paper presented at the meetings of the Association for Public Policy Analysis and Management, Pittsburgh, Pa.(October 31–November 2, 1996).

———. 1996b. "'Soft' Skills and Race: An Investigation of Black Men's Employment Problems." *Work and Occupations* 23(3).

———. Forthcoming. "Why Opportunity Isn't Knocking: Racial Inequality and the Demand for Labor." In *Urban Inequality in the United States: Evidence from Four Cities*, edited by Lawrence Bobo, Alice O'Connor, and Chris Tilly.

Move Massachusetts 2000 Walk Boston. "Central Area Surface Street Consensus Plan: December 1995." Final recommendations of the Surface Transportation Action Forum.

Muehlmann, Heinz K., et al. 1970. "Economic Changes in Massachusetts." Massachusetts Department of Commerce and Development (August).

Mullin, John R., Jeanne Armstrong, and Jean Kavanagh. 1986. "From Mill Town to Mill Town: The Transition of a New England Town from a Textile to a High Technology Economy." *Journal of the American Planning Association* (Winter).

Munnell, Alicia H., Geoffrey M. B. Tootel, Lynn E. Browne, and James McEneaney. 1996. "Mortgage Lending in Boston: Interpreting HMDA Data." *American Economic Review* 86(1): 25–53.

Neal, Derek A., and William R. Johnson. 1996. "The Role of Premarket Factors in Black-White Wage Differences." *Journal of Political Economy* 104(5): 869–95.

Nealon, Patricia. 1991. "Census: Minority Population Up in Area." *Boston Sunday Globe*, March 10, 1991.

Neckerman, Kathryn M., and Joleen Kirschenman. 1991. "Hiring Strategies, Racial Bias, and Inner-City Workers." *Social Problems* 38(4): 433–47.

Nickerson, Colin. 1996. " 'It Is Hallowed Ground': Canada Honors Victims of Irish Famine." *Boston Sunday Globe*, June 2, 1996.

O'Brien, Margaret C. 1985. "Diversity and Change in Boston's Neighborhoods: A Comparison of Demographic, Social, and Economic Characteristics of Population and Housing, 1970–1980." Report no. 169. Boston Redevelopment Authority (October).

O'Connor, Edwin. 1956. *The Last Hurrah*. Boston: Little, Brown.

———. 1991. *Bibles, Brahmins, and Bosses: A Short History of Boston*, 3rd ed. Boston: Trustees of the Public Library of the City of Boston.

———. 1993. *Building a New Boston: Politics and Urban Renewal, 1950 to 1970*. Boston: Northeastern University Press.

———. 1995. *The Boston Irish: A Political History*. Boston: Northeastern University Press.

Oi, Walter. 1962. "Labor as a Quasi-Fixed Factor." *Journal of Political Economy* 70(October): 538–55.

Oliver, Melvin L., James H. Johnson, and Lawrence Bobo. 1994. "Unraveling the Paradox of Deepening Urban Inequality: The Multi-City Study of Urban Inequality." *African American Research Perspectives*: 43–52.

Oliver, Melvin L., and Thomas M. Shapiro. 1995. *Black Wealth/White Wealth: A New Perspective on Racial Segregation*. New York: Routledge.

O'Neill, June. 1990. "The Role of Human Capital in Earnings Differences Between Black and White Men." *Journal of Economic Perspectives* 4(4): 25–46.

Orfield, Gary, Susan E. Eaton, and the Harvard Project on School Desegregation. 1996. *Dismantling Desegregation: The Quiet Reversal of Brown v. Board of Education*. New York: New Press.

Osterman, Paul. 1991. "Gains from Growth? The Impact of Full Employment on Poverty in Boston." In *The Urban Underclass*, edited by Christopher Jencks and Paul E. Peterson. Washington, D.C.: Brookings Institution.

———. 1995. "Skill, Training, and Work Organization in American Establishments." *Industrial Relations* 34(2): 125–46.

Page, Marianne. 1995. "Racial and Ethnic Discrimination in Urban Housing Markets: Evidence from a Recent Audit Study." *Journal of Urban Economics* 38(2): 183–206.

Palmer, Thomas. 2000. "Natsios Planning Review of Big Dig's Prime Ocntractors." Boston Globe, April 13, 2000, p. 1.

Peirce, Neal R. 1981. "New England's Resilience." In *Business and Academia: Partners in New England's Economic Revival*, edited by John C. Hoy and Melvin H. Bernstein. Hanover, N.H.: University Press of New England, New England Board of Higher Education.

Pettigrew, Thomas F., and Joanne Martin. 1986. "Shaping the Organizational Context for Black Inclusion." *Journal of Social Issues* 43: 41–78.

Pettigrew, Thomas F., and Marylee C. Taylor. 1990. "Discrimination." In *Encyclopedia of Sociology*, vol. 1. New York: Macmillan.

Piore, Michael J. 1976. "Immigration, Work Expectations, and Labor Market Structure." In *The Diverse Society: Implications for Social Policy*, edited by San Juan Cafferty Pastora and Leon Chestang. Washington, D.C.: National Association of Social Workers.

———. 1979. *Birds of Passage: Migrant Labor and Industrial Societies.* Cambridge, U.K.: Cambridge University Press.

Pleck, Elizabeth H. 1979. *Black Migration and Poverty: Boston 1865–1900.* New York: Academic Press.

Porter, Michael. 1991. *The Competitive Advantage of Massachusetts.* Cambridge, Mass.: Harvard Business School/The Monitor Company.

Powers, D. A., and C. G. Ellison. 1995. "Interracial Contact and Black Racial Attitudes: The Contact Hypothesis and Selectivity Bias." *Social Forces* 74: 205–26.

Powers, John. 1997. "Of Mills and Momentum." *Boston Globe Magazine*, May 11, 1997.

Pulster, Robert. 1997. "The End of Rent Control in Boston." Case Study in fulfillment of Master's Degree requirement, McCormack Institute of Public Affairs, University of Massachusetts at Boston (May 13, 1997).

Quillian, L. 1995. "Prejudice as a Response to Perceived Group Threat: Population Composition and Anti-Immigrant and Racial Prejudice in Europe." *American Sociological Review* 60: 586–611.

Radin, Charles. 1996. "From Haiti to Boston." *Boston Globe Magazine*, December 15, 1996.

Rasell, Edith, Barry Bluestone, and Lawrence Mishel. 1997. *The Prosperity Gap.* Washington, D.C.: Economic Policy Institute.

Reich, Michael. 1981. *Racial Inequality: A Political-Economic Analysis.* Princeton, N.J.: Princeton University Press.

Reid, Alexander. 1995. "Brockton Desegregation Deadlock Is Broken." *Boston Globe*, March 26, 1995.

Reidy, Chris. 1997a. "Spaghetti Tangle: Move to Shut Lowell Pasta Plant Set Stage for a Multifaceted Drama." *Boston Globe*, June 26, 1997.

———. 1997b. "Textile Firm Planning to Buy ex-Prince plant." *Boston Globe*, December 10, 1997.

Reimers, David M. 1983. "An Unintended Reform: The 1965 Immigration Act and Third World Immigration to the United States." *Journal of American Ethnic History* (Fall): 9–28.

Reskin, B. 1993. "Sex Segregation in the Workplace." In *Annual Review of Sociology*, 19. Palo Alto, Calif.: Annual Reviews, Inc.

Rexroat, C. 1993. "Race, Work, and Welfare—Attitudes Toward the Required Employment of Young Mothers Who Use Welfare." *Population Research and Policy Review* 12: 123–38.

Reynolds, Lloyd. 1951. *The Structure of Labor Markets.* New York: Harper and Bros.

Ribadeneira, Tatiana W. 1997. "Essential Shuttle Serves Chinatown." *Boston Globe*, March 9, 1997.

Ropers, Richard H., and Dan J. Pence. 1995. *American Prejudice: With Liberty and Justice for Some*. New York: Insight (Plenum).

Rosegrant, Susan, and David Lampe. 1992. *Route 128: Lessons from Boston's High Tech Community*. New York: Basic Books.

Rusk, David. 1995. *Cities Without Suburbs*, 2nd ed. Washington, D.C.: Woodrow Wilson Center Press.

Ryan, Dennis P. 1983. *Beyond the Ballot Box: A Social History of the Boston Irish, 1845–1917*. Amherst: University of Massachusetts Press.

Sagara, Carlton, and Peter Kiang. 1993. "Recognizing Poverty in Boston's Asian American Community: A Background Paper by the Asian American Resource Workshop for Beyond Poverty: Building Community Through New Perspectives, A Roundtable Series about Poverty in Boston." Boston: Boston Foundation.

Salop, Steven C. 1973. "Wage Differentials in a Dynamic Theory of the Firm." *Journal of Economic Theory* 6(August) 6: 321–44.

Sawhill, Isabel V. 1988. "Poverty in the U.S.: Why Is It So Persistent?" *Journal of Economic Literature* 26(3): 1073–1119.

Saxenian, AnnaLee. 1994. *Regional Advantage: Culture and Competition in Silicon Valley and Route 128*. Cambridge, Mass.: Harvard University Press.

Schinto, Jeanne. 1995. *Huddle Fever: Living in the Immigrant City*. New York: Knopf.

Schor, Juliet. 1991. *The Overworked American*. New York: Basic Books.

Schuman, Howard, and Lawrence Bobo. 1988. "Survey-based Experiments on White Racial Attitudes Toward Residential Segregation." *American Journal of Sociology* 94: 273–99.

Schuman, Howard, Eleanor Singer, Rebecca Donavan, and Claire Sellitz. 1983. "Discriminatory Behavior in New York Restaurants: 1950 and 1981." *Social Indicators Research* 13: 69–83.

Schuman, Howard, Charlotte Steeh, and Lawerence Bobo. 1985. *Racial Attitudes in America: Trends and Interpretations*. Cambridge, Mass.: Harvard University Press.

Scott, Otto. 1974. *The Creative Ordeal: The Story of Raytheon*. New York: Atheneum.

Sewell, William H., and Robert M. Hauser. 1975. *Education, Occupation, and Earnings*. New York: Academic Press.

Shand-Tucci, Douglass. 1988. *Built in Boston: City and Suburb, 1800–1950*. Amherst: University of Massachusetts Press.

Sharkey, Joe. 1991. *Deadly Greed: The Riveting True Story of the Stuart Murder Case That Rocked Boston and Shocked the Nation*. New York: Prentice-Hall Press.

Sharpiro, Carl, and Joseph E. Stiglitz. 1984. "Equilibrium Unemployment as a Worker Discipline Device." *American Economic Review* 74(3): 433–44.

Sidanius, James. 1993. "The Interface Between Racism and Sexism." *Journal of Psychology* 127: 311–22.

Sidanius, James, Felicia Pratto, and Michael Mitchell. 1994. "In-Group

Identification, Social Dominance Orientation, and Differential Inter-group Social Allocation." *Journal of Social Psychology* 134(2): 151–67.

Sigelman, Lee, and Susan Welch. 1991. *Black Americans' View of Racial Inequality: The Dream Deferred*. New York: Cambridge University Press.

———. 1993. "The Contact Hypothesis Revisited—Black-White Interaction and Positive Racial Attitudes." *Social Forces* 71(3): 781–95.

Sinclair, Upton. 1978 (orig. 1928). *Boston: A Documentary Novel of the Sacco-Vanzetti Case*. Cambridge, Mass.: Robert Bentley.

Smith, Tom W. 1991. "Ethnic Images." GSS Technical Report 19. Chicago: University of Chicago, National Opinion Research Center.

Sniderman, Paul M., and Michael Gray Hagen. 1985. *Race and Inequality: A Study in American Values*. Chatham, N.J.: Chatham House.

Sniderman, Paul M., and Thomas Piazza. 1993. *The Scar of Race*. Cambridge, Mass.: Belknap Press of Harvard University Press.

Solomon, Barbara M. 1956. *Ancestors and Immigrants: A Changing New England Tradition*. Cambridge, Mass.: Harvard University Press.

Squires, Gregory. 1994. *Capital and Communities in Black and White: The Intersection of Race, Class and Uneven Development*. Albany: State University of New York Press.

Stevenson, Mary H. 1984. *Determinants of Low Wages for Women Workers*. New York: Praeger.

Stoloff, Jennifer A., Jennifer L. Glanville, James H. Johnson, Jr., and Elisa Jayne Bienenstock. 1996. "Determinants of Female Employment in a Multi-Ethnic Labor Market." Paper. Chapel Hill, N.C.: Kenan Institute of Private Enterprise, University of North Carolina at Chapel Hill (January).

Streitmatter, Rodger. 1996. "Josephine St. Pierre Ruffin: A Nineteenth-Century Journalist of Boston's Black Elite Class." In *Women of the Commonwealth: Work, Family and Social Change in Nineteenth-Century Massachusetts*, edited by Susan L. Porter. Amherst: University of Massachusetts Press.

Sum, Andrew, and Paul Harrington. 1994. "The Central Artery/Harbor Tunnel Construction Projects and the Boston Metropolitan Area's Labor Market." In *Boston in the 1990's: Territorial Planning and Economic Development in the Boston Area to the End of the Century*, edited by Gustav Schacter, Allesandro Busca, Daryl Hellman, and Alberto Ziparo. Rome, Italy: Gangemi Editore.

Summers, R. J. 1995. "Attitudes Toward Different Methods of Affirmative Action." *Journal of Applied Social Psychology* 25(12): 1090–1104.

Swim, Janet K., Katherine J. Aikin, W. S. Hall, and Barbara A. Hunter. 1995. "Sexism and Racism—Old-Fashioned and Modern Prejudices." *Journal of Personality and Social Psychology* 68(2): 199–214.

Taylor, Marylee C. 1994. "Impact of Affirmative Action on Beneficiary Groups—Evidence from the 1990 General Social Survey." *Basic and Applied Social Psychology* 15: 143–78.

Taylorcarter, Mary Anne, Dennis Doverspike, and Kellie Cook. 1995. "Understanding Resistance to Sex- and Race-Based Affirmative Action: A Review of Research Findings." *Human Resource Management Review* 5(2): 129–57.

Thernstrom, Stephan. 1973. *The Other Bostonians: Poverty and Progress in the American Metropolis, 1880–1970*. Cambridge, Mass.: Harvard University Press.

Thernstrom, Stephan, and Abigail Thernstrom. 1997. *America in Black and White: One Nation, Indivisible: Race in Modern America*. New York: Simon & Schuster.

Thurow, Lester. 1975. *Generating Inequality: Mechanisms of Distribution in the U.S. Economy*. New York: Basic Books.

———. 1996. "The Crusade That's Killing Prosperity." *The American Prospect* (25, March–April).

Tilly, Chris, Philip Moss, Joleen Kirschenman, and Ivy Kennelly. Forthcoming. "Space as a Signal, Space as a Barrier: How Employers Map and Use Space in Four Labor Markets." In *Urban Inequality: Evidence from Four Cities*, edited by Lawrence Bobo, Alice O'Connor, and Chris Tilly. New York: Russell Sage Foundation.

Tomaskovic-Devey, Donald. 1993. "Gender and Racial Inequality at Work: The Sources and Consequences of Job Segregation." *Cornell Studies in Industrial and Labor Relations* 27 (December).

Treiman, David J., and Heidi I. Hartmann. 1981. *Women, Work and Wages*. Washington, D.C.: National Academy Press.

Tuch, Steven A., and Michael Hughes. 1996. "Whites' Racial Policy Attitudes." *Social Science Quarterly* 77(4): 723–45.

Turner, Margery Austin, Michael Fix, and Raymond J. Struyk. 1991. *Opportunities Denied, Opportunities Diminished: Racial Discrimination in Hiring*. Washington, D.C.: Urban Institute Press.

Turner, Marlene E., and Anthony R. Pratkanis. 1994. "Affirmative Action as Help—A Review of Recipient Reactions to Preferential Selection and Affirmative Action." *Basic and Applied Social Psychology* 15(1/2): 43–69.

United Community Services of Metropolitan Boston. 1953. "Social Facts by Census Tracts: From U.S. Census 1950." Boston: United Community Services of Metropolitan Boston.

———. 1962. "Social Facts by Census Tracts: From U.S. Census 1960." Boston: United Community Services of Metropolitan Boston.

———. 1972. "Social Facts by Census Tracts: From U.S. Census 1970." Boston: United Community Services of Metropolitan Boston.

U.S. Department of Commerce, Bureau of the Census. 1952. *General Population Characteristics*. Washington: U.S. Government Printing Office.

———. 1962. *1960 General Population Characteristics*. Washington: U.S. Government Printing Office.

———. 1972. *1970 General Population Characteristics*. Washington: U.S. Government Printing Office.

———. 1982. *1980 General Population Characteristics*. Washington: U.S. Government Printing Office.

———. 1990a. *1990 U.S. Census Database: C90STF3A.* Available on the world wide web at: http://www.census.gov/cdrom/lookup.

———. 1990b. *Census of Population and Housing, Social and economic Statistics, Metropolitan Areas.* Washington: U.S. Government Printing Office.

———. 1992a. *1990. General Population Characteristics.* Washington: U.S. Government Printing Office.

———. 1992b. *Census of Population: Historical Tables.* Washington: U.S. Government Printing Office.

———. 1993. *1990 Census of Population. Social and Economic Characteristics, Metropolitan Areas (1990 CP-2-1B).* Washington: U.S. Government Printing Office.

U.S. Department of Housing and Urban Development, Office of Policy Development and Research. 1998. *Cityscape: A Journal of Policy Development and Research—Racially and Ethnically Diverse Urban Neighborhoods* 4(2).

U.S. Department of Labor, Bureau of Labor Statistics. 1995. *Employment, Hours, and Earnings for States and Local Areas.* Washington: U.S. Government Printing Office.

U.S. Department of Labor, War Manpower Commission. Various dates (1943–1950). *Weekly Summary of Labor Market Conditions.* Washington: U.S. Government Printing Office.

Uriarte, Miren. 1992. "Contra Viento Y Marea (Against All Odds): Latinos Build Community in Boston." In *Latinos in Boston: Confronting Poverty, Building Community,* edited by Miren Uriarte, Paul Osterman, and Edwin Meléndez. Boston: Boston Foundation.

Valdes, Alisa. 1997. "Sales Down, But Loyalty Remains." *Boston Globe,* January 25, 1997.

Verkuyten, M., and K. Masson. 1995. "New Racism, Self-Esteem, and Ethnic Relations Among Minority and Majority Youth in the Netherlands." *Social Behavior and Personality* 23(2): 137–54.

Waldinger, Roger. 1993. "Who Makes the Beds? Who Washes the Dishes? Black/Immigrant Competition Reassessed." Working paper 246. Institute of Industrial Relations, University of California at Los Angeles.

Warner, Sam B., Jr. 1962. *Streetcar Suburbs: The Process of Growth in Boston, 1870–1900.* Cambridge, Mass.: Harvard University Press.

Warsh, David. 1986. "War Stories: Defense Spending and the Growth of the Massachusetts Economy." *New England Journal of Public Policy* 2(1).

Weiss, Andrew. 1980. "Job Queues and Layoffs in Labor Markets with Flexible Wages." *Journal of Political Economy* 88(3).

West, Dorothy. 1982. *The Living Is Easy.* Old Westbury, N.Y.: Feminist Press.

Editorial. 1996. "West Enders Deserve Better." *Boston Globe,* August 18, 1996.

White, Michael J. 1986. "Segregation and Diversity Measures in Population Distribution." *Population Index* 52(2): 198–221.

Whitehead, Jr., Ralph, Barbara Defoe Whitehead, and Robert J. Lacey. 1999. "Don't Underestimate 'Union' Benefits." *Boston Globe*, September 5, 1999.

Whitehill, Walter M. 1968. *Boston: A Topographical History*. 2nd ed. Cambridge, Mass.: Harvard University Press.

Whitten, Robert. 1930. "Report on a Thoroughfare Plan for Boston." Report prepared for the City Planning Board.

Wilson, William Julius. 1987. *The Truly Disadvantaged: The Inner City, the Underclass and Public Policy*. Chicago: University of Chicago Press.

———. 1996. *When Work Disappears: The World of the New Urban Poor*. New York: Vintage Books.

With, Tatiana. 1996. "From Mexico to Massachusetts: Northeast Migration Linked to Jobs, Prop. 187 and Family." *Boston Globe*, April 14, 1996.

Wolfe, Tom. 1987. *The Bonfire of the Vanities*. New York: Farrar, Straus, & Giroux.

Woods, Robert A., ed. 1970 (orig. 1903). *Americans in Process: A Settlement Study*. New York: Arno Press and New York Times.

Word, Carl O., Mark P. Zanna, and Joel Cooper. 1974. "The Nonverbal Mediation of Self-fulfilling Prophecies in Interracial Interaction." *Journal of Experimental Social Psychology* 10: 100–20.

Yellen, Janet L. 1984. "Efficiency Wage Models of Unemployment." *American Economic Association Papers and Proceedings* 74(2): 200–5.

Yinger, John. 1986. "Measuring Racial Discrimination with Fair Housing Audits: Caught in the Act." *American Economic Review* 76(5): 881–93.

———. 1995. *Closed Doors, Opportunities Lost: The Continuing Costs of Housing Discrimination*. New York: Russell Sage Foundation.

Zaleski, Alexander V. 1985. "Route 128: The Road to Nowhere?" Conference proceedings, Route 128: Moving Towards the Year 2000. Metropolitan Area Planning Council.

Zernike, Kate, and Doreen Iudica Vigue. 1999. "Ex-foes Join as End OK'd to Schools' Race Policy." *Boston Globe*, July 15, 1999.

Zimbardo, Philip G., and Michael R. Leippe. 1991. *The Psychology of Attitude Change and Social Influence*. Philadelphia: Temple University Press.

Ziparo, Alberto. 1994. "Growth Management and Environmental Quality in the Boston Metropolitan Area." In *Boston in the 1990's: Territorial Planning and Economic Development in the Boston area to the End of the Century*, edited by Gustav Schacter, Allesandro Busca, Daryl Hellman, and Alberto Ziparo. Rome, Italy: Gangemi Editore.

Zubrinsky, Camille, and Lawrence Bobo. 1996. "Prismatic Metropolis: Race and Residential Segregation in the City of Angels." *Social Science Research*. New York: Academic Press.